C000215121

PRAISE FOR *I*

'Stimulating and highly original'
Financial Times, Books of the Year

'Ruth Scurr's imaginative take on Napoleon's life serves up
fascinating insights into the man's behaviour and motivations, as
well as an illuminating account of those around him'
Penelope Lively

'A pleasure to read. The portrait of Napoleon as scientist,
scholar, soldier, savant and grubby-fingered gardener is
fresh and tremendously enjoyable'
Sue Prideaux

'Ruth Scurr has ingeniously somehow found an entirely new
prism through which to view Napoleon . . . An immensely
satisfying and captivating book'
Andrew Roberts, *Times Literary Supplement*

'A brilliantly original biographer . . . Scurr brings shades of
subtlety and nuance to a life well known, telling Napoleon's
story through his love of nature and the gardens'
The Times

'An elegant prose stylist, Scurr is above all a fabulous historian, and
a vivid storyteller with a novelist's eye for engaging detail . . .
Napoleon emerges not in his warrior guise but in his full humanity'
Claire Messud, *Harper's Magazine*

'A beautifully written account of Napoleon's
interaction with horticulture'
History Today, Books of the Year

'*Napoleon* is a delight to read and must have been an immense
pleasure to research . . . History at its most enjoyable'
Caroline Moorehead, *Literary Review*

'A strikingly original account of Napoleon's life'
Daily Mail

'Beautiful . . . Her horticultural angle allows Ruth Scurr to tell the
endlessly fascinating story of Napoleon's life anew'
Wall Street Journal

'Ruth Scurr, with her characteristic originality, has found a new
way to tell Napoleon's astonishing story: not through revolution or
war, but through the gardens he made wherever he went'
Stella Tillyard

'Ruth Scurr gives us a captivating, original perspective on
a man too often simplified as a glorious – or vainglorious –
emperor on horseback . . . [A] sparkling book'
Peter McPhee

RUTH SCURR

Ruth Scurr is an historian, biographer and literary critic. She teaches history and politics at the University of Cambridge, where she is a Lecturer and Fellow of Gonville & Caius College. Her first book, *Fatal Purity: Robespierre and the French Revolution*, won the Franco-British Society Literary Prize, was longlisted for the Samuel Johnson Prize, shortlisted for the Duff Cooper Prize and was listed among the 100 Best Books of the Decade in *The Times*. Her second book, *John Aubrey: My Own Life*, was shortlisted for the Costa Biography Award and the James Tait Black Memorial Prize. It was chosen as a Book of the Year in fifteen newspapers and magazines. She reviews regularly for the *Times Literary Supplement*, the *Spectator* and the *Wall Street Journal*.

RUTH SCURR

Napoleon

A Life in Gardens and Shadows

VINTAGE

To my daughters, Polly and Rosalind

1 3 5 7 9 10 8 6 4 2

Vintage is part of the Penguin Random House group of companies whose
addresses can be found at global.penguinrandomhouse.com

Penguin
Random House
UK

Copyright © Ruth Scurr 2021

Ruth Scurr has asserted her right to be identified as the author of this Work in
accordance with the Copyright, Designs and Patents Act 1988

First published in Vintage in 2022
First published in hardback by Chatto & Windus in 2021

penguin.co.uk/vintage

A CIP catalogue record for this book is available from the British Library

ISBN 9781784704032

Printed and bound in Great Britain by Clays Ltd, Elcograf S.p.A.

The authorised representative in the EEA is Penguin Random House Ireland,
Morrison Chambers, 32 Nassau Street, Dublin D02 YH68

'What a pity to see a mind as great as Napoleon's devoted to trivial things such as empires, historic events, the thundering of cannons and of men; he believed in glory, in posterity, in Caesar; nations in turmoil and other trifles absorbed all his attention . . . How could he fail to see that what really mattered was something else entirely?'
Paul Valéry, *Mauvaises Pensées et Autres* (1941)
Epigraph to Simon Leys's *The Death of Napoleon* (1991)

'. . . all agree that it [the art of painting] originated in tracing lines round the human shadow.'
Pliny the Elder, *Natural History* (c.77)

Contents

A note on names and measures   xi
Chronology   xiii

Introduction   1
1. First Gardens   11
2. Revolutionary Regeneration   32
3. Egyptian Gardens   61
4. Growing a Crown   94
5. Terre Napoléon   129
6. The Forest of Fontainebleau   162
7. Imperial Gardens   192
8. Gardens on Elba   219
9. The Walled Garden at Waterloo   247
10. Last Garden   274

Acknowledgements   305
Notes   307
Bibliography   329
List of Illustrations   349
Index   353

A note on names and measures

The spelling of Napoleon's name changed over his lifetime. I have used the version most fitting for each of the chronological chapters that follow.

Between 24 October 1793 and 1 January 1806, France adopted the Revolutionary calendar. Weeks became ten days long (*décades*) and the days and months acquired new names inspired by the natural world. I have given both the Gregorian and Revolutionary calendar dates for events that occurred in this period.

The metric system, based on the gram, metre and litre – measures derived from the natural world – was first introduced into France in 1799. I have adopted it throughout the text.

The decimal franc was introduced in 1795 during the Revolution and its value was set at 1.0125 livres. In today's terms, 1 franc in 1800 was worth approximately £2.77, $3.70 or €3.11.

Chronology

1769   Birth of Napoleon to Carlo and Letizia (née Ramolino) di Buonaparte, in Ajaccio, Corsica, 15 August.

1779   Napoleon enters the military school at Brienne-le-Château, aged nine, 15 May.

1784   Napoleon leaves Brienne and enters the Royal Military School of Champ de Mars in Paris, 22 October.

1785   Death of Napoleon's father, 24 February.
Napoleon graduates and joins the La Fère regiment at Valence, 28 October.

1786   Napoleon visits Corsica on leave, arriving 15 September.

1787   Napoleon returns to Corsica on leave to help his family and its failing mulberry nursery, 21 April–12 September.

1788   Napoleon returns to Corsica again, 1 January.
He joins his regiment in Auxonne, in eastern France, 1 June.

1789   The French Revolution begins when France's largest representative body, the Estates General (comprising delegates from the clergy, the nobility and the Third Estate, or commoners), meets at Versailles, 5 May.

The Third Estate swears the Tennis Court Oath, refusing to disband until France has a new constitution, 20 June.

Napoleon is granted leave for six months and returns to Corsica, 9 September.

1790   Napoleon requests an extension to his leave, 16 April.

He meets the Corsican freedom fighter Pasquale Paoli, in Bastia, Corsica, 17 July.

1791   Napoleon returns to France and rejoins his regiment in Auxonne, 31 January.

He returns to Corsica after 30 September.

1792   Napoleon is registered absent without leave from his regiment, 1 January.

Revolutionary France declares war on the Holy Roman Empire, 20 April.

Napoleon returns to France and is reincorporated into the army as a captain, 10 July.

He witnesses the fall of the French monarchy in the Tuileries gardens, 10 August.

Convocation of the National Convention to design a republican constitution for France, 20 September.

Napoleon returns to Corsica, 10 October.

1793   Execution of Louis XVI, 21 January.

France declares war on England and the Dutch Republic, 1 February.

France declares war on Spain, 7 March.

Establishment of the Committee of Public Safety, an emergency government for France, 6 April.

Napoleon and his family are banished from Corsica by Pasquale Paoli, 27 May.

Foundation of the Muséum d'histoire naturelle at the Jardin des Plantes, 10 June.

Napoleon and his family arrive in Toulon and he rejoins his regiment in Nice, 26 June.

France adopts the Revolutionary calendar (backdated to 22 September 1792), 24 October.

Siege of Toulon, 29 August–19 December.

Napoleon is promoted to the rank of battalion commander (7 Brumaire, Year 2), 28 October.

1794   Robespierre attempts to introduce a new religion to France with the Festival of the Supreme Being (20 Prairial, Year 2), 8 June.

French victory at the Battle of Fleurus (8 Messidor, Year 2), 26 June.

Arrest of Robespierre and his brother and other associates (9 Thermidor, Year 2), 27 July.

Execution of Robespierrists (10 Thermidor, Year 2), 28 July.

Napoleon is briefly arrested, accused of complicity with the Robespierre brothers (3–13 Fructidor, Year 2), 20–30 August.

1795   Proclamation of the constitution of the Year 3, 23 September.

Napoleon suppresses a royalist revolt in Paris (13 Vendémiaire, Year 4), 5 October.

Napoleon succeeds Barras as commander of the Army of the Interior (4 Brumaire, Year 4), 26 October.

A five-member Directory is appointed to govern France (12 Brumaire, Year 4), 3 November.

1796   Napoleon appointed commander of the French Army of Italy (12 Ventôse, Year 4), 2 March.

He marries Joséphine de Beauharnais in a civil ceremony in Paris (19 Ventôse, Year 4), 9 March.

Start of Napoleon's first Italian campaign (13 Germinal, Year 4) 2 April.

Battle of Montenotte (23 Germinal, Year 4), 12 April.

Battle of Mondovi (2 Floréal, Year 4), 21 April.

Battle of Lodi (21 Floréal, Year 4), 10 May.

Napoleon asks the Directory to appoint a commission to supervise the removal of works of art from Italy (22 Floréal, Year 4), 11 May.

Battle of Arcole (25–27 Brumaire, Year 5), 15–17 November.

1797 Battle of Rivoli (25–26 Nivôse, Year 5), 14–15 January.

Treaty of Tolentino (1 Ventôse, Year 5) 19 February.

Battle of Tagliamento (26 Ventôse, Year 5), 16 March.

Napoleon and Josephine visit the gardens of Isola Bella (30 Thermidor, Year 5), 17 August.

He is elected to the Institut de France (5 Nivôse, Year 6), 25 December.

1798 Napoleon appointed commander of the Army of the Orient (23 Germinal, Year 6), 12 April.

He leads his army into Alexandria (14 Messidor, Year 6), 2 July.

Battle of Chobrakit (25 Messidor, Year 6), 13 July.

Battle of the Pyramids (3 Thermidor, Year 6), 21 July.

Festival of Arts and Sciences in Paris to celebrate Napoleon's triumph in Italy (9 Messidor, Year 6), 27 July.

Battle of the Nile (also called the Battle of Aboukir Bay), (13–14 Thermidor, Year 6), 1–2 August.

Napoleon founds the Institut d'Égypte, (5 Fructidor, Year 6), 22 August

Cairo Revolt (30 Vendémiaire, Year 6), 21 October.

1799   Napoleon leads his soldiers into Gaza (7 Ventôse, Year 7), 25 February.

He captures Jaffa (17 Ventôse, Year 7), 7 March.

He visits plague victims in Jaffa (21 Ventôse, Year 7), 11 March.

The Directory declares war on Austria (22 Ventôse, Year 7), 12 March.

The siege of Acre begins (29 Ventôse, Year 7), 19 March.

Josephine purchases Malmaison (2 Floréal, Year 7), 21 April.

End of the siege of Acre (28 Floréal, Year 7), 17 May.

Napoleon makes a second visit to plague victims in Jaffa (8 Prairial, Year 7), 27 May.

He slips out of Egypt, leaving General Kléber in command (5 Fructidor, Year 7), 22 August.

He visits Ajaccio on his way back to Paris (9–14 Vendémiaire, Year 8), 1–6 October.

Coup of 18 Brumaire, 9 November.

Napoleon expels the legislature from the orangery at Saint-Cloud (19 Brumaire, Year 8), 10 November.

The Directory is replaced by three consuls: Napoleon, Cambacérès and Lebrun (20 Brumaire, Year 8), 11 November.

Proclamation of the constitution of the Year 8 (24 Frimaire, Year 8), 15 December.

Napoleon becomes First Consul (3 Nivôse, Year 8), 24 December.

1800   Creation of the Banque de France (28 Nivôse, Year 8), 18 January.

Plebiscite acceptance of the constitution of the Year 8 (29 Pluviôse, Year 8), 18 February.

Napoleon's second campaign in Italy begins (16 Floréal, Year 8), 6 May.

He crosses the Alps at the Great St Bernard Pass (30 Floréal, Year 8), 20 May.

Battle of Marengo (25 Prairial, Year 8), 14 June.

Assassination of General Kléber in Cairo (25 Prairial, Year 8), 14 June.

A commission established to draw up the Civil Code (24 Thermidor, Year 8), 12 August.

Napoleon and Josephine visit the gardens at Ermenonville (10 Fructidor, Year 8), 28 August.

Departure of the Baudin expedition to Australia (17 Vendémiaire, Year 9), 19 October.

Attempt to assassinate Napoleon in the Rue Saint-Nicaise, known as the Plot of the Infernal Machine (3 Nivôse, Year 9), 24 December.

1801   The revolutionary leader Toussaint Louverture establishes a new constitution for Saint-Domingue (Haiti) (18 Floréal, Year 9), 8 May.

The new King of Etruria visits Malmaison (14 Prairial, Year 9), 3 June.

The concordat, an agreement between Napoleon and Pope Pius VII reconciling France and the Roman Catholic Church, is signed (26 Messidor, Year 9), 15 July.

Napoleon establishes a home in the chateau of Saint-Cloud (20 Fructidor, Year 9), 7 September.

Napoleon's brother-in-law, General Leclerc, appointed commander of an army sent to re-establish control over Saint-Domingue (2 Brumaire, Year 10), 24 October.

1802   Leclerc and his army arrive in Saint-Domingue (17 Pluviôse, Year 10), 6 February.

Signing of the Peace of Amiens, ending the war between France and Britain (6 Germinal, Year 10), 27 March.

Establishment of the Legion of Honour (29 Floréal, Year 10), 19 May.

Napoleon re-establishes the slave trade in French colonies, which had been abolished during the French Revolution (30 Floréal, Year 10), 20 May.

Toussaint Louverture is arrested (18 Prairial, Year 10), 7 June.

Napoleon proclaimed First Consul for Life by the Senate (14 Thermidor, Year 10), 2 August.

1803 Collapse of the Peace of Amiens (22 Floréal, Year 11), 12 May.

1804 Arrest of the Duc d'Enghien (24 Ventôse, Year 12), 15 March. Execution of the Duc d'Enghien (30 Ventôse, Year 12), 21 March.

Napoleon is proclaimed Emperor (30 Floréal, Year 12), 20 May.

He receives Pope Pius VII at Fontainebleau (4 Frimaire, Year 13), 25 November.

Napoleon and Josephine are married in a secret religious ceremony (8 Frimaire, Year 13), 29 November.

Napoleon's coronation in the cathedral of Notre-Dame (11 Frimaire, Year 13), 2 December.

1805 Napoleon is crowned King of Italy in Milan (6 Prairial, Year 13), 26 May.

Start of the Ulm campaign (3 Vendémiaire, Year 14), 25 September.

Surrender of Ulm (25 Vendémiaire, Year 14), 17 October.

The French occupy Vienna (22 Brumaire, Year 14), 13 November.

Battle of Austerlitz (11 Frimaire, Year 14), 2 December.

Peace Treaty of Pressburg (5 Nivôse, Year 14), 26 December.

1806 Restoration of the Gregorian calendar, 1 January.

Napoleon commissions the Arc du Carrousel, 26 February.

First stone of the Arc de Triomphe laid, 15 August.
Battle of Jena, 14 October.
Surrender of Erfurt, 16 October.

1807   Battle of Friedland, 14 June.
Peace of Tilsit signed between France and Russia, 8 July.

1808   Napoleon is excommunicated by Pope Pius VII, 27 March.

1809   Beginning of Napoleon's bombardment of Vienna, 12 May.
Battle of Aspern, 21 May.
Battle of Wagram, 5–6 July.
Pope Pius VII arrested in Rome, 6 July.
The civil marriage between Napoleon and Josephine is dissolved by the Senate, 16 December.

1810   The religious marriage between Napoleon and Josephine is declared invalid, 9 January.
Napoleon marries Marie Louise (daughter of Francis II of Austria) in Vienna by proxy, 11 March.
Their civil marriage is celebrated at Saint-Cloud, 1 April.
Their religious marriage is celebrated at the Louvre, 2 April.

1811   Birth of Napoleon's only legitimate son, the King of Rome, 20 March.
Start of construction of the palace for the King of Rome on Chaillot Hill in Paris, 7 May.
Celebration of the birth of the King of Rome in Rome, 8 June.
Baptism of the King of Rome in the cathedral of Notre-Dame, 9 June.

1812   Pope Pius VII arrives as a prisoner at Fontainebleau, 19 June.
Start of Napoleon's Russia campaign, 24 June.

Battle of Smolensk, 16 August.
Battle of Borodino, 7 September.
Burning of Moscow, 14–15 September.
Start of the retreat from Moscow, 19 October.

1813   Prussia declares war on France, 27 March.
Battle of Leipzig, 16–18 October.

1814   Battle of Brienne, 29 January.
Battle for Paris, 30–31 March.
Napoleon abdicates unconditionally, 6 April.
Treaty of Fontainebleau, 11 April.
Napoleon signs the Treaty of Fontainebleau, 13 April.
He arrives on the island of Elba, 3 May.
Louis XVIII, the restored Bourbon king, arrives in Paris, 3 May.
Pope Pius VII returns to Rome, 24 May.
Opening of the Congress of Vienna, 3 November.

1815   Napoleon leaves Elba to return to France, 26 February.
Louis XVIII leaves the Tuileries Palace and Napoleon returns, 20 March.
Festival of the Champ-de-Mai, on the Champ de Mars, 1 June.
Battle of Ligny, 16 June.
Battle of Waterloo, 18 June.
Napoleon abdicates for a second time, 22 June.
Louis XVIII returns to France, 25 June.
Napoleon surrenders to the British at Rochefort, 15 July.
Napoleon sets sail for St Helena on HMS *Northumberland*, 7 August.
He arrives on St Helena, 16 October.

1821   The death of Napoleon, 5 May.

Napoleon

Introduction

'Truly his life is a rainbow; the two extreme ends touch
the earth, the intervening arc spans the skies.'
Charlotte Brontë, 'The Death of Napoleon'[1]

Gardening was the first and last passion of Napoleon Bonaparte, a
figure still recognised by his silhouette two hundred years after his
death. Between cultivating his first garden at school in Brienne-le-
Château, in the Champagne region of northern France, and his last
in exile on the South Atlantic island of St Helena, he won and lost an
empire. He was born Napoleone di Buonaparte, in Ajaccio on the
island of Corsica, on 15 August 1769. He simplified the spelling of
his last name to Bonaparte after his first marriage, became Napoleon
Emperor of the French in 1804, and abdicated a decade later. In 1815
he escaped from a brief exile on the island of Elba to reclaim his
empire for almost a hundred days, lost the Battle of Waterloo, and
was sent to St Helena, where he died on 5 May 1821.

At the beginning and end of his extraordinary life, gardening offered
Napoleon a retreat from the frustrations of powerlessness. A clever
Corsican boy, who won a scholarship to a military school in France,
he spoke French slowly with a heavy accent. He wanted, at times, to
shut himself off from his peers, to read, think and remember his home
and family on the island of Corsica. He was powerless in the ordinary

sense; a child from a secure but modest background with an unknown future ahead of him.

After he was sent into exile on St Helena at the age of forty-six, gardening was Napoleon's last burst of activity before he died. On the advice of his doctor, he made an elaborate garden where sunken paths helped him evade the surveillance of the British guards. He swapped his iconic bicorne hat for a battered straw one and set about cultivating the only patch of ground remaining to him. His interactions with the natural world at the end of his life resonate with those of every man or woman who enjoys gardening in retirement or in retreat from the stresses and strains of the world. But Napoleon was no everyman. Earlier in his life, his relationship with nature was determined by his ambition, first to advance himself within the chaotic aftermath of the French Revolution, and then to become the most important and feared man in Europe. Even in exile, there were echoes of grandeur in the extensive and meticulous plans he laid out for his last garden.

Napoleon spent five years at the military school in Brienne-le-Château and six on St Helena. These blocks of time enclose his life like bookends. They are the periods during which he had little control over the conditions of his everyday life and found refuge in growing plants. In between his first and last gardens, the arc of his life rose towards the sky, before falling back down to earth. As his power grew, then declined, he rarely had time for gardening himself; but he passed through many gardens, large and small, public parks or private green spaces, admiring them. Often he ordered improvements, commanding other people's labour, always imagining a grander garden than the one that existed. He was a garden-watcher and enthusiast, alert to the science and art of cultivation. He valued gardens as places to walk in at his own pace as he reflected on the frenetic events by which he hoped to secure the future of France. For someone almost always in motion and in a hurry, more often at war than not, gardens offered rare opportunities for calm and pleasure. They were a counterpoint to the many battlefields; discrete settings in which the terrain and the weather were as important as they were in combat, but for creative not destructive purposes. On two significant occasions, one at the start of Napoleon's career, the other at the end, a garden became a battlefield and the distinction was lost. The first was the Tuileries gardens in central Paris, where in 1792 he witnessed the massacre of Louis XVI's Swiss Guard and the fall of the French monarchy; the second was the walled garden of Hougoumont at Waterloo. In both these gardens the piles of dead and mutilated bodies formed a terrible contrast with horticultural attempts to impose order on the natural world.

Napoleon wanted to impose order on France and dreamed of expanding the nation's territory within Europe and beyond. In 1802, when he was First Consul and not yet Emperor, Samuel Taylor Coleridge described him as 'Poet Bonaparte – Layer out of a World-Garden'.[2] Almost a decade later, despite his dismay at the violent outcome of Napoleon's power, Coleridge proposed 'a series of lives from Moses to Buonaparte of all those great men, who in states or in the mind of man had produced great revolutions, the effects of which still remain, and are, more or less, distant causes of the present state of the World'.[3]

Napoleon was a modern-day Alexander the Great whose life also epitomised the ideal of a self-made man; the corporal from Corsica who came to rule over Europe and crowned himself Emperor of the French. His authority was not inherited, but hard won through military and political genius. His rise to power would not have been possible without the French Revolution, but when he made himself hereditary ruler of France he betrayed the revolutionary ideals that gave him his first opportunities.

As a biographical subject, Napoleon has always attracted great male writers who identify with him. Walter Scott travelled to Paris to interview Napoleon's former colleagues and published *The Life of Napoleon Buonaparte, Emperor of the French* in 1827. Stendhal followed in Napoleon's footsteps and claimed, 'I am writing this *Life of Napoleon* to refute a slander.' In his autobiography Stendhal declared, 'I fell with Nap[oleon] in April 1814.'[4] William Hazlitt drank himself into a stupor for weeks after the Battle of Waterloo, then never drank again. He later published a three-volume life of Napoleon. Thomas Carlyle, who declared that 'The history of the world is but the biography of great men', included Napoleon in *On Heroes, Hero-Worship and the Heroic in History* in 1841.[5] But Carlyle's attitude to Napoleon was ambivalent: sometimes he characterised him as 'our last Great Man', at other times he criticised him for 'grandiose Dick-Turpinism, revolutionary madness, and unlimited expenditure of men and gunpowder'. Ultimately he saw Napoleon as a reckless gambler whose immense temporary success ended in him 'losing his last guinea.'[6]

Carlyle asked that Napoleon be judged according to 'what Nature with her laws will sanction. To what of reality was in him; to that and nothing more.'[7] *On Heroes, Hero-Worship and the Heroic in History* was published the year after Napoleon's remains were brought back to Paris from his modest grave on St Helena to be interred in Les Invalides, in a sarcophagus and setting worthy of a world-changing emperor. In 1842, a year after Carlyle's book was published, Charlotte Brontë, aged twenty-six, went to Brussels to improve her French. Sixteen kilometres from Waterloo, she wrote a short essay on 'The Death of Napoleon', which began by asking: 'How should one envisage this subject? With a great pomp of words, or with simplicity?' She distanced herself from great orators, writers and politicians, and set out from the perspective of 'the ordinary person' for whom Napoleon would always be a soldier of fortune:

> Let her then approach with respect the tomb hollowed out of the rock of St. Helena and, while refusing to bow down in adoration before a god of flesh and clay, preserving her independent though inferior dignity of being, let her take care not to cast a single word of insult at the sepulchre, empty now, but consecrated in the past by Napoleon's remains.[8]

Brontë contrasted the glory of Napoleon which grew overnight, 'like Jonah's vine', to the glory of the Duke of Wellington which grew 'like one of the ancient oaks that shade the mansion of his fathers on the banks of the Shannon'.[9] Wellington was her hero, but Napoleon, the outsider, the young soldier with nothing behind him but courage and talent, was closer to her own experience of the world. On 4 August 1843, the teacher she was in love with, M. Heger, gave her a fragment of Napoleon's coffin from St Helena, which had been given to him by a friend who had been Napoleon's nephew's secretary.[10] She turned it over in her hand and reflected that we all have only the idea of Napoleon we are capable of having. There are no definitive biographical portraits, only one person looking at another – mediocrity looking at genius perhaps – and casting a cold eye.

Brontë's cold eye inspired me to write about Napoleon. 'What are you going to find to say that hasn't already been said?' an older, male, supportive but sceptical colleague asked at the outset. But if there are no definitive biographical portraits, no final word or conquest of another person's life, then there is always something new to say, no matter how many regiments of biographers have marched across the same ground. Napoleon is the most masculine of subjects and very few women have written his biography: a fact that would have pleased him. He condescended to and dismissed bookish women of the time, especially the novelist and liberal political theorist Madame de Staël. When she first met the young hero, de Staël tried to talk to him about revolutionary politics. In response he asked her how many children she had.[11] He believed women should be concerned with childbearing, not politics or literature. 'I do not like women who make men of themselves, any more than I like effeminate men,' he told his secretary.[12] In retaliation, de Staël wrote eloquently about Napoleon's egoism. 'He regards a human being as an action or a thing, not as a fellow-creature. He does not hate more than he loves; for him nothing exists but himself; all other creatures are ciphers.'[13]

In *A Room of One's Own*, Virginia Woolf evoked the subservient
role women have played in the lives and biographies of great men:

> Women have served all these centuries as looking-glasses
> possessing the magic and delicious power of reflecting the figure
> of man at twice its natural size. Whatever may be their use in
> civilised societies, mirrors are essential to all violent and heroic
> action. That is why Napoleon and Mussolini both insist so
> emphatically upon the inferiority of women, for if they were not
> inferior, they would cease to enlarge. That serves to explain in
> part the necessity that women so often are to men.[14]

Seeing Napoleon in gardens helps to strip away the distorting mirrors
which Woolf complains are essential to all violent and heroic action.
Instead of mirrors there are shadows in the gardens. Sometimes the
shadows are long, stretching over an expanse of time and space, sometimes they are short, falling over only the people closest to him. The
other people who enter his story, women especially, are not treated
as inferior foils or ciphers, but as individuals whose lives were as
precious to them as his was to him. A shadow is a dark area or shape
projected by a body coming between rays of light and a surface.
Napoleon was often compared to the sun and his first wife, Josephine,
adopted the heliotrope as her emblem with the motto '*Vers le Soleil*'
(Towards the Sun).[15] But in this book he is not the sun. Instead, he
is firmly situated within the natural world. He is seen by tracing the
shadows that he cast over the lives gathered around his and the
shadows that he threw across the lawns of specific gardens, a brooding
and mysterious presence.

Napoleon's shadow, unlike his instantly recognisable silhouette, is
not singular or monolithic. The enormity of what his life meant for
France, Europe and the world cannot be disputed. But is his shadow
great or monstrous? There are many thousands of books about him
and almost all of them come down on one side or the other of this

question. Rather than weighing Napoleonic questions, or reconstructing the motives behind his world-changing actions, I have set out to ground his life by situating it in a series of gardens where the shadows he casts are various and changeable, plural not singular.

Napoleon: A Life in Gardens and Shadows draws on a wealth of scholarship, historical and contemporary, inviting the reader to look at the trajectory of his extraordinary life from unfamiliar perspectives. During the French Revolution ideas about nature – human nature, the natural world and exchanges between the two – were at the centre of fierce political debates and events. Nature was both venerated and desecrated. The Ancien Régime, the old allegedly natural social order, was destroyed, and a new meritocratic order, centred on the revolutionary values of liberty and equality, came into existence, in name if not always in fact. Napoleon's personal nature and his relationship with the natural world developed in this dynamic context. He came to see himself as an agent of healing, a patron of the sciences and progress, a person capable of bringing an end to the violence of the Revolution and binding up its wounds. In fact he unleashed a new era of dreadful destruction. The Napoleonic Wars caused somewhere between three and six million unnatural military and civilian deaths.

If Napoleon had not become one of the greatest military generals in history, he would have been a scientist. When he was young, he wanted to be a scientific discoverer, like Isaac Newton, more than he wanted to follow in the footsteps of Alexander the Great. Although his military career had to take precedence in adult life, he never abandoned his adolescent dreams. He carried them with him across battlefields and campaign trails, into the debating chambers, corridors and throne rooms of political power. There was, he thought, a 'world of details' to be explored, and when he considered what his contribution could have been to advancing human understanding of the natural world, he was full of regrets. 'Thinking about it, I feel pain in my soul,' he told his friend the naturalist Étienne Geoffroy Saint-Hilaire.[16]

In this book I offer a portrait of the emperor drawn from oblique angles. A series of chronological chapters, framed in gardens, forests or botanical expeditions, explore particular passages in Napoleon's life. After his first garden at school, there is his family's garden and a mulberry nursery on Corsica; the botanical garden in Paris, the Jardin des Plantes, one of the few royal institutions to survive the Revolution; gardens in Cairo during the Egyptian campaign; gardens just outside Paris at Malmaison, which became his marital home; gardens and the forest at Fontainebleau, where at the height of his power he installed a throne room; gardens in Rome and palatial gardens in Paris for his son, the King of Rome, which were never finished; gardens during his first exile on Elba; the walled garden at Waterloo, the site of a battle within the battle; and his last garden at Longwood House on St Helena's Deadwood Plateau. These gardens were places of refuge, or conquest and control; scenes of scientific enquiry, or the pursuit of pleasure; and sometimes their orderliness was besmirched by blood.

Within these widely defined gardens Napoleon's life is described through the shadows he cast over the people around him. His relationship with the natural world was mediated through family, friends and lovers, many of them professional or amateur scientists, determined to push forward the frontiers of knowledge, just as he was determined to expand his territorial control. His dealings with all these people, over gardens, horticultural projects, scientific research or experiments, offer unguarded and unusual opportunities to see what Napoleon was like. Sometimes the focus of the story shifts away from him so that his effect on other lives can be explained. The lives surrounding his are not static surfaces or mirrors; they do not just reflect his power or passively accept it; they are valued in their own right and are part of the context within which his achievements were possible.

Plutarch, the father of biography, often put a great life against a less celebrated one. This book builds on that biographical tradition by putting a series of lesser-known or forgotten lives up against Napoleon's to reveal the contours of his personality and power. Many of these people are intermediaries in Napoleon's relationship with the natural world: gardeners, botanists, scientists and researchers. Others are politicians or diplomats, ordinary soldiers or generals; some are female survivors and victims, outsiders or foreigners; some are loyal members of his family or household, architects and garden designers; others are remote inhabitants of different continents who never met or knew the person whose hard-won authority changed their lives. Some left letters, diaries or memoirs slanted from their own perspective, but others left no personal records and are known only through anecdotes. Figures from this crowd of lives weave in and out of Napoleon's as he seizes precious moments of rest and reflection in the gardens he encountered or made.

Napoleon's life was epic in its intensity and impact, but a mere speck of time within the history of the natural world. When he was dying on St Helena, when the power and will to garden even a small plot of land had left him, he knew that he was surpassed by nature, but that he had claimed a place in history: his shadow would continue to fall over the world for centuries beyond his death. By going back to the gardens Napoleon made at the beginning and end of life, by watching him pass through other gardens on his rise to and fall from power, I have sought to return him to the context within which he lived. I have accepted that there were, and are, many Napoleons. He can be – and often is – described in what Charlotte Brontë called 'a great pomp of words'. That, certainly, is what he intended. But he was also fascinated by details: the empirical facts that he would have classified and collated if he had been free to pursue a scientific career. By narrowing my focus to gardens, I have found space for the small details that are pushed aside in grander, more conventional narratives. All gardens combine basic facts – the type of soil, the kinds of plants – with abstractions: the seasons, time, eternity. In tracing Napoleon's shadows in gardens I have neither bowed down in adoration nor proscribed him. I have looked carefully at his effect on others in various green spaces and I have found that Madame de Staël was wrong to write: 'In every respect it is war, and only war, which suits him.'[17] Gardens suited him too and the shadows he cast within them yield new ways of seeing his life.

1

First Gardens

'The garden is the smallest part of the world and the whole
world at the same time.'[1]
Michel Foucault

His first garden was not much bigger than a grave. At boarding school
in Brienne-le-Château, between the ages of nine and fifteen, Napoleone
di Buonaparte was allocated a small plot of land. He could sit or lie
down in it, learn to grow flowers and a few vegetables, nothing more.
Other boys had similar allotments, lined up in rows, like beds in
dormitories or barracks. The school was one of twelve sponsored by
the French state to prepare pupils for the military academy in Paris.
It was run by monks, Les Minimes de Brienne, who considered
gardening an educative pastime which would supplement the curricu-
lum of French, Latin, Mathematics, History, Geography, Music,
Drawing and Fencing. Some of the boys neglected their gardens, soon
losing interest, letting them turn to dust or be overrun by brambles,
but Buonaparte took enormous pride in his. Perhaps he had help from
a kindly monk with horticultural expertise; perhaps he did not need
it after spending his early years in orchards and olive groves on Corsica.
He spoke French poorly with a thick Corsican accent. He pronounced
his own name Napoilloné, so his peers nicknamed him *la paille au
nez*, 'straw-nose'.[2] He was homesick. He missed his parents and their

house in Ajaccio, the room he was born in and the gardens he had played in with his siblings before being sent away to school. 'To be deprived of your childhood room, of the garden in which you roamed in your early years, not to have a personal home, is to have no homeland,' he later claimed.[3] He longed for the Corsican terrain, sea, sky and climate; the winters in Champagne were hard. But once they were over, gardening helped him feel better. He was a scholarship boy from a modest but aristocratic family. If he had a small amount of pocket money, he used it to improve his garden, to screen it with fencing or shrubs and cultivate flowers in his hours of recreation. Within two years he created an arbour, a green sanctuary, where he could read and be alone.[4]

The fact of this first garden is not robust. It has been passed down through the memoirs of people claiming to remember Buonaparte before he simplified his name to Bonaparte, and long before he became Napoleon, Emperor of the French. Like most hints about the early lives of the famous or infamous, the idea of Buonaparte gardening at school has been embellished. Some suggest that Buonaparte's appropriative and expansionist ambitions were already evident when he took over the neglected plots on either side of his own and tripled the size of his garden. In the book based on his failed play about Napoleon, the novelist and playwright Alexandre Dumas, whose father was a general in Napoleon's army, imagined him alone in his garden arranging pebbles in military order, size designating rank.[5] When one of the other boys climbed the fence to spy on him and laugh at his pastime, Buonaparte responded by throwing a stone at the intruder, who carried a scar on his forehead from the wound for the rest of his life. Twenty-five years later, Dumas's story goes, when the Emperor Napoleon was at the peak of his power, he recognised his former schoolfellow as 'a General-in-chief that I struck on the head'.[6] Dumas was building on the memoirs of Louis Antoine Fauvelet de Bourrienne, who was born the same year as Buonaparte in 1769, was at school with him in Brienne-le-Château, and afterwards became his private

secretary. Bourrienne's accuracy and veracity have long been questioned, not least because he relied on ghost writers to turn his notes
into published memoirs. While Bourrienne mentioned Buonaparte's
enjoyment of outdoor recreation and his dismay when snowfall
prevented him from gardening, he did not suggest that the fence
Buonaparte erected was tall and substantial enough to be scaled by a
schoolboy, or that inside that fence, Buonaparte was already practising
for war, marshalling pebbles like soldiers.[7]

Another story has Buonaparte retreating into his garden as 25
August 1784 approached and the whole school became excited about
preparing for the Festival of St Louis, a feast day celebrated by pupils
across France.[8] The monks allowed boys who were fourteen or over
to buy small amounts of gunpowder to use in miniature cannon and
pistols. No one spoke of anything else. Guns and petards were cleaned
in anticipation. A banner celebrating the thirty-year-old reform-
minded king, who had been crowned in 1774, was strung across the
facade of the school, proclaiming '*À Louis XVI, notre père*' (To Louis
XVI, our father). But on the day itself Buonaparte played no part in
the celebrations. He had recently turned fifteen, he could have sourced
some gunpowder and joined in with his peers, but instead he chose
to spend time in his garden. That evening around 9 p.m. he was
disturbed by a party of twenty or so boys who had crowded into an
adjacent plot to set off a firework. Embers fell from the sky and ignited
a box of gunpowder on the ground which exploded and caused a
stampede into Buonaparte's garden. He was enraged at the destruction,
all the trampled plants and flowers, and chased the intruders back out
of his plot, brandishing a gardening tool like a pike.[9] With the benefit
of hindsight, Buonaparte's refusal to join in with the Festival of
St Louis has been interpreted as an early indication of his republican
sympathies: 'straw-nose' was a child from Corsica who resented the
French monarchy for conquering his native island.

Then there is the school snowball fight anecdote that some biographers dismiss and others work up into the earliest example of

Napoleon's genius for military operations.[10] Allegedly, during the especially bitter winter of 1783, Buonaparte organised his schoolfellows
into a mock siege in the school grounds. They dug trenches and raised
a fortress of snow, then divided into platoons and fought for control
of the frozen stronghold. The game continued for many days and it
was only after the snow began to melt and gravel got mixed in with
the snowballs causing serious cuts and abrasions that it stopped. None
of this seems unlikely in a military school for boys. Any one of the
participants who went on to become a soldier might have looked back
and claimed responsibility for masterminding a memorable snow
siege. But even if true, the snow story adds nothing to our understanding of Buonaparte's character. In contrast, Buonaparte's passion
for gardening is more distinctive. People disagree about how clever
he was, how early his mathematical abilities were evident, whether he
was isolated and bullied or popular and charismatic. Most of the
disagreements about Buonaparte's early life will never be resolved.
But at the heart of the highly embellished claim that he loved and
tended a small garden at school, there is a kernel of truth. It is not the
sort of pastime someone would invent for him because it is so incon-
gruous, so irrelevant to his later military and political conquests.

Among the many books he read in his garden, or with his back
against one of the fruit trees that thrive in Champagne, was Jacques
Delille's *Les Jardins* (1780). Delille was professor of Latin poetry at
the Collège de France before the Revolution and was well known for
his translation of the *Georgics*, Virgil's poem of nature and nationalism.
In *Les Jardins*, Delille described a Tahitian man, Potaveri, who was
brought to Paris by the explorer the Comte de Bougainville, and allegedly moved to tears by the sight of a banana tree in the king's arboretum
because it reminded him of his home and early years.[11] Buonaparte
later referred to *Les Jardins* in the essay on happiness he wrote at the
age of twenty-one in 1791, hoping to win a prize from the Academy
of Lyons. He claimed that, snatched from Tahiti and overwhelmed by
cares, the only thing Potaveri found to alleviate his suffering was not

a banana but a paper mulberry tree, which he embraced crying, 'Tree of my country! Tree of my country!'[12] This, according to Buonaparte, who used the word 'nature' almost fifty times in his hundred-page essay, illustrates the sentiments we have for our natural surroundings, our country and the people close to us. He was disappointed when the judges decided none of the essays entered deserved a prize.

Buonaparte encountered the work of the philosopher Jean-Jacques Rousseau at school. He was nine when he first read *La Nouvelle Héloïse*, and it made a deep impression on him. In the novel, the character Julie has a fictional estate named Clarens in which there is an old orchard, a gated wilderness, called her Élysée. Julie has allowed flowering shrubs and climbing plants to grow among the trees, and meandering moss-covered paths and a stream wind their way through the deep shade. When her lover Saint-Preux visits the orchard for the first time he thinks he is seeing 'the most wild, the most solitary place in nature', and feels as though he is the first mortal ever to have entered it. He tells Julie that nature seems to be the sole author of her Elysée, to which she replies: 'It is true that nature has done everything, but under my direction, and there is nothing here that I have not ordered.'[13] Julie's orchard is a deliberate challenge to the traditional formal style of French gardening, which relied on parterres, geometrical shapes and neatly clipped topiary. Instead of serried trees sculpted into parasols and fans, her plants and shrubs seem to grow naturally without artifice.[14] Her Élysée has many features in common with the informal style of gardening known in the eighteenth century as the *jardin à l'anglaise*. Later in life, Buonaparte would always favour the French style, but solitude in green spaces was important to him too. In his imagination he could retreat into the secluded garden at the heart of the Clarens estate, just as he withdrew to his own small garden when his fellow pupils irked him.

Although he was unhappy and homesick at school, Buonaparte later looked back on his time at Brienne-le-Château with affection. He stayed in contact with some of his teachers, among them the mathematician Louis Monge, whose more distinguished brother Gaspard became a close friend and scientific adviser. He also maintained his acquaintance with some of his peers, Bourrienne above all. When he visited his old school and first garden, on the way to Milan for his coronation as King of Italy in 1805, he found the school had been partially destroyed during the Revolution and had closed in 1790, because of its close association with Louis XVI and the Ancien Régime. He granted 12,000 francs for repairs and galloped off into the surrounding woods without his escort to be alone with his memories.[15] He returned to Brienne-le-Château in January 1814 to fight invading Russian and Prussian forces. The town's chateau, like the legendary school snow fort, was besieged. He won a narrow victory, but did not succeed in driving the enemy back beyond the French border. In exile on St Helena, he reminisced about the Battle of Brienne, which was fought close to the grounds of his old school. He claimed that he was nearly killed – by a cannonball, according to one account, or a Cossack, according to another – near the exact same tree where he had liked to sit reading as a schoolboy.[16] In the midst of a bloody battle, he recognised a particular tree – it might have been an apple, a pear or a plum – from his schooldays.

For the five years that he was at Brienne-le-Château, Buonaparte did not return to Corsica. After he graduated and moved to the military academy in Paris in 1784, he started to go back for holidays and to become involved with his family again and with the island's politics. Buonaparte's parents, Letizia and Carlo di Buonaparte, had thirteen children. Of the eight who survived into adult life, he was the second eldest. He had one older brother, Joseph; three younger brothers, Lucien, Louis and Jérôme; and three younger sisters, Eliza, Pauline and Caroline. The family had two homes – one in Ajaccio and one called Les Milelli in the hills outside Ajaccio overlooking the sea. They owned other property including an olive grove, a vineyard and a mill, employed servants and were well connected to the island's elite. The

Archdeacon of Ajaccio, Joseph Fesch, was Buonaparte's mother's half-brother. After Corsica was invaded by France in 1769, the year of Buonaparte's birth, the new governor, the Marquis de Marbœuf, became a family friend who helped secure his place at school in Brienne.

Both the Buonaparte family houses had gardens. The one in Ajaccio was smaller, a town courtyard garden, but spacious enough for tall drought-tolerant palm and fragrant orange trees. The garden at Les Milelli was much bigger. This was the family's summer residence, approached through a gated avenue of overhanging cacti. There was a beautifully laid-out lawn, surrounded by shrubberies and an orchard: the name 'Les Milelli' means little apple trees in Corsican. Clematis climbed through almond trees while Corsican violets and rich-scented curry plants flourished in the flower beds. Thickets of olive trees wrapped around the estate, protecting its privacy.

Somewhere in the 120,000 square metres, hidden under a green canopy of shrubs, there was a small opening in an isolated granite rock, where Buonaparte liked to seclude himself. Later it acquired the name 'Napoleon's Grotto'. An early tourist found the remains of a small summer house built beneath the rock and a flourishing fig tree that had nearly closed off the entrance. In his biography, Walter Scott wrote: 'How the imagination labours to form an idea of the visions which in this sequestered and romantic spot must have arisen before the hero of a hundred battles!'[17] Today the location of 'Napoleon's Grotto' has migrated from Les Milelli to the Place d'Austerlitz in Ajaccio, where it can be found at the foot of an imposing monument erected in 1938. A steep inclined expanse of stone, rising between two columns topped by eagles bearing the dates of Napoleon's birth and death, lists his battles and achievements:

MONTENOTTE	MILLESIMO
LODI	CASTIGLIONE
MONDOVI	ARCOLI

RIVOLI   LES PYRAMIDES
PASSAGE DU SAINT BERNARD
MONTEBELLO   MARENGO
ULM   AUSTERLITZ   JENA
EYLAU   FRIEDLAND   MADRID
ECKMUHL   ESSLING   WAGRAM
LA MOSKOVA   LUTZEN
BAUTZEN   DRESDEN   BRIENNE
CHAMAUBERT   MONTMIRAIL
NANCIS   CRAONNE   LAON
   LIGNY SOUS FLEURUS

CODE CIVIL   UNIVERSITE
   BANQUE DE FRANCE
   LEGION D'HONNEUR
   COURS DE COMPTES
CONCORDAT CONSEIL D'ETAT

The monument is flanked by tall stone steps for visitors to climb to a pyramid and statue at the top, where there is an inscription that almost deifies him: 'Napoleon I Emperor of the French 1804–1815. We have seen you rise to the Empyrean.' Back down on the ground, from inside the grotto, the emperor's familiar silhouette can be seen high against the skyline. The modern-day 'Napoleon's Grotto', so conveniently close to the monument, is an invention for tourists. But somewhere at Les Milelli there was a sheltered, secluded place where he went to think and write, unsure whether his future would be on Corsica or in France, clear only that he must work and make the best of himself, delighting always in the beauty of the natural world. It would please him to know that today Les Milelli is a botanical garden with pleasant places to stroll, an arboretum for educating children planted in 1993, and organic vegetable gardens made available to the public since 2003. The species of trees in the arboretum include horse chestnuts, cedars of Lebanon, Atlas cedars and Judaean date palms. A sign at the entrance reads: 'Here Nature is King. Thank you for respecting this place.'

Buonaparte stayed at Les Milelli for a year when he returned from France in September 1786. He took extended leave from the La Fère regiment, garrisoned at Valence, on the left bank of the Rhône, which he had joined after graduating from the military academy the previous year. During this time he worked on writing a history of Corsica, constructing it as a chronological gallery of great men, but lamenting the current state of the island.[18] 'I was born when my country was dying,' he wrote.[19] Overtaken by melancholy and dismayed by what he had heard of Corsican politics under French rule, he contemplated killing himself:

> What is there to do in this world? Since I must die, is it not just as well that I should kill myself? If I had already passed my sixtieth year, I should respect the prejudices of my contemporaries and wait patiently until nature had finished its course; but since I begin to experience misfortune, and since nothing is a pleasure to me, why should I support a life in which nothing prospers for me? How far men are removed from nature! How cowardly they are, how abject, how servile![20]

The teenage Napoleon idolised Corsican patriots, whom he imagined leading simple lives of public virtue, close to nature and full of love. He thought the French had robbed and corrupted Corsica. He had dreaded returning – 'What attitude am I to hold? What language am I to use?' – and indulged thoughts of suicide to alleviate his feelings of disgust and isolation.

The short-lived Republic of Corsica had been established in 1755, after declaring independence from Genoa, under the leadership of the freedom fighter Pasquale Paoli. The small republic was conquered by France at the beginning of May 1769, three months before

Buonaparte was born on 15 August. He was a naturalised French citizen, but grew up mourning Corsican independence. In 1784, before he left Brienne-le-Château, Buonaparte wrote to his father asking him for a copy of the Scottish biographer James Boswell's *Account of Corsica* (1768), which he read in the French or Italian translation.[21] Boswell had visited Corsica in 1765, approving of a small island asserting its liberty and wanting to meet the patriot leader Paoli. During his time on Corsica, Boswell noted that gardening had been greatly neglected in the fight for independence. At the time of his visit there was an ordinance by which 'every man who possesses a garden, or other enclosure, is obliged to sow every year pease, beans and all sorts of garden stuff, and not less than a pound of each, under the penalty of four livres, to be exacted by the Podestà'.[22] The Supreme Council of the Republic appointed two officials in each province to superintend the cultivation of land and to encourage especially the planting of mulberry trees, in the hope that Corsica might be able to produce silk from the worms that feed exclusively on mulberry leaves. The dream of a silk industry on the island survived the demise of the republic.

On the coast, north-east of Ajaccio, there was marshland known as Les Salines, separated from the sea by a sandbar. Between the reeds, salt pans stretched across roughly ten acres of land, bordered by vineyards on one side, sand on the other. In living memory there had always been pestilence rising from Les Salines. Local people wondered if the land could be sanitised by draining, or if the marsh could be transformed into a fish pond or saltworks. Few people in Ajaccio had the money for such an enterprise, but Buonaparte's father Carlo was one of them. He laid claim to the land with an old title deed dating back to 1584.[23] The French state accepted his document and in the name of Louis XVI he was granted a concession in Les Salines in perpetuity. He immediately applied for government help to drain the land, then in 1782 he took an interest-free loan from the French state for the establishment of a mulberry tree nursery. He promised to grow

100,000 mulberry trees in ten years and received 8,500 livres plus 2 sols per graft.[24]

In addition to mulberry trees, Carlo planned to include other fruit trees and exotic plants in the nursery. Two years later, he had spent around 30,000 livres and Les Salines was still not properly drained. The pestilence continued, claiming the life of one of the gardeners who worked on the fetid land.[25] Carlo estimated he needed almost as much money again as he had already spent to complete the project. But on 24 February 1785, he died from stomach cancer, aged thirty-nine. Buonaparte, in Paris at the military academy, deeply regretted that he had not been able to close his father's eyes.[26] The mulberry nursery was a troublesome inheritance for his family and he was soon drawn into the struggle to secure the money that had been promised by the French state. When his mother wrote to request the remainder of the loan in October, just nine months after her husband had died, she was told the nursery was underperforming: only 25,330 trees had been supplied, and of those only 7,850 were viable. Les Salines was still too wet and the nursery was failing. The French state simply cancelled the loan and demanded repayment. In addition to their bereavement, the Buonaparte family was now close to bankrupt.

Buonaparte fought on his family's behalf. The following year, after further petitions and demands for damages, a French official travelled to Corsica to inspect Les Salines. He found the drained part of the land covered with beautiful saplings. At the end of his report the official wrote: 'I can only applaud the care and intelligence employed by the eldest son of Madame Buonaparte, whom she retained in the country to watch over the establishment which suffered from the death of the father Monsieur Buonaparte.'[27] Buonaparte was not the eldest son, but he had been on Corsica since 15 September 1786. He was more diligent in helping his mother than his indigent elder brother, so it is possible that the official who inspected Les Salines was praising him, not Joseph, for his careful cultivation.

Buonaparte disapproved of the way he and his fellow trainee soldiers had been waited on and pampered at the military academy in Paris. Looking back, he thought it would have been more appropriate for the cadets to learn to prepare and grow their own food. His family on Corsica took pride in never buying bread, wine or olive oil. Apart from a small number of items that could not be produced on the island – coffee, sugar and rice – everything else on the table in Ajaccio or at Les Milelli came from the local land or sea.[28] At the start of his career, when he should have been advancing himself through the ranks in his regiment, Buonaparte's family pulled him back to Corsica, where he did his best to rescue their mulberry nursery on unsuitable land. However much the reeds were cleared and the ditches filled with soil, the water kept reclaiming Les Salines, rotting the saplings which sank slowly into the earth.

Buonaparte tried to persuade the authorities to advance the rest of the loan, so that more grafting could take place. He attempted to secure compensation for the thousands of mulberry trees his family had already supplied to the French government. He hoped that in 1787, when Louis XVI replaced his controller of finances (*contrôleur général*), sacking Charles-Alexandre de Calonne and promoting Archbishop Loménie de Brienne, there would be a new opportunity to recoup some of his family's losses. But all these hopes for justice and compensation from the French state came to nothing. 'Last year we delivered four or five thousand trees, although we had ten thousand ready to transplant. This year we have delivered only hundreds, although the king should still have taken ten thousand. This cultivation is ruining us,' he complained to the French *intendant* of Corsica, 'and I cannot hide from you that the plantation is now in a very bad state. But something must be done and it is not just that we should continue to suffer.'[29] In 1789, when Louis XVI agreed to address the threatened bankruptcy of his kingdom by summoning the Estates General, the nation's largest representative body which had not met since 1614, Buonaparte was back in France stationed with his regiment in Auxonne, a town in Bourgogne. His Corsican background and early experience of familial finances left him sympathetic to calls for reforming the Ancien Régime. He hoped the summoning of the Estates General would revive the fight for Corsican independence. He idolised the legendary Paoli, who was living in exile in London, and dreamed of Corsica throwing off French dominion, just as it had once thrown off Genovese.

When he was training at Auxonne, Buonaparte wrote a dissertation on royal authority and a treatise on the uses of artillery. 'I have no resource but work,' he wrote to his uncle back on Corsica in March 1789.[30] He continued researching his history of Corsica. He also took extensive notes from the encyclopedia *Histoire Naturelle*, by the great naturalist Georges-Louis Leclerc, the Comte de Buffon, which concentrated on the formation of the planets, of the earth, rivers, seas, lakes, winds, volcanoes, earthquakes and human beings.[31] As the Third Estate, or commoners, in Paris invented a new meaning for the term 'revolution' – a complete rejection of the Ancien Régime and the establishment of a new social and political order – it was the old meaning of the term that Buonaparte encountered in Buffon's description of the planets:

The earth is about 3,000 leagues in diameter and is situated 30 million leagues from the sun, around which it makes a revolution in 365 days. This movement is the result of two forces: one from top to bottom, called attraction, the other from left to right . . . the revolution is always on a small axis which is 1/175 less than the axis of the equator.[32]

He noted Buffon's theory that the planets had arisen from the oblique collision of a comet with the sun, resulting in parcels of molten matter that had become rapidly rotating satellites revolving around the sun. He made notes on the cooling and formation of the earth, the emergence of human life, human reproduction and the development of foetuses. He even made notes on dental and linguistic development after birth, and took a special interest in castration. In this work, Buonaparte encountered the history of humanity situated in the history of the natural world. As Buffon wrote:

> Six hundred centuries were necessary for Nature to construct her great works, to cool the earth, to fashion its surface and arrive at a tranquil state; how many will be necessary for men to arrive at the same state and stop annoying, agitating and destroying one another?[33]

Buffon underestimated the age of the world, but not the elusiveness of peace on earth. In his *Epochs of Nature*, he argued that every country, every society, should strive for the best possible form of government, 'one that would be able to make all men, if not equally happy, at least less equally unhappy', but he was not an enthusiast for revolution and had no political programme or form of government to propose. He simply hoped that the time had come for mankind to recognise that 'his true glory is science and peace his true happiness'.[34] Buonaparte in his studious youth at Auxonne would have agreed. He maintained a lifelong interest in the progress of the sciences. But he would have been the first to admit that peace was not what he contributed to human history.

In early April 1789, Buonaparte, a number of other officers and three hundred soldiers under their command were sent to the town of Suerre, forty kilometres south of Auxonne, to quell the food riots that were taking place alongside the elections to the Estates General that opened in Versailles on 5 May. Buonaparte stayed in the town for a couple of months to maintain order, threatening to fire on the rioters if they did not disperse. He was not in Paris for the Tennis Court Oath on 20 June, when representatives of the clergy and aristocracy (the First and Second Estates) were invited by representatives of the commoners (the Third Estate) to join them in drafting a new constitution for France. Locked out of their debating chamber, the representatives of the Third Estate reassembled in an indoor tennis court at Versailles and swore not to disband until France had a new constitution. For many this oath, afterwards depicted in a dramatic painting by the artist Jacques-Louis David, marked the beginning of the Revolution. The Tennis Court Oath was not a rebellion that could be suppressed, nor a reform movement that could be addressed through compromise; it was the assertion of the rights of the Third Estate which now renamed itself the Nation.

Buonaparte followed the early revolutionary events from a distance. He could not afford to travel to Paris to observe them at first hand. For him the important questions were: How would the Revolution affect Corsica? How would it impact on his family and the unresolved problem of the mulberry nursery? On 12 July he wrote a fan letter to Paoli explicitly identifying himself as a Corsican patriot. 'I was born as the fatherland perished. Thirty thousand French, vomited onto our shores, drowned the throne of liberty in waves of blood, such was the hateful spectacle that first struck my eyes.'[35] Perhaps, one day, he might visit Paoli in London, his letter went on to suggest.

When the Bastille, the prison that symbolised the oppression of the Ancien Régime, fell on 14 July, Buonaparte was probably studying. He heard the news from Paris the next day when two of his comrades rushed into his room and read it to him. He was astonished and alarmed. Reports of the troops that were in Paris to maintain order mingling with the people and exchanging fire with soldiers from other regiments seemed to him an unprecedented level of chaos and uncertainty. When riots broke out in Auxonne less than a week later, Buonaparte's general called on him to restore order. Aged seventy-five, tired and reluctant to use excessive force, General du Teil was pleased to rely on the judgement of his junior officer, who was prepared to harangue and arrest the troublemakers. Writing to his elder brother, Buonaparte expected two or three of them to be hanged. He was no royalist, but he was instinctively on the side of law and order.[36]

*

Buonaparte obtained leave of absence to go home again in September 1789. This time he remained on Corsica until 30 January 1791. The French Revolution had a paradoxical effect on the island: whereas the French had previously been seen as oppressors by those arguing for Corsican independence, suddenly they were defenders of freedom. 'Regeneration: truly you are the king of Nature,' Buonaparte wrote.[37] He finally met Paoli on 17 July 1790, not as he had imagined he might in London, but in the town of Bastia, after the legendary patriot had been persuaded to return to Corsica. Paoli travelled via Paris where he was honoured across the whole political spectrum by Louis XVI, the National Assembly and the radical revolutionary Maximilien Robespierre who said he had 'defended freedom at a time when we did not yet dare hope to achieve it'.[38] Aged twenty-one, Buonaparte was proud to be included in Paoli's retinue. In exile on St Helena he claimed that Paoli had said to him: 'Oh Napoleon! There is nothing modern in your character! You are formed entirely on Plutarch's model.'[39] But in 1790 the future Napoleon was still only Buonaparte, infinitely less certain of becoming a biographical subject than he was before he died. While it is unlikely that Paoli recognised Buonaparte as a future figure in world history, he still helped his elder brother, Joseph, get elected as the president of the administration in the Ajaccio district. Buonaparte went back to France in February 1791, returned to Corsica nine months later, then went back once again to France the following spring to resume his career in the French army.

Buonaparte arrived in Paris shortly before revolutionary France, in a pre-emptive strike, declared war on Austria on 20 April 1792. This increased the likelihood that a young soldier, even one who had been absent without leave, would soon be employed again. Seeking reinstatement in the army, drawing on all the contacts he had, he went to meet the mathematician Gaspard Monge, Minister of the Navy and elder brother of Louis Monge, who had taught him mathematics at school. Monge received the unknown, impoverished young man very politely. Buonaparte's appearance was shabby: a simply made grey greatcoat buttoned up to his chin, a clumsily tied cravat and a round hat, pulled far down over his face, or else balanced on the back of his head. His badly powdered hair hung lankly over the collar of his coat.[40] Monge, the son of a pedlar, was a pioneer of descriptive geometry, which serves two purposes: the calculation of the dimensions of solid bodies; and methods for representing three-dimensional objects on a two-dimensional piece of paper. For many years his ideas were classified as military secrets because descriptive geometry was so useful for improving artillery and fortification techniques. A theory of shadows was central to his work. By shadow he meant what is understood by the term in ordinary speech: the projection of one body onto the surface of another as when 'for example, while walking in the sunshine, one remarks that the shadows are short at noon.'[41] When he first met Buonaparte, Monge could not have guessed at the shadows that this dishevelled young man would cast over his own life.

At this time, Buonaparte and Bourrienne, who knew each other from school, renewed their acquaintance in Paris. They were now both twenty-three, with little money and even less to do. Buonaparte had been removed from the army's lists on 6 February 1792, after overstaying a period of leave on Corsica that had technically expired at the end of the previous year. In his unreliable memoirs, Bourrienne boasts that Buonaparte was even poorer than he was himself, but admits they were both living like vagabonds, struggling to pay their landlords.[42] Buonaparte hoped to find work at the War Office, Bourrienne at the Office of Foreign Affairs. Again, Bourrienne brags that of the two, he was the more successful. They met regularly and went for walks or sat about, on the lookout for moneymaking opportunities. Buonaparte had a scheme to rent and sublet several houses in the Rue Montholon. He was reduced instead to selling his watch through Bourrienne's brother Fauvelet, who ran a furniture warehouse on the Place de Carrousel, very near the Tuileries Palace gardens, where people needing to leave Paris in a hurry were advanced money against the sale of their possessions.

Buonaparte rejoined the army in May, and a few weeks later, on 20 June, the third anniversary of the Tennis Court Oath that had signalled the start of the Revolution in 1789, he and Bourrienne went for one of their walks, meeting at a restaurant in the Rue Saint-Honoré, near the Palais Royal. As they were setting out, they encountered a crowd dressed in rags and armed with impromptu weapons. Buonaparte quickly calculated the size of the gathering at five or six thousand. The friends followed it to the Tuileries gardens, where they positioned themselves on the terrace alongside the River Seine to watch the confrontation between the king and the protesters.[43]

Louis XVI had been living in the Tuileries Palace since October 1789, when he was forced to move from Versailles to Paris, and had been under strict surveillance since June 1791 when he had tried to escape to the French border, where forces hostile to the Revolution had gathered. He had formally, if reluctantly, accepted his new role in the constitutional monarchy in September 1791, and on 18 September there had been a night-time festival in the Tuileries gardens to celebrate the new constitution. On that occasion the royal family was cheered by the crowd, but less than a year later the king started to use his executive veto in a way that inflamed revolutionary senti-ment. After the declaration of war on Austria, when crowds collected in the Tuileries gardens, demonstrating their support for the war, they were driven out by the king's Swiss Guard, who had special respon-sibility for protecting the royal family. As a result, on 24 April 1792 the Legislative Assembly, which met in the Salle du Manège, the riding hall at the north end of the gardens, west of the palace, had decreed the Tuileries gardens a 'national good'. The deputy Kersaint declared: 'The nation houses the King in the Tuileries, but nowhere do I see that she has given him exclusive enjoyment of the garden.'[44] The gardens were renamed 'Jardin National'. Floral decorations were removed from the beds on the parterres and replaced with vegetable crops to provide food for Paris's hospitals. Shops and stalls appeared in the gardens, turning them into a marketplace. The small remaining private sections of the gardens, reserved for the royal family, were separated from the public by a fragile tricolour ribbon.

The Tuileries gardens dated back to the mid-sixteenth century, the time of Catherine de' Medici, the wife of Henry II of France, and mother of Francis II, Charles IX and Henry III. A hundred years later the designer André le Nôtre transformed them into a formal garden in the French style known as *jardin à la française*, for the Sun King, Louis XIV. Favouring straight lines and symmetry, typically including long avenues of trees, often chestnuts or elms, and closely cut hedges, of privet or beech or boxwood, formal ponds or fountains, gravel paths and parterres, Le Nôtre's gardens reflected the orderly triumph of man's will over nature. Interspersed among the geometrically arranged plants were beautiful marble statues. The gardens were works of art designed to be seen from above, from the terrace, or the first-floor salons of the palace. Easily accessible from the surrounding roads, including the Rue Saint-Honoré, the Tuileries gardens had been open to the public since 1667 and used for concerts, firework displays at the Feast of St Louis on 25 August, and even for an early balloon flight in 1783.

The crowds that gathered at the Tuileries on 20 June were critical, not celebratory, demanding that Louis XVI demonstrate his loyalty to the Revolution. Buonaparte was shocked and outraged when the king was forced to appear at the palace windows overlooking the gardens full of protesters, wearing not a crown but the revolutionary *bonnet rouge*, the red cap of liberty, a symbol borrowed from classical antiquity, when it was worn by freed slaves. When one of these caps was placed on the head of Maximilien Robespierre, the rising star of the increasingly radical Jacobin Club devoted to debating revolutionary principles, he tore it off and threw it to the ground; but Louis XVI was in no position to reject or challenge the emblems of the Revolution.[45] He agreed to drink a glass of wine to the health of the nation. Bourrienne claims that Buonaparte could not understand why the protesters had been allowed to enter the palace gardens. 'Why don't they sweep off four or five hundred of them with the cannon,' he wondered aloud, 'the rest would then set off fast enough.'[46]

Over dinner that evening, which Bourrienne paid for, Buonaparte talked of nothing else. He discussed the causes and consequences of the unrepressed insurrection and predicted that the monarchy would soon collapse, which it did on 10 August 1792. By this time, Bourrienne had been appointed to a diplomatic post at Stuttgart, so Buonaparte went back to the Tuileries Palace gardens alone to witness the violence that finally deposed Louis XVI. Later in life, he told his brother Joseph that the carnage he saw in the garden that day affected him more profoundly than any of the subsequent battles he participated in.[47] Early in the morning, as soon as he heard of the attack on the Tuileries, he had hurried to Bourrienne's brother's warehouse, from where he could be sure of a clear, safe view of what was happening.[48] Here, surrounded by the belongings of people who had already fled France, he watched the death throes of the monarchy. Around nine hundred Swiss Guards attempted to protect the royal family from the revolutionary crowd. A hundred and fifty of them had already accompanied the king on his sad walk across the garden to the Legislative Assembly in the Salle du Manège where he resigned his crown. As he left the Tuileries for the last time, the king remarked that the autumn leaves were falling early that year. The rest of the Swiss Guard remained at the now empty palace. Despite having cannon and ammunition, hundreds were slaughtered in the Tuileries grounds. This was because they had received the order from Louis XVI to lay down their arms and return to their barracks. They obeyed, and almost seven hundred of them were killed, their bodies piling up by the round pond in the formal garden while the palace was pillaged. The contrast between the geometrical precision of the garden layout, with its neat, symmetrical topiary, and the corpses of the dead and dying was shocking.

With retrospect, Buonaparte was not sure if it was the smallness of the space, the unusual spectacle of a bloody battle inside a garden, the density of dead bodies piled on top of one another on the ground, or the fact that he was still young and inexperienced and this was the first time he had ever seen bloodshed, which accounted for the deep and lasting impression of horror that the massacre of 10 August made on him.[49] Men and women participated in the violence. Théroigne de Méricourt, a flamboyant female revolutionary, who founded a club with the mathematician Charles-Gilbert Romme called Société des amis de la loi (Society of Friends of the Law), was later awarded a civic crown for her courage.[50] Buonaparte remembered walking through the garden in the aftermath and seeing well-dressed women behaving with gross indecency, mutilating the genitals of the murdered Swiss Guards, seemingly civilised people descending to bestial behaviour. Afterwards, making the rounds of the nearby cafes, he noticed the anger in people's faces, sensing revolutionary rage in every heart. He thought he caught people looking at him with hostility and defiance, as though he was somehow suspicious for remaining calm and not sharing their anger.[51] He was more likely in shock, unsure of his future and of what to think in the midst of the Revolution. But the sense that the crowd might suddenly turn on him, as it had turned on the king and his Swiss Guards in the Tuileries gardens, never left Buonaparte, it only got stronger, more plausible and haunting over time.[52]

2

Revolutionary Regeneration

'O, Nature, this immense people, assembled in the beams
of the first light of day, is worthy of you, is free!'[1]

At the heart of revolutionary Paris, on the left bank of the River
Seine, there was a botanical garden. Before the Revolution it was
the Jardin du Roi, the King's Garden. Louis XIII's doctors established
it in the mid-seventeenth century to grow medicinal plants. Later
the Comte de Buffon transformed it into one of the greatest gardens
in the world. For fifty years, until his death in 1788, the year before
the Revolution began, Buffon planted, propagated and researched
in the garden. He introduced into France the first hydrangea from
China, the dahlia, the plane tree, the sweet-acorned oak. He remod-
elled the greenhouses, laid out avenues of lime trees and extended
the grounds by negotiating with the abbot of the neighbouring
monastery. When Buffon was away at his private estate in Montbard,
working on the many volumes of his *Histoire Naturelle*, the person
who cared most for the Jardin du Roi was André Thouin, the head
gardener, whose father had been head gardener before him. Thouin
had been born in the Jardin du Roi and never wanted to live
anywhere else.[2]

Under Thouin's care the garden thrived during the Revolution while
other royal institutions were destroyed. It was given a new name – the

Jardin des Plantes – a menagerie of animals was added and Louis-Jean-Marie Daubenton, who had been demonstrator of the king's cabinet (or collection) of natural history under the Ancien Régime, was charged with establishing a modern museum, the Muséum national d'histoire naturelle.[3] Thouin quickly became a committed revolutionary. He was forty-three when the Revolution began, a tall man with grey-brown hair, brown eyes, a high forehead and an aquiline nose. A distinguished botanist, he was determined to protect the garden he had known since childhood. He wanted the Jardin des Plantes to contribute to the public good without being interfered with by the new government. For public enjoyment, he laid out the grounds with topiary and flower beds. In the early years of the Revolution, Parisians found the Jardin des Plantes a green paradise amid political turmoil.

Thouin played a prominent part in the design of the Revolutionary calendar which replaced the Gregorian calendar on 24 October 1793. The new system for marking the division of days, weeks and years was inspired by the natural world and backdated to the foundation of the French Republic on 22 September 1792, so that when the new calendar began, France was already into its second year of revolutionary regeneration. The revolutionaries were determined to make both a substantial and symbolic break from the corrupt Ancien Régime. In addition to designing a new constitution for France, they hoped to erase all vestiges of clerical and aristocratic privileges. The mathematician Charles-Gilbert Romme directed the commission that designed the new calendar. Others involved included Gaspard Monge and the playwright Philippe Fabre d'Églantine – who had added 'eglantine' (wild rose) to his name after winning a poetry prize. 'We could not go on reckoning the years during which we were oppressed by kings as part of our lifetime. Every page of the old calendar was soiled by the prejudices and falsehoods of the throne and the church,' Fabre d'Églantine claimed.[4] The new Republican calendar year began on the day of the autumnal equinox in Paris. It was divided into twelve

months of thirty days each with names that were neologisms inspired
by nature:

Vendémiaire	(month of vintage)	30 days beginning	22, 23 or 24 September
Brumaire	(month of mist)	30 days beginning	22, 23 or 24 October
Frimaire	(month of frost)	30 days beginning	21, 22 or 23 November
Nivôse	(month of snow)	30 days beginning	21, 22 or 23 December
Pluviôse	(month of rain)	30 days beginning	20, 21 or 22 January
Ventôse	(month of wind)	30 days beginning	19, 20 or 21 February
Germinal	(month of seeds)	30 days beginning	20 or 21 March
Floréal	(month of flowers)	30 days beginning	20 or 21 April
Prairial	(month of meadows)	30 days beginning	20 or 21 May
Messidor	(month of harvest)	30 days beginning	19 or 20 June
Thermidor	(month of heat)	30 days beginning	19 or 20 July
Fructidor	(month of fruit)	30 days beginning	18 or 19 August

In the new calendar, the weeks were ten days long and each of the
days was named after a plant, animal or tool used by agricultural
labourers. Because of his horticultural expertise, Thouin had special
responsibility for proposing the names of plants to replace the names
of the Christian saints in the old calendar.[5] He chose fruits and vegetables that would already be well known throughout France: turnip,
chicory, medlar, cauliflower, truffle, olive, orange and so on. Every
tenth day was a day of rest. The extra five (or six in a leap year) days
left over from decimalising the Gregorian calendar were called
'Sansculottides', or without-breeches days, in honour of the nickname
given to the ordinary revolutionaries who turned out on the streets
wearing their *bonnets rouges*, who would, if necessary, use violence to
protect the new republic.

One symbol of regeneration early in the Revolution was the Liberty
tree. These trees were planted high on mounds of earth, in the hope
they would grow isolated, straight and tall, symbolising the vitality
of the new regime. Soon there were about 60,000 Liberty trees

throughout France, many of them failing to thrive. No one, least of all the Convention elected to govern France after the fall of the monarchy, wanted to see Liberty trees wilting or dying and Thouin was pleased to give advice on which species were most suitable for transplanting.[6] He disagreed with the suggestion that Liberty trees should only be oaks. He saw an opportunity for introducing new varieties of tree across France, trees that would be novel and interesting for locals. He imagined that some of these new varieties might become as popular as the elm, which, after a difficult introduction, now grew abundantly throughout the country. He emphasised the importance of choosing trees that were strong and able to survive French winters, and trees with generous and long-lasting foliage so that citizens could shelter under them from rain and sun. He drew up a list of sixty-six trees, suitable for different parts of France, and a list of nurseries where they could be obtained. He was an essential horticultural expert for the new state.

Bonaparte was introduced to Thouin and the Jardin des Plantes through his friend Jean-Andoche Junot who became his aide-de-camp during the siege of Toulon in late 1793. Toulon was Bonaparte's first major opportunity to distinguish himself in combat. In Year 1 (mid-September 1793), when he was still only an officer in his artillery regiment escorting a slow-moving convoy of gunpowder wagons along the south coast from Marseilles to Nice, he stopped to see his fellow Corsican, Antoine Saliceti, at Beausset. Saliceti was one of the Convention's powerful representatives-on-mission, invested with extraordinary power to impose order in the provinces or the army. He was close to the revolutionary leader Maximilien Robespierre and his brother Augustin Robespierre.[7] Maximilien, a provincial lawyer before the Revolution, was now the most feared man in France owing to his membership of the infamous Committee of Public Safety that orchestrated the Terror. Augustin was a deputy of the Convention who had been sent on mission to suppress the counter-revolutionary revolt in southern France. Saliceti was in Beausset because it was the headquarters for an army under the command of General Carteaux, a painter and policeman, entrusted with putting down the revolt and defending the country against foreign invasion. Within hours, Bonaparte, through his own determination and with Saliceti's help, was promoted from convoy escort to a commander in Carteaux's artillery. He was sent to Toulon, where counter-revolutionary royalist supporters had taken charge of the city and opened its port to the allied force of an Anglo-Spanish fleet.

Bonaparte knew Toulon well because it was from there that he sailed to and from Corsica on his many voyages between the island and mainland France.[8] Thinking about the position of the port he realised that they could only regain control of the city by laying siege to the promontory and fort of L'Éguillette, a narrow point from where they would be able to police access to and from the harbour. By aiming to take the promontory with his artillery forces he sought to cut off communication between the insurgents of Toulon and the Anglo-Spanish ships. The plan was simple and its successful enactment saved France from foreign invasion, but it was only adopted after a protracted struggle. The young battalion leader did not have the authority to override the decisions of his superiors whose lack of competence deeply frustrated him.

During the construction of one of the first of Bonaparte's batteries against the English, he asked for a volunteer with outstanding clerical skills and beautiful handwriting. Jean-Andoche Junot, a 22-year-old sergeant, stepped forward and began writing down Bonaparte's orders, leaning on the retaining wall, not flinching when shots and dirt fell down around him onto the paper. 'At least I have no need of sand to dry the ink,' he quipped.[9] It was soon afterwards that Bonaparte made Junot his aide-de-camp and the two became close friends. They built more batteries, one called 'Jacobins', another 'Men Without Fear', and managed to push back the enemy until the British General Charles O'Hara was captured. O'Hara then began negotiations with Augustin

Robespierre. On the night of 26 Frimaire, Year 2 (16 December 1793) Bonaparte, who had been promoted to the rank of colonel, launched an assault and the British abandoned L'Éguillette. Two days later, on 28 Frimaire, the Anglo-Spanish fleet fled Toulon. Afterwards, Bonaparte was promoted to the rank of *général de brigade*.

Junot's uncle, the Bishop of Metz, was a distinguished naturalist and a close friend of Daubenton's, who was now settled into his museum in the Jardin des Plantes. When Junot and Bonaparte were in Paris together they often went for walks in the Jardin des Plantes, where Daubenton and Thouin received them kindly. Daubenton strolled around the garden like a patriarch, overseeing the planting, while Thouin worked so hard he could have been mistaken for a common labourer.[10] Bonaparte loved to go on tours of the greenhouses with Thouin. The greenhouses were not yet what Junot's future wife Laure Martin de Permond would later describe in her memoirs as 'the finest temple ever raised to nature in the midst of a city', but they were already filled with rare and fascinating plants. The most recent greenhouse, built in 1788, was named after the Comte de Buffon. It was 7.8 metres long, 3.8 metres wide and 4.6 metres tall. It contained a magnificent collection of ferns, including the golden-leafed *Gymnogramma chrysophylla*. It also held the great bougainvillea (*Bougainvillea spectabilis*), the climbing, flowering vine that was discovered in Brazil during Louis Antoine de Bougainville's expedition around the world in 1772. Its flowers were pink and hairy on the outside, yellow on the inside.

In 1786, the Comte de Buffon had put Thouin in charge of a seedling garden, sheltered from the sun and wind, with instructions to expand the range of vegetables grown in France. Wandering through the Jardin de Plantes, Thouin showed Bonaparte vegetables from all over the globe being propagated in frames and under coverings that replicated their natural climates. Some were from tropical regions, others from mountainous snow-covered terrain. Alongside the edible plants were ornamental ones: northern ferns, daphnes, alpine

geraniums, yellow flowering violets, rock jasmine, primroses, saxifrages
of the Pyrenees, alpine soldanellas, glacial absinthes, buttercups and
dwarf willows.[11]

One of Buffon's successors at the Jardin des Plantes was the naturalist and novelist Jacques-Henri Bernardin de Saint-Pierre. He was
the author of *Paul et Virginie*, a romance set in Mauritius, then known
as the Île de France, which had captured Bonaparte's imagination. The
novel, published in 1788, describes a child of nature corrupted by the
sentimentality of the French privileged class. The characters live off
the land in Mauritius, treating their slaves kindly and telling the time
by the shadows of trees. 'Paul and Virginie had no clocks, no almanacs,
no history or philosophy books. Their lives were regulated by nature.
They knew the hours of the day by the shade of the trees, the seasons
by the flowering and fruiting of the trees, and the years by the number
of harvests.'[12]

When he was appointed to run the Jardin des Plantes, Bernardin
de Saint-Pierre was determined to create a zoo alongside the gardens
and new natural history museum. In Year 1 the Commune of Paris
passed a law banning people from exhibiting wild animals in the streets
of Paris.[13] The owners of the animals were invited to bring them to
the Jardin des Plantes, where they were accommodated in old stables
or makeshift cages until more permanent buildings could be
constructed. Bears, wolves, foxes, marmots and birds began arriving.
The animals from what had been Marie Antoinette's old menagerie at
the palace of Versailles and the Duc d'Orléans' menagerie at the
Château du Raincy were also moved to the gardens. In total, about
sixty insecurely housed animals and many more birds spread out
through the Jardin des Plantes. People kept arriving with more dona-
tions. Sometimes they were motivated by patriotic zeal, sometimes
by self-interest. Some brought along common cats hoping for a reward.
In the midst of the Terror, as more and more people were guillotined
for counter-revolutionary activity or sentiments, the Jardin des Plantes
remained a relative enclave of civilisation. It offered public lectures

and a vibrant, if increasingly chaotic, assembly of wildlife among the carefully tended trees and plants.

In Pluviôse, Year 2 (February 1794), Augustin Robespierre wrote to his elder brother in Paris praising the brilliant young officer responsible for the victory at Toulon. 'I would add to the list of patriots the name of citizen Buonaparte, general in chief of the artillery, an officer of transcendent merit.'[14] Augustin met Bonaparte in Nice. They became friends and Augustin did his utmost to promote Bonaparte, arranging for him, after the success of his strategy at Toulon, to be put in charge of planning an attack on the fortified town of Coni on the Piedmontese plain.[15] Bonaparte never met the elder Robespierre, but through Augustin he formed a strong and favourable opinion of the man most closely associated with the reign of Terror. He approved of Robespierre's attempts to stabilise revolutionary France through a strong central government, and attributed to him a plan for 'regenerating both the century and the country'.[16] Influenced by Augustin, Bonaparte saw Robespierre as the Incorruptible imagined himself: a man selflessly committed to the triumph of the Revolution. Nevertheless, he was careful to keep himself at a distance from the fervid politics at the heart of the Revolution. When Augustin tried to persuade him to return to Paris with him in Prairial, Year 2 (May 1794) to take over command of the National Guard, Bonaparte thought about it for an evening and declined. 'I didn't care to get mixed up in revolutionary plots that I had up to that point stayed out of.'[17]

During the Revolution, Parisian promenades and gardens were frequently used to stage public celebrations.[18] On 20 Prairial, Year 2 (8 June 1794), a papier-mâché statue of atheism, designed by the artist Jacques-Louis David, was ceremoniously burnt in the Tuileries gardens. The site of the massacre that marked the end of the monarchy was deliberately chosen as the venue for the Festival of the Supreme Being, the inauguration of Robespierre's new religion. Presenting himself as a high priest in a sky-blue coat and carrying a bouquet of wheat and wild flowers, Robespierre made a long speech before setting fire to atheism. As the statue burned another emerged inside the flames representing wisdom. Afterwards the crowds followed Robespierre to the Champs de Mars, the scene of another massacre earlier in the Revolution. There a huge artificial mountain had been constructed with a Liberty tree planted at the summit.

Bonaparte approved of Robespierre's attempts to reverse the rise of atheism in France by introducing this new revolutionary religion organised around the worship of the Supreme Being. Robespierre hoped his deistic religion would replace both Roman Catholicism and the atheistic Cult of Reason that had developed during the Revolution. Bonaparte, like Robespierre, thought belief in the existence of God and the immortality of the soul were useful for the stability of the state. Where many found the worship of the Supreme Being ridiculous, and some members of the Convention were seen tittering as Robespierre ascended the artificial mountain with his bouquet, Bonaparte praised the Incorruptible for trying to reintroduce religion and raise morality in France. He read the printed version of Robespierre's discourse on the Supreme Being with great interest and concluded that Robespierre was no ordinary man, but a courageous and politic one. 'He was very superior to everything around him.'[19]

Robespierre's power, however, was nearly spent. Since his arrival in the port city of Bordeaux in Vendémiaire, Year 2 (September 1793), the young Representative on Mission, 24-year-old Jean-Lambert Tallien, sent from Paris to subdue insurgency, had delighted in feeding the infamous instrument of revolutionary punishment. But after an initial period of bloodletting, the guillotine was suddenly quieter and Tallien seemed less keen on the methods of the Terror. People said this was because he had fallen in love with the wealthy and beautiful Thérésa Cabarrus, the former wife of the Marquis de Fontenay, who was intent on saving her friends from the guillotine and used her influence over Tallien. When this came to Robespierre's attention, he recalled Tallien to Paris. Thérésa was arrested and imprisoned, which would almost certainly have led to her being guillotined. But from prison she sent Tallien a dagger and a letter that read: 'I die in despair at having belonged to a coward like you.' Tallien's determination to redeem himself in the estimation of his mistress by saving her from death contributed to the coup that brought down Robespierre on 9 Thermidor, Year 2 (29 July 1794). Tallien was one of the members of the Convention, which still nominally governed France, who denounced Robespierre as a traitor and conspirator against the Revolution. Many members of the Convention had reason to believe that Robespierre was going to proscribe them and send them to their deaths and it was for this reason that they moved against him first. The next day, Robespierre went to the guillotine accompanied by his younger brother. Bonaparte was in Nice when he heard the news. 'I have been somewhat moved by the catastrophic fate of Robespierre, whom I liked and thought pure, but had he been my father, I would have stabbed him myself if he aspired to tyranny,' he wrote to the French chargé d'affaires in Genoa.[20] It was Bonaparte's view that Robespierre fell not because he was a tyrant, but because he was more moderate than some of his fellow Jacobins and had being trying to stop the disruptive effects of the Revolution.[21]

Whatever Bonaparte's good opinion of Robespierre was, many owed their lives to his downfall. Thérésa Cabarrus was just one of those released from prison in the immediate aftermath of Thermidor. Bonaparte's future wife Josephine was another. Because of his association with Augustin, Bonaparte himself was arrested on 22 Thermidor, Year 2 (9 August 1794), accused of complicity with the Robespierre brothers. He was imprisoned for only two weeks, either in Fort Carré in Antibes, or under house arrest in his lodgings in Nice. During this time he wrote to his aide-de-camp Junot, to tell him his conscience was clear and he would make no effort to escape.[22] He also wrote at length to the Representatives of the People who had suspended him from his duties and ordered his arrest. He declared that during a revolution there are just two classes of people – suspects and patriots – and he was definitely a patriot who had been attached to the principles of the Revolution since it began.[23]

Bonaparte esteemed Junot's friendship highly, sometimes claiming that a faithful friend is the true image of God.[24] During his walks with Junot in the Jardin des Plantes, he became communicative and confiding. When they passed through the garden gates into the deep green shade they felt as if heavy burdens were left behind and they could inhale purer air. On one of these visits, Bonaparte told Junot that he was deeply in love but that his feelings were not requited. His voice trembled with emotion, but Junot thought 'there was within him an extraordinary force that struggled against his weakness'. Yet when Junot reciprocated and confided his love for Bonaparte's beautiful sister Pauline (Paulette), as they left the garden, Bonaparte became steely and rational. The friends crossed the Seine in a boat and walked north towards the new Chinese baths. Outside the enclosed, peaceful space of the Jardin des Plantes, beyond its 'odoriferous shades', the harsh realities of life reclaimed Bonaparte. He refused to write to his mother to recommend Junot as a marriage prospect for his sister. 'The truth is, you have nothing but your lieutenant's pay,' he told him, 'and Paulette, she has not so much. So to sum up; you have nothing, she has nothing. What is the total? Nothing. You cannot marry at present. You must wait.'[25] Junot would later point out the place on the Boulevard des Italiens they had reached when Bonaparte spoke these words to him.

In the spring of Year 3 (1795), Paris was starving. At the Jardin des Plantes there was nothing to feed the animals in the menagerie, not even horsemeat, and over half of them died and became specimens in the museum.[26] Less than a year after the fall of Robespierre, famished citizens looked back with fondness to the regime of Terror, remembering that then there was at least bread. 'Balls, theatres and concerts were nightly crowded, while famine was staring us in the face, and we were threatened with all the horrors of anarchy,' Laure Martin de Permond recalled in her memoir.[27] She was a precocious young girl whose caustic wit and great beauty were already evident at the age of ten. She came back to Paris in Year 3 with her mother Panoria, while her father attended to business in Bordeaux and waited to hear if it was safe for him to join his family. Panoria, who was of Greek descent, had spent time living on Corsica and knew many Corsicans in Paris before the Revolution. When she returned, these acquaintances called on her and her daughter in the rooms they were renting, on the second floor overlooking a garden, at the Hôtel de la Tranquillité in the Rue des Filles Saint-Thomas. Bonaparte was among the regular callers. He visited almost every day. He was a long-standing friend of the family, having once stayed with them for three weeks when he sprained his ankle at military school.[28] With the cruelty of youth, Laure thought him emaciated and decidedly ugly. Sometimes he brought Panoria a bouquet of violets, flowers he was particularly fond of. Laure knew that Bonaparte's vehement political talk annoyed her mother and yet he was indulged. Despite the fact he was a general, Bonaparte was broke, living off handouts from his elder brother Joseph, who had recently got married.

Laure's memoirs also noted the fate of Jean Bertrand Féraud, who had been close to Robespierre, but had deftly dissociated himself after 9 Thermidor to become part of the new government. He had recently been given the unenviable task of overseeing supplies for Paris. On 1 Prairial, Year 3 (20 May 1795), Féraud, once described as 'the maddest colleague you could dream of', was trying to talk down an angry crowd that had broken into the Convention demanding food, when a hungry woman, who had brought a pistol with her, shot him dead. The crowd fell upon his body and cut off his head, fixed it to a pike and paraded it into the debating chamber of the Convention. A locksmith in his fifties was arrested for carrying Féraud's head on the pike and afterwards guillotined. No one knows what happened to the woman with the pistol.

Laure remembered that while these violent scenes were occurring in the Convention, respectable Parisians, people who still had something to lose, locked themselves away with their valuables, anxiously waiting for news. Her brother returned in the evening, having eaten nothing all day, full of stories of the uprising in the streets, especially in the Faubourg Saint-Antoine. But it was not until Bonaparte arrived later, also unfed, that they learned of the murder in the Convention. According to Laure, Bonaparte was clear that 'if we continue to sully our Revolution, it will be a disgrace to be a Frenchman'.[29] He thought it would be a terrible mistake for the Convention to bombard the Faubourg Saint-Antoine because then the violence would spread more widely through Paris.

One of those arrested after the uprising was Gilbert Romme, who had chaired the committee that invented the Revolutionary calendar and had also designed an agricultural almanac based on the new calendar. He had supported the insurrection and the crowd's demands for bread. He pledged to commit suicide if he was condemned, and did so, plunging a dagger into his heart on the staircase of the courtroom, declaring 'I die for the republic', on 29 Prairial, Year 3 (17 June 1795). In her version of the story, Laure claimed that Romme's last words were 'Vive la liberté!', and that her brother was standing so close to him when he died that his coat was spattered with blood. Bonaparte was away from Paris for a few days in Saint-Maur, but when he got back and learned of Romme's death he was deeply moved. He eulogised Romme and turned vehemently against Saliceti, whom he accused of trying to revive the policies of the Terror. Recording all this, Laure wanted to overturn the negative portrait of Bonaparte as a cold, unfeeling character that Bourrienne's wife provided. The Bourriennes, newly married, had returned to Paris from Stuttgart for a visit shortly before Romme's trial and they socialised with Bonaparte, though bread was so scarce dinner guests had to be asked to bring their own, and went on many trips to the theatre. Madame Bourrienne found Bonaparte reserved and gloomy and did not share her husband's warmth towards his old school friend. 'There was always something eccentric in Bonaparte's behaviour, for he often slipped away from us without saying a word; and when we were supposing he had left the theatre, we would suddenly discover him in the second or third tier, sitting alone in a box, and looking rather sulky.'[30]

That autumn Bonaparte wrote a novel, *Clisson et Eugénie*, a wishful-thinking, loosely autobiographical romance, strongly influenced by Bernardin de Saint-Pierre's *Paul et Virginie*. 'From birth Clisson was strongly attracted to war' is the opening sentence. But soon it is love, not war, that the novel focuses on. Clisson likes nothing better than to wander in the woods, 'there he felt at peace with himself, scorning human wickedness and despising folly and cruelty'.[31] He appreciates the sunrise and sunset, 'the changing seasons, the varying vistas, the concerts of birdsong, the murmuring waters'.[32] He realises that in his previous battle-filled life he was blind to beauty and 'insensible to the pleasures of nature'.[33] Clisson meets Eugénie at a spa and compares her to a piece of music by Paisiello, 'which elevates only those souls born to appreciate it'.[34] He renounces all thoughts of war and glory for Eugénie and they live together for years having many children and remaining deeply in love. 'They spent every day together, bringing up their children, tending their garden and running their household.' They delight in love, nature and rustic simplicity. Eventually this domestic idyll is shattered by war and Eugénie's infidelity. Clisson goes off to die in battle.

The character of Eugénie was probably based on Eugénie Désirée Clary, to whom Bonaparte was briefly engaged. She was the sister of his elder brother Joseph's wife. It is unclear if Eugénie was the woman whom Bonaparte discussed with Junot during their walks in the Jardin des Plantes, but if his love was initially unrequited, it was he, not Eugénie, who ended their engagement on 20 Fructidor, Year 3 (6 September 1795). The reason was Josephine. The woman who would become Bonaparte's first wife was born Marie Josèphe Rose Tascher de la Pagerie to a wealthy Creole family who owned slaves and a sugar plantation in Les Trois-Ilets, Martinique. She married Alexandre de Beauharnais in 1779 and had two children with him, Eugène and Hortense. During the Terror, Alexandre was arrested and accused of counter-revolutionary activity on 29 Germinal, Year 2 (18 April 1794), and his wife was arrested three days later. Alexandre was guillotined five days before Robespierre. Josephine (who was known as Rose until she met Bonaparte, who changed her name to one he preferred) was released from prison in the immediate aftermath of Robespierre's fall from power. By the time Bonaparte met her in the autumn of Year 3, she was well connected to the new government through her close friend Thérésa Cabarrus, Tallien's beautiful mistress, now his wife, and through her own affair with Paul Barras, a member of the Convention and commissioner to the French army.

The romantic and pragmatic sides of Bonaparte's nature coincided in his attraction to Josephine. He was entranced and besotted by her, but her connection to Barras, whom he knew from Toulon, made her a savvy practical choice too. Since the fall of Robespierre, Barras's power had only increased and he was now in command of the troops that guarded the Convention. When Josephine became his lover, he paid off her debts (even though she had an annual income of 25,000 francs a year), and gave her a deposit for a lease on a house in the Rue Chantereine. But he was promiscuous and soon after their affair began his interest moved on to Thérésa Cabarrus, whose marriage to Tallien was already in difficulty after a year. Barras actively encouraged a relationship between Bonaparte and Josephine, doubtless hoping to divest himself of further responsibility for her. She was thirty-three with two adolescent children. For Bonaparte these mundane concerns were not obstacles. Marrying a woman six years older than himself did not perturb him. Laure Permond claimed that after her father's death, Bonaparte proposed marriage to her mother, who was his own mother's age and a friend of hers.[35] Laure would have been a child at the time and even in her much later memoirs the incident is presented as a semi-joke in the context of Bonaparte searching for a way to unite the two Corsican families, and claiming that when he got up that morning 'a marriage-breeze had blown on him'.[36] There was nothing jocular in his proposal to Josephine. He saw in her someone incomparable, whose kisses fired his blood and stirred deep and uncontrollable feelings of tenderness and desire.[37] She liked sex and was good at it. 'She had the nicest little cunt imaginable,' he confided to Comte Henri Gatien Bertrand on St Helena, long after she was dead.[38]

Inside the Tuileries, on 12 Vendémiaire, Year 4 (4 October 1795), Bonaparte looked out on the gardens where Louis XVI's Swiss Guards had been slaughtered and asked: 'Where is the artillery?' The new republican Constitution of the Year 3 had been officially accepted ten days ago, but the five Directors of the executive committee that was to govern France had not yet been chosen. Royalist opponents of the new constitution, die-hard supporters of a constitutional monarchy, chose this time to try and seize power. Bonaparte was one of the Jacobin generals charged with defending the Convention, which was still meeting, pending elections under the new constitution. The Convention had gone into permanent session and was now seeking protection from an uprising of around 30,000 armed citizens inside the Tuileries. Of Paris's forty-eight sections, forty-four were in revolt against the Convention, backed by the National Guard. Amidst the chaos, Bonaparte was taking orders only from Barras, the general-in-chief of the Army of the Interior. In Toulon, Barras had been impressed by Bonaparte and had started to rely on him. When Barras was called upon to save the government, Bonaparte was at the theatre. Barras sent someone to ask him to help and in the carriage on the way to the Tuileries Bonaparte made up his mind. He saw himself as Barras's second in command. He would fire on the crowd if he had to.

Outside the Tuileries the supporters of the uprising seemed to outnumber the defenders of the Convention six to one. Bonaparte thought, as he had done back in 1792, that a small number of cannon, skilfully deployed in the narrow streets surrounding the Tuileries, could disperse the crowd. But where were the cannon? Knowing there were about forty in the camp of Les Sablons ten kilometres away, he sent the cavalry officer Joachim Murat to fetch them. The insurgents had the same idea, but Murat at full gallop, leading a squadron of soldiers on horseback, overtook them and reached the cannon first. They dragged them back to Bonaparte, waiting in the Tuileries, still mindful of the carnage in the gardens that had ended the monarchy. He had the cannon in place by the afternoon of 13 Vendémiaire, when the armed crowd marched down the Rue Saint-Honoré. There was a brief exchange of musket fire, then came the signal for the cannon to fire. The signal was repeated two or three times before the rebels dispersed. Afterwards Bonaparte claimed that there were fewer casualties than there might have been because after firing the first few rounds of shot on the crowd, he ordered the artillery to use powder only. Shot first, scare tactics second, was his strategy. The other way round, he was convinced, was a disaster: if no one was killed the first time the cannon fired, the crowd would become complacent, and many more would have to die before they took the threat seriously.[39] For some, for Bonaparte especially, Vendémiaire proved that the monarchy could have been saved in 1792, and the Terror, perhaps even the foreign and civil wars, avoided.

Following the success of Vendémiaire, Bonaparte was officially named second in command of the Army of the Interior, and soon afterwards he succeeded Barras, who resigned to focus on forming the new government of the Directory, as general-in-chief. The five members of the Directory were: Barras, La Révellière-Lépeaux, Rewbell, Le Tourneur and Carnot. It took over the offices of the infamous Committee of Public Safety in the Luxembourg Palace in central Paris and tried to stabilise the city and the country. Its most urgent problem was the continuing revolutionary war against the coalition of Britian and Austria which had begun in 1792, before Louis

XVI was executed. The foreign war had long been causing economic hardship and domestic unrest. The original remit of the Army of the Interior, comprising approximately 40,000 soldiers, was to keep the peace in Paris and police the delivery of food supplies. There were many riots because winter was deepening and the people were still hungry, many of them starving. Bonaparte did his best to distinguish counter-revolutionary troublemakers from ordinary desperate people 'moved by need or a moment of giddiness'.[40] It was not so long ago that he had been hungry too. Now he had a salary and a residence that came with his appointment. He set about organising support for the Directory, creating a special guard to protect it and disbanding the National Guard which had supported the insurrection. He imposed as much order as he could on Paris, even visiting the theatres at night, checking that no one was singing anything other than La Marseillaise, or stirring up trouble for the Directors.[41]

Bonaparte continued his courtship of Josephine and proposed in Nivôse, Year 4 (January 1796), after having known her for less than a year. The gold engagement ring, which he struggled to afford, was decorated with a diamond and a sapphire in an eighteenth-century setting called 'Toi et Moi'. (In 2013 it was sold at auction for $1.17 million.) Bonaparte's family, smaller-minded than he was, disapproved of the engagement. His mother and sisters had hoped for a younger, less sophisticated bride whom they could influence; instead they got a beautiful, experienced woman, far beyond their control. The marriage took place on the evening of 19 Ventôse (9 March), Bonaparte arriving late for the civil ceremony at the town hall on Rue d'Antin, because he had recently been appointed commander-in-chief of the French army in Italy and was preoccupied with planning his campaign against Piedmont and Austrian Lombardy. He owed his promotion to the support of General Lazare Carnot, who was known as 'the Organiser of Victory' in the French revolutionary wars and was now a member of the Directory. As she waited for her 26-year-old groom, Josephine, now aged thirty-two, but claiming to be only twenty-eight, wore violets in her hair and asked that her new husband always give her violets, only violets, on their wedding anniversaries.[42] Her wedding ring – last seen on the corpse of Napoleon III, and probably interred with him in Farnborough Abbey in Hampshire – was reputedly inscribed '*au destin*' (to destiny). After a thirty-six-hour honeymoon, Bonaparte left for Italy.

'On 15 May, 1796, General Bonaparte entered Milan at the head of that young army which had lately crossed the Lodi bridge and taught the world that after so many centuries Caesar and Alexander had a successor,' wrote Stendhal at the beginning of *The Charterhouse of Parma*.[43] Yet Bonaparte's appearance was less than heroic. Very thin, he wore a tight tunic with narrow gold facings and a hat with a tricolour feather. The French envoy and scholar Miot de Mélito met him at Brescia. 'My first impression was that he was anything but good-looking; but his strong features, keen questioning look and quick decisive gestures revealed a flame-like spirit; his broad and reflective forehead was that of a deep thinker.'[44] As he conducted his conquering march through Italy, Bonaparte collected natural history specimens and fine art. The Directory appointed a Commission of Arts and Sciences to help him, which included his friends the mathematician Gaspard Monge and the botanist André Thouin, along with other scientists, naturalists and artists. In Parma, Piacenza, Modena, Bologna, Ferrara, Milan, Verona, Perugia, Loreto, Pavia and Cento, the commission rounded up paintings, books, manuscripts, artefacts and specimens to be sent back to Paris.

Thouin went to Italy to join Bonaparte's army on 2 Prairial, Year 4 (21 May 1796), and participated enthusiastically in the selection of spoils and trophies to bring back to Paris and the Jardin des Plantes.[45] As soon as the commission arrived in Milan, Bonaparte had lunch with its members to honour them. After the lunch, Thouin went to see the cathedral. From Bologna, Thouin wrote to his brother Jean about a box of fifty cuttings from two unusual varieties of vine that he hoped to propagate in France. He asked Jean to consult the notes he had made in his journal and already sent to their other brother Jacques, adding that if the vine cuttings were dry when they arrived, they needed to be soaked in water for thirty-six to forty-eight hours then potted and kept warm and moist. He regretted that he had to devote a great deal of his time to the arts and the army, and much preferred to be out in the fields collecting cuttings and specimens. As he crossed the Alps at Mont Cenis, he collected alpine anemones, *Draba alpina, Gentiana nivalis, Viola cenisia, Saxifraga oppositifolia* and many other plants in full flower.[46]

Towards the end of this year, in Brumaire, Year 5 (November 1796), the French were fighting the Austrians south of Verona at the Battle of Arcole. To win the battle, French forces needed to cross a bridge over the Adige River occupied by enemy forces. Bonaparte grabbed a flag and stood in the line of fire to inspire his men. This was a near-suicidal act. At the end of Bonaparte's novel, Clisson sends a final letter to his unfaithful wife and 'dutifully placing himself at the head of a squadron, threw himself headlong into the fray – at the point where the victory would be decided – and expired, pierced by a thousand blows'.[47] Perhaps Bonaparte thought of Clisson as he stood waving the French flag. In one version of events, his aide-de-camp Colonel Muiron saved him by taking a bullet that would otherwise have hit the general, dying in his place. Afterwards Bonaparte fell off the bridge into the mud. In another version he was dragged down into the mud by an unknown officer intent on saving him. With hindsight, Bonaparte decided it was at Arcole that he became aware of his extraordinary destiny. He had reckoned with death and escaped. In reality, his escape might have been pure luck, or the good judgement and self-sacrifice of others, but hindsight wiped away the mud and the banality of random chances. He had faced death on the bridge at Arcole and triumphed.[48]

Arcole was a narrow victory, but the Battle of Rivoli, two months later, proved decisive. On the eve of Arcole, Bonaparte had admitted in a dispatch to the Directory: 'We may be on the point of losing Italy.'[49] After Rivoli, he could reassure the Directory that Austria had no more resources, no more troops to fight. At Rivoli, the French were outnumbered by Austrian forces intent on relieving the city of Mantua which had been under siege since Thermidor, Year 4 (July 1796). The Austrian troops trapped in the city were starving, reduced to eating rats. Bonaparte was at Verona when the Austrian army, commanded by Jozsef Alvinczi, first attacked the French forces at Rivoli comman-ded by General Barthélemy Joubert. Alvinczi had almost three times the number of soldiers: 28,000 to Joubert's 10,000. Bonaparte sent General Berthier with reinforcements, before following with his own, arriving on the Trambasore Heights at 2 a.m. on 25 Nivôse, Year 5 (14 January 1797). The fighting that ensued lasted ten hours. Still outnumbered, the French owed their success to Bonaparte's clever tactics and deployment of the artillery, and the victory boosted his fame and reputation dramatically, both on the battlefield and back in Paris. He still took orders from the Directory, he was still one among many generals, but after Rivoli he stood out as the bright hope of the Republic. Having pushed Austria out of northern Italy, Bonaparte turned his attention south to the Papal States. Under the Treaty of Tolentino, signed on 1 Ventôse, Year 5 (19 February 1797), Pope Pius VI ceded Romagna, Bologna, Avignon and Ferrara to France, together with 30 million francs and a hundred works of art.

Bonaparte did not go to Rome, but sent his commissioners, including Thouin, to confiscate the works of art for Paris. He asked specifically for the bronze bust of Lucius Junius Brutus, founder of the Roman Republic, and the marble bust of Marcus Junius Brutus, leader of the assassins of Julius Caesar, from the Capitol.[50] Back in France this flamboyant plundering of Italy proved controversial. The artist Jacques-Louis David was one of around fifty signatories to a petition calling for the Directory to reconsider its policy. But a counter-petition appeared in the newspaper the *Moniteur Universel*, arguing that 'The French Republic, by virtue of its strength, its superior enlightenment, and superior artists, is the only country in the world that can provide inviolable sanctuary for these masterpieces'.[51] The priceless loot was sealed into crates and transported on specially made carts to Livorno, then to Marseilles by frigate, and onwards by barge to Paris. Thouin watched nervously as the crates were loaded. In Rome his mind had still been largely on gardens; he was unimpressed by the Borghese gardens, comparing them unfavourably to French gardens at the Petit Trianon in Versailles and at Ermenonville, outside Paris, where the philosopher and botanist Jean-Jacques Rousseau died.[52] He was also disappointed by Rome's botanical garden which seemed to him incompetently run.[53] But he was impressed by what he found in Rome's libraries.

Crossing the Tagliamento River in Ventôse, Year 5 (March 1797) with cavalrymen, artillery officers and combat engineers, Bonaparte carried his campaign from Italy into Austria and established himself as the saviour of the Republic, which he compared to 'the sun in heaven'.[54] If the Republic was the sun, Bonaparte was certainly growing in stature under it, casting ever longer shadows over the many soldiers and citizens who looked to him to rescue their country from ignominy and turmoil. The principal Austrian force was stationed on the banks of the Tagliamento. Engaging the French on the Tagliamento plain should have provided the opportunity for Archduke Charles to deploy the cavalry that had long been the strength of the Austrian army.[55] But Bonaparte tricked the enemy into thinking that, exhausted, his soldiers had withdrawn for the night. Then, in the dead of night, 'when all seemed profoundly quiet', his infantry boldly crossed the river, protected by the French cavalry. Meanwhile, General Masséna, on Bonaparte's orders, had crossed the Tagliamento River higher up, at its source in the Julian Alps, cutting off communication between the archduke and Vienna. Describing these events thirty years later, Walter Scott claimed that the archduke still hoped 'to derive assistance from the natural or artificial defences of the strong country . . . through which he was retreating'.[56] It was reasonable for the archduke to think that the deep and furious torrent of the Lisonzo, surrounded by impassable mountains, would be a natural barrier to Bonaparte's advance. 'But nature as well as events fought against the Austrians. The stream, reduced by frost, was fordable in several places.' Once he had taken the town of Grandisca, Bonaparte persuaded, or forced, the local people to donate food and other supplies for his army. With Bonaparte within 120 kilometres of Vienna, the archduke sued for peace.

Four months later, in Thermidor, Year 5 (July 1797), Josephine arrived in Milan, the capital of Lombardy, to join her triumphant husband. Even though they were so recently married, Bonaparte had had to beg her to come. They set up home together in the Castle of Montebello and Thouin noticed how delighted Bonaparte was by Josephine's presence. Soon after she arrived, she hosted an official reception for the commissioners, asking each of them to choose a distinguished local artist or savant to bring to the dinner.[57] Thouin and his colleagues brought a young doctor, a sculptor, a mineralogist, the secretary of the Milanese Society for Agriculture and Arts, and the architect of the La Scala theatre. When they arrived they found Barnaba Oriani, the astronomer, and the painters Andrea Appiani and Antoine-Jean Gros among other guests. The table was set for twenty-five. Bonaparte led the conversation, reminding the assembled company of each one's major achievements. There was just one course, no excess, no ostentation, and the dinner lasted only an hour and a half. The conversation continued afterwards for a further two hours, and Thouin was amazed at how much Bonaparte knew of science, chemistry and mineralogy.[58]

Josephine and Bonaparte loved excursions into the countryside. They set off with a retinue of sixty or so soldiers and servants from Milan along the shores of Lake Como to Lake Maggiore. On 30 Thermidor, Year 5 (17 August 1797), they reached Isola Bella and, without advance warning, invited themselves and their followers to stay at the Palazzo Borromeo, where ten tall terraces of baroque gardens overlooked the town of Stresa. Tons of earth had been moved to the island to create these gardens in the seventeenth century. Bonaparte was entranced by them: the grandeur and order of the terraces, beautifully lined with balustrades, obelisks, sculpture and topiary, rising one after another towards Carlo Simonetta's magnificent statue of a unicorn, thirty-seven metres above the level of the lake, outlined against the sky. He was delighted to discover a theatre where light operettas were performed on the top terraces. It was built from black stones and limestone and decorated with colossal shells. The garden was exactly to his taste. By the end of the year, he would revoke the Borromeo family's jurisdiction within the Duchy of Milan, but he left them their private palaces and islands.

The Victorian statesman and author Edward Bulwer Lytton wrote a poem about Bonaparte at Isola Bella, published in 1845. He imagined 'the wondrous Corsican' invited to make a wish and carve it on the trunk of a giant laurel, or 'prophet', tree:

> Slow moved the mighty hand – a tremor shook
> The leaves, and hoarse winds groaned along the wood;
> The Pythian tree the damning sentence took,
> And to the sun the battle-word of blood
> Glared from the gashing rind.[59]

Lytton imagined the bloody word 'battle' disappearing from the tree over time as it continued growing. The laurel tree's bark would expand and shrink 'the chronicle of ill', and the record of Bonaparte's graffiti would rot away. Given his appreciation of the Palazzo Borromeo gardens, it is hard to imagine Bonaparte taking out a knife to deface a majestic tree. But when Lytton wrote he was looking back on the bloodshed of the Napoleonic Wars and wanted to suggest that the natural world would eventually triumph over Bonaparte and his destructive ambition.

*

When he returned to Paris from Italy on 15 Frimaire, Year 5 (5 December 1797), Bonaparte found himself famous and feted. One of the many people who approached him for a favour, within a week of his return, was the writer Bernardin de Saint-Pierre who sent him copies of his books, claiming to be very hard up and hoping for patronage.[60] Bonaparte was flattered that the author of his favourite novel now wanted to meet him. But when they met he was disappointed. He found in Saint-Pierre nothing of the delicate sensibility that had impressed him in *Paul et Virginie*. He tried discreetly to give him some money and was mortified to find himself ridiculed; everyone in Paris, except himself, seemed to know that Saint-Pierre was shameless in his leeching off others. Bonaparte was embarrassed that he had been flattered by the author's attention. He remembered reading part of Saint-Pierre's book *Études de la Nature* at about the same time that he read and annotated Buffon's *Histoire Naturelle*.[61] He had been shocked by the mistakes in it, especially the suggestion that the cause of the ebb and flow of the tides was the melting of the polar ice caps during the day and the refreezing of them at night. For the rest of his life, Bonaparte maintained that Saint-Pierre was ignorant of mathematics and a poor scientist.

Years later, walking in his garden in exile on St Helena, Bonaparte would reminisce to Emmanuel de Las Cases about the composition and spirit of the Institut de France, to which he was elected, as a member of the Mechanical Arts Section of the First Class (the Physical and Mathematical Sciences), on 5 Nivôse, Year 6 (25 December 1797).[62] The institute had been created by the constitution of 1795 to replace the royal academies which had existed before the Revolution. Bonaparte boasted that he provided Parisian circles with a remarkable spectacle: the young general of the Army of Italy in the ranks of the institute, discussing profound metaphysical matters in public with his colleagues. As a result, he acquired new nicknames: the Geometer of Manoeuvres (or Battles), the Mechanic of Victory.

The Prussian philosopher and linguist Wilhelm von Humboldt was visiting Paris and happened to see the new member arriving at the institute the day after his election, accompanied by the French naturalist Bernard Germain de Lacépède. They entered during a session, which continued, but all eyes were on Bonaparte. Humboldt recorded a long precise physical description, as though he were observing a rare species of animal:

He is small and lean, has a small head, and it seemed to me for such a figure his hands were small and delicate. His face is more oval than round and very spare. His hair is brown and thin. His forehead, as far as I could see from the hair over it, is flatter than it is prominent, and the arch of his eyebrows is strong, marked and well curved, such that his forehead protrudes above his nose. His eyes are large, deep-set and finely contoured, his nose curved, but not hooked, though it is cleanly and strongly contoured. His mouth and chin are very masculine, strong, and his chin is especially strong and roundly contoured. His upper lip stands out over the lower one and the line between the corners of his mouth and his nose is rather straight, though without giving an air of harshness or pride. As he is rather lean, his cheekbones are pronounced and all of the muscles of his face move when he speaks, even his nose, and to an astonishing degree. He often makes a blinking movement that makes his lower eyelid rise . . . though this does not evoke grandeur, but rather makes him look much smaller. He was dressed very simply, in a blue coat and overcoat with sleeves reaching almost his fingers, and in boots and spurs. His hair was in a pigtail and powdered. His physiology has nothing large about it, or heavy, or determined, and he seems to exude more intellectual than moral qualities. He seems calm, pensive, decisive, and, although he has a strong and justified pride, he seems relaxed, perceptive and very serious, as if he is committed only to his work, without any other penchants or interests. Sometimes his expression takes on a harder and cutting edge, especially when he is moving. It would be difficult to imagine him in an action, and even more difficult to imagine him enthusiastic. His face is quite modern, and in my opinion is more French than Italian. In terms of the intellectuality of his expression, he could be an example of the ideal of the modern.[63]

The following spring, Humboldt saw him again, walking in the Jardin des Plantes with Josephine and her son, Eugène Beauharnais, and their friend the artist Jacques-Louis David. Times were hard for the garden and its menagerie. There were severe food shortages because of the war. Some animals had been shot to feed others. A gazelle was sacrificed to a hyena and a pheasant to a jackal. But amid the grimness, new animals arrived, including the elephant couple Hans and Marguerite. Bonaparte wanted to see them.

Hans and Marguerite were originally captured by the Dutch in Sri Lanka (Île de Ceylan) in 1784.[64] The elephants had lived in Holland at the court of William V, then in the Menagerie du Stathouder near Apeldoorn, until the French revolutionary army invaded in Year 3. The French Republic formally appropriated the menagerie on 16 Prairial, Year 3 (4 June 1795), and the following year Hans and Marguerite were moved in a convoy of animals and birds that took twenty months to reach Paris, arriving in Ventôse, Year 6 (March 1798). The journey was very difficult; at one point Hans, in a great rage, destroyed his cage and refused to enter his new rapidly constructed one until tricked into doing so, and there was a terrible storm as the convoy sailed down the North Sea coast. But once in the Jardin des Plantes, the elephants were delighted to be reunited. They settled down and became celebrities. Their attachment to each other and their seemingly modest refusal to mate in public resonated with republican morality.

Humboldt met Bonaparte's party in the Jardin des Plantes in front of the elephant enclosure and chatted to Josephine, whom he found extremely polite, pretty and delicate. He noted in his diary that:

Nonetheless, she has a face of a woman of the world, one with a certain amount of experience. Her complexion is yellow. She must be over forty years old. She took pleasure from seeing my children and thought, when my son was speaking German, that he was English. She admired Li's [Karoline, Humboldt's daughter's] blond hair, stroked her head, and, with her hand on her hip, let her head rest under her arm.[65]

On 9 Thermidor, Year 6 (27 July 1798), the Directory celebrated its four years in government since the fall of Robespierre with a two-day Festival of Liberty. The procession began in the Jardin des Plantes at the Muséum national d'histoire naturelle, where live animals, including camels, ostriches, lions and gazelles, and forty-five cases of specimens were loaded onto wagons decorated with tricolour ribbons and garlands. Then came a detachment of troops and more wagons carrying rare books, manuscripts and medals. Precariously, antique marble statues, including the *Capitoline Venus* and *The Dying Gaul*, were included in the parade, as were the lion and the four bronze horses from St Mark's Basilica in Venice. Even though no one could see or appreciate them, there were also wagonloads of paintings: Raphael's *Transfiguration*, Veronese's *Wedding at Cana*, Poussin's *The Martyrdom of St Erasmus*. It was raining. But the crowds came anyway and sang: 'Rome is no more in Rome. It is all in Paris.' Thouin walked at the head of the procession carrying a tricolour flag.[66] He led it along the Seine to the Tuileries gardens, and finally onto the Champs de Mars. In the place where Robespierre had ascended an artificial mountain with a Liberty tree at its summit, there was now an imposing Altar of Victory decorated with the bust of Junius Brutus, transported from the Capitol. The inscription read: 'Rome was first governed by kings: Junius Brutus gave it liberty and the Republic.' Thouin read a short speech presenting the trophies of Bonaparte's Italian campaign to the nation. The message was that France was the new Rome. But where was Bonaparte? Without his conquests, Rome would still have been in Rome and there would have been no loot to parade. Surely, like Robespierre at the Festival of the Supreme Being, he should have been walking slightly ahead of the other dignitaries, perhaps holding a bouquet or laurel wreath to place on the Altar of Victory next to the bust of Brutus? Instead he was nowhere to be seen; he had already set sail from Toulon for Egypt on a voyage of exploration, leaving his growing reputation for military glory to hover over the festivities. The parade included two floats that bore enormous representations of the rivers Tiber and Nile. On behalf of the Republic, Bonaparte had dominated the land watered by the Tiber; next would come the land watered by the Nile.

3

Egyptian Gardens

'I promise to each soldier who returns from this expedition
enough to purchase six arpents [20,520 m²] of land.'[1]
Napoleon

They told him it would be easy, that 'the valley of the Nile would soon
be transformed into a garden', and this was what he wanted to believe.[2]
Invasion of England was not practicable; he had looked into it and
concluded that the strength of the English navy could not be overcome
close to home.[3] But in Egypt, the English could be thwarted, their
trade route to India blocked, and the valley of the Nile cultivated to
provide produce and pleasure for France. When he was training in
the military academy at Auxonne, he had read and admired the Comte
de Volney's *Voyage en Égypte et en Syrie*, about his travels in the early
1780s, and before he left Italy he demanded all the books about Egypt,
Syria and the Red Sea from the library of the Duomo in Milan.[4] He
knew that the travel writer Claude-Étienne Savary had described Egypt
as 'the tranquil garden promised by Mohammed'.[5] 'The time is not far
away that we will feel that, in order truly to destroy England, we must
take Egypt,' Bonaparte informed the Directory on 29 Thermidor, Year
5 (16 August 1797).[6] 'The vast Ottoman Empire, which dies every
day,' he continued, 'lays an obligation on us to exercise some fore-
thought about the means whereby we can protect our commerce with

the Levant.'[7] The army of 30,000 soldiers set sail from Toulon, Genoa, Civitavecchia and Corsica the following year. In total the convoy, including ships of the line, frigates and smaller warships, was around four hundred vessels. Not since the Crusades had so large an armament appeared in the Mediterranean.[8] Almost two months later, on 14 Messidor, Year 6 (2 July 1798), Bonaparte, leading in person in the tradition of Alexander the Great and Caesar, took his army into Alexandria on foot because it had not been possible to land the horses. 'Great reputations are only made in the Orient; Europe is too small,' he said.[9]

Besides soldiers, Bonaparte brought scientists and scholars to Egypt. From the beginning, the French conquest of Egypt was considered a voyage of discovery. One of the many books Bonaparte took with him was Captain Cook's *Voyages*. His travelling Commission for Arts and Sciences was formed by order of the Directory, but according to his own wishes. According to the list compiled by the army paymaster, there were 167 members of the commission.[10] At its centre were two of his close friends: the mathematician Gaspard Monge and Claude Berthollet, a chemist. As they set about recruiting their colleagues for a secret journey to an undisclosed destination, these two knew they were going to Egypt. André Thouin refused Bonaparte's invitation, citing the fact that he had only just returned from Italy, the illness of his sister and pressing work in the Jardin des Plantes as his reasons.[11] He made some discreet enquiries about the proposed voyage and was told it was Bonaparte's intention to colonise Egypt, to use it as a route for commerce with the Indies, and to open a canal for this purpose between the Nile and the Red Sea, thereby destroying England's trade opportunities.

The soldiers were envious of the scholars and annoyed that Bonaparte placed his title as a recently elected member of the National Institute before his title as commander-in-chief of the army, signing his letters 'Membre de l'Institut National, Général en Chef', as though scholarship came before soldiering. To avoid further disgruntlement, he divided the scholars into five ranks, and paid them in accordance with army grades. Scholars who were members of the First Class were allocated cabins, but the rest had hammocks like the ordinary soldiers.

The first meetings of the travelling commission were at sea. The scholars visited each other's ships during calm weather and Bonaparte convened seminars on board the flagship *L'Orient*. This vessel, carrying tons of explosives and 120 cannon, had been fitted out with a ballroom, library and suite for Bonaparte. His friend Junot fell asleep and snored at one of the seminars. '[Bonaparte's] damn Institute would send anyone to sleep,' he complained when woken.[12] In a letter to his wife back in France, Monge described the team of scholars as strong and cheerful, singing revolutionary hymns together and falling asleep happy at sea. From on board *L'Alceste*, the young naturalist Geoffroy Saint-Hilaire wrote to his friend and colleague Georges Cuvier, the great zoologist and palaeontologist who had stayed in Paris: 'I am just as comfortable here as at the Jardin des Plantes.'[13] He was proud to be setting out on an expedition with 'the man of the century'.[14] On reaching Alexandria, the scholars were forgotten, and amid the heat, dust and chaos, it took them five days to get common soldiers' rations for themselves from the ships. When they complained, they were promised that things would improve in Cairo. But rations were not the only difficulty. By 18 Messidor (6 July), Bonaparte was already writing to the Directory admitting: 'This country is anything but what travellers and storytellers represent it to be.' Letters home from soldiers and others involved in the expedition were now full of disappointment and doubts:

This country, so much celebrated, is by no means worthy of the character it has obtained; the most savage and uncultivated spot in France is a thousand times more beautiful. Nothing on earth can be so gloomy, so wretched and so unhealthy as Alexandria, the most commercial spot in Egypt! Houses of mud with no other windows than a hole here and there, covered with a clumsy lattice; no raised roofs, and doors which you must break your back to enter; briefly, figure to yourself a collection of dirty, ill-built pigeon houses, and you have an adequate idea of Alexandria.[15]

Among the tired band of scholars was the diplomat and artist Dominique Vivant Denon. Aged fifty-four, he was the oldest of the savants to accompany Bonaparte to Egypt. He owed his invitation to his friendship with Josephine. When he saw Pompey's Column for the first time on the approach to Alexandria, he felt his imagination go back to the past:

> I saw art triumph over nature; the genius of Alexandria employ the hands of commerce, to lay, on a barren coast, the foundations of a magnificent city; the Ptolemies invite the arts and sciences and collect that library which it took barbarism so many years to consume.[16]

But Denon could not help but notice that Alexandria's present was far from its illustrious past, that the shoreline was not punctuated by a single tree or single house and had the appearance 'not of the melancholy of nature, but of her ruin, of silence and of death'.[17] On his first full day in Alexandria, Denon and the geologist Déodat de Dolomieu discovered a sarcophagus covered in hieroglyphics that was being used as an ablution tank in a mosque that had once been a Coptic church. They thought they had found the sarcophagus of Alexander the Great; in fact it was the sarcophagus of King Nectanebo II.[18]

Monge and Berthollet joined Bonaparte on the four-day desert crossing from Alexandria to Cairo, 'under a burning sky, over sands, and arid deserts, without water and without bread'.[19] There was nothing to eat but watermelon: 'watermelons for our dinner, and watermelons for our dessert'.[20] Many soldiers died from dehydration or were driven to suicide on the march.[21] The survivors blamed the Directory and the scholars for their suffering, imagining that it was Monge and

Berthollet's interest in antiquities that had inspired the expedition. In vengeance they named their donkeys savants, or half-savants.[22] British commentators also mocked the scholars for being under-informed about Egypt and expecting, like the mythical Phaethon, 'to meet with pleasing woods / And stately fanes, and cities fill'd with Gods'. Instead they found 'a general conflagration and a river'.[23]

Whatever their state of ignorance or unpreparedness, Monge and Berthollet were singled out in Bonaparte's report to the Directory for their bravery at the Battle of Chobrakit.[24] Both scholars were on board *Le Cerf* on 25 Messidor (13 July) when she was attacked by Mamelukes with guns mounted on the riverbed. The Mamelukes were an elite equestrian Islamic fighting force that had governed Egypt for hundreds of years. In 1517, the Turks had conquered Egypt and incorporated it into the Ottoman Empire, but had never succeeded in subordinating the Mameluke warriors.[25] At the time of the French invasion, Murad Bey was commander of the Mameluke army. 'War with the Mamelukes, peace with the Arabs!' was the French strategy for occupying Egypt.[26] They hoped to present themselves as liberators of the Egyptians from Mameluke oppression at the same time as they were competing with the British for control of the territory. Bonaparte's army, fresh from recent victories on land, came to the rescue of *Le Cerf*. Afterwards, Monge and Berthollet were not present for the Battle of the Pyramids, fought near Embaba on 3 Thermidor (21 July). Here the French won a decisive victory against the Mamelukes, causing Murad Bey to flee into upper Egypt with the remnants of his army. Monge and Berthollet then rejoined Bonaparte for his triumphant entry into Cairo. The fourteenth-century scholar Ibn Khaldun had described Cairo as 'the metropolis of the universe, garden of the world, swarming core of the human species, a city embellished with castles and palaces, bedecked with convents and colleges, illuminated by the moons and stars of knowledge'.[27] Arriving five centuries later, Bonaparte wrote to Admiral Brueys reassuring him that there was no need for further worry about subsistence for the army because the country was 'rich in wheat, pulse, rice and cattle, almost beyond imagination'.[28]

In Cairo Bonaparte found a newly built, freshly furnished palace that seemed almost to be waiting for him. This was the palace of al-Alfi Bey on Azbakiyya Square in western Cairo. The Azbakiyya area, close to the lake filled by the Nasiri Canal during the annual flooding of the Nile, had been gradually rebuilt after a fire in 1776. The Alfi Palace was on the waterfront and had just been finished according to the owner's taste, and was, conveniently, still uninhabited when Bonaparte arrived.[29] The chronicler and scholar Abd al-Rahman al-Jabarti, who was born in Cairo and lived there for most of his life, was forty-four at the time of the French invasion. To him it seemed as though the Alfi Palace had been built for Bonaparte.[30] The residents of the Azbakiyya area were ordered to vacate their homes, so the French could occupy them and live together in one part of the city, which would make them feel safer.[31] Altogether, the French confiscated 298 residences in Cairo and set up the army headquarters next to Bonaparte's residence.[32] The palace Bonaparte appropriated had a very large garden, which became known as the 'Jardin du Général en Chef'. He compared it to the gardens of nunneries in Italy; full of magnificent trees, great arbours, and the most glorious grapes in the world, but completely lacking in paths and alleys.[33] He ordered improvements, arranging for the installation of walkways, marble basins and fountains, grafting French features onto the existing garden. In his memoirs he claimed that 'the natives of the East are not fond of walking; to walk when one might be sitting appears to them an absurdity which they can only account for from the petulance of the French character'.[34] He did not mention that before his time, the waterfront of the Alfi Palace had been a public promenade.

Beyond Bonaparte's personal garden, trees were planted around the edge of the lake, and the Maghribi Bridge over the Nasiri Canal was restored in its original Mameluke style.[35] A new wall-lined road was laid out between the lake and the bridge. The French found the winding streets of Cairo dangerous and inconvenient, so they built thoroughfares to connect their headquarters with the city's various districts, and their fortifications and road-building involved demolishing the surrounding houses as well as several mosques.[36] 'They destroyed the windows and the gates,' wrote al-Jabarti, 'and they burnt all the beams so that destruction proliferated in all these places and the owl hooted in them and the raven croaked.'[37] Orders were given to remove the cemeteries of Azbakiyya, considered unhygienic in an urban area.[38] Many trees were felled, including those in the garden of Ibrahim Efendi, the official in charge of registering spices, and the palm trees in the fields of al-Ma'diyya and Misbah. The mosque of Zahir Baybars was turned into an observation tower and mounted with cannon. There were also plans to redesign the whole Azbakiyya area, with broader, straighter streets, lined by newly planted trees. According to al-Jabarti, the French planned 'a large road with shops and caravanserais on either side, colonnades, trellises, arbors and gardens', running through the city from the south-west corner of the Birkat al-Azbakiyya to the Muski Bridge. Lack of time and resources meant that this was never realised.[39] But even so, there was more than enough change and destruction to send Cairo's chronicler back to poetry eulogising Azbakiyya in the old days:

> Azbakiyya was full of joys and jolly company
> Water and sky floating together and flowers enveloped by heaven;
> Surrounded by splendid houses as the halo of the moon,
> In the green brocade of its fields the doves are cooing,
> The breeze refreshed by its flowing waters catching the light sparkling through the trees,
> Glittering as a silvery armour with roses marking the red of wounds.[40]

There was nothing metaphorical, or rose-like, about the wounds the French inflicted on the people and city of Cairo.

*

Bonaparte's victorious land battles and his command of urban administration were not matched at sea. During the Battle of the Nile, which
began on 14 Thermidor (1 August) in Aboukir Bay, thirty-two kilometres north-east of Alexandria, almost the entire French fleet was
destroyed by the British. The explosion of the splendid *L'Orient*, which
was packed with ammunition below deck, was heard and seen from
the port of Rosetta.[41] One witness described the 'pitchy darkness' and
'profound silence' that followed the explosion and lasted for about ten
minutes, until the sound of gunfire started up again.[42] Jean-Lambert
Tallien, who had been instrumental in the fall of Robespierre in 1794
and the official, if not the actual, end of the French Revolutionary
Terror, was watching from a promontory overlooking the sea, when
he saw the explosion and knew it would fall to him to tell Bonaparte.
Bonaparte was in Salahiyya when he heard the news, which came 'like a
thunderbolt', over a week later. He learned that *L'Orient* was destroyed.
Only two of the thirteen French ships of the line engaged in the battle
and two of the four frigates had survived the British attack led by
Admiral Nelson. Bonaparte and his army were now stranded in Egypt.
Presented with reports of the debacle, he was completely silent at first.
Later he said, 'The important thing is to safeguard the army from a
discouragement that would contain the germ of its destruction.'[43]
Egyptians gossiping about the destruction of the French fleet were to
have their tongues cut out. When it came to recriminations, Bonaparte
focused on General Blanquet, who had been a lone voice of opposition
to the plan of mooring the fleet in the sheltered bay. Bonaparte himself
had hesitated: would the fleet be safe in the bay, or could British ships
corner it there? Would the French have been safer in open water? The
majority of the ships' captains thought not. They had outvoted
Blanquet, who was subsequently unfairly blamed by Bonaparte for
surrendering without a fight. In fact, Blanquet had fought: his face was
disfigured and half his nose was shot off before his ship was captured.
But Bonaparte had to blame someone and Admiral Brueys, first in
command of the now non-existent fleet, was dead.

Bonaparte himself was one of the sources for the story of the boy who stood on the burning deck 'whence all but he had fled', celebrated in Felicia Hemans's poem 'Casabianca' (1826). The poem, learned by heart by generations of British schoolchildren and therefore the subject of much pastiche, presents the boy as doggedly obedient to his father:

> Yet beautiful and bright he stood,
> As born to rule the storm;
> A creature of heroic blood,
> A proud, though childlike form.
> The flames rolled on – he would not go,
> Without his father's word;
> That father, faint in death below,
> His voice no longer heard.

The boy was a Corsican child sailor named Giocante, the son of the commander of *L'Orient*, Luc-Julien-Joseph de Casabianca. Bonaparte had formed attachments to these fellow Corsicans on the long sea voyage to Egypt. 'Say a thousand kind things to . . . Casabianca' is how he ended a letter to Admiral Brueys on 9 Thermidor (27 July).[44] When the Battle of the Nile began, Giocante was ordered by his father to stay safe in a section of the ship until he was called for, which he did, not disobeying his father's orders, even after the guns had been abandoned and the ship had caught fire. Bonaparte reported the deaths of father and son to the Directory: 'Casabianca died with calm and sang-froid amidst the burning of his ship. He perished with it. His son aged 11, who never wanted to leave his father, was devoured by flames in his arms.'[45] Bonaparte's version of the story, sentimental wishful thinking perhaps, did not picture the boy alone on the burning deck, but allowed father and son to die in each other's embrace.

Tallien worried that when news of the Battle of the Nile reached France, Bonaparte's enemies would agitate public opinion against him.[46] 'The parties, the half-extinguished factions, will reinvigorate their mutual rage, and our unhappy country will again be torn to pieces by new dissentions!' Writing home to his wife, Thérésia Cabarrus, Tallien pledged his loyalty to Bonaparte: the commander-in-chief had suffered a reverse with the loss of the fleet, but this was just an additional reason 'for attaching myself more firmly to him, and for uniting his fate with my own'. Nevertheless, his revolutionary past had taught Tallien that should 'an ambitious chief arise, aiming to enchain his country, or to turn the arms of its defenders against its liberty', he would need to join the opposition immediately:

> You see my girl, that I know how to choose my party, but I declare to you, with the most perfect openness of heart, that I had rather a thousand times be with you and your daughter, in some retired corner of the world, far from all the passions and intrigues which agitate mankind; and I assure you that if I ever have the happiness of placing my foot once more on the soil of my native land, nothing shall induce me to quit it again. Of the forty thousand Frenchmen who are here, there are not four whose determination on this subject is not the same as my own.[47]

Letters like this went back and forth to France, but some were captured by British ships. Among the intercepted naval and military intelligence missives were personal communications from the soldiers, including a letter from Bonaparte to his brother Joseph alluding to reports of Josephine's infidelity. 'I have a great, great deal of domestic sorrow as now the veil has been completely lifted.'[48] From the beginning there had been problems in Bonaparte's marriage, but there is all the difference in the world between suspicion and certainty of sexual infidelity. In the desert, on the march to Cairo, Bonaparte had been presented with evidence, in the form of a letter, of his wife's affair with a young soldier, Lieutenant Hippolyte Charles. He wrote to Joseph asking him to find a secluded country residence outside Paris or in Burgundy where he could stay after his return from Egypt, professing himself 'tired of human nature', on the brink of becoming misanthropic. He wanted somewhere isolated and scenic to lock himself away for the winter.[49] He needed solitude to recover his wounded spirits. Another intercepted letter was one from Bonaparte's stepson Eugène Beauharnais to his mother seeking reassurance that she was not being as wicked as was rumoured. Bonaparte was a devoted stepfather to Josephine's two children from her previous marriage and Eugène was in Egypt as Bonaparte's aide-de-camp.

In London, the intercepted letters were pored over and shown to Lady Holland, Elizabeth Vassall-Fox, 'under the strictest promise of secrecy'.[50] After an early unhappy first marriage, Elizabeth had married Lord Holland, the nephew of the Whig statesman Charles James Fox, and become a leading socialite and hostess of literary and political gatherings at Holland House. Bonaparte's letter 'places that extraordinary man in a far more amiable point of view than I had seen him before', she noted in her diary.[51] 'At 29 he has exhausted the *attraits* of ambition and glory, and . . . been deceived by those he trusted most.' She hoped the letters would not be published and thought it would be fitting for the British ministers to send them to their addressees. Nevertheless, sections from the letters were published in the British press. The *Morning Chronicle* took the moral high ground, arguing that 'It derogates from the character of a nation to descend to such gossiping'. But others fed the public appetite for scandal and delighted in presenting Bonaparte as a cuckold.

It was rumoured that, soon after arriving in Cairo, Bonaparte was offered sex with a sixteen-year-old girl named Zeinab.[52] She was the daughter of Sheikh al-Bakri, Egypt's most eminent clergyman and a chancery member, keen to ingratiate himself with the leader of the invading army, who was said to be hoping to make love not to slave girls but 'to some teenagers who belong to the Egyptian elite society'.[53] It is unclear whether Bonaparte accepted the sheikh's offer. According to one account, Zeinab, who had a 'lithe body and firm, well-placed breasts', was dressed up in a Parisian costume and presented to him, hardly able to walk in the unfamiliar foreign clothes and shoes.[54] There is little evidence for this episode, which seems like an orientalist fantasy of sex and violence.[55] But three years later, after Bonaparte had left Egypt, Zeinab was arrested and accused of having been debauched by the French. Forced to appear before an impromptu court at her mother's house after sunset, she was interrogated, and when her father's advice was sought, he disowned her. Aged nineteen, she was beheaded, a victim of war, betrayed, then destroyed, by the men who had power over her.[56]

In his memoirs, Bonaparte calculated that the surface of the valley of the Nile was a sixth of the size of ancient France (by which he meant Gaul), 'but in France there are mountains, sands, heaths and uncultivated land, whilst in Egypt everything is productive'.[57] The valley of the Nile, made fecund by water, mud and sun, was more fertile than the best land in France. If the irrigation canals were well maintained, not stopped up by rubbish or neglect, the land could be even more successfully cultivated. 'There is no country in which government has more influence on agriculture, and consequently on population, than Egypt.' Bonaparte was sure that 'under a good administration the Nile gains on the desert; under a bad one the desert gains on the Nile'. The Nile was good, the desert was evil. He aligned himself with the Nile. He knew that Egypt had been the granary of Rome, but was lacking in wood, coal and oil. Cairo was an interim destination for trading caravans from Morocco, Fez, Tunisia, Algiers and Tripoli, en route to Mecca. Caravans also came to Cairo from Arabia, India, Africa, Abyssinia, Tagaste and the Cape. They brought the produce of their countries and slaves to trade for the goods of Europe and the Levant. Bonaparte had read that in Ptolemy's time the canal from Suez to the Nile was open, removing the need for land carriage of merchandise. It was his ambition to reopen it.[58]

'It never rains in Egypt,' Bonaparte claimed in his memoirs, dictated during his exile on St Helena.[59] This was an exaggeration; his own scientists reported that it rained in Rosetta: 'It is an earthly paradise! The temperature of our May reigns here, and it is raining!'[60] But rain was a rarity. The *Description de l'Égypte*, the vast encyclopedic record of the discoveries that the scientists and explorers made during the French occupation, notes that 'the atmosphere in Egypt is hardly ever refreshed by rain, and its humidity arises only from the Nile'.[61] Bonaparte too wanted to emphasise that the Egyptian earth is rendered fertile only by the inundation of the Nile, which rises between the summer solstice and the autumnal equinox. He remembered going to read the Nilometer at Roudah Island, considered since the time of the Pharaohs to be a measure of how the Egyptian economy would fare for the year. On 1 Fructidor, Year 6 (18 August 1798), when the height of the river had reached the requisite 16 cubits on the Nilometer, he presided over the Festival of the Nile together with the chief deputy of the Ottoman viceroy and other notables, parading to the dam at al-Sadd Bridge, observed by thousands of spectators. He gave the signal to break the dyke to let the waters of the Nile cascade into the Khalidj Canal that surrounded Cairo. As tradition demanded, an effigy of a young virgin was thrown into the fast-moving water, a symbolic sacrifice to the God of the Nile. The ceremony marked the peak of the annual flood, 'the life-giver to Egypt'.[62] The French newspaper in Cairo, the *Courrier de L'Égypte*, reported that Bonaparte tossed out large quantities of small coins to the people, as well as throwing pieces of gold at the decks of passing boats. He delivered a speech in praise of Allah and marched back to Azbakiyya Square for a firework display.[63]

Bonaparte entrusted Monge and Berthollet with 5,000 francs to finance activities related to the Commission for Sciences and Arts, and with finding premises for the new branch of the National Institute he was determined to establish in Egypt.[64] They chose the adjoining palaces of Qasim Bey and Hassan Bey Kachef, surrounded by beautiful gardens in the al-Nasiriyya quarter, about two kilometres east of Bonaparte's headquarters in Cairo. At the time, the vast walled gardens, bordered by countryside stretching towards the Nile, were already divided up in the manner of agricultural fields and planted with willows and a variety of crops.[65] There was a complex system of canal irrigation and cascades of water several storeys high. These waterfalls were surrounded by pavilions and terraces shaded by trees.[66] Qasim Bey had opened his magnificent garden to the public, so there were coffee houses, seating areas and latrines for general convenience. Everything was confiscated and converted into the new institute, the main purpose of which was 'to foster the spread of Enlightenment and knowledge in Egypt'. Scientific discovery, rigorous classification of phenomena and the application of reason to understanding the natural world were among the aims of the institute, but so too were the more worldly goals of local administration and governance. Bonaparte instructed Monge and Berthollet to establish a French and Arabic press, a physics and a chemistry laboratory, a library and an observatory in the garden of the new institute. 'The real conquests, the only unregretted ones, are those against ignorance. The worthiest and most significant occupation for nations is to enlarge the frontiers of human knowledge,' he declared.[67]

Al-Jabarti visited the institute and was shown the library, the many books on Muslim history and science, and saw the efforts the French scholars were making to learn Arabic. He was also shown the laboratories and the observatory. In his chronicle he wrote: 'They possess extraordinary astronomical instruments of perfect construction and instruments for measuring altitudes of wondrous, amazing and precious construction.'[68] Describing the site of the institute, the naturalist Saint-Hilaire remarked that the immense well-watered garden, planted with many species of trees and full of birds, would soon surpass the Jardin des Plantes back in Paris.

The menagerie was filling up with animals. Elephants, lions, tigers, giraffes, hippopotami and foreign birds had been brought to Egypt for millennia and exchanged as diplomatic gifts.[69] Egypt had a long tradition of zoos, reaching as far back as the world's first zoo in c.2500 BC.[70] The vast walled garden of the institute covered approximately thirty acres. The scholars could walk in it deep into the evening, admiring the beauty of the sky, the perfume of the orange trees, the mildness of the temperature. 'It is our garden academus,' Saint-Hilaire wrote proudly to his father. The botanist Alire Raffeneau Delile was director of the garden, and naturalists, architects, chemists, inventors, engineers and geographers came here to debate ancient and modern civilisation. Writing to his wife, Monge described this garden of the institute, after it had been flooded with the waters of the Nile, as charmingly verdant, almost an earthly paradise. Soon a fully fledged botanical garden, filled with animal and vegetable curiosities, it was considered a realisation of the highest goals of the Enlightenment.[71] In contrast, the scholars were dismissive of other gardens they found in Cairo. In the *Description de l'Égypte*, the cartographer Jomard recorded that there were twenty-two important gardens in the city, but warned readers not to imagine gardens in the European sense; instead these gardens were more like plantations 'consisting of dense shrubs and vines, bananas, orange and lemon trees, acacias and syca-mores'.[72] He echoed Bonaparte's complaint that Egyptian gardens were not designed for walking in, but for enjoying from a seat inside a trellis-covered kiosk.[73]

On 5 Fructidor, Year 6 (22 August 1798), Bonaparte signed a decree formally establishing the institute dedicated to the sciences and arts in Egypt; the inaugural meeting was held the next day at 7 a.m. in the harem hall of the palace of Hassan Bey Kachef, which, according to al-Jabarti, had been 'built to perfection'.[74] The architect and draughtsman Jean Constantin Protain made a sketch of that first meeting, depicting Bonaparte, slim and elegant at the centre of the gathering of scholars, and himself in the window seat, wearing his glasses and drawing. In the garden of the main building the scholars erected a giant sundial with the inscription 'L'AN VII RF' (Year Seven of the French Republic).[75] The institute had thirty-six members and four sections: mathematics, physics and natural history, political economy, and literature and the arts. Monge was the first president;

Bonaparte was the first vice-president and a member of the mathematics section. It would look better in Europe, he thought, not to have made himself president. But still the soldiers resented the institute, referring to it as their general's favourite mistress. Its objectives were to assist the military and administrative occupation of Egypt, to study the country and to propagate European progress.[76] Bonaparte himself was either in denial or unaware of the irritation his institute caused among the soldiers. In his memoirs he claimed that: 'The simple manners of the scientific men, their constant occupations, the respect which the army paid them, their usefulness in the works of art and manufactures . . . soon gained them the good will and respect of the whole population.'[77]

Bonaparte proposed six subjects for research: improving the baking of bread; finding an alternative to hops in brewing beer; purifying the water of the Nile; the construction of wind and water mills; the manufacture of gunpowder; and the reform of the Egyptian legal and educational systems. He asked the scholars to concentrate on a number of practical problems, such as cultivating vines, repairing the aqueduct carrying water from the Nile to Cairo, and a detailed comparison of methods for growing grain in Europe and Egypt. The scholars set to work on these projects and also pursued their own interests. Berthollet, for example, performed chemical experiments several times a week, attended by Bonaparte and many officers.[78] Bonaparte thought that local residents assumed the scientists were alchemists trying to discover the art of making gold. At an early meeting, Monge read a paper on the phenomenon of mirage based on his recent experience in the desert, where he had seen cruelly illusory visions of water when most in need of it.[79] When Bonaparte suggested presenting a paper himself, Monge tactfully dissuaded him. He was also dissuaded from appearing in Egyptian dress after one experiment that made the soldiers burst out laughing.[80]

Bonaparte declared himself a lover of Islam and attempted to govern Egypt by using religious language and quotations from the Koran. He invited the leading sheikhs and other powerful administrators to join the diwan, or council, he established to run the country.[81] His decrees were issued in both French and Arabic, frequently emphasising 'his respect for God [Allah], his Prophet and the Koran'. He even claimed to have converted to Islam, arguing later that a 'change of religion for private reasons is inexcusable. But it may be pardoned in consideration of immense political results.'[82] After the debacle of the Battle of Nile, the Turkish sultan in Constantinople declared war on the French, and Bonaparte extended his rhetoric in response: he was now not just on a mission to liberate Egypt from the Mamelukes, but fighting for the freedom of the Arabs from their Turkish oppressors too.[83] Bonaparte thought he could combine respect for Islam with the project of translating Enlightenment and revolutionary values from France to Egypt. The members of his institute assumed they were superior to the Egyptians, showing little or no respect for the current state of learning in the country, and conceiving of themselves as tutors who would help Egypt return to its ancient glory.

After the Battle of the Nile, Bonaparte's urgent need to win Egyptian approval for the French form of government led him to mount large-scale celebrations in Cairo to mark the sixth anniversary of the foundation of the French Republic on 1 Vendémiaire, Year 7 (22 September 1798). A wooden *arc de triomphe* was constructed on Azbakiyya Square, facing a second arch on which was written in French and Arabic: 'There is no god but God, and Muhammed is his prophet'; the Genoese painter Michel Rigo decorated it with scenes from the Battle of the Pyramids.[84] The foundation of the Republic was presented to the Egyptians as the day on which the French chased out their own oppressors, and in this way the privileged orders of Ancien Régime France were equated with the Mamelukes. Originally, the programme had included a demonstration of balloon flight, but this had to be postponed as the scientists, who had lost most of their equipment at the Battle of the Nile, were not ready in time.[85]

At 7 a.m. Monge led the members of the institute out into Azbakiyya Square to take their places for the ceremony, which included a military parade and a specially composed hymn. Bonaparte made a speech, followed by cries of '*Vive la République!*' and volleys of gunfire. Later in the day there was a feast in the Jardin du Général en Chef, with a table set for two hundred people on the richly decorated terrace. During the sumptuous meal two orchestras took it in turns to play various symphonies. Bonaparte proposed a toast: 'To the prosperity of the Republic and the glory of its armies!'[86] Afterwards, soldiers were sent to place the French flag on top of the pyramids. The next day, Bonaparte decided to visit the pyramids and the Sphinx, still buried in sand up to its neck, and invited the members of the institute to accompany him. When he had first seen the pyramids at Giza, on the march from Alexandria to Cairo, he had addressed his troops grandly: 'Soldiers! From the heights of these pyramids, forty centuries of history are looking down on you.' But this time he asked, 'Who can be the first to the top?', provoking a scramble up the ancient stones. Bonaparte did not join the race, staying on the ground, laughing at the others with General Caffarelli, who did not join in either because he had a wooden leg. The Egyptians called the general Abu Khashaba, or 'Woody'. Bonaparte, with his heavy Corsican accent, called him 'Gaffarelli'.[87] In his memoirs, he claimed that the pyramids were the greatest work of art he ever saw. If the French had won the Battle of Waterloo, he would have commemorated the victory with a pyramid of white stones.[88]

The Cairo Revolt, an uprising of the people of Cairo against the French, began on 30 Vendémiaire (21 October) when Bonaparte was out of the city surveying the Nile. At first there seemed to be no threat to the institute and the angry crowd focused on General Caffarelli's residence, next to the Grand Mosque, into which a convoy of books, manuscripts and scientific instruments had been moved. But the next day, after a number of French soldiers had been murdered in the streets and the violence had spread through the city, it became clear that the institute itself needed defending. The engineer Villiers du Terrage remembered hearing the cries and threats of the women of the neighbourhood and withdrawing to a pavilion on the far side of the institute gardens.[89] Monge and Berthollet convinced their colleagues that it would be disgraceful to flee the premises and abandon their research and resources; instead they barricaded themselves inside, waiting for external help, which arrived when Bonaparte returned to his headquarters. Among the several hundred dead French were a few members of the Commission of Sciences and Arts and one member of the institute. Writing home, Saint-Hilaire condescendingly reported: 'The miserable inhabitants of Cairo did not know that the French are the tutors of the world in how to combat insurgencies. They learnt to their cost.'[90] Bonaparte surrounded the area around the Grand Mosque and shelled it, then ordered the execution of all citizens who had been arrested carrying weapons. Their headless cadavers were thrown in the Nile. More than 3,000 Egyptians died and some accounts estimate the number at 5,000.[91] Afterwards, Bonaparte was determined to govern through terror:

> Every day I cut off five or six heads in the streets of Cairo. We had to manage them up to the present in such a way as to erase that reputation for terror that preceded us. Today, on the contrary, it is necessary to take a tone that will cause them to obey, and to obey, for them, is to fear.[92]

A few months after the Cairo Revolt, spectators gathered in Azbakiyya Square for the demonstration of balloon flight which had been postponed from the celebrations the year before. Monge had been working with the inventor Nicolas-Jacques Conté to develop balloon flight for military purposes. Conté had been a precociously talented child artist, who thought he would grow up to be a gardener, as his father was.[93] Instead he became a chemist and inventor who saved revolutionary

France when it had run out of graphite by inventing a new form of
pencil. He was one of the few French scientists to succeed in learning
Arabic. With limited resources, Conté and Monge managed to
construct a spherical hot-air balloon out of paper, twelve metres in
diameter and patriotically coloured red, white and blue. The balloon
ascended over Azbakiyya Square, but soon fell from the sky, spreading
panic among the spectators. Al-Jabarti wryly commented: 'Their claim
that this apparatus is like a vessel in which people sit and travel to
other countries in order to discover news and other falsifications did
not appear to be true. On the contrary, it turned out that it is like the
kites which household servants build for festivals and happy
occasions.'[94]

Bonaparte was present for the embarrassing display and overheard
his stepson talking to another soldier about a pretty Frenchwoman in
the crowd. This was Marguerite-Pauline Fourès, who had accompanied
her newly-wed lieutenant husband to Egypt, disguised in a cavalry
uniform. Since arriving in Cairo she had reverted to feminine dress.
Intrigued, Bonaparte arranged to meet her in the Egyptian Tivoli
gardens. These gardens, close to Azbakiyya Square, were modelled on
the Parisian Tivoli gardens and designed to amuse the disgruntled
soldiers. They were managed by a schoolmate of Bonaparte's from
Brienne, ex-guards officer Dargevel.[95] It was Bonaparte's idea to set
up the gardens, where, at the end of every ten-day revolutionary week,
there would be fireworks. He also hoped a theatre could be established
to perform a repertoire suited to the available actors. He attached great
importance to festivities in Cairo.

The Egyptian Tivoli gardens were in the grounds of a former
Mameluke palace, the Ghayt al-Nubi. They included baths, a menagerie and hippodrome, and became the centre of entertainment for
the army, filled with promenades, games, amusements, fireworks,
swings, jugglers, snake-charmers and dancers.[96] There was also a
gambling room and library with copies of newspapers. The off-duty
soldiers could stroll around, eating ices beneath citrus trees hung with

lanterns, listening to a military band. Al-Jabarti describes these gardens as 'places for amusement and licentiousness including all kinds of depravities and unrestricted entertainment, among them drinks and spirits, female singers and European dancers and the like'.[97] He remembers a man on the gate selling tickets for ninety nisf fiddas, which gave the purchaser the right to come and go for the day, occupying himself with 'food, drink, fornication and gambling according to his heart's desire and he would pay for each of these services according to what it cost'. It was also possible to rent a private booth inside the gardens at a monthly rate and furnish it as one pleased. 'This service was not restricted to the French only, but was available to anyone who wanted it, whether he be European, Muslim, Copt, Greek or Jew.' There were far fewer women in the Egyptian Tivoli compared to the Parisian. Most of the officers' wives had been left behind in France, and local women either were forbidden from entering the garden or showed no interest in doing so.[98]

In these circumstances, Madame Fourès, very attractive, twenty years old, stood out dramatically and Bonaparte began courting her with gifts and letters. He arranged for her husband to be sent back to Paris, organised a lunch party the following day, upset a carafe of water over her dress, and insisted on taking her into a side room to change. According to one observer: 'they paid some regard to appearances but unfortunately their absence was so prolonged that the guests who remained at the table entertained grave doubts as to the genuineness of the accident'.[99] Madame Fourès soon moved into a house close to Bonaparte's headquarters and walked in his newly modified gardens with him. When her husband returned sooner than expected, having been intercepted by the English and sent back to Cairo, she promptly obtained a divorce and reverted to her maiden name, Bellisle. The soldiers called her Cleopatra. She became Bonaparte's regular companion, appearing at his side, richly attired, in his carriage and at his table. Eugène Beauharnais was tactfully excused from his duties as aide-de-camp on public occasions when Bonaparte's mistress was present. No letters from Bonaparte to Josephine survive from this period, either because they were lost or destroyed, or because they never existed in the first place. But there were many from him to Madame Fourès, which she burned at the end of her long life, before dying in Paris in 1869.

Bonaparte was so impressed by and grateful to the artist Dominique Vivant Denon that he later made him director of the Louvre, which had become a museum to display the nation's art collection during the French Revolution. Denon accompanied the contingent of soldiers led by General Desaix that chased Murad Bey and his Mamelukes into upper Egypt, where they had fled after the Battle of the Nile. The French got as far as modern Sudan, before returning to Cairo. When they arrived on the island of Philae, the Nubian community was so terrified that many of them drowned themselves and their children in the Nile. Denon sketched frantically, on the move, amid the fighting, drawing hundreds of accurate sketches and panoramas as fast as he could while keeping up with the troops and avoiding the bullets. The eyes through which Denon saw and recorded the ruins of ancient Egypt were often sore and inflamed. He tried to treat his ophthalmia with vinegar and honey, when available, because the surgeons in the army had no drugs. Many of the soldiers suffered from eye infections in the desert and some of them went blind.[100]

When the army arrived at Thebes in Ventôse, Year 7 (March 1799), Denon recorded that the soldiers spontaneously dropped their weapons, 'as if the possession of the remains of this capital had been the object of its glorious labours'.[101] Higher up the river at Dendera later in the year, Denon recognised the importance of the zodiac bas-relief in the Temple of Hathor, hoping that it contained clues to the age of the site.[102] The aridity of the desert formed a sharp contrast with the fertile parts of Egypt and heightened the sensitivity of the soldiers and scholars to the natural world. 'After a sojourn of eight days in the silence of the desert, the senses are awakened by the most trifling sensations; I cannot describe what I experienced when, in the night, lying by the banks of the Nile, I heard the wind shake the branches of the trees, and cool itself by filtering through the thin leaves; life was in the air, and nature seemed to breathe,' wrote Denon.[103] Many of his drawings were worked up for publication in the *Description de l'Égypte*, and they were the source for the decoration of the Sèvres porcelain Egyptian Service that Bonaparte, as Emperor, commissioned in 1804. The miniaturised and perfected images were reproduced on plates, coffee cups, saucers, sugar bowls and creamers. Scenes of pyramids, temples and the Sphinx were surrounded by borders of hieroglyphics, selected at random before the meaning of these symbols had been unlocked by the deciphering of the Rosetta Stone.

Henri-Joseph Redouté was a zoological draughtsman, appointed to the Muséum national d'histoire naturelle in Paris as painter of animals. His elder brother, Pierre-Joseph Redouté, later renowned for his botanical drawings and known as 'the Raphael of flowers', was painter of plants at the museum. The botanist Étienne Geoffroy Saint-Hilaire recommended that Henri-Joseph Redouté join the Commission for Arts and Sciences and he became a member of the institute in Egypt, making many detailed studies, including one of the fish of the Nile. But the work of the French naturalists in Egypt was impeded by the loss of their equipment before it reached the institute, when the ship carrying their scalpels, microscopes, tweezers, jars, pins and pressing frames from France sank. In addition, the soldiers were often unwilling to act as escorts for the naturalists' collecting expeditions, regarding the work of guarding birdwatchers and insect-hunters as beneath them.[104] Nevertheless, the naturalists, unlike the engineers, chemists and inventors, were free to pursue their scientific interests uninterruptedly most of the time. As soon as they arrived they began collecting seeds to send back to the Jardin des Plantes in Paris.

The British naval blockade, which dated back to 1793, early in the revolutionary wars, did not extend to ships carrying botanical specimens and seeds back to France. Despite his knowledge of her infidelity, despite his own affair with Madame Fourès, Bonaparte reputedly sent

Reseda odorata seeds home to Josephine, who was delighted by the strong and beautiful scent of the plant's flowers and named it 'Mignonette d'Égypte' (little darling of Egypt). The plant is an annual, listed in *Description d'Egypte* as growing spontaneously in Syria and Barbaria.[105] Custom has it that Bonaparte's gift to Josephine marked its introduction into France and afterwards Europe, but according to the *Transactions of the Horticultural Society*, the plant was cultivated in France earlier in the century and was already called 'Mignonette d'Égypte' in the sixth edition of Miller's *Gardener's Dictionary*, in 1752. The plant's essential oil, reseda oil, was important in the preparation of perfume. Perhaps it was one of Bonaparte's favourites, maybe he did send seeds back to Josephine, but if so the gesture was less original and less romantic than has been claimed.

Monge and Berthollet joined Bonaparte on his expedition to investigate the remains of the ancient canal that once connected the Gulf of Suez with the Nile, but to spare them the arduous journey, he arranged for them to travel in a coach drawn by six horses. On the night of 5 Nivôse (25 December), the French convoy came to rest close to a tall solitary acacia tree which had come into view many hours earlier on a high stony plain. The Egyptian guides explained that the tree, which marked the pilgrim station of Haura, was venerated, its branches adorned with bits of clothing left by those en route to Mecca, and anyone who harmed it would be treated with opprobrium.[106] Trees were rare in the desert, except around wells where a few palms could be found.[107] Bonaparte pitched his tent close to the trunk to protect it from any of the soldiers who might have been tempted to mutilate it for firewood. It was too cold to sleep. In the absence of wood, the scholars gathered a large number of camel bones and tried to burn them to generate some heat. Monge even sacrificed some of the strange animal skulls he had collected on the journey and stored in the carriage. There were a great many human and animal bones in the desert that could be used for fuel.[108] The smell of the burning bones was unbearable, but there was no question of wasting water putting out the fire once it had been lit. The march resumed at three in the morning. They reached Suez on 6 Nivôse (26 December).

Bonaparte claimed to be the first to find the ruins of the ancient Canal of the Pharaohs that connected the Nile to the Red Sea via the Bitter Lakes. He put the engineer Jacques-Marie Le Père, the brother of Gratien Le Père, another of his schoolmates from Brienne who had accompanied him to Egypt, in charge of surveying the possibility of a new canal cut straight across the Suez Isthmus, which would connect the Mediterranean and the Red Sea without following the winding route of the Nile.[109] Le Père calculated that the level of the Mediterranean was significantly lower than that of the Red Sea and warned that the proposed canal could lead to dangerous flooding in the Nile Delta.[110] This was an error, but Le Père persisted in it, despite challenges from some of the other scholars at the institute, and as a result, Bonaparte was eventually dissuaded from continuing with the project. From Suez, he also visited the Fountains of Moses near Sinai, which could only be reached by fording the Red Sea on horseback. The party of French soldiers spent several hours by the biblical fountains and made bitter undrinkable coffee with salty water drawn from them. Then they misjudged the timing of the tide and were almost drowned. General Caffarelli lost his wooden leg in the commotion.[111]

In Suez, where he spent much of his time scouting out trade, Bonaparte encountered some Arabs escorting a caravan on camels. Noticing the agility and suitability of these animals for travelling through the desert, he ordered Eugène Beauharnais to try riding them, then found himself having to gallop his horse to keep up.[112] He decided to form a dromedary regiment, which was decreed less than a month later, on 20 Nivôse, Year 7 (9 January 1799), charged with policing Egypt and pursuing the Bedouin insurgents who continued to make raids, even into Cairo. The regiment was divided into two squadrons of four companies each, armed with sabres, pistols, bayonets and lances. The uniform included a turban and cloak. The camels, which had been stolen from the Bedouin, could go long distances without food or water, and the Bactrian camels with two humps could carry two soldiers at once, back to back. In theory, this meant that the soldiers could fight assailants from whatever angle they approached. When given the command, the camels would kneel down instantly, to allow the soldiers to dismount and continue the fight on foot.

Bonaparte acquired his own, single-hump, camel. After he left Egypt, it was allegedly brought back to Paris in 1801, and kept at the Jardin des Plantes. When it died it was stuffed and displayed in the Muséum national d'histoire naturelle, until it was moved to the Musée Africain de l'île d'Aix in 1932. There is no evidence that the stuffed camel that can still be seen on the Île d'Aix was Bonaparte's, and it seems unlikely he would have noticed if the one that arrived in Paris was different from the one he rode in the desert. Nevertheless, the nameless camel is as plausible a relic as the skeleton of Bonaparte's horse, Marengo, also supposed to have been brought back to Paris from Egypt. At the Battle of the Pyramids, Bonaparte was so impressed by the beautiful Arab horses on which the Mamelukes led their charges that he could hardly bear to order his artillery to fire at them.[113] After the battle, many of the cavalry horses were appropriated by the French. Bonaparte, displaying his erudition, named one of them Tamerlan after the conqueror who invaded Asia Minor in 1402 and defeated the Ottomans.[114] But it was a different horse, a six-year-old light grey barb, that became Bonaparte's personal steed. Marengo was said to have been captured after the Battle of the Nile and subsequently ridden by Bonaparte until the Battle of Waterloo. Barbs were named after the Barbary Coast and considered inferior to pure Arab-bred horses, but Bonaparte preferred them to larger horses and kept about ten that he rode interchangeably. His riding style was free, frantic and graceless, his habits having been acquired on Corsica before the formal training he received at military school. The skeleton of Marengo is in the collection of the National Army Museum in London. Enduring fascination with the remains of a camel and a horse, which might or might not have been ridden by Bonaparte, reflects the afterlife of his status as hero and celebrity, a status that he was only in the early stages of creating in Egypt.

One of the motivations behind Bonaparte's extension of his campaign into Syria was the search for timber. The French needed to build fortresses to protect themselves from attacks along the Nile, and they also hoped to replace their lost frigates, but there was a shortage of wood in Egypt. According to the Bible, there were forests of cedar in Lebanon, which was part of Ottoman Syria.[115] During the Suez Canal expedition, he heard that Ottoman forces had seized the desert fort of El-Arish on what was then the Egyptian and Syrian border. War with the Ottoman sultan was imminent and he decided attack was the best form of defence. He prepared a force of 13,000 for the invasion, including divisions under the command of General Kléber and General Caffarelli.

Bonaparte's invading forces never reached modern-day Syria, only the lands known today as Gaza, Israel and the West Bank.[116] His army arrived in Jaffa on 17 Ventôse, Year 7 (7 March 1799), after marching ninety-six kilometres across the desert and laying siege to the city. In forty-eight hours of bloodletting approximately 4,500 prisoners were executed. Many of the French soldiers caught bubonic plague during the siege and Bonaparte established a hospital on the site of the Carmelite monastery at Mount Carmel to treat them. He visited the sick himself, an act of dutiful bravery amid the brutality and bloodshed, later immortalised in Antoine-Jean Gros's hagiographic painting, *Bonaparte visitant les pestiférés de Jaffa* (1804), which was exhibited at the Louvre between the proclamation of Napoleon as emperor and his coronation. In it he is depicted touching the bubo under a victim's armpit, in a gesture recalling the Royal Touch, by which monarchs of the Ancien Régime were believed to be able to cure scrofula. But at the time of the suffering in Jaffa, there were no miracles to be had, only natural resources and limitations. Bonaparte discussed merciful killing with the military doctor René-Nicolas Dufriche Desgenettes, who refused to administer fatal doses of opium. More personal than his staged and afterwards mythologised visits to the hospital were Bonaparte's private visits to Monge who was ill and feverish for weeks. The future emperor checked on his friend during the night and offered him water to drink.

When General Caffarelli was wounded in the Battle of Acre, Monge and Berthollet read aloud from Montesquieu and discussed political economy by his bedside, but he died from an infection soon after his arm had been amputated. Bonaparte ordered the mummification of Caffarelli's heart so it could be taken back to Paris. By late May, he had reluctantly accepted defeat at Acre. His forces simply could not take the fortress, and without it could not hope to take Syria. He returned to Cairo, his troop strength much depleted by battles and plague, though he put out propaganda about the campaign having been a glorious success. He and his bedraggled soldiers did a victory lap around the Egyptian capital and he issued a decree promising to build a huge mosque to commemorate his triumph. But at a meeting of the institute in June Desgenettes confronted Bonaparte about what had happened in Jaffa. Excluded from a committee charged with reporting on the plague, the doctor leapt to his feet and 'with a vehemence that astounded the numerous audience' accused the general of covering up his military defeats and failures, which he referred to as crimes.[117]

On 24 Thermidor, Year 7 (11 August 1799), in the garden of the institute, Bonaparte confided in Monge and Berthollet his intention of returning to France. He planned to leave his army behind, under the command of General Kléber, who would be informed of this by letter after Bonaparte had left. He proposed taking Monge, Berthollet and Denon with him, but some scholars would remain in Egypt. Saint-Hilaire guessed Bonaparte's plans and handed him a manuscript to take back to Europe and publish. Bonaparte also discussed with Monge and Saint-Hilaire his long-standing ambitions as a scientist and discoverer of the natural world. As an adolescent he had wanted to compete with Newton but circumstances compelled him to follow a military career. If he had followed his dreams, he would have discovered 'a world of details': Newton had discovered the world's uniformities, but Bonaparte would have explored its varieties. Bonaparte's idea of 'a world of details' was precious to him. Saint-Hilaire thought that what he meant by it was the contrast between the astrological world of fixed laws and the phenomenal world of infinite detail, all the things and actions in the universe, to be studied not from a priori principles, but from systematic survey. Newton had elevated the mathematical sciences above the others, but Bonaparte thought this was wrong. The study of botany, zoology, hydrology, embalming, hieroglyphics was just as important. Newton's discoveries were abstract, whereas Bonaparte wanted to engage with the real world. In a similar story, Bonaparte is said to have confided to Monge while inspecting the Mokattam quarries of the pyramids in Cairo that: 'I found myself a conqueror in Europe like Alexander; it had been more to my liking to march in the footsteps of Newton.'[118]

Twelve years earlier, aged eighteen, Bonaparte's interest in science was reflected in a short story he wrote in Ajaccio. His story was inspired by the Abbé Marigny's *Histoire des Arabes sous le gouvernement des califes* (1750). Called 'Le Masque Prophète' (The Veiled Prophet), it begins by describing the just, peaceful, science-promoting rule of the medieval Caliph al-Mahdi in Baghdad. 'Feared and respected by his neighbours, he occupied himself with making the sciences flourish and accelerating their progress.'[119] The caliph's progressive rule is challenged by a prophet from Khurasan in eastern Iran. Attractive, statuesque and eloquent, the prophet pleases the multitude by preaching moral purity and equality of ranks and wealth. The caliph tries unsuccessfully to quell the growing insurrection. After the prophet is disfigured by illness, he takes to wearing a veil, but this does not detract from his powerful sermons. He tells his followers he is wearing the veil to protect them from being dazzled by the light emanating from his face. He tells them they are the chosen ones, but poisons them at a last supper before committing suicide by throwing himself into a vat of acid. When the caliph arrives to restore order he finds the city gates open and only the prophet's mistress still alive. Those who continue to believe in the prophet imagine he has been taken up to heaven. Bonaparte's conclusion is: 'This example is incredible! How far the fury of being illustrious can lead.' The word *incroyable* (incredible) is ambiguous in both French and English. Just over a decade after he wrote this story, Bonaparte was furiously pursuing his own illustrious career, addressing his troops with rousing speeches, promising them quantities of land, exposing them to war and plague. His purposes were still those of scientific enlightenment and progress, but his methods were barbaric.[120]

When Bonaparte slipped away from Egypt, leaving his letter of instruction for General Kléber, the horses that conveyed him and his chosen companions to the shore were turned loose to make their own way back to Alexandria. It is not clear whether the horse later called Marengo was taken on board *Le Murion* with Bonaparte. His camel was not, but his pet Egyptian antelope was.[121] Under cover of night the small ship carrying him back to France hugged the Egyptian coastline to avoid attracting the attention of the British blockade, then turned north after passing the ruins of Carthage. Among those on board was Roustam Raza, an eighteen-year-old slave of Armenian descent who had been trained as a Mameluke and given to Bonaparte by Sheikh al-Bakri after the siege of Acre. Roustam was already Bonaparte's bodyguard, sleeping outside the door of his cabin. He was excited to be travelling towards a new life in France, but regretted leaving Cairo in a hurry because he had hoped to persuade his new master to offer positions to some of his friends. The artist Denon also left Cairo with a mixture of relief and sorrow. Back in Paris he reviewed his Egyptian hoard, including a papyrus from Thebes and his many sketches. For his friend and patron Josephine, he brought back a small monkey which had been trained to seal letters.[122]

General Kléber was furious. Without warning, he had been left in charge of the stranded, embattled, despairing army. He enjoyed a brief dalliance with Madame Fourès, but before long she too succeeded in slipping out of Egypt. She remarried, divorced again in 1816, and then went off to Brazil to start a lumber business before returning to France in 1837, where she lived to be ninety-one.[123] General Kléber was not so fortunate. He was assassinated in the Jardin du Général en Chef at the Alfi Palace on 25 Prairial, Year 8 (14 June 1800).[124] He had moved into the palace when he stepped, unwillingly, into Bonaparte's shoes as general-in-chief. He was walking on the terrace with the army architect Jean Constantin Protain, discussing necessary repairs and possible improvements to the building, when he was approached by someone he assumed was a beggar. Kléber held out his hand to receive the supplicant's kiss and was repeatedly knifed, as was his companion, who initially threw himself to the ground, then tried to beat off the assassin with a stick. By the time the guards reached him, Kléber was dying. Protain survived his injuries, and the assassin was found hiding in the garden behind a ruined wall, his clothes bloodied and the dagger lying in the earth nearby.

Sulayman al-Halabi was a young man from Aleppo. He was accused of having followed Kléber around all day with the dagger concealed under his galabiya.[125] During the investigation, for which Protain was able to testify, it emerged that three Azharite sheikhs in Cairo were aware of Sulayman's murderous intentions. Al-Jabarti, controversially, treated Sulayman's actions as criminal in his chronicle, not as representative of Arab rebellion against French repression.[126] His account includes the reports of the trial that were distributed by the French administration. He refers to Sulayman as a 'religious enthusiast', but more recently there have been moves to rehabilitate Sulayman as a hero, including a statue in his honour in Aleppo. Sulayman's supposed conspirators were sentenced to beheading, but he was condemned to a long, torturous death by impaling after his right arm had been burnt off to the elbow. The French, whose revolution had outlawed such punishments, in favour of the more humane instrument of the guillotine, justified this decision by reference to local customs. The accounts of Sulayman's horrific punishment recall those of Ancien Régime executions. In Egypt, the French, so proud of their scientific enlightenment, reverted to barbarous practices. Sulayman's death took four hours and only afterwards was he beheaded, so that his skull could be taken back to Paris, to be studied as the head of a criminal. Later it was displayed in the Musée de l'Homme as an artefact of scientific interest.

General Kléber's funeral was held on 28 Prairial (17 June). His remains were carried on a chariot through the streets of Cairo, covered with a black carpet and surrounded by his military trophies. The mathematician Fourier delivered a eulogy, asking the assembled soldiers: 'How many of you would have aspired to the honour of throwing himself between Kléber and his assassin!'[127] At this there was an outpouring of grief for the distinguished general who had fought so many battles for the French Republic. Afterwards the embalmed corpse was shipped back to France. Bonaparte was shocked by the assassination and remembered how often he had been in Kléber's position, walking unprotected on the terrace of the Jardin du Général en Chef. When he was told the news, in the middle of the night, his secretary read in his face the thought: 'Egypt is lost!'[128] Bonaparte was mindful too of Kléber's fame as a soldier, which reached back as far as the beginning of the revolutionary wars in 1792, and decided that the general's remains could not be brought to Paris, lest his tomb become a focus for revolutionary sentiment. Instead Kléber's body was kept offshore for eighteen years at the Château d'If on a tiny fortified island near Marseilles, before being buried at last in his home town of Strasbourg, in the Place Kléber, where he is commemorated by a statue.

After the French left Egypt in 1801, Muhammad Husraw was sent as governor from Istanbul and took up residence in the Alfi Palace. The building was gutted by fire soon afterwards, so when his successor

Muhammad Ali became governor in 1805, he did not live in the ruined palace, but close by. Muhammad Ali completed the French initiative of removing the Azbakiyya cemeteries for reasons of urban hygiene, and he filled in the lake, which was considered pestilent, especially when the water level sank, and turned it into a large public garden: 'to give the public of Cairo and particularly the Europeans a promenade'. By the end of his long reign, Azbakiyya Lake had become a park *à l'européenne*.[129] In 1849 Samuel Shepheard, an English pastry chef and entrepreneur from Preston, opened a hotel on the site of the old Alfi Palace. First it was called Hôtel des Anglais, then Shepheard's Hotel. It was renowned for its terrace, overlooking Azbakiyya Square, as the original Alfi Palace had been, even before Bonaparte took up residence. The poet Gérard de Nerval, whose father had served as a doctor in the French army, stayed at the hotel in 1842. He saw posters announcing a charity performance to benefit the blind of Cairo at the theatre Bonaparte had built in the Egyptian Tivoli gardens, whose name had been changed to Jardin Rosetti, and went to the performance. The menagerie the French had created was still there and Muhammad Ali's medical expert had added some giraffes.[130] The gardens themselves de Nerval found an oasis of palm, orange and sycamore trees.

4

Growing a Crown

'I found the crown [of France] in the gutter. I picked it up
and the people put it on my head.'[1]
Napoleon

Josephine bought Malmaison, the 'mala domus' or 'bad house', before
Bonaparte returned from Egypt. It became their marital home. They
had visited it together in Nivôse, Year 6 (January 1798), before he
left, but reached no agreement on the purchase, which he considered
too expensive.[2] On 2 Floréal, Year 7 (21 April 1799), she promised
to pay 225,000 francs for the house, which could be dated back to the
fourteenth century, situated eleven kilometres north-west of Paris,
surrounded by parkland, forests, fields and streams running into the
River Seine. She had to borrow the deposit of 15,000 francs and wait
for her husband to come back to settle the remainder of the debt. The
previous owner, Jacques-Jean Le Couteulx du Molay, a wealthy finan-
cier, had had a garden of great beauty laid out in the English style.
The designer, Jean-Marie Morel, was a leading advocate of the *jardin
à l'anglaise* and the author of *Théorie des Jardins*, published in 1776.
Instead of the strict formality of the traditional French style, which
Napoleon much preferred, the *jardin à l'anglaise* included winding
paths, asymmetric plantings, groves, lakes and follies. When Josephine
bought it, Le Couteulx's garden had been neglected but there was still

a vegetable patch, an orangery, a greenhouse and a pavilion, octagonal on the outside and circular inside.

Le Couteulx's garden had been neglected because he and his wife were arrested at Malmaison during the revolutionary Terror. Their library and bedroom were sealed, as was usual for those accused of counter-revolutionary activity. Josephine herself had been imprisoned at that time of denunciations, sham trials and executions. But although her first husband, the Vicomte de Beauharnais, was guillotined, Josephine, Le Couteulx and his wife all escaped the revolutionary tribunal. When she bought the house of her dreams from her fellow survivors, Josephine was determined to make an even more enchanting English garden than the one that had existed before the Revolution.

At first, Josephine lived in Malmaison with her daughter Hortense and her younger lover, Hippolyte Charles, whom the villagers in nearby Rueil assumed was her son. Bonaparte arrived back in Paris on 24 Vendémiaire, Year 8 (16 October 1799), furious about his wife's affair and house purchase. But over time he came to love Malmaison and allowed Josephine to spend some 3.5 million francs renovating it, until their divorce in 1809, when it became exclusively hers. Between Years 8 and 10, Malmaison, along with the Tuileries Palace, would be the headquarters of the French government. Despite the disasters, Bonaparte managed to pass off the Egyptian campaign as a success and became First Consul – the head of an authoritarian, centralised republican government – through the coup of 18 Brumaire (9 November 1799), less than a month after his return. Appointed for ten years, he was hailed as the saviour of the country by both the pro-revolutionary Jacobin faction and the royalists. The ex-priest and political theorist, the Abbé Sieyès, whose revolutionary pamphlets had helped destroy the Ancien Régime in 1789, thought that in Bonaparte he had found a general who would at last implement his constitutional ideas. Sieyès, not for the first time, was wrong.

Sieyès was one of five members of the ruling Directory, for whom Josephine had given two lavish dinners at Malmaison while Bonaparte was still abroad.[3] Sieyès already knew Malmaison. He went there in June 1789, invited by Le Couteulx and his wife, to discuss the Revolution in its earliest days.[4] Ten years later, there had been bloodshed and destruction beyond anything he could have imagined. Fearing a royalist backlash and electoral victory against the failing government, he was ready to support a coup against the Directory he was part of. But for it to succeed, all five of the directors would have to resign, and the legislative bodies (the Council of the Ancients and the Council of Five Hundred) would have to accept a new constitution. Sieyès and two other directors resigned voluntarily; the remaining two were arrested. The councils were tricked into thinking that they were at risk in central Paris and would be safer on the outskirts of the city at the chateau of Saint-Cloud. Bonaparte followed them there on 19 Brumaire (10 November 1799) and stormed into their meetings. He accused the recalcitrant Council of the Ancients of having violated their own constitution, and told them, 'The Revolution is fixed to the principles on which it began. It is finished . . . We have reached the end of the novel of the Revolution, and must now begin its history.' At the Council of Five Hundred meeting, which was taking place in the orangery of the chateau, he was physically assaulted and almost fainted. His brother Lucien took charge and used military force to expel the deputies from the orangery. In a contemporary English cartoon Bonaparte, newly returned from Egypt, was portrayed as a large crocodile, wearing thigh-high boots and, prophetically, an imperial gold crown. The large crocodile is backed by a line of smaller crocodiles in military dress and depicted expelling a council of frogs. Some of the frogs are wearing red cloaks and the revolutionary *bonnets rouges*, decorated with cockades, as they flee from the 'Corsican crocodile'. Only a single little frog brandishes a tiny dagger, scarcely bigger than one of the many teeth in the mouth of the invading reptile. The anonymous cartoonist suspected what Sieyès, an intellectual, did not: Bonaparte's imperial ambitions were stirring.

The constitution of Year 8 was adopted on 22 Frimaire (24 December 1799). It gave Bonaparte extensive power and was the first constitution since 1789 not to be prefaced by a Declaration of Rights. By this point, Bonaparte was the de facto ruler of France, despite the fact there were two other consuls: Jean-Jacques-Régis de Cambacérès and Charles-François Lebrun. Classical Roman terms were used in the drafting of the constitution to evoke the autocratic republic of Caesar Augustus, the first Roman emperor. The legislative branch was divided into three, but effectively Bonaparte, as First Consul, could rule by decree. His ever helpful brother Lucien organised a plebiscite on the new constitution on 18 Pluviôse, Year 8 (7 February 1800). The official results were over 3 million French citizens in favour and only 1,562 against. These results might have been exaggerated, but there could be no doubt that the overwhelming majority had had enough of revolution and hoped Bonaparte would bring peace and stability to France after a decade of political turmoil.

Busier than ever, Bonaparte welcomed the distraction of Malmaison for Josephine. When she acquired the estate it was approximately 105 acres, but she immediately set about acquiring adjacent land until, by the time of her death in 1814, it had almost trebled in size to 294 acres, an expansion that required over five hundred contracts of sale and exchange.[5] Even before the coup of 18 Brumaire, she started improving the estate by trying to trade a piece of woodland for the Saint-Cucufa Pond and neighbouring marsh.[6] She bought surrounding woodland, farms and parks and eventually purchased, from twelve different landowners, the whole of the Hudrée Valley, through which a small river ran from the Saint-Cucufa Pond to Malmaison. When Bonaparte allowed her to buy the nearby palace and estate of Bois-Préau, he wryly referred to her passion for English-style gardens: 'I'll let you do it because it makes you happy, but now it is bought do not have it torn down in order to have some rocks put in its place.'[7]

On a frosty day early in Frimaire, soon after the coup of Brumaire, the artist Jacques-Louis David travelled to Malmaison with two architect friends, Charles Percier and Pierre-François-Léonard Fontaine, to offer Josephine advice about renovating her house. The architects had known each other as students in Paris; they had won prizes to study in Rome and were there when the Revolution began. They both came back before the Terror. Percier's father had been a gatekeeper at the Tuileries Palace and his mother a laundress to Queen Marie Antoinette. His main source of income was rent paid by the restaurant of the Swiss Guard, which closed after the massacre that ended the monarchy in the Tuileries gardens.[8] As young architects in unstable times, Percier and Fontaine had accepted a commission to redesign the seating of the Convention and found work producing stage sets for the opera. To cheer themselves up and maintain their connection with Rome during the Terror, they began work on a book about the ancient city's villas and gardens. Like David, they were determined that regime change would not interrupt their artistic ambitions. They may or may not have been lovers; their business partnership lasted decades.

Walking around Malmaison, the architects decided it was a beautiful site, the gardens were pleasant, but the house itself was in a parlous state. The walls were crumbling, there were missing and broken beams and the floors needed repairing. They agreed to come up with some renovation plans. A few days later, Josephine and David took Percier and Fontaine to meet Bonaparte. Instead of the great war hero they were expecting, he seemed to them a smallish man, wearing a long grey coat, double-breasted and full-skirted, buttoned up against the cold.[9] It was around this time that he started wearing his signature bicorne hat, distinctive for being worn sideways and for its extreme simplicity: no decorative brocade or feathers, only a revolutionary cockade attached to the black felt. He spoke to the architects at length about his plans for improving Paris and the problem of where to place the spoils that had returned from Italy. Should the statue of Laocoön, the horses and lion of Venice, and other ancient sculptures be permanently housed in the army's church at Les Invalides as war trophies or in the Louvre? Fontaine, affable and articulate, spoke his mind: the museum would be more suitable. Percier, tall and shy, kept silent, as he often did.[10]

The architects came up with grandiose plans for Malmaison inspired by their studies of Roman villas in the Tuscan countryside. They wanted to erect a whole new building to mirror the existing one across a courtyard garden. North of both buildings, they planned a Palladian pavilion, which would house Napoleon and his wife in separate but connected quarters decorated according to their different tastes. They envisaged all three structures surrounded by Italianate gardens laid out with symmetrical topiary, water features and long avenues of trees. Bonaparte approved. He enjoyed the straight lines of the Tuileries gardens and would have happily seen them reproduced at Malmaison. He wanted to extend the grounds and include a large lake. Precision and order were central to his aesthetic. But Josephine's vision was different. She wanted to develop the informal English style initiated by the estate's previous owner. Fontaine complained that in her planting schemes Josephine wished only for 'groups, effects, oppositions and especially sentiment'.[11] He was dismayed when she employed a Scottish head gardener, Alexander Howatson, and horrified when she had a tulip tree planted in the middle of one of the lawns.

Josephine set about acquiring plants for her garden: roses, eucalyptus, laurel, hibiscus and four varieties of magnolia, including *grandiflora* and *tripetala*.[12] She commissioned a new heated orangery from Percier and Fontaine, who sourced some of the stone for its pillars from the Tuileries gardens. But from the start there was conflict over the garden between Josephine and the architects. She was upset to discover that they had arranged for paths to be laid in straight lines. An avenue leading directly from one place to another was not to her taste, she considered it barbaric and against the rules of sophisticated gardening. She wanted meandering, curving paths in her *jardin à l'anglaise*.[13] She engaged another architect, Louis-Martin Berthault, hoping that Percier and Fontaine's work could be confined to the house and kept out of the garden. To address Bonaparte's complaints, she organised a more orderly garden for him, separated from the rest by a small drawbridge over a stream.[14]

Every tenth day, Decadi, the day of rest in the Revolutionary calendar, Napoleon went to Malmaison with Josephine, his four brothers, his mother, his half-uncle Joseph Fesch, who later became an archbishop and then a cardinal, his aide-de-camp Junot and other close friends and supporters. He got up early and went for long walks in the woods, often alone, sometimes accompanied by Fontaine and the estate manager/bailiff, who had worked for Le Couteulx. Fontaine considered the estate manager a coarsely clever character.[15] Bonaparte enjoyed discussing his plans for Malmaison with both of them, but there was a big gap between the grandeur of his projects and his budget. He hated wasting money and complained constantly about the cost of the renovations. By spring Fontaine had already lost hope of realising the design he and Percier had drawn up for Malmaison. He confided to his diary that instead of building a grand house worthy of France's extraordinary First Consul, they faced rescuing a ruined house which had only ever been intended for an ordinary person.[16]

Bonaparte left Paris again in Floréal (May) for the start of his second Italian campaign. He planned to surprise and defeat the Austrian army by crossing the Alps, which had not been attempted by a general since Hannibal in ancient times. He met his reserve army, six regiments under the command of General Lannes, at Lausanne. The soldiers had been force-marched to meet him. Thousands of other soldiers needed for the expedition joined the reserve army, many of them conscripts. Before setting off across the Alps, Bonaparte reviewed his 40,000 troops just outside Lausanne at Saint-Sulpice. To honour the occasion, Étienne de Loys, a powerful local landowner, arranged for a 22-year-old oak (*Quercus robur*) to be uprooted and replanted in the middle of his Doringy estate, where he had recently finished renovating his country chateau and gardens. Legend has it that Bonaparte visited and sat on the stone bench beneath the transplanted oak.[17] The magnificent tree survives and is now over thirty metres tall with a trunk circumference of seven metres. It is known as Le Chêne Napoléon.

Bonaparte's position as First Consul was consolidated by the Battle of Marengo, fought near the city of Alessandria, in Piedmont, on 25 Prairial, Year 8 (14 June 1800). General Kléber's assassination in Cairo also occurred on this date, but for the purposes of securing his recently acquired power, what was happening in Italy mattered much more to Bonaparte than the mess he had left behind in Egypt. Finalising the conquest of northern Italy was now his military and political focus. After the daring crossing of the Alps in May, the French army's occupation of Milan, and a successful battle at Montebello, Bonaparte engaged the Austrian army, led by Field Marshal Michael von Melas, in a decisive conflict. The battle took place on a plain east of Alessandria, crossed by the Bormida River and a small stream, the Fontanone. The French were outnumbered by the Austrians until General Desaix arrived with reinforcements, and while the French had only fifteen guns, the Austrians had a hundred. Despite this, there were heavy losses on the Austrian side during twelve hours of fighting, advancing and retreating across the Bormida and Fontanone, until finally the Austrians were defeated. On the morning of 26 Prairial (15 June), Bonaparte rushed back to Paris, leaving General Berthier to negotiate the Convention of Alessandria, which committed the Austrians to withdrawing from northern Italy beyond the Ticino River. No other army general had been able to inflict this kind of a defeat on the Austrian or allied forces. Bonaparte's military luck had run out in the Middle East, but closer to home he had rescued his reputation. In 1805 he laid the first stone of a pyramid to commemorate the site of the Battle of Marengo, but it was never finished and has now disappeared.

At Malmaison, Josephine commemorated the Battle of Marengo by planting a cedar of Lebanon which grew into the mighty specimen that still stands in the grounds of the chateau. She also organised a big celebration in the garden. Percier and Fontaine had to borrow tents from their colleague Étienne Lecomte, who was the government's chief architect in charge of renovating the Tuileries Palace, to protect the tables of food positioned under the trees. Tents were quick to erect, inexpensive and evocative of military campaigns. They soon became a feature of Percier and Fontaine's renovations at Malmaison.[18] They positioned two tent-like structures, either side of the entrance to the estate, for a porter and a guard. Bonaparte was surprised and furious. He wanted to know who had given the architects permission to construct buildings of such poor quality. They also designed a glass portico shaped like a campaign tent over the entrance to the chateau. The end columns looked like bundles of pikes. When Bonaparte saw it for the first time, he said it reminded him of an animal lodging at a country fair.[19] He was more approving of the way Percier and Fontaine converted his bedroom into a council room by lining it with striped fabric draped, tent-like, over the ceiling and walls. He had envisaged Malmaison as a retreat, a private house for relaxation at the end of the working week, but he was receiving more and more visitors and conducting a mass of complicated state business from the house. His council room recalled his campaign quarters on the battlefield.

The artist Jacques-Louis David depicted Bonaparte, commanding and victorious, in his *First Consul, crossing the Alps at Great St Bernard Pass*. There are five versions of this iconic propaganda painting; the first, originally commissioned by France's ally Charles IV, King of Spain, was bequeathed to the museum of Malmaison in 1949. David showed Bonaparte in military dress, armed with a Mameluke-style sabre, swathed in a swirling golden cloak, his bicorne hat adorned with matching braid, astride a rearing piebald horse, modelled on the famous barb Marengo. In fact, Bonaparte had crossed the Alps on a mule, which was safer and more practical. Horses like Marengo, transported from Egypt, would not have been ready for battle in Europe so soon. At the bottom of the painting, the names Hannibal, Karolus

Magnus Imp. (Emperor Charlemagne) and Bonaparte are carved in stone. Once again, an artist intuited the First Consul's imperial ambition. Bonaparte refused to sit for the painting – that would have been a waste of his time – and anyway what he wanted was a representation of his character and genius, not a physical likeness. The canvas was finished by Nivôse, Year 9 (January 1801), having taken four months. It was exhibited later that year in Prairial (June) and extensively reproduced.

During the summer of Year 8, the poet and member of the institute, Louis-Jean-Népomucène Lemercier, sent a copy of his *Homère, Alexandre, Poèmes* to the Tuileries and was invited to dinner at Malmaison the next evening. Walking among the distinguished guests in the gardens, Lemercier began discussing the differences between epic and didactic poetry.[20] Bonaparte was interested in Lemercier's views. He complained that whereas Alexander the Great chose Homer as his poet, and the Emperor Augustus chose Virgil, the only epic poet left for him was Ossian. Ossian was the narrator of a cycle of poems in Scottish Gaelic, reportedly translated and published by the Scot James Macpherson from 1760. Lemercier restrained himself from pointing out that the First Consul would have displayed more taste if he had chosen Milton or Tasso. After dinner, Bonaparte asked Lemercier to stay behind to continue their conversation. He loved to find parallels between himself and the ancient heroes. The Roman general Scipio, who defeated Hannibal at the Battle of Zama in 202 BC, was known as 'Africanus'. Bonaparte pointed out that French citizens were referring to him as 'Italicus' following his victory at the Battle of Marengo. Lemercier later claimed to have warned the First Consul against those encouraging him to invade Britain and hoping to give him the further title 'Britannicus'.

Bonaparte believed Hannibal was the greatest of all the great men of antiquity. Caesar, he thought, was the poets' hero, and Brutus the democrats' hero, but Hannibal was the greatest military captain in the ancient world. When it came to deciding who was the greatest captain in the modern world, Bonaparte was not looking for flattery. First he wanted to have a serious conversation about the claims to this title of Prince Eugène of Savoy, Turenne, Condé and Montecuccoli, then he wanted to discuss the great generals of the revolutionary wars. Finally, coming to himself, he seemed content with Lemercier's representation in verse of his own battles – Arcole, Rivoli and Marengo – and pleased that the poet had placed him in the company of heroes. Lemercier found himself consumed with curiosity to get inside the First Consul's 'gigantic dreams'. After a discussion of his tragedy *Charlemagne*, he concluded that Bonaparte was dreaming of re-invading Egypt by land not sea, and 'of making Constantinople the capital of a combined Eastern and Western Empire', with France as a viceroyalty within the division of grand prefectures. All Bonaparte's other ambitions, the poet thought, were 'simply stages towards this imaginary goal'.

On 10 Fructidor, Year 8 (28 August 1800), Bonaparte and Josephine made a pilgrimage of sorts to Ermenonville, an estate about forty-eight kilometres north of Paris, where the philosopher Jean-Jacques Rousseau spent the last months of his life and was buried twenty-two years earlier. Ermenonville was one of the first landscape gardens in the *jardin à l'anglaise* style in France, created by a wealthy admirer of Rousseau, René de Girardin, the Marquis of Vauvray, who modelled his extensive gardens on the idyllic scenes described in Rousseau's books. He built a small cottage in one of the wildest parts of Ermenonville, to evoke the house occupied by the character Julie in the novel *La Nouvelle Héloïse*, and it was there that Rousseau died in 1778. As a young lawyer, Robespierre is said to have visited Rousseau at Ermenonville just before he died. But this story, which appears in Henri Béraud's 1825 memoir, *Mon ami Robespierre*, is even less likely to be true than the claim that Robespierre slept with a copy of Rousseau's *Du contrat social* under his pillow while orchestrating the Terror. During the Revolution, Rousseau's body was removed from its tomb, inscribed 'Here lies the man of Nature and of Truth', on a small island, the Île des Peupliers, in a lake at Ermenonville, and transferred to the Panthéon in Paris; but the estate continued to attract visitors wanting to pay their respects to the philosopher who had asserted the nobility of nature: 'Everything is good when it leaves the hands of the Creator. Everything degenerates in the hands of Man.'[21] The gardens at Ermenonville, inspired by his philosophy, liberated plants and flowers from the strict formality of the traditional French style of gardening. Near the entrance a pedestal was inscribed with Enlightenment sentiments:

> Gardens, tastes, customs,
> May be English, French, Chinese;
> But the waters, the meadows, the woods,
> Nature and the landscape,
> Are of all time and all lands:
> Hence, in this wild place,
> All men will be friends,
> And all languages admitted.[22]

Bonaparte had read *La Nouvelle Héloïse* in his youth and admired it along with many other works by Rousseau. He might even have seen himself, as a teenager and young adult, as Rousseau's 'Virtuous Man', withdrawing from the public realm to concentrate on work and love. But when he came back from Egypt he had changed his mind. 'Natural man is a dog!' he declared.[23] Rousseau's insistence on the natural goodness of man no longer convinced Bonaparte, who had seen and participated in so much horror, on and off the battlefield. At Ermenonville, visiting the room in which Rousseau had died, he complained to Girardin, for whom Josephine later arranged a pension, 'He was a mad man, your Rousseau; it is he who brought us to the state we are in.'[24] Bonaparte now blamed the controversial philosopher for preparing the road to the Revolution, to which he owed his own power. 'It would have been better for the peace of France if that man had never existed,' he told Girardin, who boldly replied, 'I would have thought, Citizen Consul, that it is not for you to complain about the Revolution.' To which Bonaparte said, 'Time will tell if this earth would have been a more peaceful place if Rousseau and I had never existed.' Bonaparte's rejection of Rousseau did not stop Josephine from honouring the philosopher at Malmaison. Georgette Ducrest, one of Josephine's ladies-in-waiting, remembered a finely carved bust of Rousseau, carefully positioned so that vines and foliage would play around it and form 'a natural crown'.[25]

It is unclear exactly when Bonaparte's solution to France's problems evolved to include the idea of crowning himself; but Ducrest knew that the last thing her mistress wanted was for Bonaparte to acquire a crown, natural or otherwise. While he was away in Egypt, Josephine told close friends about the predictions a fortune-teller had made when she was a young girl growing up in Martinique: she would marry a nobleman who would die an unnatural death, she would live a miserable and perilous life, but eventually become a queen, greater than a queen, but she must 'Gare la chute' (Beware of downfall).[26] The warning haunted her. Her failure to produce an heir left her terrified that Bonaparte would divorce her if he became king. Unkind commentators remarked on the irony of the First Consul's wife propagating so many fine and rare plants at Malmaison, surrounding herself with fecundity when she was herself unable to reproduce with Bonaparte. Ducrest later published an undated letter in which Josephine, reversing the role of Lady Macbeth, urged her husband to forgo monarchical ambition:

I have read over your letter, my dear, perhaps for the tenth time, and I must confess that the astonishment it caused me, has given way only to feelings of regret and alarm. You wish to raise up the throne of France, and that, not for the purpose of seating upon it those whom the Revolution overthrew, but to place yourself upon it! You say, how enterprising, how grand and above all how useful is this design! But I should say, how many obstacles oppose its execution! What sacrifices will its accomplishment demand! And when realized, how incalculable will be its results?[27]

On 3 Nivôse, Year 9 (Christmas Eve 1800), one young girl was definitely sacrificed. Afterwards, people argued about how many others were killed or wounded, but there was never any doubt about the girl. It was cold and misty in the streets. Her mother sent her out on an errand early that evening wearing a skirt with blue-and-white stripes, a grey woollen jacket and a blue scarf over her red hair. They were going to stay up late for a midnight feast with friends, like families used to before Mass was forbidden. Aged fourteen, she had no memories of the old days. She was three when the Revolution started, seven when the king was guillotined and the Republic and the new calendar began. That evening Parisians were celebrating the first anniversary of the constitution of the Year 8. The girl was looking forward to the midnight feast.[28]

Heading home to the Rue du Bac, where her mother sold vegetables and fresh-baked bread, she found the Rue Saint-Nicaise more crowded than usual. People were lining the street and looking out from their apartment windows. The Café d'Apollon, the shops for hats, wigs, culottes and watches, were full of customers in good spirits. She asked what was happening and was told there had been an announcement in the newspaper that First Consul Bonaparte would attend that evening the widely publicised first performance in Paris of Joseph Haydn's *The Creation*. The Rue Saint-Nicaise was on the route between the Tuileries Palace, where Bonaparte lived when not at Malmaison, and the Théâtre des Arts, where an audience of almost 1,500 people had assembled, their wealth and elegance far beyond her own experience. She dithered about whether to wait and catch a glimpse of Bonaparte or hurry home. She had never seen him before, but it was dark and getting late and her mother might need her help. Then as she was passing a shabby two-wheeled cart on one side of the street, a man offered her twelve sous to hold the reins of the black mare harnessed to it. He said he would be back soon and the horse would give her no trouble, as it was old and tired.

She was pleased to be paid while she waited. She heard the nearby bell of the Church Saint-Roch in the Rue Saint-Honoré strike 8 p.m., then cries of 'Vive Bonaparte!' She saw his carriage, drawn by two horses, and an escort of cavalrymen, coming up the Rue Saint-Nicaise very fast, too fast for her to see the First Consul as he flashed past. She tightened her grip on the reins of the black mare and wondered when its owner would return to release her. The next minute, from nowhere, from above, from behind her, came a deafening crash, a blinding white light: an explosion, like the beginning or the end of the world. Her body was thrown into the air and torn apart. It fell to the ground, mutilated and nude: the skin ripped from her face and her skull broken open. Nothing was left of her clothing or red hair. Scattered arms and legs and horseflesh were spread across the street. The onlookers were injured and their apartments damaged. One woman who had been watching for Bonaparte in her shop doorway was blinded; another had her breasts ripped off. In the carriage that was following Bonaparte's, Josephine fainted. His sister, Caroline Murat, in her ninth month of pregnancy, was severely traumatised and later gave birth to an epileptic son. Josephine's daughter, Hortense, had her hand lacerated. Some say there were only two fatalities; others say nine, a dozen, or twenty. The number wounded was somewhere between six and fifty-two.[29] Bonaparte declared there would be vengeance 'like a thunderbolt': the perpetrators of this plot against his life would be discovered and 'blood must run'. But that was later; too late for her. No one ever doubted that Marianne Peusol died instantly, as obscure and dispensable to history as the old black mare.

Bonaparte had had a long and tiring day. Earlier in the evening he had been minded to miss the concert, but Josephine insisted that they go. He had been slumbering when the cart, horse and girl exploded in the space between his carriage and his wife's. He had been dreaming that he was drowning in the Tagliamento river in Italy.[30] Waking, he cried out to those travelling with him – General Berthier, General Lannes and Colonel Lauriston – 'My friends, we have been mined.'[31] The carriage windows were shattered but he ordered the driver to carry on towards the Théâtre des Arts, leaving his entourage behind, wasting no time. The driver, who was drunk, assumed the crash and flash of light in the sky was a military salute in honour of his illustrious passenger. He delivered Bonaparte to a standing ovation at the Théâtre des Arts, only about ten minutes late. When the audience heard the bang they too assumed it was a round of artillery, perhaps announcing peace or victory in the war with Austria. But by the time Bonaparte took his seat, word of the assassination attempt had spread. He stayed long enough to reassure the audience, then went back to the Tuileries to plan his response while Haydn's oratorio came alive onstage. The libretto, based on the Book of Genesis and Milton's *Paradise Lost*, had been translated into French. The prelude, 'The Representation of Chaos', is followed by God creating order: heaven and earth, the sun and the moon, the water and the weather, animal and plant life, and, finally, Adam and Eve. Bonaparte too determined to bring order out of chaos. Haydn's music might have been too elaborate for his taste, and it is hard to know how much of the performance he stayed for, but possible that he at least heard the spectacular creation of the sun in the first part: 'In splendour bright is rising now the sun and darts his rays, an amorous joyful, happy spouse, a giant proud and glad to run his measured course.'[32]

From the outset, Bonaparte insisted it was obvious who was behind the carnage: the diehard Jacobins, the old revolutionary trouble-makers, purveyors of chaos, who had long 'dishonoured the Republic and sullied the cause of liberty by all kinds of excesses'. After all this time, they were still trying to destabilise France, but this was his opportunity to subdue them once and for all, the dawn of a new order.

A crowd of senators, legislators, tribunes, state councillors and ministers joined Bonaparte at the Tuileries after Haydn's oratorio finished
to discuss what should be done in the wake of the assassination
attempt. Pierre-Louis Rœderer, a political survivor with a revolutionary past, was not one of them. When the monarchy fell in 1792
Rœderer, then *procureur-général-syndic* of the Department of Paris,
had led Louis XVI from the besieged Tuileries, across the palace
gardens, to seek sanctuary in the National Assembly. He also played
an important part in bringing Bonaparte to power as First Consul
through the coup of 18 Brumaire (9 November) that resulted in the
constitution of Year 8. In his memoirs he boasted: 'I spent the last
night of Louis XVI's reign with him, and the first of Bonaparte's with
him in turn.' Rœderer was canny and circumspect; he did not rush to
the Tuileries because he did not want to seem importunate. Instead
he went to find Charles-Maurice de Talleyrand-Périgord, who had
also been instrumental in the coup of 18 Brumaire and was now
Bonaparte's Foreign Minister. They talked until 10.30 p.m.; then
Talleyrand went off to the Tuileries and found Joseph Fouché, the
Minister of Police, still there.

On the evening of 4 Nivôse (25 December), Rœderer went to see
Josephine. Relations between Bonaparte and his wife were strained
– after the extramarital affairs there had been on both sides, he had
decided 'Power is my mistress' – but she was still of political importance, close to the First Consul and able to grant access to his time and
favour. When Rœderer arrived, Bonaparte was sitting on a sofa at one
end of Josphine's salon, while she was at the other, close to the door
of her bedroom, surrounded by women. According to Rœderer,
Josephine was always surrounded by women. She asked politely after
his wife. Bonaparte got up and left. Then Rœderer spoke poisonously
of Fouché: the Minister of Police was surely to blame for the assassination attempt, it would not have happened if he had been doing his job
properly, and if he stayed in office another two months, they would
all have their throats cut. Fouché, for a whole year, had failed to act

against suspected terrorists, who were intent on destabilising the constitution of Year 8. This was untrue – a large number of terrorist attacks had been prevented, including one to kill Bonaparte at Malmaison with a blunderbuss.[33] But Rœderer insisted that the Minister of Police was too lenient and it would be better to risk injustice to a good man than to tolerate monsters. Josephine laughed bitterly and said: 'Sir, you are so severe!' 'Yes, Madame,' he replied, 'I am.' He accused her of being surrounded by courtiers who hid the truth from her. He, on the other hand, spoke it courageously. She turned on him angrily, saying: 'It is not against the Minister of Police that Bonaparte must protect himself, but against more dangerous sycophants who encourage him towards ambitions he does not have.' Everyone knew that by 'sycophant' she meant Rœderer, and by 'ambitions' she meant a crown.[34]

Bonaparte's speech during an extraordinary session of the Council of State on 5 Nivôse (26 December) was carefully transcribed in Rœderer's memoirs. Bonaparte argued that the assassins had struck not only against him, but against the hundred or so people killed or wounded and the twenty buildings ruined or damaged:

> There must be as many sacrifices as there were victims, otherwise people might think that the government is not concerned with avenging the public. Paris and France will not be tranquil until the hundred or hundred and fifty scoundrels who caused general terror have been shot or deported. The nation needs peace: that is the purpose for which we are invested with power. The law that has been proposed only deals with those who were immediately implicated in the affair, not with all the scoundrels who were their accomplices. Why not invest the Consuls for five days with a power similar to that the Romans entrusted to Roman Consuls? *Caveant consules*, etc.[35]

Bonaparte asked Fouché to draw up a list of 130 Jacobins to be proscribed and deported without trial. Both men had once been fervent Jacobins. When Fouché demurred, Bonaparte accused him of trying to save his old friends, insisting, without any evidence or investigation, that he knew who was behind the explosion in the Rue Saint-Nicaise. 'This is the work of the Jacobins! It was the Jacobins who tried to assassinate me! . . . I know the truth of it, and nobody can make me change my mind. It is those low scoundrels who have been in open revolt, in a constant conspiracy, in armed rebellion against all the governments that have followed one another. If they can't be put in chains, they must be annihilated. France must be purged of that vile scum. No pity for the villains!'

The novelist and liberal political theorist, Madame de Staël, was conversing with friends in her salon when she heard the sound of the explosion. Supposing it to be 'merely the firing of some cannon by way of exercise', she continued with her discussion. She already knew that Bonaparte disliked her and disapproved generally of clever women. When she tried to impress him with her intellect, he asked her if she had any children. She had supported him before the coup of Brumaire, but was increasingly concerned that he would betray the first principles of the Revolution. She was shocked when he used the assassination attempt as an excuse to rid himself of 130 Jacobin opponents. 'When the arbitrary transportation of one hundred and thirty citizens is submitted to, there is nothing to prevent . . . the application of the same treatment to the most respectable persons.'[36]

To discover the real culprits, Fouché launched the first forensic criminal investigation into an act of terrorism in France. Marianne Peusol's widowed mother had presented herself to the police the morning after her daughter did not come home. She gave a detailed description of Marianne and explained that she usually sent her daughter out to sell bread rolls in the street; on that particular evening she had sent her in the direction of the Rue Saint-Nicaise. With his *préfet de police*, Louis-Nicolas Dubois, Fouché followed the clues left in the remnants of the horse and cart. They had them collected from the bloodstained street. They called in a veterinary artist to examine the horse's shattered carcass and provide a portrait of what it would have looked like alive. The day after the explosion they put up posters describing the horse and asking anyone with information to come forward. Two days later, a local resident named Lambel recognised the black mare as one he had sold the previous month, on 23 Frimaire, along with a cart for 200 francs.[37]

A blacksmith named Legros said he had shod the horse recently. A man who rented carriages and stables recognised it too. Then they found the supplier of the barrels of gunpowder. Guards in the Rue Saint-Nicaise claimed to have seen a long fuse hanging down behind the cart, but thought nothing of it before the explosion. All these clues and witnesses pointed to three conspirators: Pierre Robinault de Saint-Régent, Chevalier Pierre Picot de Limoëlan and François-Jean Carbon (formerly in the service of Limoëlan). They got hold of Carbon first, on 28 Nivôse (18 January). He was already in the police files, so it took only a short time to find him. They interrogated his eldest niece who held out for a while, but finally admitted that her uncle was hiding with some nuns on the Rue Notre-Dame-des-Champs. He was tortured and soon gave the names of his co-conspirators. It was Limoëlan who had enticed Marianne Peusol to hold the reins of the black mare, but all three had been involved in constructing the bomb and planning to explode it in Bonaparte's path. These men were royalists, not Jacobins, whatever Bonaparte chose to believe.

Fouché took the evidence to him. This is what Bonaparte told the Council of Ministers: 'It's a mistake to think I would behave like Louis XVI and offer no resistance. I am a man of the people, and I would never let myself be insulted like a king.' There was no question of pardoning the proscribed Jacobins. The First Consul turned everything to his advantage: he never admitted he was wrong. After Carbon's confession, they arrested Saint-Régent, who was found wandering the streets not daring to ask anyone to hide him, and about a hundred other royalists. Only Limoëlan escaped to America where he became a priest and spent every Christmas Eve in church on his knees, praying for forgiveness for the sacrifice of Marianne Peusol. But even with two of the three suspects apprehended, it was too late to save the victimised Jacobins, who were proscribed not for any direct link with the assassination attempt, but in the interests of public safety. The Council of State refused to pronounce on their proscription, declaring that it was not a legislative matter. The Legislative Assembly was not summoned to vote on the law of proscription because Bonaparte could not be absolutely sure that it would be accepted. So he asked the Senate to ratify the act as a 'measure tending to preserve the Constitution'. As 'guardian of the constitution', the Senate tacitly invested itself with the power to modify or violate it. The Senate's acceptance of the proscription of the Jacobins in the decree of 13 Nivôse, Year 9 (5 January 1801), was the first in a series of steps that made it possible for Bonaparte to legislate without the Legislative Assembly. In this way he began to revise the constitution of Year 8 to suit himself. The Jacobins were deported to the Seychelles, or 'the bottom of the sea' as Madame de Staël speculated, since they were never heard of again.[38]

Fouché did not believe Bonaparte had imperial or monarchical ambitions at this time. He knew for a fact that Josephine did not. But it was clear that the First Consul was determined to increase his power. He used the attempt on his life to vanquish enemies on the left and the right. The Jacobins and the royalists were equally punished. Carbon and Saint-Régent appeared before a criminal tribunal. One of the witnesses called was the widow Peusol who said several different people had told her that her daughter was offered twelve sous to hold the horse for the assassins. She was asked if she had identified the body and said no, she had asked her brother to do that. She was asked if she was aware that her daughter's limbs had been torn off in the blast and she said yes, she was. Ordinary women in the crowd were more outraged by the sacrifice of Marianne Peusol than by the attack on the First Consul. When Carbon and Saint-Régent were guillotined on 1 Floréal, Year 9 (21 April 1801), there was rapturous and prolonged applause from the spectators. Public anger turned on the cowards who had used an innocent fourteen-year-old girl to hold the reins of their infernal machine. People became afraid of what would happen if Bonaparte was assassinated; the idea that the future of France depended on protecting him started to spread. Fouché continued to blame the English for the attempt on the First Consul's life.

Bonaparte was afraid of Fouché, who had not lost his attachment to the revolutionary past. Fouché wanted to save what he could of the Revolution and prevent the aristocracy from regaining control of the state. He was nostalgic for the time when he too spoke in the name of the sovereign people. He had done personal favours for many people in Paris, who would have been loyal to him, if he had chosen to assert his independence. His revolutionary past was more extreme than Bonaparte's. He had organised the massacre of thousands of counter-revolutionaries in Lyons. He had been involved in bringing down Robespierre after the Incorruptible expelled him from the Jacobins on 26 Messidor, Year 2 (14 July 1794), and he had helped bring Bonaparte to power. Bonaparte was watching Fouché closely. Fouché's passions were the ordinary ones: money and power. Bonaparte's ambition was much greater. He told himself he wanted to 'close the romance of the Revolution', to heal the wounds, correct the extravagances and secure the conquests.[39]

In the immediate aftermath of the explosion, Josephine wrote directly to Fouché to plead for clemency for those accused of the assassination attempt. 'I cannot help feeling distressed and uneasy beyond measure at the prospects of the dreadful punishments which must await the perpetrators of the crime, who belong, I am told, to families with whom I have formerly been in habits of intimacy. I shall be appealed to by mothers, sisters and disconsolate wives, and I shall be grieved by my inability to grant all the favours I should wish.'[40] She was confident that Bonaparte was merciful and his attachment to her was great, but even so, she knew that awful examples would have to be made following such a crime. She asked Fouché to limit his investigations, not to be too rigorous in his hunt for the accomplices. Surely, she insisted, it was enough to punish the ringleaders. Bonaparte, newly invested with power, should seek to consolidate friends, not to triumph over adversaries. 'Having myself narrowly escaped the dangers of the Revolution, it is perfectly natural that I should feel interested on behalf of those whose lives may be spared without danger to the existence of my husband, which is so precious to me and to France.'[41] Finally, she pleaded with Fouché, 'Endeavour, citizen minister, to diminish the number of victims.' When it came to healing the wounds of the Revolution, Josephine, who had been much closer to the guillotine than Bonaparte, had a different vision from him as to what was needed. Her call for clemency was deeply humane. Her dreams were haunted by her fellow inmates, her first husband among them, who had been so much less fortunate than she was.

In *The Interpretation of Dreams*, Sigmund Freud discusses the dream Bonaparte was having as he slumbered in the carriage on the way to the Théâtre des Arts.[42] There were two sources for the dream. The first was Adolphe Garnier, a philosopher and psychologist, who claimed in his book on the capacities of the human soul, *Traité des facultés de l'âme* (1852), that Bonaparte was dreaming of his traumatic crossing of the Tagliamento River and the bombardment of the Austrians. By crossing the river in Ventôse, Year 5 (March 1797), with cavalrymen, artillery officers and combat engineers, Bonaparte had carried his campaign from Italy into Austria and established himself as the saviour of the Republic. According to Garnier, when the explosion in the Rue Saint-Nicaise happened, Bonaparte incorporated it into his dream of battle before he woke crying, 'My friends, we have been mined.' The second source, unnamed by Freud, claimed that when Bonaparte heard the deafening noise it caused him to dream of the thunder of the guns at the Battle of Arcole in Brumaire, Year 5 (November 1796). At Arcole, Bonaparte had grabbed a flag and stood in the line of fire inspiring his men until an unknown officer dragged him down into a ditch. Freud conflates the two sources and argues that one way or another the sound of the explosion was divorced from reality and woven into a dream sequence to prolong sleep momentarily. Freud believed that Bonaparte was an exceptionally good sleeper: someone who could dispose of his waking thoughts simply by deciding to go to sleep. Freud imagined that once Bonaparte was asleep his robust ego would have resisted anything that attempted to wake him up, even the infernal noise of an exploding cart, horse and girl.

After the assassination attempt, the atmosphere inside the Tuileries Palace was one of paranoia and denunciation, reminiscent of the Terror. One of the people suspected of having conspired against Bonaparte was the government's chief architect Lecomte. Bonaparte decided to sack him and replace him with Fontaine. Believing this unjust to his colleague, against whom there was no evidence, Fontaine tried to stand up for him. Bonaparte was furious. 'I've heard enough about Lecomte,' he shouted. 'I have put my trust in you. Take care not to lose it!'[43] Realising there was nothing further he could do for Lecomte, Fontaine shifted his focus to Percier. They were business partners, they worked together, Fontaine could not accept a promotion that did not apply to Percier too. Josephine tried to help, but Bonaparte ignored her. His mind had moved on to other matters. Fontaine went away determined to share the honour of his new position as chief architect with Percier. Another architect, Guillaume Trepsat, was one of those injured in the attempt on Bonaparte's life. He was coming out of a cafe on the corner of the Rue Saint-Nicaise when he was hit by debris from the exploding cart that shattered his leg and led to it being amputated. His injuries left him unable to work and destitute. Fontaine agreed to interest Bonaparte in his plight. He set up a meeting at Malmaison to suggest that the injured architect could be put in charge of Les Invalides, but was dismayed to find Bonaparte in a foul mood before Trepsat arrived. That morning, Bonaparte had tried to open a window in his newly renovated library – which he was generally pleased with even though the wood panelling reminded him of a sacristy – only to discover that it had been replaced by a fixed pane of glass. Once again he was furious with Fontaine who apologised profusely and promised that there would be a functioning window again by the next morning. Bonaparte calmed down enough for the injured architect to flatter his way into a job. Asked what had gone through his mind when the bomb exploded, Trepsat claimed to have thought only of the great man who had escaped the darkest of plots.[44] He was just one of many citizens now accustomed to living under Bonaparte's protective shadow. A threat to the First Consul's life was widely perceived as a threat to national security and stability.

While Fouché was busy tracking down the culprits behind the assassination attempt in the Rue Saint-Nicaise, a pamphlet entitled 'A Parallel among Caesar, Cromwell, Monck and Bonaparte' appeared.[45] The pamphlet arrived in an official envelope on the desk of every prefect in the Republic, openly advocating royalty and hereditary succession. It announced that, after ten years of upheaval, the person who could simultaneously call a halt to the Revolution and preserve its achievements had at last appeared:

> Bonaparte, like Caesar, is one of these dominating characters before whom all obstacles and all wills subside; their inspiration seems so supernatural that, in classical times, one would have considered them as living under the protection of a genie, or a God.[46]

Caesar had been dictator for life and had named his heir. Bonaparte, now aged thirty-one, was still only First Consul. The path towards consolidating his power was clear. Fouché quickly discovered that this pamphlet had been instigated by Lucien Bonaparte, now Minister of the Interior, and that a draft had been corrected by Bonaparte himself. Lucien was hoping that he would be named as his brother's heir if the opportunity arose. There was a terrible row between the three men and at the end of it Lucien was sent off, effectively into exile, as ambassador to Madrid. Bonaparte dissociated himself from the pamphlet, and Fouché arranged for copies of it to be rounded up and destroyed. The First Consul reflected on the poor timing of his first step towards absolute power: 'I have broken ground too soon. The pear is not yet ripe.'[47] The crown, like an unripe fruit, was still growing, no longer concealed deep in Bonaparte's imagination or dreams, but now a future prospect. 'The French can be governed only by me,' he told Rœderer. In his journal Rœderer noted that Lucien claimed to have taken the original draft of the pamphlet, with corrections in his brother's handwriting, to Spain with him, 'and I believe him'.[48]

The first crown Bonaparte created was not for himself, it was for Louis I, King of Etruria. Until Year 9, there was no kingdom of Etruria. After Bonaparte's successful campaigns in Italy, France controlled Tuscany, Parma, Savoy, Sardinia, Lucca and Modena.[49] The Duchy of Parma had been occupied by French forces since Year 4, but now that Bonaparte had conquered most of the rest of Italy, he sought to compensate the House of Bourbon. Ferdinand, Duke of Parma, reluctantly ceded his duchy to France and in return his son Louis became king of what had formerly been the Grand Duchy of Tuscany. The kingdom of Etruria took its name from the ancient Etruscans. Louis, who was sickly and epileptic, arrived in Paris for his coronation with his wife, Maria Luisa, who was one of the daughters of Charles IV, King of Spain. The couple travelled through France with their small son incognito, Louis disguised as the Count of Livorno.

Bonaparte received them at Malmaison. As usual, preparations for the reception were rushed and last-minute. Percier and Fontaine commissioned an enormous fifteen-metre-wide octagonal tent, pitched next to the lawn like a huge umbrella, but when it was half erected Bonaparte decommissioned it. Embarrassed and frustrated, the architects asked the carpenter to store it in his workshop in case it was needed for a future occasion.[50] Shortly before the guests arrived,

Percier and Fontaine decided to hang two new paintings by Nicolas-Antoine Taunay in the salon. One represented Bonaparte exhausted and asleep during the crossing of the Alps before the Battle of Marengo, the soldiers marching past trying not to wake him. The other depicted him at the summit of the Alps, showing his soldiers the rich plains of Lombardy below. When Bonaparte entered the salon and saw the paintings he laughed and demanded they be taken down. There was a scramble to rehang the green toile they had replaced before the future King of Etruria arrived.[51]

The coronation astonished Parisians who, seven years earlier at the height of the Terror, had seen citizens condemned by the Revolutionary Tribunal and guillotined for royalist sympathies. Madame de Staël believed that Bonaparte wanted to 'exhibit to the French the spectacle of a prince of the ancient dynasty humbled before the First Consul'.[52] Beyond France, many were shocked by the idea that a military general, the First Consul, but still only a consul, could create a monarch. Louis was criticised for accepting his crown from the hands of Bonaparte, and Maria Luisa, struggling to care for her child and her sick husband, was horrified by having to visit the city where Louis XVI and Marie Antoinette had been executed. Parisians gossiped about the blunders of the new King of Etruria. He was taken on a visit to the Muséum national d'histoire naturelle at the Jardin des Plantes, where he asked questions about quadrupeds and fish that would have been embarrassing from a twelve-year-old child.[53] During this time of transition from revolutionary customs to monarchical ones, Bonaparte attended a performance of *Oedipus* at the theatre and the audience broke into spontaneous applause at the line: 'I have made kings but do not want to be one.'[54]

Bonaparte came round to the view Percier and Fontaine had held from the start: Malmaison would never be a grand enough house for a person of his stature. He asked his architects to switch their attention to renovating the chateau of Saint-Cloud, the scene of the coup that

The fall of the French monarchy in the Tuileries Palace and gardens,
10 August 1792

The Jardin des Plantes, formerly the Jardin du Roi, remained
a place of tranquillity during the Terror in 1794

The gardens of the institute in Egypt, established in Cairo in 1798
during Bonaparte's occupation of the city

The interior of the institute in Egypt with the architect and
draughtsman, Jean Constantin Protain, drawing in the window
seat and Bonaparte at the centre of the meeting

Porcelain plates from Napoleonic France showing, clockwise from top left: dromedaries, also known as Arabian camels, from the Sèvres Egyptian Service; French scientists measuring the Sphynx, from the Sèvres Egyptian Service; *Mesembryanthemum carinatum*, from the Sèvres Exotic Plants Service; *Iris Susiana*, from the Sèvres Liliacées Service

An English satirical print depicting Bonaparte as a crocodile – recently
returned from Egypt, dispelling the Council of Five Hundred and already
wearing a crown – in the orangery of the chateau of Saint-Cloud
on 19 Brumaire, Year 8 (10 November 1799)

Napoleon and George III as rival gardeners separated by the
English Channel in 1803

Napoleon and his wife Josephine in the garden at Malmaison after he became First Consul in 1799. The couple extensively renovated the house and garden during the Consulate and after their divorce in 1809 it became Josephine's

An allegory of the Empress Josephine as patroness of the garden at Malmaison with her spectacular greenhouse in the background

The frontispiece to the *Voyage de Découverte aux Terres Australes*
by François Péron, published in 1807 (on Napoleon's orders many
of the plants, birds and animals brought back to France from
Australia were reserved for Josephine's garden)

Napoleon Crossing the Alps by Jacques-Louis David, an image which idealises the events of May 1800 when Bonaparte led his army through the Great St Bernard Pass, riding on a mule

Napoleon meeting Pope Pius VII (who was persuaded to travel to France for Napoleon's coronation on 2 December 1804) in the Forest of Fontainebleau

The celebration of Napoleon's second marriage to Marie Louise, daughter of Francis II of Austria, in the Tuileries gardens in 1810

had brought him to power. They were more than happy to do so. They had had enough of the arguments at Malmaison, and were particularly affronted when Josephine hired Jean-Marie Morel, the small, robust garden designer in his seventies responsible for Malmaison's enclosed park under the Ancien Régime. Josephine brought him out of retirement in Lyons to oversee her *jardin à l'anglaise*. Morel thought the vogue for informal gardens reflected the social and political status of the émigrés who had fled the Revolution, but were now returning to France.[55] Before the Revolution, he had worked at Malmaison for five years, contributing, among other designs, a rustic hamlet, similar to the one Queen Marie Antoinette had had at Versailles before the Revolution. When he returned he criticised everything that had been done in the garden recently. The trees were not planted in the right combinations of species and all the effects Percier and Fontaine had been aiming for seemed to him tasteless. Even the new greenhouse was in the wrong place, according to the patriarch of English-style gardens. The architects scathingly referred to Morel as a Dendrologue and resolved to resign their position as chief government architects and finish the book on Roman country villas which they had started during the Terror. They wrote two letters of resignation, one to Josephine and one to Bonaparte's secretary Bourrienne. They expected to be disgraced and replaced, like their colleague Lecomte. But they heard nothing. They remained in their post and concentrated on the new project of Saint-Cloud.[56]

When Bonaparte walked alone in the woods near Malmaison he felt 'amidst the solitude of nature'. He was a spiritual agnostic, accepting that, as human beings, 'we do not know where we come from, or where we are going'.[57] One evening he heard the distant bells of the church of Rueil ringing through the trees and felt overcome with emotion. He reflected on the power of early habits and associations, and on how such feelings and sentiments must be even stronger in more credulous people. Afterwards, relating this episode to the

Councillors of State, he said: 'I am no believer in particular creeds; but as to the idea of a God, look to the heavens, and say who made that.' He proposed the restoration of the Roman Catholic religion in France, which the Revolution had dismantled, but not destroyed. He told the councillors that when he was in Egypt he was a Muslim, but in France he would be a Roman Catholic and bring about a reconciliation with the Pope: 'the people will sing God save the Gallican church'. There was fierce opposition among the councillors who thought that the Revolution had done too much damage, there could be no forgiveness from the clergy or re-establishment of the Church. The councillors argued for religious freedom, insisting that 'the Spirit of the Age is wholly opposed to a return to Catholicism'.[58] But Bonaparte disagreed. 'We have seen republics and democracies; history has many examples of such governments to exhibit, but none of a state without an established worship, without religion, and without priests.'[59]

On 26 Messidor, Year 9 (15 July 1801), despite continued opposition from a significant proportion of the Councillors of State and the legislature, Bonaparte agreed the concordat with Pope Pius VII. The concordat was drawn up by a commission comprising three representatives from each side; among the French was Bonaparte's brother Joseph. Under the concordat, Roman Catholicism was acknowledged to be the religion of the majority of French citizens, but was not given the status of official state religion. Church property which had been confiscated during the Revolution was not restored, but the émigré priests who had fled were able to return to their parishes. According to the new agreement, Bonaparte, not the Pope, would select bishops and supervise the Church's finances. Rœderer was irritated that he was not consulted about these arrangements.[60] The first he heard about the concordat and the re-establishment of the clergy was during a conversation in the gardens of Malmaison with the First Consul and Antoine Claire Thibaudeau, another revolutionary survivor who had voted for the execution of Louis XVI and served briefly on the notorious Committee of Public Safety during the Terror. Thibaudeau was one of the Councillors of State who disapproved of the concordat, but it was to Rœderer that Bonaparte turned first. 'It is said that you are the leader of the opposition to the re-establishment of the clergy.' Rœderer replied, 'I am opposed to the insults spoken everyday by false apostles against philosophers, otherwise I am not opposed to anything.' Bonaparte insisted that the people needed a religion. 'It is absolutely essential to have a religion for the people; and not less so, that that religion should be directed by the government.' Robespierre, who had tried in the depths of the Terror to establish worship of the Supreme Being, would have agreed with him.

People gossiped that the restoration of the clergy was a prelude to the return of the crown, that the concordat might herald the revival of the Ancien Régime. When the concordat finally became law it was celebrated with a Mass in Notre-Dame on 28 Germinal, Year 10 (18 April, Easter Sunday, 1802). The cathedral bells had not been rung for ten years. When they sounded again they announced a celebration more lavish than any that had been seen since the start of the Revolution. Bonaparte made his journey from the Tuileries to Notre-Dame in a carriage drawn by eight horses, an honour reserved for the king under the Ancien Régime.[61] Each of the eight horses was led by a servant in superb livery. The Archbishop of Paris met Bonaparte as he arrived at the cathedral door. The First Consul was sprinkled with holy water and proceeded under a canopy to his seat, followed by the other two Consuls, the Councillors of State, the legislature and the army generals. There were some notable absences, though. The staunch republican General Lannes, for example, who had commanded the reserve army and been in Bonaparte's carriage en route to Haydn's *The Creation*, refused to attend, and was tactfully given a mission outside Paris to explain his absence. General Masséna, a veteran of many battles, including those of Arcole and Rivoli, was one of Bonaparte's most trusted military commanders. He had a house in Reuil from which he joked that he could piss on Bonaparte at Malmaison. He caused a disturbance when he arrived and found no seat had been reserved for him. Bonaparte turned round and glared disapprovingly.[62]

During the Revolution, the cathedral had been stripped of its twenty-eight statues of kings and queens, and rededicated, first to the Goddess of Reason, then, very briefly, to Robespierre's Supreme Being. Afterwards it had been left to deteriorate. The ban on organised religion during the Revolution also led to the collapse of the cathedral schools, and by Year 10 there was a serious shortage of trained church musicians.[63] Music for the *Te Deum* to celebrate the concordat was composed by the Italian Giovanni Paisiello, Bonaparte's new *maître de chapelle*. Bonaparte had insisted that Paisiello relocate to Paris from Italy, as he approved of his quiet and monotonous music, which was not too intrusive or demanding. He also approved of a new book, *Le Génie du christianisme* (*The Genius of Christianity*), published just four days before the celebratory Mass, by the young writer François-René de Chateaubriand. Chateaubriand was an émigré, descended from an aristocratic family from Brittany, who had recently returned to France. He had left France in 1791, after the Revolution but before the Terror, visited America, studied botany and wrote beautiful descriptions of nature in the Deep South. He had also spent time in England and was strongly influenced by Milton's *Paradise Lost*. Impressed by his book, which made a timely argument for the artistic superiority of Christianity on account of its beautiful ceremonies and majestic cathedrals, Bonaparte made Chateaubriand secretary of the legation to the Holy See. The second edition of *Le Génie du christianisme* appeared in Year 11, dedicated to the First Consul.

By Year 10, Britain was France's only unvanquished enemy. The two countries had been at war for almost a decade, since the execution of Louis XVI and the start of the Terror early in 1793. The Peace of Amiens, under which Britain finally recognised the French Republic, ended hostilities, but only lasted just over a year. It was signed on 4 Germinal, Year 10 (25 March 1802) and it ended on 28 Floréal, Year 11 (18 May 1803). During that brief interval of peace, Britain could afford to ridicule and dismiss the threat of Bonaparte. On 21 Pluviôse, Year 11 (10 February 1803), Samuel William Fores published a satirical print in London, part of a folio of caricatures that could be loaned out for an evening's entertainment, called *The Rival Gardeners*. The artist, Charles Williams, depicted George III and Bonaparte in their gardens on opposite sides of the Channel, each growing a crown in a tub hooped with gold. George III is plainly dressed, wearing a gardening apron and leaning on a spade. Bonaparte is in military dress, but has also donned a gardening apron and over-sleeves. George III's crown thrives at the top of a vigorous oak sapling; but Bonaparte's crown droops, unsupported by a wilting plant. Behind Bonaparte are rows of red flowers in pots, labelled 'Military Poppies', and a wheelbarrow, filled with coins, into which he has stuck his sabre. On the side of the wheelbarrow is written: 'This is manure from Italy and Switzerland.' The caption above Bonaparte's head reads: 'Why I don't know what is the reason – my Poppies flourish charmingly – but this Corona Imperialis is rather a delicate kind of plant, and requires great judgement in rearing.' George III, pointing to his healthy crown, replies: 'No – No – Brother Gardener – though only a ditch parts our grounds – yet this is the spot for true Gardening, – here, the Corona Britanica [*sic*], and Heart of Oak, will flourish to the end of the World.' Floating in the Channel between Britain and France is a cudgel carved with the words 'British Oak'.

Madame de Staël noticed how 'monarchical institutions were rapidly advancing under the shadow of the republic'.[64] There was now a praetorian guard, crown diamonds had been used to decorate the First Consul's sword, and his dress, covered with gold, echoed the Old, pre-revolutionary, Regime. He seemed to her a parvenu with all the audacity of a tyrant. She left a withering account of his smile:

His smile has been cried up as agreeable; my own opinion is that, in any other person it would have been found unpleasant; for this smile, breaking out from a confirmed serious mood, rather resembled an involuntary twitch than a natural movement and the expression of his eyes was never in unison with that of his mouth; but as his smile had the effect of encouraging those who were about him, the relief which it gave them made it be taken for charm.[65]

Within a year, de Staël's outspokenness would result in Bonaparte exiling her from Paris for a decade, insisting that she stay at least forty leagues away. On the day she was given twenty-four hours to leave, she was struck by the beauty of the sun and flowers. 'How different are the sensations which affect us from the combinations of society, from those of nature!'[66]

Following the Peace of Amiens, Bonaparte's tenure as First Consul was extended, first for a further ten years, then for life. Aside from General Carnot, who declared 'I will vote against the re-establishment of monarchy', on 22 Floréal, Year 10 (12 May 1802), the tribunate voted unanimously in favour of this lifetime extension, and a plebiscite on 14 Thermidor (2 August) was also overwhelmingly in favour.[67] Bonaparte's birthday that year was celebrated by another *Te Deum* in Notre-Dame marking the 'Birthday of the Consul for Life'.

During the peace, thousands of English visitors crossed the Channel to visit France. Among them were the Whig statesman Charles James Fox, his nephew Lord Holland, and the latter's wife Elizabeth, Lady Holland. On 15 Fructidor (2 September), Fox was granted an audience with the First Consul who received him politely, making a bland pre-prepared speech complimenting Fox as 'the greatest man of one of the greatest countries', an advocate for humanity, justice and peace. Fox was slightly irritated by and envious of Bonaparte's grandeur, describing him as 'a young man considerably intoxicated with success'.[68] De Staël thought no one could doubt Fox's 'talents and goodness of heart', but that he paid too much attention to Bonaparte and failed to recognise that he was an enemy of the first principles of the French Revolution: liberty and equality.[69]

The meeting between Bonaparte and Fox was cruelly satirised by Gillray in his cartoon *Introduction of Citizen Volpone & his Suite at Paris*, which represents Lady Holland as having been present, obese and obsequious, bowing down before a skinny man, a quarter of her size, seated on a throne, wearing an enormous bicorne hat instead of a crown. In fact Lady Holland only saw Bonaparte from a distance, riding a fine white Arabian horse, plainly dressed in his undecorated black hat. She was impressed by the public dinners given in the Tuileries gardens to hundreds of soldiers. She admired the celebratory illuminations. She was less impressed to see the four bronze horses brought to Paris from Venice, now standing on the gates to the Tuileries. 'The Brazen Horses from Venice are placed upon the Grille which runs across the Carrousel; they stand separate, and produce a very poor effect.'[70]

Now that there was peace, Bonaparte turned his attention to the arts and sciences. The astronomer William Herschel and his wife Mary came to Paris as guests of honour of the institute. Bonaparte granted Herschel and some other scientists, including the mathematician Laplace, an audience at Malmaison, where they came upon him supervising the irrigation of some newly planted flower beds in a heatwave. It was 28 degrees in the shade and over ice creams they discussed the construction of canals.[71] Bonaparte summoned Antoine Canova, the best sculptor in Europe, to Paris to model his bust. Canova did not want to leave his studio in Rome, and Pope Pius VII and Cardinal Consalvi, the Secretary of State for the Papal States, had to plead with him to consider the consequences for Italy if he refused the First Consul's summons. Canova arrived in the autumn, to the delight of Percier, Fontaine, David and other Parisian artists. He went to the chateau of Saint-Cloud to fulfil his commission, but Bonaparte found sitting for him extremely boring, and would only do it for very short periods.[72] Canova got to know the gardens and garden statues of Saint-Cloud very well while he waited for his impatient subject.

Bonaparte was spending more and more time at the chateau of Saint-Cloud, where he had overturned the Directory in the orangery during the coup of Brumaire. In Vendémiaire, Year 10 (October 1801), he had issued a decree redesignating the chateau as the official centre of consular power. The estate, which dates back to the sixteenth century, is on a hill overlooking Paris and the Seine, surrounded by gardens and terraces, including the renowned garden designer Le Nôtre's Grand Cascade. Marie Antoinette had acquired Saint-Cloud in 1785, believing that the air would be good for her children, and although the contents of the chateau were sold or looted during the Revolution, the gardens were preserved 'at the expense of the Republic for the pleasure of the people'. One visitor to the chateau during the Consulate was overwhelmed by its magnificence and could not help noticing that the room which was destined to become the emperor's throne room had been fitted up with a cornice 'ornamented by a cock (France) on the back of a crouching lion (England)!' Four compartments of the ceiling of the same room had been decorated with the imperial arms 'before the people willed so kindly that he should be urged to do them the favour to accept the Empire'.[73] When Lady Holland visited Saint-Cloud before leaving France she found that 'the gardens are insignificant, but if the Consul continues to like living there, I doubt not he will find means to extend them, tho' as yet I only look upon St. Cloud as a halt on the road to Versailles'.[74]

5

Terre Napoléon

'Poet Bonaparte – Layer out of a World-garden.'
Samuel Taylor Coleridge[1]

Among Bonaparte's juvenilia is a detailed summary of the Abbé Nicolle de la Croix's textbook guide to the globe, *Géographie moderne* (1752). Aimed at young people, the book presents geography as 'one of the eyes of history' and provides a sketch of the extent, manners, customs and religion of individual countries, listing their principal cities and characterising their natural history. As a schoolboy, Bonaparte copied out and underlined the reference to St Helena, 'a little island', and noted the countries of the southern hemisphere grouped under the name Australasia: 'La Nouvelle Guinée, la Carpentaire, la Nouvelle Hollande.' In 1785, aged sixteen, just after graduating from his military academy, he applied to join the Comte de La Pérouse's voyage around the world. He hoped that his aptitude for mathematics and his artillery training would qualify him for La Pérouse's crew. Both skills were in demand at sea: mathematics for navigating and artillery training in case of attack. He made the longlist for the voyage, but not the final selection. La Pérouse set out to complete the discoveries of Captain Cook in the Pacific. After reaching modern-day Chile, Hawaii, Alaska, California, Korea, Japan, Russia and Australia, his ships, *Le Boussole* and *L'Astrolabe*, set sail from the coast of New South Wales in March

1788, expecting to be back in France by June 1789. But those ships disappeared without trace. 'Any news of La Pérouse?' Louis XVI asked, on the morning of his execution in January 1793.[2] If Bonaparte had been accepted on that voyage, he would have drowned before the Revolution began.

Soon after his appointment as First Consul, on 4 Germinal, Year 8 (25 March 1800), a delegation of Bonaparte's colleagues from the institute asked him to sanction an expedition to the uncharted coasts of New Holland (the western part of Australia that had not been incorporated into the British colony of New South Wales). Since the Revolution, scientific exploration had become a national priority. The revolutionaries had sent an expedition to the Pacific in 1792 to search for La Pérouse; the regenerated nation was determined not to forget or abandon him 'to the fury of the seas or the rage of cannibals'.[3] But the rescue expedition failed to find La Pérouse, and the sailors and scientists returned to a country governed by Terror two years later. As France struggled to recover from the Terror, scientific exploration as a measure of national ambition became even more important because it seemed to offer an opportunity to revive the values of human progress and reason that had characterised the early Revolution before it descended into chaos.[4] Bonaparte's increased power was a new opportunity for the scientists at the institute. The delegation was led by Captain Nicolas Baudin, a seafaring merchant and commoner from the Île de Ré. Baudin, who had previous experience of the Pacific and Indian oceans, argued that France needed to catch up with other nations, especially in the natural sciences. Bonaparte was pleased to give his support and he requested that when the French explorers came into contact with the inhabitants of remote places, they take care to meet them as 'friends and benefactors'.[5] Preparations for the expedition were elaborate and expensive. Two ships were selected from the port of Le Havre: Le Géographe, a 450-ton corvette carrying thirty guns, and Le Naturaliste, a slower storage ship for the collection of plant and animal specimens. The ships were well stocked with scientific instruments, necessities and luxuries for the long journey. Baudin even had specially designed headed notepaper for his letters back to France, which pictured his two ships sailing beneath a banner suspended between the revolutionary values, 'Liberté' and 'Égalité'. Printed across the banner were the words 'Bonaparte Premier Consul'.

Among the carefully chosen crew of sixty-one, there were twenty-four savants, including five artists, five gardeners, five zoologists and three botanists. The German naturalist Alexander von Humboldt, the younger brother of the linguist and philosopher Wilhelm von Humboldt, would have liked to join the expedition, but had a low opinion of Baudin.[6] The official purpose of the voyage was 'observation and research relating to Geography and Natural History'. Baudin, who had spent only a brief time in the French navy, was proud of his status as an amateur scientist. 'I have not learnt the sea at school, nor the natural sciences in laboratories. I have crossed the ocean on merchant ships. I have picked up plants in the Americas and New Holland myself.'[7] During his previous travels he had become a keen and knowledgeable botanist, been shipwrecked several times and participated in the slave trade. Because France and Britain were at war in 1800, *Le Géographe* and *Le Naturaliste* needed passports from the British Admiralty to secure immunity from British attack and guarantee them a favourable reception in British ports outside Europe; Sir Joseph Banks, the president of the Royal Society, a veteran explorer and naturalist who had sailed with Captain Cook, advised the British Admiralty to grant these.

Ill winds prevented the expedition from leaving Le Havre until 27 Vendémiaire, Year 9 (19 October 1800). At a goodbye banquet on 7 Fructidor, Year 8 (25 August 1800), Baudin raised a toast to Bonaparte: 'First Consul of the French Republic and protector of the expedition.' The guests also drank to the 'amelioration of the lot of savage races' and the hope that 'civilisation will result from the visit the French are about to pay them'. La Pérouse was honoured in silence. At another banquet, while the ships were still waiting to set sail, a Chinese man named Ah Sam, who had been found on board a captured British frigate, proposed a toast to his good friends, the French. Bonaparte had personally entrusted Baudin with taking Ah Sam back to his own country.[8] It took the ships 220 days to reach Australia, and by the time they did many on board were suffering from scurvy. Sir Joseph Banks had written ahead to the British governor, Captain Philip Gidley King, in Port Jackson (Sydney), to warn him that it was possible the French ships had a political as well as a scientific purpose. Banks thought it likely that First Consul Bonaparte was hoping to secure allegiance to the Republic from the Île de France (Mauritius) and the Île de Bourbon (Réunion).

Bonaparte's new power also benefitted natural science and scientists closer to home. As First Consul, he was in a position to authorise funds for the Jardin des Plantes, to revive projects that had been interrupted by political turmoil, to increase its size and enrich its collections.[9] Mindful of his own origins, soon after he became First Consul he ordered the creation of a botanical garden on Corsica, the Jardin d'Expériences.[10] It was situated in Ajaccio in the walled grounds of the old convent of St François, which had been converted into a military hospital. Exotic plants grew so well here that six years later, after Bonaparte had become the Emperor Napoleon, he passed a decree making the Jardin d'Expériences a branch of the Jardin des Plantes.[11]

Since his return from Italy and refusal to go to Egypt, Bonaparte's friend and colleague at the institute, André Thouin, had devoted himself to the Jardin des Plantes and the Muséum national d'histoire naturelle. He lived with his family in an apartment in the grounds, prepared a course on cultivation and helped establish the Société d'Agriculture et d'Économie Rurale. It was typical of Thouin, a humane and literally down-to-earth man, that one of the first things he requested from the new regime was the decommissioning from the army of the son of one of his gardeners. On 8 Nivôse, Year 8 (29

December 1799), Thouin signed a certificate confirming that Louis Serjent, originally from Pontoise in the Department of Seine-et-Oise, aged sixty-nine, had worked diligently in the Jardin des Plantes for twelve years. He and his wife were now old and frail and their only son had been away fighting for the Republic in the 12th Battalion since 1793. Thouin hoped he could be sent home to his parents who needed him even more than the Republic.[12]

Thouin was invited by the government to form the Société d'Agriculture et d'Économie Rurale in 1798, to promote public discussion of agriculture and scientific research into cultivation in the aftermath of the Terror. Renamed the Société Libre d'Agriculture du Département de la Seine in 1803, it too had notepaper printed with the words 'Liberté' and 'Égalité'.[13] Thouin was a deeply committed republican. He had seen friends die for the Revolution, not least of all Gilbert Romme, with whom he had collaborated on the creation of the new calendar, suggesting agricultural names for the days of the year, celebrating flowers, trees, plants, animals and farming tools. Much as he valued the stability and opportunities that Bonaparte's rise to power offered the Jardin des Plantes, the Muséum national d'histoire naturelle and the institute, he could not reconcile himself to the prospect of an increasingly hierarchical and authoritarian regime.

The Revolution had brought bloodshed and destruction to France, but also some achievements. The abolition of titles and distinctions of social rank was considered by republicans eager to keep the spirit of 1789 alive to be one of the most important. In these circumstances, Bonaparte's determination to introduce a Legion of Honour met with vehement opposition. His proposal, which involved extending the system of military honours to the civil sphere, came before the Council of State in Floréal, Year 9 (May 1801). It was seen as an attempt to reintroduce ranks into society by resurrecting a system of nobility, a meritocratic nobility, but nevertheless a nobility, that would distinguish citizens from their equals and so unravel one of the foundational principles of the Revolution. Bonaparte defended his proposal by insisting on the importance of mental over physical qualities in modern warfare. 'The general who can now achieve things is possessed of shining civil qualities,' he told the Council of State. It was these qualities that soldiers respected, and it was no longer necessary to be close to two metres tall to command on the battlefield.[14] Referring back to his time in Egypt, Bonaparte remembered the bafflement of Mourad Bey, who could not understand how someone as physically mediocre as Bonaparte functioned as a general, until he understood the importance of intellect in the French system of war. Showing no awareness of how irritating his soldiers found his pride in being a member of the institute and his sense of himself as a man of knowledge and science, Bonaparte claimed, 'I knew well what I was about, when, though only a general, I took the title of Member of the Institute; I felt confident of being understood by the lowest drummer in the army.' It would be a mistake, he was sure, to divide society into soldiers and citizens, and therefore the military system of honours should be extended to high-achieving civilians.

The tribunate and the legislature were as opposed to Bonaparte's Legion of Honour as the Council of State. One concern was that 'under the pretence of effacing the last traces of the old nobility, it [the Legion of Honour] will establish a new one, and strongly confirm the old'.[15] And ultimately there was the fear that 'The proposed order leads directly to a monarchy. Crosses and ribbon are the pillars of an hereditary throne: they were unknown to the Romans who conquered the world.' Bonaparte fiercely rejected the claim that a system of honours was unknown to the Romans. Never, he insisted, had there been a nation in which they mattered more. 'The Romans had patricians, the equestrian order, citizens and knights; for each class they had a separate costume, different habits. To reward achievements they awarded all sorts of distinctions, surnames recalling great services, mural crowns, triumphs.' People were dismissive of his proposed honours, 'they call them baubles', Bonaparte reflected, 'but it is with baubles that men are led'.[16] He presented his Legion of Honour as a step towards rebuilding a broken society. 'Everything has been destroyed, we must commence the work of creation.'[17]

The Legion of Honour was passed by a small majority in the Council of State, the tribunate and the legislature, and finally instituted in 1802. It was loosely modelled on a Roman legion, with legionaries, officers, commanders, regional cohorts and a grand council. All Frenchmen could qualify for an honour, the only criteria being merit or bravery (the first recorded award to a woman, Angélique Brûlon who fought in the Revolutionary wars disguised as a man, was in 1851; women who joined the army received awards before this date, but the records have been lost). The small cross of the Legion of Honour was made from white enamel and hung from a red silk ribbon. The design involved five quadrangles, evenly arranged on top of a circular laurel wreath and centred on a small circular bust of Bonaparte. This design was copied by the architect Jacques Molinos for the construction of a new building in the Jardin des Plantes, the Rotunda, begun in 1802, to house part of the menagerie. The decision to build it in the shape of the cross of the Legion of Honour united two of Bonaparte's passions: science and meritocracy.

Bonaparte was respectful of his scientist friends, but sometimes overlooked them. Despite his meritocratic principles, his first choice as Minister of the Interior was his brother Lucien. This caused panic among the professors at the institute and at the Jardin des Plantes who feared that, under Lucien, scientific research would be centralised and controlled by the government, just like public health and the police. Thouin worried that if the new Minister of the Interior sacked him, he would lose his home and position at the Muséum national d'histoire naturelle, and the hard-won autonomy of the Jardin des Plantes would be compromised. Fortunately, Bonaparte found his brother too wilful and soon replaced him with the chemist, agronomist and member of the institute Jean-Antoine Chaptal, who worked to represent the interests of scientists. In Messidor, Year 9 (July 1801), Chaptal travelled to England to purchase pairs of tigers and lynxes, a leopard, a panther, a mandrill, a hyena and various birds for the Jardin des Plantes. The total cost was 175,000 francs. He also allowed Joseph Banks to add a collection of rare plants to the shipment. Under Chaptal, Thouin kept his job until his death in 1824.[18]

Private as well as public gardens were changing. As Bonaparte's power grew, so too did Josephine's ambitions for her garden at Malmaison. She wanted it to be 'the most beautiful and curious garden in Europe' and a rival to the best botanical gardens in the world, Kew in London and the Schönbrunn and Belvedere gardens in Vienna. Thouin was a helpful contact, happy to supply the wife of the First Consul with plants from the Jardin des Plantes. She asked him for foreign plants to stock her orangery and greenhouses. But the exchange was not one way; from the beginning there was close cooperation between Malmaison and the Muséum national d'histoire naturelle, enthusiastic sharing of samples and botanical knowledge. Sometimes Josephine's requests included plants that were not ready to move, but otherwise the professors were happy to send her what she asked for, knowing that the plants would be well cared for at Malmaison.[19] When Thouin wrote an article on national collections of heath (genus *Erica*) and heather plants originally imported from the Dutch colony the Cape of Good Hope (Cap de Bonne Espérance), he placed France third in the world, after England and Holland, largely due to successful propagation at Malmaison.[20]

The war did not interrupt all international botanical and other scientific exchanges. In 1801 Thouin received a letter from his colleague Carl Peter Thunberg in Uppsala, lamenting the effects of the war, which Sweden was not yet involved in, and wishing that he was still young, so that when peace finally came he could travel to Paris to see the collection of plants and animals at the Jardin des Plantes.[21] On 19 Vendémiaire, Year 10 (11 October 1801), Josephine wrote to Louis Otto, a diplomat and the French government's commissioner for the exchange of prisoners in London, thanking him for finding time to concern himself with her requests for plants in the midst of the war. She hoped that once peace had been established between France and England, he might ask King George III to send her some plants from Kew Gardens. Plants had been sent to Malmaison from the renowned Lee and Kennedy Vineyard Nursery in Hammersmith, London, throughout the war, sometimes arriving in poor condition, leading to dispute about payment.

With the declaration of the short-lived Peace of Amiens on 4 Germinal, Year 10 (25 March 1802), Otto arranged a special passport for the plantsman John Kennedy, whose father had co-founded the Vineyard nursery, allowing him to travel to France with rare plants and seeds for Josephine. During this visit, Josephine and Kennedy agreed to co-fund a research trip to the Cape of Good Hope. The agreement was that Malmaison and the Vineyard nursery would share the cost of sending a botanist to the Cape, and would also share the resulting samples. They chose James David Niven, a Scottish botanist who had already been on a collecting trip to the Cape, and he spent six years there, sending plants and seeds back to Europe via the island of St Helena, which was owned and governed by the East India Company.[22] Niven found thirty *Erica* plants not previously known to science for Josephine's collection, including *elegans, pellucida, blandfordia, hibbertia* and *niveniana*.[23] She also had a share of the ixias, pelargoniums and other plants. Later, the firm Lee and Kennedy would instruct a lawyer to try and recover from Josephine's heirs the money she had promised but never paid. But during the Peace of Amiens, and for a long time afterwards, it was impossible to imagine that the wife of the First Consul, soon to be Emperor of the French, would renege on her side of a contract.

Meanwhile the ships continued their voyage of exploration. After *Le Géographe* and *Le Naturaliste* reached Van Diemen's Land in Nivôse, Year 10 (January 1802), they entered the d'Entrecasteaux Channel and captured an albatross.[24] The scientists conducted hydrographic work and also recorded meetings with indigenous peoples. Afterwards the ships became separated. The scientists on *Le Géographe* went on to explore the eastern and southern coast of New Holland, renaming it Terre Napoléon. On 18 Germinal, Year 10 (8 April 1802), while anchored in a bay south-east of modern Adelaide, the crew saw a ship flying the English flag approach. She was under the command of Captain Matthew Flinders and had left England in Thermidor, Year 9 (August 1801). It was easy to believe that the English ship had been sent in pursuit of the French.[25] Neither Captain Baudin nor Captain Flinders knew about the Peace of Amiens, but despite their mutual assumption that their countries were still at war, the captains met on friendly and cooperative terms and the site of their meeting became known as Encounter Bay. As Flinders shared his maps with Baudin and told him about his discovery of Kangaroo Island, it became clear to the French that the English had pre-empted much of their exploration of the uncharted coasts of New Holland. On 9 Messidor, Year 10 (28 June 1802), Le Géographe and Le Naturaliste were reunited at Port Jackson. The exhausted and sickening French crews were well looked after for five months in the English colony. During this time the French scientists could devote themselves to their botanical, anthropological and other research, and Baudin eventually decided that enough progress had been made to warrant sending Le Naturaliste back to France with a cargo of natural history collections, maps, memoirs and observations.

Le Naturaliste set sail for Europe on 25 Frimaire, Year 11 (16 December 1802), while Le Géographe headed for Kangaroo Island. The captain of Le Naturaliste was Jacques Hamelin, who was more affable and much better liked than Baudin. When his ship reached Le Havre five months later on 17 Prairial, Year 11 (6 June 1803), Thouin was sent from Paris to welcome Hamelin and supervise the division of the cargo between the Jardin des Plantes and Malmaison. The professors at the Muséum national d'histoire naturelle had been politely invited by the Minister of the Interior, Chaptal, to prioritise Josephine's claims over the specimens.[26] The request was repeated on 18 Thermidor, Year 11 (6 August 1803).[27] On the journey from Paris to Le Havre, Thouin was struck by how much freedom of movement had been reduced under the First Consul's authoritarian regime.[28] Even compared to the restrictions imposed on citizens during the revolutionary Terror, the need for passports and documentation to justify his journey seemed excessive. Already disconcerted by Bonaparte's purge of the diehard Jacobins after the assassination attempt in the Rue Saint-Nicaise, and by the concordat reconciling France and the Pope, Thouin found the new police measures uncomfortable. He felt ever more strongly that the revolutionary values of Liberté and Égalité were being eroded. The documents he needed to make the journey to Le Havre included a detailed physical description: aged 56, 1.76m tall, grey-brown hair, brown eyebrows, brown eyes, high forehead, aquiline nose, round chin, oval face.[29]

The Australasia expedition had already cost the lives of a number of the crew, including two gardeners, two zoologists, a botanist, an astronomer and a painter, who all died at sea or from illnesses that caused them to leave the ships. Eventually, only six of the original twenty-four savants made it back to France. So it was a relief when Thouin and other institute colleagues of the deceased judged the cargo of Le Naturaliste to be of outstanding scientific significance. There were 180 cases of minerals and animals, four cases of dried plants, three casks of timber specimens, two boxes of seeds and sixty tubs of living plants.[30] Thouin helped prepare the inventory. There were no kangaroos among the living specimens because they had died on the journey when attempts to force-feed them had failed.[31] Among the living birds sent to Malmaison, there was an emu (the large species, *Dromaius novaehollandiae*) that had been loaded onto *Le Naturaliste* at Port Jackson.[32] On 27 Thermidor, Year 11 (15 August 1803), a report on the expedition was published in *Le Moniteur*, which was the official newspaper for Bonaparte's regime. And yet, in contrast to the great send-off their expedition had received, the grand feasts as they waited to set sail from Le Havre, Hamelin and his returning crew were disappointed by the lack of attention and congratulations they received outside the institute. But they had returned to a nation once again in deep turmoil. Bonaparte was busy preparing for battle because the Peace of Amiens had collapsed on 28 Floréal, Year 11 (18 May 1803), when England declared war on France.

At Malmaison, Josephine was developing a menagerie to rival the one at the Jardin des Plantes. She was also echoing Marie Antoinette's pre-revolutionary passion for collecting animals. She favoured animals and birds that could peacefully coexist and roam as freely as possible throughout her gardens. She kept a flock of merino sheep at Malmaison and the sale of their wool became one of the sources of revenue for the estate. The project of importing Spanish sheep was inherited from the Ancien Régime. It had long been recognised that the merino breed had particularly fine fleeces and was responsible for the success of the Spanish wool trade, but until the late eighteenth century there was a ban on exporting merinos from Spain. After the ban was relaxed, Sir Joseph Banks introduced the first British flock at Kew Gardens in 1792. But Marie Antoinette had had a flock at Versailles from 1786. Breeding merinos at Malmaison was a self-conscious imitation of Marie Antoinette on Josephine's part, but it was also a practical business venture. Bonaparte was interested in the possibility of producing more and better wool in France for supplying the makers of army uniforms. Another imitation of Marie Antoinette was the dairy Josephine established at Malmaison. Three Swiss staff and a herd of Swiss cows arrived in 1803. Josephine, like the queen before her, took great pleasure in showing visitors her farm and consuming her own milk and cream.

Josephine was the first to breed black swans in captivity.[33] A pair that arrived in France on *Le Naturaliste* were taken straight to Malmaison. There was no record of their origin, but it was probably Port Jackson. The Minister of the Interior, Chaptal, told Thouin explicitly that these birds were reserved for Josephine. Five years later she was able to offer black swans she had bred at Malmaison to the Muséum national d'histoire naturelle for the national collection. The original birds reproduced twice and one of them was preserved by the ornithologist and pioneer taxidermist Louis Dufresne when it finally died in 1814. Alongside living birds, Josephine received a large number of dead specimens from *Le Naturaliste*, which were sent to the Muséum national d'histoire naturelle where Dufresne and his wife worked to preserve them. In 1803 Dufresne introduced the neologism 'taxidermy' into a textbook, *Nouvelle Dictionnaire d'Histoire Naturelle*, explaining that the difference between embalming and taxidermy is aesthetic.[34] The Dufresnes aimed not merely to preserve their specimens with arsenical soap, but to capture the magnificence and individuality of each of them in a realistic mount.[35] Taxidermy, Dufresne argued, is an art as well as a science. In addition to all the work on Josephine's birds from *Le Naturaliste*, the Dufresnes also prepared a further fifty for the Muséum national d'histoire naturelle. Some were in a terrible, rotting state after months in transit, but Dufresne hoped his colleagues and Josephine would be happy with the ones that could be rescued as evocative exhibits.[36] Josephine was so pleased with the results that she began to spend thousands of francs on stuffed birds. She had the obsessive tendencies of many collectors: she could not stop enlarging and refining her collections of plants, animals and natural history specimens.

Josephine wrote to the French sub-commissioner in Portsmouth, New Hampshire, in Year 12:

> Please send me a collection of American seeds . . . for I want to convert part of the land at Malmaison into a nursery . . . of exotic trees and shrubs which could be grown in our climate. The First Consul takes the greatest interest in this project . . . it is a new source of prosperity for France . . . I count on your enlightened help and patriotic zeal.[37]

Bonaparte was certainly supportive of Josephine's plant collecting at Malmaison. He wrote on one occasion to the Versailles et du Roule nursery ordering that the plants requested for Josephine be delivered; between Brumaire and Ventôse, Year 12, over 2,000 individual plants were supplied to Malmaison.[38] Another of her aims was to collect every variety of rose in the world. She had 167 gallicas, 27 centifolias, 22 chinas, 11 wild species, 8 albas, 4 spinosissimas, 3 mosses, 3 damasks, 3 foetidas and 1 musk.[39] She entrusted management of her expanding botanical establishment to Charles-François Brisseau de Mirbel, the founder of microscopic plant anatomy in France. He became the *super-intendant* of the gardens and all their staff. When Bonaparte was cross about paying a bill at Malmaison, he blamed Mirbel.[40]

Bonaparte's interest in introducing new plants to France was more economically focused. He wanted to know if potatoes and sugar beets could be grown more widely to provide alternative sources of food for a nation still heavily dependent on bread. 'An army marches on its stomach' is a saying sometimes attributed to Bonaparte, sometimes to Frederick the Great. But even if the attribution to Bonaparte is false, there is no denying the patriotic zeal with which he addressed the crucial question of food for the army. He wanted 'to give some real encouragement to agriculture' and for this reason wanted to understand regional differences. He thought it was a mistake for land to be owned by small-scale cultivators who cared only about making a living and never invested in improving their holdings. 'These are not the people to be encouraged. It is the rich land-owners, who do something to increase the value of their property, and who are the only class to think about their interests, and to be concerned for the future of themselves and their children.'[41] Such people, he thought, would not be motivated by grants, but by medals, decorations and honours. A letter of congratulations or the Legion of Honour was to be awarded to agriculturalists throughout France who distinguished themselves by the extent and skill of their farming or livestock rearing.

Josephine's hopes to naturalise the exotic plants that had returned from Australasia throughout the departments of France were shared by André Thouin. In 1806, Thouin's School of Practical Agriculture was set up at the Jardin des Plantes to research the use of plants in rural and domestic economies.[42] The school's objectives bridged revolutionary values and those of Bonaparte's new regime. Plants were considered potential resources for the poor, sources of enjoyment for the rich and beneficial to the Republic in general. Thouin defined geography as a science informing the choice of 'the most appropriate methods of conservation and multiplication of plants that come to us from different parts of the earth, plants that it is useful or pleasant to introduce into our agriculture'.[43] There were hopes that botanical nomenclature could be standardised both inside France and internationally, and plans to naturalise new plants throughout the departments of France for human and animal consumption. Eucalyptus, from the myrtle family, was a candidate for acclimatising in southern France and perhaps in other departments. *Phormium tenax* (New Zealand flax), long used by the Maori to make textiles and more recently for making sails and ropes, had been successfully introduced to St Helena, and Mirbel, the director of the Malmaison garden, hoped it could be grown in France too.[44] French botanists often appealed for Bonaparte's help through Josephine. Alire Raffeneau Delile, who had been with Bonaparte in Egypt and directed the botanical garden in Cairo, was appointed French Vice Consul to Wilmington, North Carolina, in 1802. He was charged with forming a herbarium of American plants that could be naturalised in France. A year later, Josephine was asked to support an increase in his stipend so that he could afford a horse on which to pursue his research into American plants suitable for growing in France.

In Frimaire, Year 10 (December 1801), Bonaparte sent warships and troops commanded by his brother-in-law, General Charles-Victoire-Emmanuel Leclerc, to Saint-Domingue (now Haiti). Madame de Staël noticed that in his decree, Bonaparte used the royal 'we' when referring to 'our' brother-in-law. She found the suggestion that France was now associated with the prosperity of a particular family 'a bitter pill'.[45] The purpose of the expedition was to reassert French power over the Caribbean island and to re-establish exclusive trading rights for France. Slavery on the island had been abolished during the Revolution, but there were widespread fears it would be reinstated by the Consulate. Led by the formidable Toussaint Louverture, himself a former slave, anti-colonial insurgents had drafted a revolutionary constitution for Saint-Domingue, which Bonaparte thought flouted French authority. Under the new constitution, Louverture had been proclaimed governor for life without severing ties to France; he thought of himself as 'the Bonaparte of Saint-Domingue'.[46] Josephine was personally grateful to Louverture because he had helped her Martinique relatives restore order and production on the sugar plantations they owned in Saint-Domingue, which benefitted her financially.[47] Louverture established his headquarters in a splendid house in the Ennery commune, with long walkways and beautiful rose gardens to rival those of Malmaison, and from here he governed and held court.[48] Bonaparte's sister, Pauline, accompanied her husband on the expedition to Saint-Domingue. Before the flagship *Océan* sailed from Brest, the poop deck, normally reserved for cannon, was turned into a garden for Pauline and her small son to enjoy during the voyage, which took almost two months.[49]

After arriving in Saint-Domingue in Pluviôse, Year 10 (February 1802), Leclerc and his family lived in Port-au-Prince (known as Port-au-Républicain after 1793) in a luxurious home with extensive grounds, including fresh springs and a magnificent forest, approached through an avenue of citrus trees. Pauline planned a menagerie of exotic animals. But the beautiful setting belied the ugliness of what the French had come to do. Bonaparte had entrusted Leclerc with restoring French authority in Saint-Domingue, which involved removing Louverture, who was declared an outlaw.[50] Louverture was arrested on 18 Prairial, Year 10 (7 June, 1802) and deported to France where he died in prison less than a year later. William Wordsworth, who supported the abolition of slavery, wrote a sonnet to Louverture, willing him to live and promising:

> Though fallen thyself, never to rise again
> Live, and take comfort! Thou hast left behind
> Powers that will work for thee – air, earth and skies;
> There's not a breathing of the common wind
> That will forget thee![51]

But despite abolitionist arguments, after the Peace of Amiens, Bonaparte passed laws maintaining slavery in French colonies that still had it and reintroduced the slave trade in Martinique, Tobago and St Lucia, followed by Guadeloupe and Guyana.[52] In Saint-Domingue the freedoms the Revolution had granted were being destroyed.

Alongside the colonial gardens and the plantations in Saint-Domingue, there were the gardens of ex-slaves, on poor, mosquito-infested land. The people who struggled to subsist in such wretched circumstances were determined not to forgo their liberty. They left their small plots and joined the rebels in the mountains. Leclerc and his soldiers resorted to atrocious torture and murder, but could not make French authority prevail. He wrote to Bonaparte insisting many more troops would be needed. Leclerc told himself he would be going home soon, but he died of yellow fever on 11 Frimaire, Year 11 (2 December 1802) and Pauline returned to France alone, a widowed single mother at the age of twenty-one. Leclerc's successor lost against the insurgents and Saint-Domingue was declared independent on 10 Nivôse, Year 12 (1 January 1804).

The 45-acre forest garden at L'Habitation Leclerc was abandoned. Almost a century and a half later, in 1944, it was purchased by the American dancer and anthropologist Katherine Dunham, who turned it into a resort for the wealthy, with villas and a spectacular swimming pool. But at the end of her life, she wanted it to become a botanical garden, a verdant legacy for the people of Haiti. The trees at L'Habitation Leclerc are its last remaining coastal forest. Over the years they have been protected from pillaging and commerce by the voodoo belief that spirits live among the enormous mapou and mango trees. The forest is considered a dangerous place. When Dunham bought it, it was still haunted by the ghosts of slaves and ex-slaves mutilated and killed by the French colonial regime. She was warned, 'the master of Leclerc will never be happy'.[53] In exile on St Helena, Napoleon admitted that the invasion of Saint-Domingue was a great stupidity on his part.[54] But this was a retrospective assessment: at the time, he was determined to reintroduce slavery, arguing that the revolutionaries had not understood what they were doing when they abolished it in 1794.[55]

Three months after the declaration of Saint-Domingue's independence, on 4 Germinal, Year 12 (25 March 1804), the second ship of the Australasia expedition, Le Géographe, arrived at the safe anchorage of Lorient, no longer captained by Baudin. Exhausted and ill, Baudin had abandoned the expedition in Messidor, Year 11 (July 1803), reached the Île de France on 9 Fructidor, Year 11 (27 August 1803), and died three weeks later. The instructions for the division of Le Géographe's cargo were exactly the same as they had been for Le Naturaliste's cargo: Josephine's wishes were to take priority over those of the professors at the Muséum national d'histoire naturelle.[56] Before reaching France, Le Géographe, now captained by Pierre Bernard Milius, stopped at the Cape of Good Hope, and from there Governor Janssens sent Josephine a bird called secrétaire du Cap and a mountain zebra.[57] There was also a cassowary bird on board, a wildebeest, three kangaroos, two emus of a rare variety (Dromaius novaehollandiae minor), smaller than the commoner kind, and various other birds and animals.[58] This time Étienne Geoffroy Saint-Hilaire, who had been with Bonaparte in Egypt, went to meet the returning ship and made an inventory of the live animals on board. Some that had survived the arduous journey from Australasia died in transit from Lorient to Paris. Two of the three kangaroos did not survive. After receiving the animals she had requested for her menagerie at Malmaison, Josephine soon sent the zebra and the wildebeest on to the Muséum national d'histoire naturelle. In just a few days she had discovered that neither of these animals was suitable for ranging freely around her garden. She swapped them for two kangaroos which had been imported from England by Dufresne during the Peace of Amiens.[59] She hoped they would settle and breed in her garden. But less than a year later, the male kangaroo was attacked by a dog and died. Its body was sent back to the Muséum national d'histoire naturelle for taxidermy.

For Josephine, Malmaison was a place of peaceful sanctuary where she hoped rare plants and animals could coexist in harmony. Her garden was her antidote to the Terror, an intensely personal approach to healing political trauma through interacting with the natural world. For Bonaparte, Malmaison was also a sanctuary, but when he retreated there it was sometimes to contemplate extreme violence, even murder. He was at Malmaison when he was told that the arrest of the Duc d'Enghien, which he had ordered, was about to be carried out. The Duc d'Enghien was a member of the House of Bourbon, doubly descended from Louis XIV, the Sun King. During the Revolution, he had commanded émigré forces that attempted an unsuccessful invasion of France led by the Duke of Brunswick, but since Year 9, when he privately married Charlotte de Rohan, the niece of the French Bishop of Strasbourg, he had left military service and was living quietly at Ettenheim in Baden. Bonaparte nevertheless suspected him of being in England's pay and of involvement in the Cadoudal Affair, yet another royalist conspiracy to assassinate him, this time on the road to Malmaison. For these reasons Bonaparte sent kidnappers across the Rhine to seize the duc in his own home and bring him to France.

The Duc d'Enghien was taken straight to the Château de Vincennes, a fortress in east Paris, where he was tried by court martial and immediately executed in the early hours of 30 Ventôse, Year 12 (21 March 1804), by firing squad, beside a hole in the ground that had already been dug. Bonaparte did not want to risk a more protracted trial in case public opinion in Paris turned against him in favour of the Bourbons. This swift condemnation to death by a military tribunal recalled the summary executions of the Terror. Josephine had begged Bonaparte to show mercy. To her lady-in-waiting, Madame Rémusat, she confided: 'I have done what I could to induce him to promise me that the Prince's [sic] life shall not be taken, but I am greatly afraid his mind is made up.'[60] Bonaparte believed that the consolidation of his power required the death of the Duc d'Enghien. He was at Malmaison when he was told that the execution had taken place and that the duc's request for a face-to-face meeting with him had been denied. Much later, in exile on St Helena, Bonaparte claimed that he felt no regret. 'I was assailed on all sides by enemies whom the Bourbons had raised up against me. Threatened with air-guns, with infernal machines, and treacherous plots of all kinds, I seized the occasion to strike terror even as far as London.'[61] He insisted he would have done the same again, even though the execution was widely condemned at home and abroad, especially by the Tsar of Russia, Alexander I, who immediately broke off diplomatic relations with France. Throughout Europe opinion hardened against Bonaparte into an unrelenting determination to remove him. 'It was worse than a crime. It was a blunder,' Bonaparte's Minister of Police, Fouché, concluded.

Madame de Staël was living in exile in Berlin in an apartment on the Spree Quay when she heard the news of the execution. At first, she could not believe it and insisted it must be a story spread by the enemies of France. But when she was shown the death sentence announced in Le Moniteur she was overcome by horror.[62] One of her friends told her that at the Château de Vincennes, a few days after the Duc d'Enghien was shot and buried, some children were playing quoits on the mound of earth that was his unmarked grave. An old invalid with silver hair watched them until, with tears in his eyes, he led them away, saying, 'Do not play there, my children, I beseech you!'[63]

On 28 Floréal, Year 12 (18 May 1804), the Senate adopted the constitution of Year 12, giving the French Republic an emperor, Napoleon Bonaparte. Claiming that there was a royalist plot to restore the Bourbon monarchy, Napoleon presented himself as the saviour of the Revolution. The new constitution declared that 'the government of the Republic is entrusted to an Emperor.' It was put to the people in a plebiscite vote: 3,572,329 for and 2,579 against. One of those voting against was Thouin: the diehard republican botanist could not reconcile himself to the imperial regime, but resolved to continue his work at the Jardin des Plantes.[64] In this he was helped by Josephine, despite his disapproval of her spouse's elevation to emperor. The resumption of hostilities between France and England after the collapse of the Peace of Amiens meant that all correspondence between the two countries was officially suspended, but once again the botanists made use of networks of prisoners of war to continue their scientific exchanges.[65]

Thouin's republican unease caused him to turn down the Legion of Honour when it was offered to him as a member of the institute. He also refused one of the new uniforms that Napoleon introduced for his institute colleagues after he became emperor. Thouin received the brochure from the embroiderer and lace dealer, but was not prepared to be measured up for the uniform. He did not want to flatter his own vanity or become a puppet of the government.[66] Turning down the Legion of Honour proved extremely difficult. Thouin's fellow naturalist Lacépède, now Grand Chancellor of the Legion of Honour, tried to persuade him to accept. Thouin listed his reasons for refusing in a note to Lacépède that he had the good sense not to send:

1. Pre-eminences and exclusive privileges have for a long time, and will always be, against my principles.

2. The honour cannot be held in common like money or science, because each keeps for themselves what they have acquired.

3. And finally, I have no ambition, I am content with the honour common to six million French citizens who acquired it by fulfilling the duties of free men.[67]

Instead of this indirect indictment of Napoleon for betraying revolutionary values, Thouin sent an emollient reply to Lacépède, expressing gratitude for the honour, but still politely refusing it. He kept turning down invitations to ceremonies and dinners, pretending to be ill, or else explaining that he did not have the appropriate costume. Finally, he sent Lacépède a short parable about the different milieux inhabited by eagles and farmers.[68] The eagle naturally inhabits the high regions of the Empire, approaching and staring fixedly at the sun; from a great height the bird casts its shadow on the ground. Whereas the farmer, bent towards the earth, limits his ambition to fertilising it and is content to enjoy the reflected light of the sun, without having the temerity to look at it directly. And so, Thouin concludes, it would be uncomfortable for a farmer to be obliged to wear the effigy of the eagle with which he has so little rapport, and to which he is averse because it kills and eats lambs. Thouin could not have been more pointed or clear. He wanted to be left alone in the Jardin des Plantes to write his lectures on agriculture and pursue his research; he wanted nothing to do with the new emperor's court. Even so, the state sent him the stipend of 125 francs which accompanied the Legion of Honour. He passed it on to a relative in need. In private he wrote his profession of faith on the subject of social distinctions, explicitly criticising the emperor and referring to him by the outdated name of Bonaparte. Persisting in his determination to concentrate on farming and botany and to stay out of politics, Thouin published a paper in Year 12 in the *Annales du Muséum national d'histoire naturelle* on the introduction of the dahlia to France.[69] He listed three varieties – *Dahlia rosea, ponceau* and *pourpre* – which had been imported from Mexico

via Madrid. At the Jardin des Plantes he began grafting dahlias successfully and named each new cultivar after someone he admired. Thomas
Jefferson and naturalists Georges Cuvier and the Comte de Buffon
were among the dedicatees. Napoleon Bonaparte was not.

In dark moods it seemed to Thouin as though twenty-five years of
revolutionary struggle for equality had come to nothing. He had a
particular expertise in grafting, which he considered the most delicate,
astonishing and precious of all horticultural techniques.[70] But he did
not care for the political grafting that now preoccupied Napoleon: the
grafting of a new empire onto the old roots of the French monarchy.
Napoleon's coronation plans were entrusted to his favourite architects,
Percier and Fontaine. After the Senate proclamation that made him
emperor and before the ceremony, Napoleon addressed the question
of imperial symbolism. On 23 Prairial (12 June) his Council of State
considered which bird, animal or plant he should adopt as the emblem
of his power and incorporate into his coat of arms. An eagle, a cockerel,
a lion, an elephant, a bee, an oak, a fleur-de-lis were all possibilities.
At first, Napoleon favoured a lion, but a few weeks later he changed
his mind and chose the eagle, the symbol of imperial Rome. After his
coronation an eagle was added to the shaft of every flag standard in
the Grande Armée that he was amassing in camps around Boulogne
on the north coast. The bronze eagles were made from six separately
cast pieces and measured twelve inches by ten. Napoleon urged the
soldiers to defend his eagles with their lives. Eagles were added to the
chain of the Legion of Honour, reserved for the emperor and princes
of the imperial family; the chain was composed of sixteen trophies
linked by eagles, each with the ribbon and cross of the Legion of
Honour around their necks. Napoleon also revived the bee, a symbol
of immortality and a link to the Merovingian dynasty, the oldest kings
of France. In 1653, depictions of bees had been discovered in Tournai
in the tomb of Childeric I, the founder of the Merovingian dynasty
in AD 457. Napoleon had them copied and added into his coat of
arms. Bees too were added to the chain of the Legion of Honour.

Napoleon now hoped to invade England with his Grande Armée. His preparations in the camps near Boulogne intensified when Britain declared war on France in Floréal, Year 11 (May, 1803) and the Peace of Amiens collapsed. Forts were built along the French coast and a flotilla assembled. Napoleon went on ceremonial visits and made awards of the Legion of Honour, but the waiting troops were getting bored and restless. They were encouraged to take up gardening. In Year 12 the *Journal de Paris* carried a detailed description of the import-ance of gardening in the French military camps around Boulogne. The encampment near the coastal town of Ostend, now on the coast of Belgium, had been 'nothing but unfruitful plains, stagnant waters and barren downs', until the presence of the French soldiers trans-formed it:

> The astonished traveller now beholds long avenues of tents, constructed in a manner both solid and agreeable. Obelisks, pyramids and columns, in the best state, surmounted with statues of the Emperor, everywhere delight the eye, and for the first time on this spot, the spectator beholds charming gardens, delicious parterres, and green turf bounding the sands of the ocean . . . Every regiment has its garden, each company its square bed, and a little well for watering the plants and flowers which it cultivates.[71]

Gardening, the *Journal de Paris* reported, made the soldiers' lives more agreeable and was a source of pride. It was rewarding to watch the obstacles of nature yield to active industry.

Napoleon considered using a fleet of air balloons to drop troops into England. By now he had sacked his 'Aeronaut of Official Festivals', André Jacques Garnerin, and replaced him with a woman, Sophie Blanchard (née Armant), the wife of the aeronautical pioneer Jean-Pierre Blanchard, who had made the first balloon flight across the Channel in 1785. Her own first balloon flight was on 6 Nivôse, Year

13 (27 December 1804). Napoleon consulted Sophie about the viability of invasion by balloon and might even have made her Chief Air Minister of Ballooning. She warned that aerial invasion of England was not likely to succeed owing to unpredictable winds. In the British press, Napoleon's invasion plans were relentlessly mocked. An etching of Year 11, entitled *Hop, Step and Jump*, pictured the indigent Corsican, hopping across the sea to France, rising through ambition and power, before attempting to jump the Channel and ending up skewered on John Bull's sword. Another, called *Conversations Across the Water*, shows Napoleon and John Bull at their respective coasts, Napoleon wearing comically big boots, and John Bull saying, 'Damn your boots and your shoes too – where I sit is my own little land in the ocean.' In the background, on the horizon, Royal Navy ships are ready to protect England.

However tense the relations between France and Britain, Josephine's botanists found a way round the hostilities and the garden at Malmaison continued expanding. In the year in which she became Empress of France, it was reasonable for Josephine, always extravagant, to assume that money was no obstacle. She wanted the greatest greenhouse in the world, and had run out of space in her existing glass houses and orangery.[72] So she asked Jean-Marie Morel, the septuagenarian landscape designer, to begin work on the Grand Serre Chaud, which would become one of the most celebrated and visited attractions near Paris until it was partially demolished when the estate was sold in 1824, then disappeared completely three years later.[73]

When Napoleon examined Malmaison's household accounts for the Year 12–13 he had a tantrum and demanded cuts. He had a rigorous eye for detail. Noticing that 140,000 francs had already been spent on the Grand Serre Chaud, he insisted that Morel be dismissed and replaced by the architects Jean-Thomas Thibault and Barthélemy Vignon.[74] The magnificent greenhouse, which involved innovative use of glass and metal, was finished according to their plans. Fifty metres long and nineteen wide, it was divided into two sections:

a glass section in which trees could grow up to five metres tall, and a series of lounges and reception rooms from which the plants could be viewed and enjoyed. It was heated by twelve coal-burning stoves. Josephine's grandson (the five-year-old future Napoleon III) ruined his teeth on the sugar cane she grew to remind her of the plantations on Martinique, just as she had done as a child.[75]

Napoleon made it clear that he expected Josephine to reduce the expenditure at Malmaison. From 1805, after the period of expansion that followed the return of Baudin's ships, she started to shrink her menagerie. In February she sent the emus she had received from King Island and Kangaroo Island to the Jardin des Plantes, where one of them survived until 1822. The skeletons of these emus, known as King Island emus, belong to a dwarf species hunted to extinction and are among the Muséum national d'histoire naturelle's most important specimens.[76] She also sent the Muséum, 'for public benefit', a pelican, three ostriches and a cassowary casque.[77]

In 1805 a new edition of *Géographie moderne*, the textbook Napoleon had used at school, was issued, updated to explain his position as Emperor of the French.[78] The textbook reproduced a lengthy extract from the constitution of the Year 12, including Title 2, Statute 3 which made the role of emperor hereditary within Napoleon's family:

> The imperial dignity is hereditary in the direct natural and legitimate lineage of Napoleon Bonaparte, from male to male, by order of primogeniture, and to the perpetual exclusion of women and their descendants.[79]

The problem was that Napoleon had no legitimate children. Josephine had been unable to become pregnant again. For this reason Statute 4 stipulated that he could adopt the children or grandchildren of his brothers, providing they had reached the age of eighteen, and that they would enter into his direct line of descendants. If afterwards Napoleon produced his own legitimate son, these adopted male relatives would cede their places. Adoption was forbidden for Napoleon's successors, its use limited to addressing his own predicament. In the absence of his own natural or adopted heir, the title of Emperor would pass to his elder brother Joseph and his male descendants, and afterwards to his younger brother Louis and his male descendants. The phrase 'to the perpetual exclusion of women' occurs twice.

In 1805 there was deep animosity between France and England, but still the scientists found a way round it. Napoleon himself was prepared to accede to requests from savants. Sir Joseph Banks, a corresponding member of the institute, wrote: 'I have obtained the release of five persons from the gracious condescension of the Emperor, the only five, I believe, that have been regularly discharged from their parole.'[80] On 1 Floréal, Year 13 (21 April 1805), David d'Anjou, a resident of Grenoble, offered Josephine an eagle for her menagerie. The eagle was either an *Aquila chrysaetos* (golden eagle) or an *Aquila heliaca* (eastern imperial eagle) from the south of Spain, but it was referred to as an 'Aigle Impérial' in the *Moniteur*.[81] It had a wingspan of 2.3 metres, and as a predator it was caged. It cannot have been a welcome addition to Josephine's peaceful menagerie at Malmaison, but it would have been hard to refuse such a gift.

The same year, Napoleon decreed that an impressive monument be built on the site of the Battle of Marengo, near Alessandria. Since 1801 there had been a commemorative column, topped by an eagle, but now he envisaged something grander: a pyramid. Accompanied by Josephine, wearing the uniform he had worn on the battlefield, he laid the first stone himself in honour 'of the shades of those who died defending their fatherland'. The pyramid, which was never finished, was to be part of a new 'City of Victories', with boulevards named after other battles in the Italian campaign.

The first time a standard with one of Napoleon's military eagles was captured was at the Battle of Austerlitz on 11 Frimaire, Year 14 (2 December 1805). Here Napoleon's Grande Armée defeated a larger army of combined Russian and Austrian troops led by Alexander I and the Holy Roman Emperor, Francis II, but lost the eagle standard of the Fourth Line Regiment. Earlier in the year, Napoleon had once again abandoned plans to invade England and deployed the forces he had amassed in northern France in the east, in the Ulm campaign in Austria. He occupied Vienna and waited for Russia to come to the aid of its Austrian allies. Feigning weakness, Napoleon tricked the allies into battle and won a decisive victory on the Pratzen Heights, a hill of ten to twelve metres. He told his marshals: 'Examine this ground carefully, it is going to be a battlefield and you will have a part to play upon it.'[82] He concealed some of his forces in dead ground opposite the Pratzen Heights.[83] Much depended on the early-morning mist, which helped hide the French troops under the command of General Soult. Napoleon's strategy also depended upon a series of streams and lakes that protected the position of his right flank, which he had deliberately weakened. The sun, later referred to by Napoleon as the 'Sun of Austerlitz', came up around 8.45 a.m., casting long shadows on the ground and dissipating the mist at exactly the right time for the French soldiers to surprise their opponents and retake the Pratzen Heights. The allied forces, who had not suspected so many French were lying in wait, fought hard but unsuccessfully. Several allied battalions were defeated in the 'Old Vineyards'. South of the battlefield, retreating Russian soldiers were fleeing across the Satschan Ponds when French artillery broke the ice. French soldiers saved some of the drowning men. After the battle, Napoleon had the ponds drained, hoping to find Russian guns, but only the corpses of a few men and about 150 horses were recovered. Addressing his victorious troops he said: 'Soldiers, I am pleased with you! On the day of Austerlitz you lived up to all my expectations of your bravery and boldness; you have decked your eagles with a glory that shall never die.' He rewarded his officers, soldiers and the war widows with generous payments and personally adopted any children who had been orphaned, allowing them to add 'Napoleon' to their names.[84]

Napoleon was close enough to the fighting to see the eagle of the Fourth Line Regiment captured. The eagle-bearer was cut down defending it with his life.[85] A lieutenant tried to save it, but was also killed. Another French soldier seized it from the lieutenant's dead hands, then was slashed by a Russian cavalry officer's sabre. The eagle was carried off, first to Tsar Alexander on the battlefield, and afterwards to the Kazan Cathedral in St Petersburg. The Fourth Line Regiment was known for its steadiness and loyalty – Napoleon had appointed his brother Joseph as its colonel after the collapse of the Peace of Amiens – but when its eagle was lost the soldiers panicked and rushed backwards in retreat. The emperor's aide-de-camp De Ségur claimed both he and Napoleon were almost knocked down in the chaos. Then the French cavalry charged in vengeance. 'Avenge them! Avenge our standards!' they cried, driving their horses at full gallop towards the Russians. What ensued was a desperate cavalry battle, hand-to-hand combat, until the Russians gave way. Other eagles at Austerlitz narrowly escaped capture. The Chasseurs à Pied eagle of the First Battalion was reputedly saved by a mongrel called Moustache, who was the regiment's pet and particularly attached to the eagle-bearer. When the eagle-bearer was shot, Moustache and two soldiers guarded the eagle until it was rescued from under the dead man's body. The dog lost a paw in the fighting and was awarded a medal by Marshal Lannes commemorating its bravery at Austerlitz.[86] The eagle of the 24th Light Infantry was lost when it was trampled by Russian cavalry. It was recovered later from the battlefield, by soldiers of the Fourth Line Regiment desperately hunting among the 15,000 corpses for their own eagle, and returned to what was left of the battalion.[87]

After Austerlitz, Napoleon moved into the Schönbrunn Palace in Vienna. On 4 Nivôse, Year 14 (25 December 1805), he reviewed a parade of General Soult's corps. When he came to the Fourth Line, ashamed to be the only battalion without an eagle, he berated the soldiers. 'What have you done with the eagle which I entrusted to you?' he thundered in his still heavily accented French. In their defence the colonel pointed out that these soldiers had captured two Austrian standards, but for Napoleon that was no compensation for the loss of one of his eagles. They begged to be given another. He demanded reassurance than none of the survivors had seen the eagle fall and failed to sacrifice their life to protect it. Eventually he relented.[88]

On her way to join the emperor in Vienna after Austerlitz, Josephine met Frederick I of Württemberg in Stuttgart, a fellow naturalist and menagerie enthusiast. He offered her another pair of kangaroos to add to her collection at Malmaison.[89] In return she sent him exotic birds, and later some black swans, which displeased the professors at the Muséum national d'histoire naturelle who thought such rarities should not be sent outside France.[90] The gardens of the Schönbrunn Palace were among the finest in the world. Marie Antoinette's mother, the Empress Maria Theresa, had launched a redesign of them in the 1770s to include a Roman ruin, a Neptune fountain and an obelisk fountain. Many plants and even some trees would be moved from Schönbrunn to Malmaison at Josephine's request.

Determined to detach France from the legacy of the Revolution, Napoleon suppressed the Republican calendar and ordered a return to the Gregorian on 1 January 1806. For all its beauty, the Republican calendar was unpopular and unwieldy: every year began on a different day to coincide with the autumn equinox. For Thouin, already so disconcerted by the Empire and grieving for the Revolution, this was like a second death for his friend Gilbert Romme.[91] The calendar had been Romme's revolutionary legacy: a secular celebration of the natural world. Among Thouin's papers there is a letter that marks the transition from one calendar to the next.[92] On 3 Brumaire, Year 14, the Minister of the Interior wrote to Thouin from the Bureau for Agriculture, asking him to send to the Prefect of Haut-Rhin the seeds he had requested for the department's nursery. Thouin has annotated the letter in the margin, noting that eighty-six species of grain were sent three months later on 22 January 1806. Between receiving the letter and fulfilling its request, the Republican calendar became a relic of the recent past.

Napoleon officially adopted Josephine's son and daughter, Eugène and Hortense, on 12 January 1806. Two days later, Eugène married Princess Augusta, the daughter of the emperor's ally, the King of Bavaria. Eugène was explicitly excluded from Napoleon's line of succession as he was not a blood relative. The emperor also adopted Stephanie de Beauharnais, second cousin to Eugène and Hortense, and arranged her marriage to the grandson of the Prince-Elector of Baden, another of his allies. As a wedding gift, Josephine gave Stephanie a botanically themed Sèvres dinner service known as the Liliacées service because it reproduced some of the illustrations from the first volume of the artist Pierre-Joseph Redouté's book of that name. First published in 1802, it celebrated the plants at Malmaison, including the lily, amaryllis, orchid, iris and other flowers. The dinner service was manufactured between 1802 and 1805 and Josephine had been using it for a year when she gave it to Stephanie in 1806. She replaced it the following year with an even grander service, for which designs were copied from another of the botanical publishing projects that she sponsored, Étienne Ventenat's *Jardin des Plantes de la Malmaison* (1803–5), in twenty volumes, each containing six plates by Redouté. Josephine sent a copy of the first volume to Joseph Banks, thanking him for his help with the Malmaison garden.[93]

The new service celebrated plants that naturally grow high in the mountains. From the Pyrenees, the Alps, Tyrol, Salzburg and Switzerland came andromeda, *Azalea procumbens*, *Primula integrifolia* and *Ranunculus aconitifolius*. From the Indies and Peru, plants collected by Alexander von Humboldt and Aimé Bonpland included *Befarua caracassana*, *Calceolaria alba*, *Gentiana corymbosa*, *Valeriana globiflora*. The service included dinner plates and soup bowls, but also large vases, pots on pedestals modelled on ancient Roman pottery, and a bust of the emperor. This second botanical service, manufactured in 1807, was more international than the first, celebrating plants from

America, Australia, China, Mexico, Japan, Europe and the Cape of Good Hope. There were seventy-two different plants in total, camellias, geraniums, irises, mimosas, pelargoniums, phlox and roses among them. The expansion in ambition between the two dinner services reflected the expansion of the Malmaison gardens, which in turn reflected the rising power of the Empire.

On 11 March 1806, Napoleon signed a decree ordering the return of Captain Flinders's ship and his release from prison. Flinders had been arrested when he stopped at Mauritius in December 1803, but after Napoleon's decree, he spent a further three years in prison. In the meantime, much of the credit for his discoveries in Australasia was appropriated by the publication of French maps in 1807. The first volume of *Voyage de Découvertes aux Terres Australes* was accompanied by an atlas that included the first complete map of Australasia. The frontispiece for the atlas was a medallion depicting Malmaison with three kangaroos, two emus and five black swans on the lawn in the foreground. Filao, mimosa and myrtle were among the foreign trees shown. The medallion acknowledged the help Josephine had provided the naturalist François Péron and the artist Charles-Alexandre Lesueur after they returned from Australasia and were entrusted with writing the official account of the exploration.[94] They chose to write very little about Captain Baudin's role and contribution now that he was dead. This atlas gave the name Terre Napoléon to the south coast of New Holland, stretching from Port Western to the Cap des Adieux, seemingly claiming for France the discovery of the part of that coast that Flinders had surveyed before he met Captain Baudin in Encounter Bay. Because Flinders had been incarcerated, he had not been able to publish his maps or an account of his circumnavigation of Australasia.[95]

When a translation of the *Voyage de Découvertes aux Terres Australes* appeared in English, there was outrage. In August 1810 an anonymous writer in the *Quarterly Review* suggested that Péron had been pressurised by the French government into what amounted to a sinister land grab in the Pacific.[96] In fact, the 1807 atlas consisted mostly of illustrations of the animals and indigenous peoples the French had encountered. But British suspicion only intensified with the publication of a second volume of the atlas by Louis Freycinet in 1811. Freycinet had been the captain of the schooner *Le Casuarina*, the smaller ship Captain Baudin purchased when he sent *Le Naturaliste* back to France, but he made no mention of Baudin whatsoever, and credited Napoleon with commissioning the expedition to New Holland. The title of the map of 'Terre Napoléon' is written on a banner, draped over Neptune's trident, carried by a ferocious eagle.[97] A further thirty-two maps in the second volume of the atlas include place names celebrating Napoleon's family and regime. Despite British suspicions, Napoleon was not directly involved in assigning these names. In many cases it was the explorers themselves who gave names associated with their head of state to the places they believed they had discovered. This was standard practice and the British certainly did the same.[98] Nor was naming an assertion of ownership. To conquer Australasia, the French would have needed to fight the British for their colonial settlement at Port Jackson and control of New South Wales. The true Terre Napoléon, the part of the south coast the French surveyed before the British, is an area from north-west of Cape Banks to the mouth of the River Murray in Encounter Bay. On a modern map names in this area are strikingly modest: M'Grath's Flat, Salt Creek, Martin's Washpool, Tilley's Swamp.[99] The name Bonaparte survives in Western Australia in the Joseph Bonaparte Gulf, the Bonaparte Archipelago and Bonaparte Basin. This is due to Captain Baudin paying tribute to the then First Consul and his family early in the expedition. The later attempts of Péron, Lesueur and Freycinet to flatter their emperor by fixing the name Terre Napoléon on a distant continent failed completely.

6

The Forest of Fontainebleau

'My English garden is the Forest of Fontainebleau and
I want no other.'[1]
Napoleon

Napoleon's boots and those of his generals and architect echoed
through the empty disused rooms kicking up the dust. The Château
of Fontainebleau, fifty-five kilometres south-east of Paris, a luxurious
hunting lodge for the kings of France since the twelfth century, was
emptied during the Revolution, its contents smashed or sold.
Afterwards it was a prison, a school and an arms store. Since Year 12
it had been a military academy. Napoleon inspected it on a cold day,
28 Frimaire, Year 12 (20 December 1803), at a time when he was
preoccupied with assembling troops for his planned invasion of
Britain. One of the decorative ponds in the formal gardens had become
a swimming pool for the cadets. There had been a fire in 1789, on
another cold day, when the pipes were frozen, which had devastated
the orangery. The roof had fallen on the fragrant trees and the high-
arched blown-out window frames were left in ruined walls against the
winter sky. The south wing of the Great Court of the White Horse
had been converted to classrooms and dormitories for boys aged
sixteen to eighteen, receiving a minimal training before being sent
straight to war. As Napoleon, always short of time, walked rapidly but

methodically through the long corridors of interconnected, formerly splendid rooms, the question in his mind was, could the chateau be restored? His architect, Pierre Fontaine, was against it. Knock it down, was his advice, build an entirely new palace on the same site beside the forest, a monument to the new Empire. But profligate expenditure was not in Napoleon's nature. 'Perhaps it is not strictly an architect's palace,' he said, 'but it is certainly a well-considered and perfectly suitable dwelling place. Small buildings must have perfect symmetry, but monuments of the centuries have the colour and the form of time.'[2] The prospect of renovating the old buildings attracted him. His own insignia, the imperial bees, the ribbon of the Legion of Honour and the capital letter 'N', would replace the Bourbon fleur-de-lis, sometimes still visible on the walls, despite the efforts of the revolutionaries to remove all traces of monarchy.

Through the windows of the Queen's Gallery, some of them broken and stripped of shutters, Napoleon looked down on the Garden of Diana. It had once been the private garden of monarchs, decorated with marble statues. Now it was neglected and overgrown by brambles. It took its name from a Roman marble statue of the huntress goddess Diana, given to King Henri II by Pope Paul IV in 1556. The gift marked an alliance between the Papal States and France against Spain. Two and a half centuries later, Napoleon had a clear idea of how useful the current Pope, Pius VII, could be to his new regime. The ancient statue, too precious to remain outside, had been moved to the Louvre long ago and a bronze replica installed at the centre of a fountain. But as Napoleon looked at the garden, all he could see was a broken water feature; the bronze Diana had been confiscated during the Terror along with the marble statues.

In the Queen's Gallery there was a place between the beams where the Sun King, Louis XIV, had marked his height between the ages of seven and forty-two. Napoleon, who still had no children with Josephine, passed by thinking about securing his power. When fully grown, Louis XIV was approximately 1.8 metres tall (significantly taller than Napoleon who was 1.68 metres) but with heels and wigs he could make himself appear much taller. He reigned for seventy-two years. Napoleon could not promise himself so long.[3] The need for an heir weighed heavily on his mind, a boy whose increasing height he could measure each year, a direct descendant who would extend his grip on France beyond the limits of his natural life. He continued his tour and reached the queen's bedroom, where Marie Antoinette last slept in November 1786, almost exactly seventeen years earlier. Beyond it was her powder room and a white marble fireplace decorated with an eagle. How long until Josephine could occupy Marie Antoinette's bed? How quickly could this derelict chateau be made ready for him?

He decided to restore Fontainebleau in the short interval between the plebiscite that confirmed him as emperor and his coronation. He dashed to the chateau with Josephine on the evening of 8 Messidor, Year 12 (27 July 1804), arriving around eleven at night. He inspected the military school again at five the next morning, then, after various meetings, went hunting in the forest at 3 p.m. The forest of Fontainebleau, criss-crossed by chains of sandstone rocks and swathes of shifting silica sand, debris from the Alps, stranded there by rivers flowing towards the sea in time out of mind, seemed to have been created for the pleasure of hunting. Galloping through thickets of enormous trees – oaks, Scots pine and European beech – Napoleon stopped in front of one of the forest's many gorges and announced: 'We are in the enchanted forest of Tasso!'[4] He was remembering his youthful enthusiasm for Torquato Tasso's epic, *Jerusalem Delivered*. In the poem the sorcerer Ismeno, a Muslim convert, enchants the forest outside Jerusalem to stop the crusading Christians from cutting down the trees to make siege towers to attack the city walls. Every time a warrior raises his axe to strike at a tree, he is overcome by the illusion that there are living human bodies incarnate in the wood.[5] When the hero Tancredi strikes a Cyprus tree with his sword, blood seems to flow onto the forest floor and he flees in horror. For Napoleon, the forest was not horrifying, but magical and deserving of his protection.

He suddenly realised it would be the perfect place to welcome Pope Pius VII to France. Against his will, the Pope had been persuaded to travel to Paris for Napoleon's coronation ceremony. No pope had anointed a French king on French soil for a thousand years.[6] Even Charlemagne had gone to Rome for his coronation. But Rome, as Napoleon quipped, was now in Paris. The Pope was en route and he planned to encounter him, as if by chance, while out hunting in the enchanted forest. On 15 Brumaire (6 November), Pierre Fontaine and Charles Percier were given nineteen days to get the chateau ready for a papal visit. Under three weeks to fix up and furnish a palace: almost impossible. An enormous team of masons, carpenters, plasterers and painters moved in, working frantically, before the furniture arrived eight days later. Fontaine and Percier scrambled to find sufficient furnishings in such a short space of time. Some of it was brought from Saint-Cloud, some bought in Paris; especially useful were the possessions of the recently disgraced General Moreau, who had been found guilty of conspiring to assassinate Napoleon in the Cadoudal Affair and banished to America. Moreau, whose father had been guillotined during the Terror, had played an important part in the coup of 18 Brumaire and then commanded the Army of the Rhine. He had amassed considerable wealth, but his republican values and criticisms irritated Napoleon. After he was disgraced, his possessions came under the control of the French state. Now Moreau's furniture, even his mahogany and bronze Jacob Frères bed, carefully transported to Fontainebleau, would contribute directly to the aggrandisement of the new emperor.

Napoleon arrived to view the progress at the chateau on 1 Frimaire, Year 12 (22 November 1804). For the next two days, he divided his time between the military school and the apartments being prepared for himself and the Pope. The Pope was to occupy the apartment of the Queen-Mothers, traditionally reserved for foreign sovereigns, but more recently a library. Fontaine reconnected the apartment of the Queen-Mothers with the large pavilion salon, to make a grand set of rooms, lined with marble and worthy of the Pope. The smell of fresh paint, which Napoleon hated, hung on the cold air in the inadequately heated chateau. Religious-themed canvases were sent from the Louvre (which had been renamed the Musée Napoléon in 1802) for the newly decorated walls – Burrini's *Le Martyre d'une sainte* and Rubens's *Le Christ en croix*, among others. The staff and pupils at the school felt immense relief when Napoleon turned his attention back to the artisans, and vice versa. He had so much energy and such an eye for detail. He was always impatient, always pressed for time.

On the morning of 4 Frimaire, Year 12 (25 November 1804), Napoleon set off on horseback, followed by Josephine in a carriage and a small hunting party, including the Mameluke Roustam, his bodyguard since Egypt. They passed the obelisk, a replica of the one outside St Peter's Basilica in Rome, that had been erected in 1785 at a crossroads in the forest in honour of Marie Antoinette and her children. During the Revolution, the bronze letters of the dedication had been removed, and a metal sculpture of a *bonnet rouge* was placed at the top of the obelisk. But that too had been removed, and now a metal eagle perched in its place, overlooking the forest, like its living counterparts. Moving on along the road to Nemours, Napoleon's party came to the cross of St Hérem, and there they met the Pope's carriage and entourage. Napoleon dismounted. The door of the carriage opened and the Pope, an ailing man of sixty-two, with black hair and black eyes, dressed entirely in white, hesitated before putting his satin-slippered foot down on the forest floor. Napoleon guided him to his own carriage and they travelled the short distance back to the chateau together. As they approached the Porte Dorée and entered the Oval Court, cannon and bells rang out.[7] Napoleon and the Pope climbed Louis XV's staircase together, then both retired to their respective apartments, which were still being made ready that morning. The Pope, exhausted from his travels, could rest at last.

Josephine asked for a private audience with Pius VII. She was more and more preoccupied by the fact that her marriage to Napoleon had not been a religious one. Could she be crowned empress alongside her husband in a religious ceremony when their wedding had been only a civil one? And behind this question was the shadow of a darker, more terrifying one: would Napoleon divorce her? Under the Ancien Régime, marriage had been indissoluble. But the revolutionaries had made divorce legal and easy. When marriages broke down during the Revolution no one needed to attribute blame, it was enough for one spouse to cite incompatibility of temperament and wait six months. There was no double standard of sexual morality for men and women, and the same law applied to rich and poor. Now Napoleon's new Civil Code, introduced in March 1804, was making divorce more difficult. Adultery, ill-treatment or condemnation to degrading forms of punishment were the new grounds, and even divorce by mutual consent required the permission of other family members. During the debates on reforming the law, Napoleon had taken a moderate position and had to argue hard against those who wanted to make marriage indissoluble again. He had tried, but failed, to retain incompatibility of temperament as a reason for divorce. It was not right, he argued, for the law to force couples to discuss their infidelities in court. But he was not all-powerful, and although he was lastingly proud of the Civil Code, it did not achieve everything he wanted.

Josephine knew that if Napoleon wanted to divorce her, he would. The Pope promised to persuade him to marry her again in a religious ceremony. Napoleon reluctantly agreed, despite the fact he was in love with his new young mistress, Madame Duchâtel, and despite the fact he needed an heir and had given up hope of producing one with Josephine. He was worried that if he refused to marry in a Roman Catholic ceremony, the Pope might not attend his coronation after all and his dream of being anointed as Charlemagne and other kings of France had been would be lost. Nothing must get in the way of the splendid coronation he had planned in Paris. Napoleon wanted no witnesses, he wanted the sacramental marriage to be as secret as a confession. Napoleon's half-uncle, Joseph Fesch, who had become Cardinal of Lyons in 1803, told him: 'No witnesses, no marriage.' But Napoleon would not give way, so Cardinal Fesch had to ask the Pope for a dispensation, one of the many he foresaw would be needed in the future.[8] At 4 p.m. on 10 Frimaire, Year 13 (1 December 1804), the day before they were due to be crowned, the emperor and empress received the sacrament of marriage in a secret ceremony performed by Cardinal Fesch in the Tuileries Palace. Josephine told herself what she wanted to believe, that her marriage was now indissoluble. The religious wedding certificate was sold at auction in 2016 for €32,500. But to Josephine it turned out to be worthless. She had got the Pope on her side, she had done everything she could to secure her position, but she knew she could not give Napoleon the heir he wanted, and religion for him was only a means to an end.

Napoleon had already asked Percier and Fontaine to plan his coronation. As usual he wanted magnificent effects and minimum expenditure. Practical as ever, he asked for a tent outside the Archbishop's palace for receiving carriages and a covered corridor between the palace and the church. He knew the weather might be bad. The architects remembered the large tent they had commissioned at Malmaison around the time of the coronation of the King of Etruria. They contacted the carpenter who had been storing it for three years, and repurposed it. The carpenter was pleased to be paid at last.[9] Four days before the ceremony, a huge gust of wind lifted the tent from its pegs and threw it onto its side. Several of the poles and rafters were broken and had to be repaired urgently despite the deteriorating weather.[10] On the day of the Napoleon's coronation, 11 Frimaire, Year 13 (2 December 1804), it was snowing. Preparations were not finished until just before his carriage arrived. He alighted under the tent, processed through the covered corridor and entered Notre-Dame, in ceremonial robes with a laurel wreath on his head. Pope Pius VII was waiting for him. Josephine was at Napoleon's side.

They were both wearing white satin embroidered with golden thread. During the ceremony a crimson coronation mantle, embroidered with bees, was placed on Napoleon's shoulders. It weighed eighty pounds, so had to be supported by attendants. A choir of four hundred voices sang Paisiello's *Mass* and *Te Deum*. The traditional crown of the kings of France, the Crown of Charlemagne, had been destroyed during the Revolution, so a newly made, mock-medieval one was waiting on the altar. When the time came, Napoleon removed the laurel wreath from his head and crowned himself. Then he crowned Josephine. In 2017 a single gold leaf cut from the Crown of Napoleon sold for £550,000 at auction, one of six removed from the crown when Napoleon tried it on before the ceremony and declared it too heavy.

After the religious part of the coronation, Napoleon swore a civil oath:

> I swear to maintain the integrity of the territory of the Republic, to respect and enforce respect for the Concordat and freedom of religion, equality of rights, political and civil liberty, the irrevocability of the sale of national lands; not to raise any tax except in virtue of the law, to maintain the institution of the Legion of Honour, and to govern in the sole interest, happiness and glory of the French people.[11]

As part of the celebrations an unmanned air balloon, ablaze with lights arranged in the pattern of the new imperial crown, was launched from the front of the cathedral. It ascended over Paris, at first more successful than the embarrassing balloon displays in Egypt, but soon blew out of control. After travelling wildly all across France and northern Italy, it eventually crashed in Lake Bracciano near Rome and inspired many jokes against Napoleon. He tried, as Roman emperors had, to turn an event that seemed like a bad omen into a good one. He ordered the smashed-up balloon to be displayed in Rome.[12]

The day after his coronation, there was a military parade on the Champ de Mars during which Napoleon distributed the famous eagle standards to his troops. Originally, the ceremony had been planned for the same day as the coronation, but Josephine, who was exhausted, asked for it to be postponed. At first, Percier and Fontaine were glad of the twenty-four-hour delay because another of their huge ceremonial tents, positioned outside the military school, was not quite ready. But they soon regretted it because on 12 Frimaire it did not stop sleeting. The painted toile decorations disintegrated and canvas drapes dripped ice-cold water onto the heads of the newly crowned emperor and empress.[13]

Pius VII had come to France hoping for political gains. The day after his arrival at Fontainebleau he tried to raise the subject of the restoration of ecclesiastical domains in Italy, but he was told that Napoleon was not prepared to discuss politics when he was concentrating on entertaining. A few weeks after the coronation he tried again. Through Cardinal Caprara, his legate in France, he pressed for a date to be set for the negotiations. But Talleyrand, Napoleon's Minister for Foreign Affairs, deployed the tactic of delay: the emperor, he said, had not yet issued any instructions. Finally, in February, Pius VII learned that Napoleon intended to crown himself King of Italy. After four months in France, he returned to Rome empty-handed.

Napoleon visited Fontainebleau again between 10 and 12 Germinal, Year 13 (31 March to 2 April 1805), on the way to Milan for his next coronation. He gave Fontaine more instructions after closely inspecting the work that had been done in his absence. Now he wanted an external spiral staircase installed to enable him to access the Garden of Diana from his library on the first floor in what had once been the Queen's Gallery. To fulfil this demand, Fontaine collaborated with another architect, Étienne Leroy, who was so proud and protective of the staircase when it was finished that he commissioned a special cover of caulked canvas to protect it in winter. Three years later, Napoleon had a second, internal spiral staircase built to connect his bedroom to his library. This meant that in the middle of the night he had a direct route into the Garden of Diana, which was reserved for his private use, just as, in the past, it had been for the monarchs of France.

In the Cathedral of Milan on 6 Prairial (26 May), Napoleon crowned himself King of Italy with the iron crown of Lombardy. He was accompanied by Josephine, but this time she was a spectator, not a participant in the magnificent ceremony. Pius VII wasn't present, having delegated his duties to Cardinal Caprara. The next day there were games and races in imitation of classical times. The coronation was followed by a month of imperial processing through the fortified cities of northern Italy, Brescia, Verona, Legnano, Mantua, Bologna, Modena, Piacenza and Genoa. Napoleon finally arrived back at Fontainebleau on 23 Messidor (12 July). Impatiently, he viewed the ongoing renovations and issued supplementary orders. He was especially interested in the placement of his bathtub with swan-neck taps, which ended up, in the English manner, in a narrow space beside one of his reception rooms.[14] The next morning, Napoleon and Josephine set off in a carriage to follow the hunt. They travelled along the route of Cascades, then up the pine-lined promenade known as the Mail Henri IV, from where they enjoyed a wonderful panoramic view of the forest.

Hunting had stopped during the Revolution, the dogs were destroyed, and poaching flourished; feudalism was dismantled and the use of guns in the forests was democratised. Napoleon reversed all this. He consulted aristocrats who had rallied to the Empire and revived the Ancien Régime hunting practices. Berthier, who had been promoted from General to Marshal of the Empire after Napoleon's coronation, was appointed Head Huntsman (*Grand veneur*), a position borrowed directly from the pre-revolutionary royal households, and handsomely remunerated.[15] Napoleon hoped that hunting parties would help him integrate into the circle of ancestral European sovereigns. The hunt also served as a military metaphor. The forest officials were assisted by one of the battalions stationed at Fontainebleau acting as beaters. The organisation of the cavalcade – 100 people, 80 horses, 180 dogs – seemed good preparation for war.[16] At the start and finish of each of his campaigns Napoleon hunted in the company of his allies.[17] Over his lifetime, he participated in about a hundred hunts, half of them between the years 1809 and 1811.

The men wore hunting livery of deep green, decorated with gold or silver buttons and braid. Napoleon decided that the women should also have hunting habits. Josephine commissioned her favourite couturier, Louis-Hippolyte Leroy, who had been responsible for her coronation costume, to design a magnificent one for her. It was a tunic made from a rich amaranth-coloured velvet, embroidered with gold, with a matching hat crowned by white feathers. Her ladies-in-waiting had matching amaranth hunting tunics.[18] Josephine's daughter, Hortense, chose blue and silver; Napoleon's sister Pauline, chose lilac and silver. The brilliant colours of these costumes flashed through the dark woods.

At Fontainebleau, hunting deer with hounds took place on fixed days. Napoleon would set off at full gallop taking the first road he came to, relishing the exercise more than the chase. He was an undisciplined hunter, galloping all over the place, not following the horn or the pack. Cooperating in a group did not come naturally to him. He was a good but ungracious rider. He would gallop down slopes at full speed and had a few severe falls which no one was allowed to mention. He was even more dangerous driving a *calèche* or small carriage. He hurtled towards obstacles, determined to overcome them, sometimes overturning himself and his horses. After one dramatic accident too many he gave up driving. 'In even the smallest things, every man should stick to his own business,' he joked.[19] Sometimes he abandoned himself to his horse and fell into a deep reverie among the trees. But he was always irate if the deer got away, and even more furious if anyone dared suggest that his own erratic riding had misled the hounds. He despised failure. Napoleon's style of shooting was as erratic and impatient as his riding. He did not take the trouble to

position his rifle securely on his shoulder, but shot rapidly and sometimes inaccurately at birds and rabbits. His valet often had to apply
cologne to the emperor's bruised and blackened arms. On one occasion, General Masséna was hit in the eye by a piece of shot from
Napoleon's gun. Like a schoolboy, the emperor brazenly blamed this
injury on Marshal Berthier, who only muttered in protest.[20]

Napoleon complained to Talleyrand: 'It is a singular thing. I have
brought together a lot of people at Fontainebleau; I wanted them to
amuse themselves; I arranged every sort of pleasure for them; and
here they are with long faces, all looking dull and tired.'[21] Talleyrand
dared to reply: 'That is because pleasure cannot be summoned at the
beat of a drum, and here, just as when you are with the army, you
always seem to say to us all, "Come, ladies and gentlemen, forward
march!"' Napoleon was in a good mood and not angered by this quip.
Behind his back, his friends and family were commenting on his new
pomposity and insistence on religious observance. The emperor was
becoming a bore. Madame de Châteaureine and three other ladies
went to visit Napoleon's favourite sister, Pauline, in Thermidor, Year
13 (August 1805). After the death of her husband General Leclerc in
Saint-Domingue, she had rapidly remarried into the wealthy Roman
Borghese family. Pauline's visitors asked after her pet parrot which
had always amused them in the past. She told them she had given it
away, along with two of her monkeys, because her brother had made
her engage an almoner and two chaplains 'and it would be too extravagant for me to keep six useless animals in my home'. She ranted against
the revival of the Roman Catholic Church; she claimed to prefer the
chatter of her parrot to the moans of her almoner, the capering of her
monkeys to the awkward bowing and kneeling of her chaplains. Her
delectable boudoir had become a chapel. 'Alas! What a change! What
a shocking fashion, that we are all again to be Christians!'[22]

Fontainebleau is one of the largest and most celebrated of the French
forests, covering 250 square kilometres, but there are many others.

Today a third of France is still covered by forest. Under the Ancien Régime, there had been bans on raking up leaves from the forest floor, gathering fallen branches for fuel, or harvesting timber, because such foraging activities were considered a risk to national security. The Sun King suppressed customary and communal uses of the forest on the advice of his Minister of Finance, Colbert, who warned in 1680: 'France will perish for want of wood!' The harsh laws hit the poorest hardest. The Ancien Régime's forest administration, the Eaux et Forêts, was one of the most hated symbols of seigneurial entitlement and oppression.

During the Revolution the restrictions on the use of forests were relaxed, the local officials who had enforced them were disgraced and often no longer paid. There ensued a decade of chaos. It was unclear whether forests would be included in the sale of land appropriated from the king and clergy. Former royal forests covered 5,000 square kilometres and ecclesiastical woodland covered a further 8,000.[23] All this now belonged to the nation and might be sold to finance its immense public debt. There was plenty of room for corruption in the new deregulated circumstances. And under the pretext of destroying feudalism, many people, from impoverished peasants to wealthy entrepreneurs, asserted their liberty to plunder the forests. 'The national interest is armed with a spade; self-interest with an axe,' argued one revolutionary, trying desperately to protect France's trees.[24] Proposals for new laws ranged incoherently from full privatisation to total reassertion of state control. Piecemeal sales of the smaller recently nationalised woodland plots went ahead and the purchasers, asserting their rights to their new property, axed the trees for commercial gain. By the time Napoleon became First Consul deforestation was widespread. In Year 8 (1799–1800), France's woodland was 1,000 square kilometres less than it had been in 1789.[25] He was determined to impose order.

After the coup of 18 Brumaire, which once again derailed reform of forest administration, those who understood how urgent it was dared to hope Napoleon might prove himself the saviour of the trees. Rougier de la Bergerie, an agronomist and opponent of deforestation, looked back with nostalgia on the way French kings had conserved the forests for posterity. He hoped the new First Consul would do the same, and there were early signs that he would:

> Have we at last arrived at the moment when it will be possible to stop the devastating hand of man, [which is] deteriorating the soil of the uplands everywhere by grievous and inconsiderate clearings and at the same time destroying the trees, woods and forests that nature has caused to grow with profusion, and which have made France the most fertile, salubrious, and happiest country in the world?[26]

On 16 Nivôse, Year 9 (6 January 1801), just a fortnight after surviving the assassination attempt in the Rue Saint-Nicaise, Napoleon instituted a new woodland hierarchy, comprising 5 *super-intendants* based in Paris, 30 *conservateurs*, 300 sub-inspectors, and 8,500 guards.[27] The new administration was placed directly under the control of the Ministry of Finance. In this matter, as in many others, Napoleon was prepared to build on ideas and reforms that had been suggested but not implemented before he came to power.

Napoleon's new forest guards were required to wear green uniforms. In an effort to fight corruption and instil discipline, all honorary or assistant guards were banned. Salaries were small and it was notoriously difficult to keep forest guards under control when they lived and worked in such remote places surrounded by brigands. Nevertheless, in the early years of Napoleon's power, after he became First Consul in 1799, forest administration was significantly strengthened. The law of 9 Floréal, Year 11 (29 April 1803), imposed a twenty-five-year moratorium on unauthorised clearing.[28] Through this clampdown on revolutionary liberty and licence, Napoleon was returning to the controversial and unpopular strictures of the Sun

King in the interests of the nation's military and strategic priorities. Under the new law the state could purchase any and all trees on private land needed for shipbuilding. There were also more personal instances of returning to the Ancien Régime. Talleyrand, for example, was trying to help his close friend the Duchess de Montmorency in her bid to repossess an extensive forest that had been seized by the state when she emigrated during the Revolution. The forest had not yet been sold and she was keen to get it back if she could.[29] She made herself agreeable at Napoleon's court and found he had a fondness for the old aristocracy.

Rougier de la Bergerie, who had supported privatisation during the Revolution, now admitted he had been wrong. He argued that there should be a strict prohibition on any further sale of nationally owned woodland:

> The revolution gave us the greatest of benefits, liberty; it inspired a universal enthusiasm that made the epoch the most memorable in the annals of all nations, but let us have the courage to admit, for we are in need of strong truths; it also developed to a great degree egoism and selfish motives, so contrary and so fatal to the public good.[30]

The Civil Code brought more changes in Year 12, not all of them welcome to the people concerned for the future of France's trees. While affirming the Revolution's abolition of feudal privileges, it introduced new laws protecting individual property rights, which meant that unless the state had an incontrovertible reason, woodland could be cleared or divided and sold by private owners as they pleased.[31] In Nivôse, Year 13 (January 1805), Napoleon complained to Fouché, his Police Minister, that the forests were still badly administered, and more would have to be done to impose order. A few days later he informed his Finance Minister Martin Gaudin that he had personally dismissed a forest inspector whom he found inadequate.[32] He wanted more thought given to how the forest inspectors were chosen and how they fulfilled their role. On 29 Messidor (18 July), he wrote to congratulate Pierre-François Réal, state councillor in charge of the first district of the police force, for his report into the forest offences of Fontainebleau.[33]

Réal was the son of a gamekeeper. He learned the ways of forests from birth. During the Revolution he was public prosecutor of the Revolutionary Tribunal. He sent many to their deaths, and would have been guillotined himself if Robespierre had not fallen from power in Year 2. Under the Directory, he was friends with Barras and Fouché. He met Napoleon through Josephine and helped with the coup of 18 Brumaire. He was helpful over the trial and execution of the Duc d'Enghien, which pleased Napoleon. This ex-revolutionary turned policeman, someone no one would want to cross walking through the trees at dusk, was the perfect person to report on the forest of Fontainebleau. Napoleon was so impressed by Réal's grasp of detail that he asked him to draw up new plans for administering the five royal forests: Fontainebleau, Saint-Germain, Versailles, Rambouillet and Compiègne, which could then be extended to other forests in France where abuses continued.[34] Napoleon thought each forest should have a captain in charge of hunting and surveillance and a deputy captain in charge of administration. He thought there should be fewer crossroads through the forests, since these encouraged poachers and foragers, and that the administrators and inspectors should report how many hours they had walked on their tours of duty. He was irritated by the weakness of the existing administration which he did not think worthy of his confidence. 'You have to propose a new, firmer supervisory administration, capable of repressing abuses,' he told Gaudin.[35]

Napoleon had a civil list of 25 million francs, and the crown lands and forests brought in a further 3 million.[36] When he went carefully through the accounts for Year 12, he noticed a shortfall of approximately 300,000 francs in the money actually received from wood-felling and the amount declared by the forestry administration. He concluded that corruption was still rife and decided to increase surveillance. While he was at the Boulogne camp in Thermidor, Year 13 (August 1805), he wrote again to his Finance Minister, reminding him that since the emperor's signature was now required on the patents for appointing forest administrators at every level, from the *conservateurs* right down to the guards, the persons proposed for these roles had better be up to scratch.[37] They should be army veterans, who had served and proved their worth. The War Minister, Alexander Berthier, would draw up a list of suitable candidates.[38]

On 24 Germinal, Year 14 (14 April 1806), Napoleon gave his newly married stepson some advice about not working too hard. He offered him the royal boxes in four Parisian theatres once a week and urged him to keep a stable and to hunt once a week too.[39] He even offered to finance the stable. 'There ought to be more gaiety in your home: it is needed for your wife's happiness and for your own health.' He sympathised with working too hard. He did that too. 'But then I have an old wife,' he wrote tactlessly to the old wife's son, 'who doesn't need me to amuse her; and I have more work to do.'[40] The following month a decree of 3 Prairial (23 May) created twelve forest inspectors, whose role was to tour France's forests reporting to the central administration. The inspectors were to monitor how well the forestry officials were doing their jobs without interfering. Napoleon was a perfectionist. Between Year 9 (1801) and 1814, 266 decrees, decisions and circulars relating to forests were issued, asserting stronger, ever more centralised control.[41] But for all his determination, hard work and organisational zeal, the forests remained wild places.

Extraordinary and frequent floods were becoming a problem in Paris and throughout France. Some people blamed the revolutionary deforestation for this change. The engineer Jean-Antoine Fabre concluded that the recent destruction of the woods that had covered the mountains was the cause of the increased flooding. He recommended a programme of replanting and wanted to see goats banned from forests, where they did such damage to young trees.[42] During the Revolution, the number of goats in France multiplied dramatically. Every time a cow, ox or sheep was requisitioned for the army, it was cheaper to replace it with a goat. In some regions in the early nineteenth century, there were four hundred times as many goats as there had been fifty years previously.[43] The voracious goats contributed to the deforestation, stripping the bark of young trees and eating the buds. Goats were resources for the rural poor, an inexpensive source of milk and cheese. It was easier to blame them for the destruction of the forests rather than the wealthy individuals who had cleared their land for financial gain. Under Napoleon's Civil Code, communal and customary use of the forests was policed and curtailed as it had not been since the time of the Sun King – the lives of people who had next to nothing to live off became even more intolerable. Napoleon's determination to impose order on the chaos bequeathed by the Revolution extended beyond the social to the natural world. At the heart of the Civil Code was the inviolable right to property. All attacks on property, even non-human ones, were to be eliminated. Goats were not the only culprits. Wolves and badgers, caterpillars and parasites, became the targets of elimination campaigns.[44]

The policing of the countryside under Napoleon reflected his regime's hierarchical, authoritarian and centralising approach to administration. He revived and reinforced state control. Between Year 10 (1802) and 1810 the presence of brigands, wolves and wild boar in the forests declined and crimes were better reported. A land survey, known as the *cadastre*, aimed to analyse and clarify taxation, ownership and access.[45] New laws restricting customary rights and private clearing were enforced by military-style personnel.[46] Local practices were disregarded. The preference for hiring army veterans as forest guards led to a battlefield mentality and encounters between the officers of the state and people trying to assert their customary rights in the woods became more violent.[47] In 1808 Napoleon asserted his rights over the royal forests even more forcibly. Ordinary people were now banned from fishing, swimming, doing their washing in streams, watering horses, collecting sticks or leaves or nuts and all other fruits in what he now considered to be his personal forests. Dogs were to be kept on leads. The hunting paths were to be kept clear at all times.[48]

At the Peace of Tilsit in July 1807, Napoleon secured an alliance with Russia and severely reduced the power of Prussia. That autumn he returned to Fontainebleau for a long stay: over a month of hunting and celebrations. On 14 October 1807 the Grand Parterre was illuminated in a spectacular festival marking the first anniversary of the Battle of Jena, which had been a decisive victory for Napoleon against the Prussian army, leading to the capitulation of Erfurt. Napoleon's brother Jérôme married Catherine of Württemberg, further securing the Bonaparte family's integration into the old royal circles of Europe. Fontaine drew up plans for installing a throne room in the chateau. The spiral staircase connecting Napoleon's bedroom to his library was commissioned and the furnishings of his private apartment were renovated in heavy velvet embroidered with branches of oleander to remind him of the trees on Corsica.[49]

A year later, in autumn 1808, Napoleon summoned the Congress of Erfurt to discuss with his new ally, Tsar Alexander, the threat posed by Austria. He wrote to Josephine to say he had just been hunting on the battlefield of Jena and had picnicked on the spot where he had slept out the night before the battle almost exactly two years earlier.[50] He was starting to feel older. There was a ball in Weimar at which Tsar Alexander danced, but Napoleon did not. 'Forty is forty,' he told his older wife, as though she didn't already know.[51] In Erfurt, he at last spoke openly of divorce with Talleyrand. 'My destiny demands it and France's tranquillity demands it also. I have no successor. Joseph [Napoleon's older brother] is nothing, and he has only daughters. It is I who must found a dynasty; I cannot found one except by allying myself to a princess who belongs to one of the great ruling houses of

Europe.'[52] Tsar Alexander had sisters, one of them young enough; she might do. He asked Talleyrand to investigate, and warned him that Josephine knew he was her enemy.

Austria had been rearming in the three years that had passed since the Battle of Austerlitz and under the command of Archduke Charles its army was now larger and better trained than it had ever been.[53] Napoleon's army, by contrast, was exhausted, full of recent, minimally trained conscripts and foreign recruits. Before Austria's army grew any stronger, something had to be done to stop it challenging France's Empire. Napoleon declared war on Austria on 12 April 1809 and arrived at the front line the next morning. After driving the archduke's army north across the River Danube, he advanced on Vienna and successfully laid siege to the city between 10 and 13 May. He conducted the siege from the Schönbrunn Palace, and had twenty howitzers bombarding the city, though they inflicted more panic than harm. Two brilliant musicians were trapped in Vienna: Beethoven who was going deaf, and Haydn who was dying. 'Children, don't be frightened, where Haydn is nothing can happen to you,' the composer unconvincingly reassured his household as the windows shook. After Vienna surrendered, Napoleon, remembering the premiere of *The Creation* from the night he was nearly assassinated by the infernal machine, positioned a guard of honour outside Haydn's house.[54] A French officer named Clément Sulémy came to sing the aria 'In Native Worth and Honour Clad' from *The Creation* at the dying man's bedside. Haydn cried tears of joy at Sulémy's sublime singing. Then the officer went back to war and was killed shortly afterwards at the Battle of Aspern. Haydn meanwhile went 'blissfully and gently' into permanent sleep on 31 May. He was buried in silence. Two weeks later, Mozart's Requiem Mass was performed for Haydn in the Schotten church with both French and Austrian soldiers in attendance. Before he was buried, friends of Haydn, who were passionate about what Napoleon considered the fake science of phrenology, stole his head. His body and skull were not reunited until 1954.[55]

For Beethoven, hiding in his brother's basement during the siege and trying to protect what was left of his hearing with pillows, Napoleon did nothing. Perhaps he did not know of the younger composer's plight. Three months later a concert was planned in the theatre at Schönbrunn, with Beethoven scheduled to conduct his *Eroica* Symphony, which had been dedicated to Napoleon until he had made himself emperor. After learning of the coronation, Beethoven vehemently scratched out the dedication, leaving a hole in the manuscript. His willingness to conduct the *Eroica* in fallen Vienna might have been bitterly sarcastic.[56] Or perhaps he hoped for recognition from the conquering emperor. Either way, Beethoven was disappointed because Napoleon was not in Vienna for the concert on the night of 8 September.

Outside the Schönbrunn Palace, on the morning of 12 October 1809, a young Viennese man could not stop trembling. He had come to watch the parade of the French occupying forces. He was eighteen, well educated, the son of a Protestant minister. He was standing in the crowd, visibly agitated, unable to control his anxiety. Suddenly, he tried to approach the emperor, seemingly to present a petition, but General Berthier stepped forward and told him to hand it to General Rapp instead. The young man, whose hand was thrust deep inside his greatcoat, said he would only speak to the emperor. He withdrew, but soon approached again with a crazed look in his eyes. This time General Rapp ordered his arrest. When he was searched they found a large carving knife concealed beneath his coat. Napoleon, oblivious, continued with the parade. Afterwards, when he was told about the arrest, he asked for a personal interview with the teenage would-be assassin, who was brought before him with his hands tied behind his back.

The teenager's name was Friedrich Staps. Aside from the knife, all he had on his person when he was arrested was a picture of his girlfriend, a wallet and a purse with a few coins. Napoleon asked, through General Rapp who could speak German, what he had intended to do with the knife. 'To kill you,' Staps replied.[57] They discussed politics and religion, but there seemed to be no traces of fanaticism in Staps, only the desire to rid Austria of the French. Napoleon raised the subject of the murder of Julius Caesar and was surprised when Staps refused to agree that Brutus, one of Caesar's assassins, was a murderer. A doctor was summoned, who pronounced Staps in good health. Napoleon asked him if his girlfriend would be distressed to hear of what had happened and was told: 'She hates you as much as I do.' He asked if Staps would be grateful to be pardoned. 'I would still find the first opportunity of taking your life' came the response. Despairing of learning more from the disturbed young man, Napoleon handed him back to the guards to be questioned when cold and hungry, then tried by a military court. Writing to Fouché in Paris, he insisted that no one was to discuss this episode. He had no desire to have Staps certified as insane. So far there had been no scandal, and he wanted to keep it that way. Four days later, Staps faced a firing squad. Unrepentant to the last, he cried: 'Liberty forever! Germany forever! Death to the tyrant!' before his body joined its shadow on the ground. The young man haunted Napoleon, who could not believe he had acted alone. He asked General Rapp for a report of his death, and told him to retain the assassin's knife.[58]

Napoleon left Schönbrunn after peace was signed, but as he turned his back on Vienna he ordered the destruction of its fortifications. He had occupied the city twice, in 1805 and in 1809, and did not want to risk having to lay siege to it again. The razed area eventually became Vienna's Volksgarten, or people's garden. Madame de Staël, still exiled from Paris, passed through Vienna three years later, on her way to Russia in the summer of 1812. She visited Melk Abbey, high on the steep banks of the River Danube, which had been Napoleon's head-quarters the first time he took Vienna. She imagined him walking on the terrace, looking down on 'the beauty of the country upon which he was going to pounce with his armies'. She claimed he often amused himself 'making poetical pieces on the beauties of nature, which he is about to ravage'. Following in his footsteps, enjoying the panoramic view of the country and the winding course of the river, she admired its fertility and 'felt astonished at seeing how soon the bounty of heaven repairs the disasters occasioned by man'. The natural world, she reflected, soon regenerates. 'It is only moral riches which disappear altogether, or are at least lost for centuries.'[59]

On his journey back to Fontainebleau, Napoleon visited his ally, Frederick I, King of Württemberg, in his palace at Stuttgart. As he looked out of the window, he noticed that a new spacious palace garden was being laid out by men working in chain gangs. He asked Frederick who these men were and learned they were rebels who had been captured and condemned to the galleys during the recent expansion of Württemberg. After he left the palace, the chained men were still on his mind. He commented to General Rapp: 'The King of Württemberg is a very harsh man, but he is very faithful: of all the sovereigns in Europe he possesses the greatest share of under-standing.'[60] At Fontainebleau there had been no preparations for the emperor's return. When he reached the chateau on 26 October 1809, there wasn't even a guard on duty. But soon afterwards his court and various family members arrived. When Josephine came, Napoleon went out hunting from dawn to dusk to avoid her. He was now deter-mined on divorce. He galloped all day in the forest, changing his horse six times and covering twenty-five leagues. He considered the benefits of an alliance with the House of Habsburg. He thought obsessively, thundering through the forest's swathes of white sand, about the need for an heir.

He broke the news, which cannot have been unexpected, to Josephine at the end of November after dinner at the Tuileries Palace. He told her their Deed of Separation must be signed on 15 December. She became completely hysterical. She fainted, or seemed to. She had never cared about his mistresses, all she cared about was not being discarded. He had to help carry her back to her rooms. He was pained by her reaction, but stuck rigidly to his timetable. As was now necessary under the new Civil Code, their respective families assembled for the signing of the deed, all of them in tears. But the Bonapartes had never liked Josephine. They didn't really feel sorry for her, especially since her divorce settlement was generous. She was given Malmaison, the Élysée Palace, the Château de Navarre in Normandy, 2 million francs to pay off her debts and 3 million francs a year to live on. 'Now you can plant whatever you like,' Napoleon remarked, remembering the arguments they had had over her gardening expenditure. At 7 p.m. on 19 December, he wrote to her from Trianon:

> Savary tells me that you are always crying. That is a pity. I hope you have been able to go for a walk today. I sent you some game from my hunt. I will come and see you when you tell me that you are being sensible, and that your courage is winning the day. Tomorrow I am busy with my ministers all day. Goodbye my dear, I am unhappy today too. I want to hear that you are satisfied, and to know that you are recovering your balance. Sleep well.[61]

Members of the institute, those who had been newly elected, and those who had recent publications, were invited to the Tuileries Palace in December 1809. They assembled in their green costumes while the emperor was at Mass. The naturalist Jean-Baptiste Lamarck, white-haired, sixty-four years old, stood in line holding his new book. Lamarck remembered the Ancien Régime; he had known the great Buffon and Daubenton; he had botanised with Rousseau and published a three-volume book on the native flowers of France.[62] As a medical student in Paris, he had become fascinated by the clouds he observed from his garret window and interested in predicting the weather. He had survived the Terror, working in the Jardin des Plantes as Professor of Invertebrates. From studying the lowly earthworm he had developed an early theory of evolution, the inheritance of acquired characteristics, which challenged the idea of the fixity of species. He knew he had enemies, fellow scientists who disagreed with and disliked him. Sometimes he thought there were conspiracies against him. Some people suspected him of atheism. He had been mocked for his interest in meteorology and his publication of weather forecasts in an annual almanac. He worried ill will would spoil the reception of his *Philosophie Zoologique*. He clutched the bound copy he was going to present to Napoleon.

Lamarck was standing near François Arago, a mathematician, physicist and astronomer, too young to remember the Revolution. Arago's election to the institute earlier that year, aged just twenty-three, had been controversial. After measuring the meridian arc in Spain, where he had been accused of being a spy for the invading French army and imprisoned on the island of Majorca, Arago had escaped and had many adventures trying to get back to France. He had only recently been released from quarantine when he received the summons to the Tuileries Palace. Some of the older scientists thought his election premature. As Napoleon processed past the line of scholars, he stopped and said to Arago: 'You are very young, what is your name?'[63] But before Arago could answer, a scientist to his right replied on his behalf. 'What science do you cultivate?' the emperor asked. Again, another colleague, desperate for attention answered. Arago was dismayed by the pushy behaviour of institute members vying to get noticed. Napoleon moved on to Lamarck. Arago watched as the naturalist well known for 'his beautiful and important discoveries' humbly presented his book. The emperor abused Lamarck in sharp sentences. Perhaps he meant to be jocular. 'What is that? Your absurd meteorology? An almanac that dishonours your old age? Do some Natural History and I will receive your productions with pleasure. As to this volume, I only take it in consideration of your white hair.' Lamarck kept trying to explain that his *Philosophie Zoologique* was actually a work of natural history. Then tears started to flow down the old man's face. They were like the tears of a gazelle Arago had seen injured and dying in Algiers. The gazelle and Lamarck produced the effect 'which is always felt when a person who is suddenly struck by an irreparable misfortune, resigns himself to it, and shows his profound anguish only by silent tears'.[64] Napoleon moved on, had a further curt exchange with another member of the institute, then went to talk to the soldiers, to avoid the rest of the scholars and civilians in the room.

Lamarck's meteorology aimed to identify the laws of nature that regulate climatic change. His attempts to make long-range weather forecasts, when there was still no means of instant communication over large geographical areas, inevitably failed. His annual almanac tried to predict the influence of the moon on the weather and the probable temperature for each day. The information and technology for doing this simply did not exist. Napoleon was interested in reliable facts, not probabilities based on scant evidence.[65] Either he did not have the intellectual sophistication to understand that trying to do something that seems impossible is part of scientific aspiration, or he was deliberately misled by Lamarck's colleagues into thinking the weather project completely absurd. Lamarck published one last forecast in 1810, explaining that his age and ill health meant that he could no longer continue with his meteorological observations.[66] But he urged others to take up the endeavour; he was sure it would benefit the public eventually. Lamarck's old age was blighted by blindness and poverty. His daughter who cared for him until the end insisted: 'Posterity will avenge you!' He was buried in an unmarked grave, but in 1909 he was at last honoured by a magnificent statue in the Jardin des Plantes.

Even if he had not mistaken Lamarck's book for an almanac and had realised that it was a pioneering work of natural history, Napoleon would still not have appreciated it.[67] Challenges to the idea of the fixity of the species risked the disapproval of the Catholic Church. If organisms could evolve by adapting to their environments, where did that leave divine agency and order? Napoleon might not have believed in God, but he certainly believed in order. And he was assured by two of the institute members he most trusted and relied on, Laplace and Cuvier, that Lamarck's understanding of the natural world was deeply flawed.[68] Lamarck's suggestion that living organisms continually and gradually transform themselves was radical, anti-authoritarian and subversive. Napoleon was more comfortable with Cuvier's vision of nature where the species are fixed and specially created to play a specific part in the order of things. According to Cuvier, catastrophes might occur and interrupt that order, but it would be reasserted afterwards, the species replenished and replaced. The history of the natural world, life itself, was not internally driven and open-ended, as Lamarck seemed to think it was. For all his interest in science, Napoleon was prepared to rely on his friends to tell him what to think. He trusted Laplace and Cuvier – they were good administrators aside from anything else – and for all he knew Lamarck was still an undependable revolutionary.

'Above all, do not touch my bible!' Napoleon warned the scientists.[69] More trouble with the Catholic Church was the last thing he needed when he had resolved to divorce Josephine. Had it not been for the sacramental marriage she had insisted on the day before the coronation, the process would have been much simpler. The civil annulment was straightforwardly approved by the Senate on 16 December 1809. But the annulment of the religious marriage was much more complicated. Even so, Napoleon, impatient as ever, managed to impose a timetable of a matter of weeks on Rome. Cardinal Fesch had to testify as to what had and hadn't happened in the private ceremony he conducted the day before the coronation. The canon lawyers found a way to deliver the required judgement, decreeing on 11 January 1810 that the sacramental marriage was invalid and had never taken place. Crucial to the case was Napoleon's insistence that the ceremony occurred without his consent, an improbable lie, as everyone from the Pope to the humblest Catholic curate knew. The judgement recommended that the emperor and empress 'rehabilitate' their marriage by consenting to renew their vows in the presence of witnesses and an official priest, but recognised that for reasons of state, this might not be what Napoleon wanted or needed to do. It certainly was not.

By autumn that year, Napoleon was back at Fontainebleau checking on the status of preparations for the reception of his new empress. As usual he complained when it seemed to him that utility had been sacrificed to decoration or fashion.[70] The architect Leroy decided he was too old to continue taking responsibility for the renovations at the chateau. His replacement was Maximilien-Joseph Hurtault, who had worked with Fontaine on the Tuileries Palace, and who was now redesigning the Garden of Diana, the private garden that Napoleon could reach down his internal and external spiral staircases. It was the emperor's middle-of-the-night garden, where he went to breathe fresh air if he could not sleep. Despite his employer's well-known dislike of the *jardin à l'anglaise* style, this was exactly what Hurtault planned. Napoleon overcame his aversion, perhaps because of the remains of the orangery. There would be no need to build an artificial ruin when a real one already existed. Also, incorporating it into the design of the garden would save the expense of demolishing it. Hurtault laid out curving paths and asymmetric lawns.[71] He repaired the fountain of Diana and put back a statue of the goddess, though not the original bronze replica because that had gone to Malmaison.[72] White marble statues produced by contemporary artists were ordered to replace the ones that had been removed during the Revolution. They were positioned amid new plantings of flowering shrubs and exotic trees, against the backdrop of the massive forest foliage. The garden descended down two gentle slopes towards ditches bordering the old orangery walls. In these ditches wide sunken paths of fine white Fontainebleau sand were created, so it was possible to walk around the irregular buildings shaded by a canopy of greenery and flowers. These walkways were a secluded alternative to the exposed pavements of the vast courtyards and parterres on the other side of the chateau.

Beyond his private garden, Napoleon took an interest in improving other parts of the estate. He embellished the area around the obelisk in the forest, regularising it with new plantations. Each of the main roads from Burgundy, Auvergne and Orléanais was marked with a military column. Louis XV's mistress, Madame de Pompadour, had created a pleasure garden at Fontainebleau, a verdant barrier against the encroachment of the sands. Napoleon too planted trees that would fix the sandy soil with their roots and built new walkways for the inhabitants of the town.[73] By the time the artist, architect and writer Antoine-Laurent Castellan wrote his historical descriptions and made sketches of Fontainebleau, Napoleon's sunken walkways around the remains of the orangery walls had been filled in, replaced by a promenade with a handrail. The ruins themselves were destroyed in 1834. Castellan regretted the loss of the stones and garden to which so many memories were attached. The epigraph of his posthumously published book is a quotation from the same Tasso poem Napoleon quoted when first encountering Fontainebleau: 'Among lonely valleys, a high forest full of ancient plants.'[74]

At Compiègne, in northern France, there is another grand chateau, built for Louis XV, bordering a vast forest where the French kings hunted for centuries. Napoleon had it restored in 1807, entrusting the work, as usual, to Fontaine and Percier. Another new garden was laid out, also in the *jardin à l'anglaise* style, so as to seem like a continuation of the forest behind it. It was to Compiègne that Napoleon brought the nineteen-year-old Archduchess Marie Louise of Austria, when she arrived in France after marrying him by proxy on 11 March 1810. Marshal Berthier had brokered the marriage, asking Marie Louise's father Francis II for her hand in marriage on Napoleon's behalf. When she arrived in France, Marie Louise was well aware that her ill-fated great-aunt, Marie Antoinette, had also been welcomed at Compiègne forty years earlier.

After celebrating their wedding in Paris in April, Napoleon and Marie Louise returned to Compiègne. 'I have married a womb,' he quipped in a vicious moment. But already he knew she was more to him than her reproductive potential. Far more. She had grown up hating him as the arch-enemy of Austria and had sobbed inconsolably when told she must marry him. But she soon reconciled herself to her fate: practical and determined to make the best life for herself that she could in his shadow. Looking out of the window of his new empress's bedroom, Napoleon decided to create a spectacular view for her, an avenue stretching from the chateau far into the forest, which would remind her of the gardens of her beloved Schönbrunn Palace, from which her family had twice fled when he occupied Vienna. At the end of the avenue, on the summit of the distant hill, he planned to build a Temple of Glory. The creation of the Percée des Beaux-Monts at Compiègne involved the destruction of four kilometres of trees. Napoleon considered this a grand romantic act. He died before the tree-felling was completed. Today the avenue through the forest remains dramatic and beautiful. It is bordered by aged oaks – some of them dating back to the Ancien Régime – that are habitats to endangered species of insects and moss. Some of the trees are named. The oak of Point de Vue is forty metres tall and thought to be four hundred years old. In the long broad corridor of empty space where thousands of trees were sacrificed, nothing is left of the sawdust and ugly stumps that once stretched like a wound gashed through the forest on a lover's whim.

7

Imperial Gardens

'The biggest, the most splendid garden in the universe.'[1]
Dominique Vivant Denon

Napoleon never reached Rome. But he planned to. He intended it to be the second city of his empire. The ancient imperial centre of government fired his imagination and shaped his dreams for Paris, but he never saw the Forum for himself. 'I wish to visit Rome,' he told the artist Canova, as he watched him sketch Marie Louise over breakfast.[2] Canova had been summoned to sculpt the new empress. He arrived in Fontainebleau on 11 October 1810 and left in early November, after completing a plaster bust of Marie Louise and conducting numerous informal and intimate conversations with Napoleon. 'Paris is the capital of the world. You must remain here: we will make much of you,' the emperor promised the artist, stopping just short of commanding him. Fifty-three years old, noticeably thinner than he had been when he visited France in 1802, Canova came back reluctantly, hoping to secure patronage and protection for antiquities, and even aspiring to make peace between Napoleon and Pope Pius VII. The previous year, the Papal States had been annexed to France, the Pope had excommunicated Napoleon, and Napoleon had arrested and deported the Pope. Afterwards there was an exodus; all the foreign ministers, forty cardinals, two hundred prelates and many other canons and ecclesiastics had left Rome. Soon grass would be growing in the already neglected streets. The emperor, the artist insisted, was the city's best and only hope.

Napoleon enquired about a recent attempt to produce cotton in Italy. Had that not generated revenue? Very little, Canova replied. Rome was in want of everything. Even the arts, long supported by the nobility, were neglected, the artists unemployed. Napoleon had heard that soldiers arriving in the city often became sick during the first year, then recovered. 'Is the air in Rome as bad and unhealthy as in ancient times?' he asked, remembering Tacitus's description of the Roman Emperor Vitellius's troops returning from Germany and falling ill after sleeping on the Vatican Mount. He called for his librarian and a copy of Tacitus, but could not find the relevant passage.[3] Canova sent him the reference afterwards pointing out that the ancients protected themselves from the unwholesome air by respecting the woods and forests which they considered sacred.

Napoleon decided that Italy could indemnify herself through excavations. He would order and finance digs to begin in Rome; any treasures unearthed would belong to him. How much, he asked Canova, had the Pope spent on excavations? The artist's answer was carefully calibrated to pique Napoleon's competitive spirit: not as much as he would have liked, owing to his want of funds, but the Pope's generous disposition had led to the establishment of a new museum. How about the Borghese family? How much had they spent? Again, Canova encouraged and flattered the emperor: the Borghese had not spent as much as it might seem since they almost always collaborated with other noble families. Canova tried to convince Napoleon that the people of Rome possessed a sacred right over the antiquities of their city, which were a species of property inherent in the soil. 'Neither the noble families of Rome, nor even the Pope himself, have a right to remove these precious remains from Rome, to which city they belong, as the inheritance of their ancestors, and the reward of their victories.'[4]

There had been a French plan to move Trajan's Column from the
Forum to Paris, but when this proved impossible, a replica was
commissioned, a celebration of the Battle of Austerlitz, made from
metal melted down from 1,200 captured Austrian cannon.[5] Out of
respect for Marie Louise, Napoleon had not attended the unveiling
in the Place de Vendôme on his birthday, 15 August, earlier that year.
He was displeased to discover that he was represented at the top of
the new column, which was 7.6 metres taller than the original, wearing
a toga. He worried that this was ridiculous. Nor did he like the four
eagles, perched in swags of foliage, at the corners of the base of the
monument, but Canova assured him these were accurately copied
from Trajan's Column. He questioned Canova closely on the progress
of the colossal statue of himself that had been commissioned in 1802.
The statue, Canova told him, was ready: it had been successfully cast
and an engraving had been made by a young artist who wished to
dedicate his work to the emperor. The renowned sculptor did not miss
an opportunity to help one of his protégés. Again he flattered the
emperor, who would surely want to encourage artists at such an unpro-
pitious time. Napoleon was concerned to hear the colossal statue was
a full-length nude. He would have preferred to be represented in
military dress. Canova explained that in sculpture the sublime style
requires nakedness. He listed several examples of ancient monuments
and the emperor seemed convinced.

Canova urged Napoleon to visit Rome, to see for himself the
Capitol, the Forum of Trajan, the Sacred Way, the columns, the
triumphal arches and the Appian Way lined with tombs. 'But what
is astonishing in this?' Napoleon asked. 'The Romans were masters
of the world.' 'It was not only power, but Italian genius and our love
of the sublime, which produced so many magnificent works,' Canova
replied. In his determined way, refusing to move to Paris, insisting
on representing Napoleon in the nude, reminding him that there is
more to accomplishment than power, Canova was one of the few
people left who came under the emperor's shadow and still stood

up to him. His reward was the patronage he needed for himself and Rome. On 6 November, from Fontainebleau, Napoleon issued imperial decrees that promised 200,000 francs for excavations in Rome and an endowment of 100,000 francs for the Accademia di San Luca, an institution that supported artists, of which Canova became principal in 1811.[6]

Both Marie Louise and Napoleon were pleased with Canova's work. He represented her as Concord, smiling. Encouraged by his success, and the free and open nature of their discussions, Canova begged Napoleon to heal the schism that had led to the arrest of Pius VII on 6 July 1809 in the early hours of the morning. 'In a short time, Sire, you will be a father,' he said, referring to Marie Louise's already visible pregnancy, which was publicly announced on 12 November 1810.[7] 'In God's name, I entreat your Majesty to protect religion and its chief, and to preserve the beautiful temples of Italy and Rome. It is far more delightful to be the object of affection than of fear.' 'That is what I wish,' Napoleon replied, breaking off the conversation. Again Canova asked to be allowed to return to Rome to make a cast of the plaster bust of Marie Louise and to work on a full-length marble sculpture, which, he hoped, the imperial couple would see soon when they came to Rome and visited his studio. 'Go then, since you will have it so,' Napoleon said, grudgingly giving his permission. But before Canova left France, he went to visit Josephine at Malmaison on 10 November. Whereas the artist had lost weight since they last met, Napoleon's ex-wife had gained it. He found her heavier and sadder than she had been in 1802, but her aesthetic judgements, her unerring eye for the beautiful, remained unchanged. Josephine had never asked Canova for a sculpture of herself. Instead she commissioned some of his most renowned work, including *Paris*, *The Dancer* and *The Three Graces*. She did not live to see the last completed, but for a short time, she had the finest collection of Canova sculptures in the world.[8] When he came to visit, she showed him her garden, her own work of art. Her garden designer, Louis-Martin Berthault, would soon be sent to Rome to assist with the project of turning the Forum and its ancient monuments into a vast garden: the Jardin du Capitole.

There were two major problems with the French excavations in the Roman Forum: first, they were underfunded; second, coordination and communication between Paris and Rome was often difficult or interrupted. Funds allocated in Paris took a long time to reach Rome and sometimes failed to arrive. Dominique Vivant Denon, Director of Museums in Paris, was named as consultant to the excavations, but refused to accept the position. He thought it was unlikely anything important would be discovered because the imperial baths and Palatine had already been explored.[9] Since air quality was such a problem, Denon advised Napoleon that the most useful thing he could do was to create a salubrious space in the centre of the city. He suggested a vast garden to include the Capitol, Forum and Palatine, stretching as far as the Oppian and Caelian hills. The ancient monuments, Rome's sole resource, would be spectacular ornaments in such a garden. Denon thought the cost would be around 3 million francs. He knew that Napoleon was particularly keen to create jobs for the poor, left vulnerable and without sustenance by the closure of convents and the end of old religious practices, but suggested that expenditure could be lowered significantly if soldiers were deployed to shift the earth. He assured the emperor that the result would be 'the most splendid garden in the universe', a sublime space containing the most magnificent monuments of ancient Rome.[10] In just three or four years, Napoleon would have done more for the Romans by creating this vast garden than the popes had ever done.[11]

Denon's plan for what became known as the Jardin du Capitole drew on suggestions from Napoleon's prefect in Rome, Camille de Tournon, and the eminent architects Giuseppe Camporese and Giuseppe Valadier.[12] Tournon had arrived in Rome in November 1810. His only previous position had been as *intendant* at Beirut and at the age of thirty-one he was the youngest prefect in the Empire, with a passion for archaeology and town planning.[13] Camporese and Valadier were almost exact contemporaries, both nearly fifty when appointed directors of the excavations in 1810. They were paid 200 francs a month each, which, they claimed, scarcely covered their travel expenses.[14] Camporese had a revolutionary past: he had been involved with designing the Altar of the Fatherland in St Peter's Square for the Festa della Federazione in 1798. Afterwards he had become a papal architect and participated in the clearing of the Arch of Severus and the buttressing of the Colosseum under Pius VII. Valadier had also been a papal architect, involved in restoring many churches and the Milvian Bridge.[15]

The Commission des Monuments et Bâtiments Civils, established to oversee the excavations and protect the ancient monuments, approved the garden plans.[16] But when they were sent to Paris, the administrator, Joseph-Marie de Gérando, queried the English-style garden concept, concerned that it might be 'torturous', 'affected' and unsuited to the grandeur of the Forum.[17] He also insisted that the Colosseum must be included in the scheme and that thought be given to drainage if the level of the Forum was to be lowered to that of the River Tiber. The call for labourers went out to each parish on paper headed by an imperial eagle clutching thunderbolts. The indigent were warned that if they refused this offer of work, they would receive no further help.[18] The poor were expected to show filial gratitude to their remote ruler for these job opportunities. Previously, under the Pope, the digging in the Forum had been done by convicts, but under Napoleon the excavations would become a source of income for the poor. Initially the workers, if they were male and aged twenty or over, were to be paid a daily rate of 20 bajocchi in papal currency (approximately 1 franc), less if they were younger, and 12 bajocchi if they were female, regardless of their age.[19]

Soon there was concern that these wages were too high and might encourage people, women especially, to abandon other, even lower-paid work. Women were paid less than men for clearing earth and rubbish, but their work was harder. A contemporary engraving of workers in the Forum of Trajan shows a male labourer pushing a wheelbarrow. Beside him is a woman balancing a large basket of rubble on her head, a toddler on her hip, and with her free hand she is holding the arm of an older child, who is also balancing a basket on his head. She is drawn calm and erect, looking appreciatively at the man. Perhaps he was the father of her children, perhaps it seemed obvious to both of them that he should be the one pushing the wheelbarrow while she worked with only a basket. But it seems likely that her serene expression did not reflect the real experience of such back-breaking work.[20]

In January 1811, there were plans to terrace or slope the ground at the foot of the Capitol.[21] Further plans were published on 12 January 1811, soon after the demolition of two modern houses that had been built in the middle of the Forum. The removal of the houses opened up a clear view from the Capitol to the Arch of Titus and made it easier to imagine the whole area turned into a picturesque garden with ancient monuments framed by newly planted trees, avenues and lawns.[22] The Forum was to become a promenade for pedestrians. By February 1811, 25,000 francs had been spent and there were already problems paying the four or five hundred poor workers, who eventually resorted to threatening to riot as the arrears in their wages accumulated.[23]

On 12 June 1811, from Saint-Cloud, Napoleon issued another decree to secure the finances of the Accademia, which was to have an annual income of over 100,000 francs, derived from the rents of forty-two houses and other properties. In August that year, Camporese and Valadier made a list of all the antiquities under the care of the Accademia, in order of urgency of repair. The list of eighty-two monuments included obelisks, theatres, temples, baths, aqueducts, arches, tombs, columns, circuses, bridges, the Cloaca Maxima, the Pyramid of Cestius and the ancient walls.[24] There were disagreements as to what should fall under the Accademia's budget for repairs, and what should be billed against the separate budget for excavations. Did work

on the Temple of Vespasian, for example, count as repair or excavation? Who was responsible for paying the workers? Amid all the
disputes and uncertainties there was ample room for corruption.

Another imperial decree increased the budget for the Jardin du
Capitole on 27 July 1811 to 100,000 francs per year.[25] The garden was
now one of the main Roman embellishment projects.[26] By October
demolition had begun and the vines and trees in the garden of S.
Francesca were due to be cleared.[27] In November, a mass of earth
placed in the Forum the year before was cleared. Sometime in 1811,
somewhere in the middle of the Forum, a stone fragment of a list of
Roman augurs was found, proving Denon wrong in his belief that
further excavations were pointless. It turned up during the digging of
a drain from the Temple of Antoninus and Faustina to the Temple of
the Dioscuri and the Column of Phocas.[28] It was part of a list of priests
from Sulla (88 BC) to Caecilius Creticus (AD 7). But this important
discovery did not interrupt the planting of the garden, which was laid
out by spring 1812 with avenues of transplanted trees.

In Paris, Napoleon wanted to build a new forum to rival that of ancient
Rome. For many years, there had been talk of connecting the Louvre
to the Tuileries Palace to make a larger centre of government at the
heart of the city. The construction of the Rue Rivoli, running parallel
to the Seine on the other side of the palace gardens, was part of this
plan. Begun in 1801, when Napoleon was First Consul and named
after his most dramatic victory in the first Italian campaign, the road
opened up a direct route between the Place de la Concorde, the
Tuileries Palace and the Louvre. The long, straight Rue Rivoli was to
be lined by strictly regulated buildings, with standardised arcades and
balconies. It would be a triumphal route and a place for Parisians to
promenade. It would also remove impediments to accessing and
defending the centre of government, making it easier to prevent revolts
of the kind that had ended the monarchy in the Tuileries gardens on
10 August 1792. As Napoleon's power increased, his architects, Percier

and Fontaine, joined in sincerely with his *rêves fantastiques*, delighting especially in the idea of redesigning the space around the Tuileries Palace and removing the traces of the Terror. In 1806, Fontaine noted in his journal that it was still possible to see holes made by cannonballs and the date, '10 Août, 1792', inscribed on the facades near the Place du Carrousel.[29] Now plans were in place to turn the centre of Paris into 'le forum Napoléon', a Roman space at the heart of the first city of the Empire.[30]

In July 1810, Percier and Fontaine won the Prix Décennal d'Architecture, for their contribution to architecture over the previous decade. Their main achievement was the Arc du Carrousel, situated between the Louvre and the Tuileries Palace, celebrating the Battle of Austerlitz. It was consciously modelled on the arches of Septimius Severus and Constantine in the Roman Forum, and on the Arc d'Orange (Arausio) of Roman Gaul which Percier had sketched on his way back from Rome. The dimensions of the Arc du Carrousel were taken directly from the Arch of Septimius Severus. Construction began in 1806, lasted for two years, and involved demolishing buildings in the Rue Saint-Nicaise, some of which had been damaged in the attempt to assassinate Napoleon in 1800. The emperor hoped that aside from the aesthetic benefits of opening up the Place du Carrousel, getting rid of ramshackle buildings and a narrow street so close to the Tuileries, where plotters could hide, would increase security.

When in Rome as a student, Percier had made a painstaking study of Trajan's Column, hanging from the structure in a basket to sketch the depictions of battles between the Romans and the Dacians. Technically, Percier's drawings belonged to the Académie royale d'architecture, but when this institution was dissolved during the Terror, he risked his life to protect his drawings, insisting that they be returned to his personal care. They were not the only available records of Trajan's Column, but they were an important source for both the Arc du Carrousel and the column in the Place Vendôme.[31] It was Denon who chose, in consultation with Napoleon, the recent military and diplomatic achievements which were to be commemorated in bas-relief on the arch: the Peace of Presbourg, the entry into Munich, the entry into Vienna, the Battle of Austerlitz, the Tilsit Conference and the surrender of Ulm.

As ever, Napoleon was in a tremendous hurry; he wanted the monument finished as soon as possible. To save time, stone and other materials that happened to be nearby were used. The eight marble columns of the Arc du Carrousel were built from blocks of Languedoc marble sourced from a marble supplier in the village of Chaillot, just west of Paris. Fontaine thought the marble was probably left over from the construction of the Grand Trianon at Versailles under Louis XIV. Accidents were inevitable. One of the columns was dropped and broken as it was being hoisted up onto its pedestal. Fontaine complained that the fracture would not have occurred if they had been using granite as he had intended in the original design. The best they could do was to stick the broken piece back on and carry on working as fast as they could, regardless of the dreadful winter weather.[32]

Napoleon saw the completed Arc du Carrousel for the first time on 1 January 1808, when he was just back from Italy. Immediately he noticed that the marble which had been used was not of the best quality, and overall he thought the arch looked more like a pavilion than a grand gate into the Tuileries Palace grounds. Nevertheless, Fontaine recorded in his journal that the emperor was pleased with the first entirely new monument to his rule. Now that more buildings had been demolished, the vista between the Louvre and Tuileries was clear. The Arc du Carrousel was at the centre of 'le forum Napoléon'. The emperor's priceless war spoils were already on display in the Louvre, where a new grand staircase was installed. The four horses of St Mark's were moved from the gates of the Tuileries gardens, where they had been placed in 1802, and repositioned on top of the Arc du Carrousel.[33] At first, a statue of Napoleon was placed in a chariot behind the four horses. But he objected to it – in the original plans the statue had been of Mars – and he insisted that the statue of himself be taken down and the chariot left empty. The rejected statue was stored in the nearby orangery in the Tuileries gardens. The point of the Arc du Carrousel, as far as the emperor was concerned, was to celebrate his army. Representations of himself in bas-relief were acceptable, a bronze statue elevated above the entire arch was not.[34]

When she was heavily pregnant, Marie Louise liked to walk on the terrace in the Tuileries gardens, but crowds of curious members of the public had started gathering, hoping to catch a glimpse of her. Napoleon, feeling intensely protective of her privacy and his own, summoned his architect Fontaine and commissioned a new underground passage from the chateau to the terrace. This would make it possible to move between the two without being observed. Fontaine was irritated that everyone in the emperor's household, from the lowest to the highest member of staff, even the doctors, had an opinion on the excavation and construction of this tunnel. Some of the critical comments reached Napoleon, who cross-examined Fontaine about his work. No detail was too small for his attention.[35] This, Fontaine reflected, was an example of how trivial things acquire great importance at court.

Marie Louise went into labour before the garden tunnel was finished. The birth was protracted and difficult. At one point, Napoleon was overheard telling the doctors to save the mother if a choice had to be made. A healthy baby boy, Napoléon François Joseph Charles Bonaparte, to be known as the King of Rome, arrived safely on the morning of 20 March 1811. Salvos of 101 cannon shots announced his birth to Paris. He was laid in a ceremonial cradle, designed by Pierre-Paul Prud'hon and decorated with rows of bees and an eaglet. Two bas-reliefs on the sides of the cradle evoked the union of Paris and Rome through the personification of the rivers Seine and Tiber. When he heard the news, Francis II, Emperor of Austria, declared that whatever his daughter Marie Louise's suffering had been, she was more than compensated for it by having produced Napoleon's heir: a judgement only she could have made. That evening there was a quick preliminary baptism for the baby, in case it died before the official christening, scheduled for Pentecost in Notre-Dame.

Fontaine, deeply engaged in designing the christening ceremony, noted that Marie Louise was up and about the Tuileries again by 19 April, when she made her first visit to church since the birth of her son. She had been bedridden or confined to her rooms for a month. Three days earlier, the tunnel between the palace and the garden terrace had been finished. Napoleon took to using it when he went out hunting. Sometimes Fontaine went with him. Together they came across the Bagatelle Pavilion, a *maison de plaisance* in the Bois de Boulogne. Immediately, Napoleon decided it should be restored for the use of his son.[36] He spoke to Fontaine of his plans for beautifying the Bois de Boulogne, which he wanted to see well planted and in good condition. He also wanted a pavilion by the Seine at the Tuileries. But when Fontaine showed him the plans and explained it would cost 500,000 francs, he was told the budget could not exceed 20,000 francs.[37]

Another of Napoleon's small building projects, directly inspired by the birth of the King of Rome, was a menagerie in the Parc Monceau. Fontaine advised him to buy up surrounding properties to completely isolate the site on all sides, then presented him with plans.[38] As always, there was conflict between Napoleon's dreams and his aversion to extravagance. The public park at Monceau predated the Revolution. It was established by Louis XVI's extremely wealthy cousin, Philippe d'Orléans, as a *jardin à l'anglaise*, featuring a large number of follies, including a fake ancient Egyptian pyramid and Roman colonnade. Even though Napoleon hated follies, he appreciated that the park was of a completely different kind to the formal Tuileries and Luxembourg gardens and the Jardin des Plantes. He thought a garden in the informal style – which he referred to as Chinese rather than English, recognising the influence on European garden design of Jesuit priests and other travellers to China – would benefit the citizens of Paris.[39]

Back in 1807 he had ordered his Finance Minister Gaudin to set aside
funds for restoring Monceau. Before the Revolution there had been
camels in the garden. Now Napoleon wanted to revive and expand
the menagerie, already anticipating the enjoyment his son would
derive from it. Fontaine tried to persuade him that Monceau could
be another *maison de plaisance* for the King of Rome, that the gardens
could be left unchanged and filled with just a small number of interesting animals.

The christening of the King of Rome, scheduled for Pentecost, had to
be postponed by a week due to the tensions between Napoleon and
the Catholic Church following his arrest of Pius VII. Canova had been
right when he urged the emperor to make peace with the Pope in
anticipation of becoming a father. The concordat was about to collapse,
but the baptism did take place. At 5.30 p.m. on Sunday 9 June 1811,
a cannon blast signalled the departure of the imperial family from the
Tuileries Palace en route to Notre-Dame. The roads had been cleared
and secured against further assassination attempts. Inside the cathedral, Cardinal Fesch was once again officiating. After the baptism,
Napoleon took his son from Marie Louise's arms and held him high
above his head in a gesture of triumphant jubilance. Later, this spontaneous act was stamped onto commemorative medals. There can be
no doubt about the sincerity of the emperor's happiness on that day.
He had secured his succession, the future of France and the future of
Rome. The cry *'Vive le Roi de Rome!'* rang out in Notre-Dame.
Afterwards there was dancing until dawn in the Tuileries Palace, illuminations in the gardens, fireworks on the Place de la Concorde and
another uncontrollable hot-air balloon ascent.

On 8 June, the day before the ceremony in Paris, the Roman Forum
was illuminated in a spectacular 'son et lumière' celebration of the
birth of the King of Rome. The Colosseum, the arches of Septimius
Severus and Constantine, the temples of Antoninus and Faustina,
Concord, Peace and Jupiter Stator, were all dramatically lit against the

night sky, using the wood-gas-burning 'thermolampe' patented by Philippe Lebon in 1799. An immense crowd gathered to see the city as it had never been seen before. Prefect Tournon felt proud of the archaeological work which had cleared the ground around the ancient monuments and made possible a stunning *coup d'œil* unique to Rome. As part of the celebrations, the Vice Regent of Rome, Bishop Atenasio, gave permission for a *Te Deum* to be sung in St Peter's Basilica, the first since the removal of the Pope. When the choirmaster of the Sistine Chapel, Niccolò Zingarelli, an Italian patriot, refused to conduct, he and his choir were arrested and taken to Paris, where Napoleon, who thought Zingarelli was the second-best living composer after Paisiello, commissioned a new Mass and *Stabat Mater* and gave him a pension.[40]

On 12 April 1811, Napoleon at last went to see Canova's colossal sculpture, which had been sent from Rome to Paris on a ship, whose crew were instructed to throw the statue overboard rather than allow it to be captured by the English. Since reaching France at the beginning of January, it had been kept at the Louvre, waiting for the emperor's approval. When he saw it, Napoleon banished it to storage, fearing that the nude athletic representation of himself as Mars the Peacemaker would cause derision.[41] With his habitual eye for detail, he also found fault with one of the arm joints. Only a few select artists were allowed to view Canova's sculpture. Jacques-Louis David was one of them. He wrote kindly to Canova:

> You have made a beautiful figure representing the Emperor Napoleon, you have made for posterity all that a mortal can make: the calumny that clings to it disregard, allow to mediocrity its little habitual consolation.[42]

David did not mean that Napoleon was mediocre, but that public opinion, which the emperor was too politically astute to ignore, was. After word of Napoleon's negative reaction to Canova's colossus spread, the plan to place a replica in the middle of the Roman Forum was cancelled.[43]

Rome was not the only city for which the emperor decreed public gardens. When he visited Venice in December 1807, Napoleon entered the city through a floating triumphal arch on the Grand Canal designed by the architect Giannantonio Selva. The 'hero of the century' was given a traditional Venetian welcome: a regatta, a banquet, a ball, a *Te Deum* in St Mark's. Selva even redesigned the city's theatre, La Fenice, to include a royal box, larger than the other boxes, which had been strictly equal under the old republic.[44] Napoleon decided that what Venice most needed was a public garden so that Venetians could have access to 'the joys of verdure'.[45] Soon after he left, plans were drawn up by Selva to turn a large part of the Castello neighbourhood into a green and salubrious space close to the Arsenale.[46] The writer Chateaubriand had recently described Venice as 'a city against nature'.[47] Napoleon's new garden would redress the city's unnaturalness.

The garden could not be created without demolition, as the area concerned was densely populated. There were humble dwellings associated with the poor: fishermen, lacemakers, glass-bead threaders and significant churches – Sant'Antonio, San Nicolò, San Domenico – as well as the seminary of the Cappuccini di Castello and the hospice for retired sailors.[48] The proposed destruction of these build- ings caused widespread dismay, but Selva's vision was fixed firmly on the future. In line with Napoleon's directives, he wanted to give Venice a grand formal garden with a magnificent vista onto the lagoon. He planned a coach house, cafe, public baths and a botanical garden, all linked by formal plantings in the orderly French style. The centrepiece of the garden was to be a *tempietto*, a small circular temple, containing a statue of Napoleon and elevated on a small hill planted with evergreens.[49]

Napoleon's stepson, Eugène Beauharnais, Viceroy of Venice, rejected the *tempietto* and the baths and reduced the overall budget for the garden in 1808. By 1810 the controversial demolitions had taken place. The Lando arch of Sant'Antonio was left standing, too beautiful to be knocked down, but the rest of the church was destroyed and the arch became a ruin, an elegant frame against the empty sky. To save money, material from the old buildings was reused in the new. The entrance to the garden, on the Via Eugenia, was designed to be impressive, gated with a tall metal fence between six columns topped by marble statues, but to the diarist Emmanuele Cicogna it looked like the entrance to a lion's cage, or a well-defended fortress.[50] Three years on, the optimism with which Napoleon had been greeted during his state visit was already in decline.

During his conversations with Napoleon at Fontainebleau in 1810, Canova discussed the plight of Venice with tears in his eyes. Commerce was proscribed, taxes were heavy, many people were struggling to sustain their lives. Napoleon promised to look into the matter. Then the subject of Machiavelli arose. Canova quoted Machiavelli approving of government by the sword. The artist himself was of the view that if the Venetians had been led by a general they would have performed more brilliant exploits, but they had been too frightened of a Caesar arising inside their republic. Napoleon agreed that military authority is dangerous. 'I told the Directory myself, that if they would always have war, some man would arise who would seize the reins of government.'[51] He had predicted his own rise to power, or at least claimed to have done. He thought that the birth of his son had consolidated that power for generations to come. In Venice the baptism of the King of Rome was celebrated with a new temporary column, commissioned from Giuseppe Borsato, an Italian artist and architect directly influenced by Percier and Fontaine. It was modelled on Trajan's Column, built in the form of a hollow spiral and illuminated from inside. On the outside were decorations painted on canvas.[52] It was not built to last.

Napoleon started to dream about a new palace for the King of Rome even before his son was conceived. Back in the spring of 1810, while at Compiègne, in the first few weeks of marriage to Marie Louise, full of optimism and high hopes for the future, he considered building the new palace at Lyons. Fontaine was asked to draw up provisional plans, but when he travelled to Compiègne to show them the emperor was too busy to see him. Later, Fontaine was told his plans exceeded the budget of 4 million francs. After further negotiations, the budget was revised upwards to 10 million francs, to include works to the gardens and parks which would surround the imagined palace.[53] When he had time, Napoleon relished scrutinising architectural drawings. He enjoyed comparing and refining plans and sometimes would discuss with Fontaine the changes of circumstance and vicissitudes to which the art of building is exposed.[54]

It was the artist David who first suggested the site of Chaillot for the new palace.[55] A small number of private estates would need to be purchased first and some houses demolished, but then there would be space for a huge palace complex on the north bank of the Seine, between Paris and Versailles. The Ancien Régime architect Marie-Joseph Peyre, who had taught both Percier and Fontaine, had hoped to rebuild Versailles. Among the additions Peyre had envisaged was a colonnade reminiscent of St Peter's Basilica in Rome. He died in 1785 and never saw his ambitious plans realised. Now his pupils, under a new regime, had the opportunity to build an imposing, epoch-defining palace from scratch. In Fontaine's fantasies, it would be far superior to Versailles.

Soon Napoleon abandoned plans for a palace at Lyons and enthusiastically pursued possibilities at Chaillot. One advantage was that the new palace grounds, which would be extensive, could be watered by the Canal d'Ourcq, which he had commissioned in 1802 to bring water to Paris. The canal was still under construction, but it was projected to flow through the Chaillot area.[56] Another advantage was that work on a second triumphal arch, much larger than the Arc du Carrousel, had already begun on the hill at Chaillot. On 15 August 1806, Napoleon's thirty-seventh birthday, the first stone had been laid in the centre of the Arc de Triomphe, a hexagonal slab measuring 3.65 metres by 1.60 metres.[57]

The stone was put in place without official ceremony on the initiative of the workers. By the end of 1807, the foundations were nearly finished. On 31 October 1808, Jean Chalgrin was appointed sole architect of the Arc de Triomphe to avoid disputes with any of his colleagues.[58] Chalgrin had previously renovated the Luxembourg Palace and gardens, creating a park at the centre of Paris that Napoleon dedicated to the city's children. Chalgrin's improvements to the Luxembourg gardens included restoring the seventeenth-century Medici fountain and formal garden and creating the most beautiful walk in Paris along the Avenue de l'observatoire. His plans for the Arc de Triomphe were approved on 27 March 1809. Napoleon wanted the inscriptions on the Arc to be in French, not a dead language. He rejected the institute's proposal to give him the titles of Augustus and Germanicus. 'I see nothing to envy in what we know about the Roman Emperors,' he declared. 'It ought to be one of the principal endeavours of the Institute, and of men of letters generally, to show what a difference there is between their history and ours.'[59] Only Caesar, in Napoleon's opinion, had distinguished himself by his character and illustrious deeds, and he was not an emperor. The only title Napoleon wanted, the only one he would allow on the Arc de Triomphe, was 'Emperor of the French'.

When Napoleon first brought Marie Louise to Paris after their wedding in 1810, Chalgrin arranged a wooden-and-canvas mock-up of the unfinished Arc de Triomphe. But he met with problems. He employed five hundred workers who went on strike and demanded two pay rises. Initially the carpenters were paid 4 francs, then they demanded 9, then 18 (which they got) and finally 24, at which point the *préfet de police*, Dubois, stepped in. Six workers were arrested and the demands ceased.[60] Chalgrin commissioned the painter and designer Louis Lafitte to do the *trompe l'œil* decor work in his workshop. Lafitte, together with many helpers, produced a whole set of painted canvases in twenty days. The life-size model gave Chalgrin the opportunity to correct flaws in his plan for the Arc de Triomphe. He died on 21 January 1811 having completed all his plans, drawings and cross-sections for the monument.[61]

Napoleon frequently visited the Chaillot construction site with Fontaine, with whom he had some revealing, and contradictory, encounters. On one of their visits, they met the furniture maker Georges Jacob, over seventy and close to the end of his life. As a friend of David's during the Revolution, he had been commissioned to make chairs for the Committee of Public Safety during the Terror. Georges had retired in 1796, leaving his two sons to run his workshop, which was known as Jacob Frères under the Consulate and Empire. The family business thrived until one of the sons died in 1803. Then Georges came out of retirement to help his surviving son oversee the many imperial commissions. Despite the fame and success of his furniture, Georges, according to Fontaine, was bankrupt. Napoleon asked many times how he could help. Fontaine was struck by the emperor's sincerity and persistence.[62] On another occasion, Napoleon and Fontaine met M. Nettement, who, since the Revolution, had owned the old convent of Des Dames St Marie. Napoleon complimented him on the house and garden he was hoping to purchase and demolish. When Nettement tried to raise the purchase price of his property, demanding compensation for the loss of his beautiful English-style garden, Napoleon flatly refused and insisted on paying only the minimum price.[63]

Fontaine's timetable, from conception of the idea of the King of Rome's palace at Chaillot to the commencement of building works, was less than a year. Percier and Fontaine's bird's-eye view plans included terraces, porticoes and fountains, echoing the Roman villas they had studied where these features linked disparate buildings and spaces.[64] They worked on a range of designs, encouraged by Napoleon to compare and contrast their proposals with other palaces past and present. One that they published showed a vast rectangular palace above stepped terraces rising up from the banks of the Seine. On one of the intermediate terraces there were two enormous fountains.[65] Another variant showed a structure rising straight up from the river with an Italian facade, reminiscent of Venetian palazzos. As the plans became more and more grandiose, Fontaine told himself that Napoleon was as engaged with the fantasy palace as he and Percier were.[66] The budget was revised up to 20 million francs with an extra million set aside for acquiring land and demolishing any existing buildings that were in the way.[67] In light of their bad experience at Malmaison, one of the things Percier and Fontaine were keen to insist on was the integration of the palace and its garden. Buildings and gardens are integral, Fontaine advised the emperor, they should be designed by the same hand.[68]

By 12 April 1811, after the birth of the King of Rome and before his christening, the architects had produced a model of the proposed palace that Napoleon had exhibited to the public for comment.[69] He summoned Fontaine to his dinner table to discuss criticisms made by himself and others. He cross-examined his architect about whether there were any remains of the dwellings of the Roman emperors. Fontaine explained that all the ruins on the Palatine Hill and those at Tivoli and Spoleto resembled a collection of different types of buildings rather than a majestic edifice built to a coherent plan. Napoleon then asked which was the most beautiful palace in the world. Fontaine was embarrassed by the unsophisticated question. He tried to evade it by giving a long answer, listing different villas, their pros and cons, and finally singling out the Farnese Palace in Rome as one of the most imposing but least convenient. The biggest villas were in Germany, the gayest in Genoa, the most habitable in France.[70] At the end of the conversation, the emperor asked his architect to construct an agreeable little pavilion in the Tuileries gardens, on the terrace near the river, where he could have breakfast.

Alongside his desire for public display and his dream of a palace to surpass all other palaces that had ever existed, Napoleon had an intense need for privacy. 'I want to be housed with dignity,' he told

Fontaine, 'but I will not be like most sovereigns, a prisoner and uncomfortable under the golden ceilings of my home.'[71] He needed two things under the same roof: first, accommodation suitable for a wealthy head of family, 'with all the conveniences of a private man who wants ease and freedom'; second, the reception and ceremonial rooms of the representative of a great nation. Fontaine set about incorporating these needs into the plans for the palace for the King of Rome. In the final version, there was a double private apartment opening onto the garden for the emperor and empress, and a double public apartment on the main facade.[72]

On 10 December 1811, Napoleon went hunting again with Fontaine in the Bois de Boulogne. He wanted updates on all the current building projects, large and small, ranging from the Bagatelle Pavilion to the construction of the palace complex on Chaillot Hill. Fontaine told him that 200,000 francs had already been spent on the first stage of terracing the site for the new palace. Lots of land and a few private houses had been acquired. For the next stage, the whole area needed to be enclosed, ramps next to the river constructed and the new park planted. Impatient as always, Napoleon complained to Fontaine about the inconvenience of living at the Tuileries while he was waiting for his new residence. There was no room, he claimed, for his maps, or any of the other things he needed. He was thinking of building an extension onto the Tuileries Palace gardens.[73]

Early in 1812, Napoleon summoned Fontaine to talk to him after dinner. They discussed the plans for the palace for the King of Rome and as usual Napoleon was acutely critical. Fontaine tried to divert attention onto the park, for which some acquisitions of private property were still needed. He asked for a budget of 3 million francs for the first stage of laying out the palace grounds. Napoleon oscillated between grandiosity and parsimony. He worried that the buildings and gardens he commissioned would not be grand enough, but scrutinised the budgets and balance sheets, always trying to cut costs.

Napoleon's visit to Rome kept being postponed. He planned to go in spring 1812. In February of that year the Jardin du Capitole was laid out between the Forum and the Colosseum and the planting began. Transplanted trees formed instant avenues.[74] The clearing of the Colosseum was finished. Then on 21 March, just as spring was under way in the vast new garden, a severe earthquake damaged the Colosseum. A few days later Prefect Tournon estimated that the garden, which had already cost 134,520 francs (and for which 100,000 had been allotted each year), would cost another 200,000 in 1812. Its total area was 0.25 square kilometres and it included the most important monuments in Rome.[75] Camporese and Valadier were asked to provide a reasoned project for further clearing of the Forum down to the ancient level. There had already been significant demolition of houses around the Temple of Saturn and the Tabularium. But other buildings, such as granaries and storerooms, remained.[76]

If he finally got to Rome, Napoleon wanted to reside in a palace as magnificent as the one he was building by the Seine. The Italian architect Raffaele Stern was put in charge of redesigning the Quirinal Palace on Monte Cavallo, a papal residence since the sixteenth century.[77] Stern came to Paris to present his plans and budget. Fontaine was sceptical about both and there was rivalry and tension between the two architects.[78] Rumours that Napoleon would at last arrive in Rome in the spring of 1812 caused a flurry of activity at the Quirinal. The renovations included a grand new staircase, paintings of tutelary gods by Felice Giani, and the ceiling of the Gabinetto delle Guerra, with a depiction of 'The Triumph of War'. One of the most decorative of the new plaster friezes in the state rooms illustrated the triumph of Caesar, with battle spoils, elephants and a triumphal arch.[79] The guiding principle of design was to compare the Napoleonic and Roman Empires, to draw parallels between Napoleon and the heroes of Roman history, Caesar above all.

Behind the Quirinal Palace, above the Piazza del Popolo on the Pincian Hill, the main point of entry to Rome, another new garden was created. There had been gardens of the rich on the Pincian Hill in antiquity. Napoleon's orders were for a public promenade. In a decree of 1811 it was named the Jardin du Grand César. Prefect Tournon wanted work to begin on Napoleon's birthday, 15 August, but he was away from Rome, in Paris for his own wedding, and could not impose his will from a distance.[80] Work on the new garden finally began at the end of September.[81] The expenditure was controversial. In the budget for 1812, Prefect Tournon estimated that another 50,000 francs would be needed to complete the project. By this point around a thousand workers had already been employed for many months. Commissioner Martial Daru, who had become Napoleon's Minister for War the previous year, complained angrily about the waste of money. What was the point of investing so heavily in a garden that would not mature quickly enough for contemporaries to enjoy? He could understand clearing the ancient monuments, but why, he asked, was it necessary to mask them with palisades and plantations? The Jardin du Capitole was in an unhealthy part of the city, so people would not want to go there. The Jardin du Grand César was better located but still, in Daru's opinion, a foolish use of public funds.

The architect Valadier, who had long been interested in beautifying the entrance to the city, drew up the plans for the Jardin du Grand César. He was influenced by Percier and Fontaine and included features in his design that would meet with their approval, such as French-style formal planning, hedged by shrubs, pools and hillocks in the adjacent Borghese gardens.[82] Because the Pincian Hill rose so steeply above the Piazza del Popolo, Valadier linked the two with formal staircases broken by generous terraces. Berthault arrived from Paris to help with some of the technical difficulties. While in Paris for his wedding, Tournon had specifically asked for a French architect skilled in garden work to be sent to Rome.[83] He was concerned that the Roman architects had grandiose visions and little regard for economy. Berthault carefully revised the plans for the Jardin du Grand César. He advised a strong vertical link between the terraces and suggested dismantling the fence between the garden and piazza. Instead of a hard barrier, trees were planted around the semicircular perimeter, blending the garden with the urban space.[84] Berthault's arrival coincided with the exposure of a scandal in the Jardin du Grand César. At the end of each working day, the attendance sheets were being left blank, then filled in by Vice Inspector Corvi with inflated numbers. Corvi was claiming the wages for workers who were not in fact labouring on the garden at all; instead they were repairing his own house, which had been damaged in the recent earthquake.[85] The labourers who were still in the garden often left after their lunch break when they received the bowl of soup that was part of their pay.[86] Many were old, ill and lacking in motivation because of their low wages, which often fell into arrears while the authorities in Rome waited for more money to be transferred from Paris.

In Paris, Napoleon approved a huge budget for his building works in 1812.[87] But he had also started preparing for the Russian campaign, in which he hoped to defeat Tsar Alexander's army and force him to join the trade blockade against Britain. On 20 January, he asked Fontaine to organise tents for the army.[88] At first the impending war did not affect the emperor's commitment to the palace at Chaillot, or any of his other projects in Paris or Rome. If anything, his determination to leave posterity impressive monuments became stronger as he got ready to go back into battle. Newly commissioned monuments, he decided, were better value than restorations to existing monuments, from which so little glory arose.[89] Fontaine agreed with him, but thought everything depended on the monument. He was highly critical of the 24-metre-tall elephant statue that was being erected on the site of the old Bastille prison to replace the revolutionary Fountain of Regeneration. So far only a plaster model had been made, under Denon's supervision, but foundations had been laid and the intention was to melt down cannon captured at the Battle of Friedland to cast the massive elephant in bronze. Fontaine disapproved on aesthetic grounds; he thought the image of the elephant would be monstrous.[90]

Napoleon left Paris for Dresden on 9 May and then joined his army. Marie Louise went with him as far as Dresden and the King of Rome was sent to the Château de Meudon with his governess, Madame de Montesquiou. Meanwhile Pius VII was brought to Fontainebleau, a prisoner, full of sad and angry memories of his first visit to the chateau en route to Napoleon's coronation eight years earlier. On 24 June, Napoleon led the Grande Armée across the Neman River and invaded Russia. Uninterrupted by the war, construction of the palace for the King of Rome began on 5 August. The first stone was laid on 15 August, Napoleon's birthday, the same day as the attack on Smolensk, a walled city 360 kilometres south-west of Moscow. Fontaine did not notice any slowing down of the project on Chaillot Hill until the following year.[91]

The French razed Smolensk. Over 80 per cent of its buildings were destroyed by artillery fire and almost all the inhabitants fled. Thousands of soldiers on both sides died. The exact numbers are disputed, but Napoleon tried to claim French losses were as low as seven hundred. He sent back triumphant bulletins and letters to Marie Louise, but the destruction of Smolensk left him without badly needed supplies for his army. After a bloody battle at Borodino, he pressed on to Moscow and entered a completely silent and deserted city on 14 September. There were fires on the outskirts, pockets of black smoke on the horizon, when Napoleon occupied the Kremlin, delighted to have taken possession of the famed palace of the tsars. He put a picture of the King of Rome on the wall in his new bedroom which had windows opening onto the Moscow River. He assumed the fires were started by pillagers and could be controlled. He ordered his soldiers to shoot anyone apprehended with a firebrand. But soon the whole of Moscow was burning. On the night of 16 September, Napoleon's valet Saint-Denis was woken by the bright light. He looked out from the Kremlin on the city. 'It was horrible! Imagine a city as large as Paris swept by flames, and one was on the towers of Notre Dame, watching the spectacle at night.'[92]

At the centre of Moscow there is a botanical garden, the Apothecaries' Garden, originally laid out by Peter the Great in the formal
style with long, straight avenues of close-set limes and elms and a
large pond. Some of the exotic plants originally came from the gardens
of the tsars, others were imported from Europe. In 1805 the botanical
garden was bought by Moscow University and a German director, the
botanist Georg Hoffmann, from Göttingen University, was appointed
to run it. Hoffmann had come to Russia hoping to escape the
Napoleonic Wars. He never imagined they would reach as far as
Moscow.[93] After the fire, Hoffmann wrote to the university: 'Not a
single chair or bench, not a single instrument is left.' But some of the
trees and plants survived, among them a tall Siberian larch, planted
by Peter the Great in 1706. Hoffmann remained in Moscow after
Napoleon's retreat, and oversaw the reconstruction of the garden.

By 1813, the effects of the disastrous Russian campaign were beginning to be felt in the first and second cities of the Empire. In Rome,
Berthault presented scaled-down, much more modest plans for
finishing the Jardin du Capitole. Other projects were halted, or
cancelled before they had even begun. The Jardin du Grand César
stalled and only restarted when Pius VII made his triumphant return
to Rome in 1814. After the French defeat at the Battle of Leipzig in
October 1813, Napoleon scaled back his plans for the palace at
Chaillot to 'a little sanctuary, a retreat for convalescence'.[94] At the
beginning of 1814, there was brief hope that Napoleon's military
prowess would recover. His first appearance on a battlefield that year
was on 29 January at the Battle of Brienne, and although he was nearly
killed, on the site of his old school, the Prussian and Russian forces
under the command of General Blücher retreated south. Afterwards,
however, Blücher managed to join his army to that of the Austrian
allies commanded by the Prince of Schwarzenberg. On 1 February,
at the Battle of Rothière, they defeated the French in freezing conditions. Later in the month, Napoleon was making plans to evacuate
the government from Paris, and by the end of March Tsar Alexander

had reached the hills above the River Seine with an invading army. After calls for Napoleon's abdication, the fantasy palace on the banks of the Seine shrank to a garden pavilion. The final plan was a landscaped garden that would have incorporated the work that had already been done on the foundations of the non-existent palace for the King of Rome.[95] The construction of the nearby Arc de Triomphe ceased in 1814 when the monument was just over five metres tall. And 'le forum Napoléon' at the centre of Paris was left incomplete, the Louvre and Tuileries still not joined or integrated, except by the unfinished Rue Rivoli.

One morning Napoleon's Mameluke bodyguard saw the King of Rome burst into his father's apartment at the Tuileries Palace. Napoleon hugged and kissed his son and took him on his knee near the windows that opened out onto the garden. 'Whose garden is this?' he asked. 'My uncle's,' said the little boy. Napoleon tweaked his son's ears and said, 'After me, it will belong to you. I hope you will have a good inheritance.' But he was already less than certain of what that inheritance would be.[96]

8

Gardens on Elba

'A garden the size of my hand.'[1]
Napoleon

In the spring of 1814 Napoleon retreated to a corner of the palace of Fontainebleau and prepared to leave for his new domain. France had been doubly invaded: the armies of Britain, Spain and Portugal had crossed the Pyrenees; and Russian, Austrian, Prussian and Swedish forces had crossed the Rhine. After the Battle of Paris, fought in the city's suburbs on 30–31 March, Napoleon was forced to abdicate. Under the terms dictated by the allies, he could have had Corfu or Corsica, but he chose Elba, the largest island in the Tuscan archipelago. He felt no connection to Corfu and too much to Corsica, his birthplace, so close to France. Elba, he thought, 22.5 kilometres long and 10 kilometres wide, could give umbrage to no one. The restored Bourbons would not be threatened by him as Emperor of Elba and he would be free to devote himself to study and repose. Besides which, it was beneath him to compare one small island to another, and a few thousand subjects, more or less, made no difference to his lost splendour. The Treaty of Fontainebleau was signed in Paris on 11 April 1814 by representatives of France, Austria, Russia and Prussia. When Napoleon ratified it two days later at Fontainebleau, in a small room in his private apartments, next to his bathroom, he made two or three scratches on the claw-footed table and a dent with the stump of his pen.[2] He abdicated his power as ruler of the French Empire and received the newly created principality of Elba. He and Marie Louise were to retain their titles of Emperor and Empress. Marie Louise was given the duchies of Parma, Placentia and Guastalla. Their son, the King of Rome, became the Prince of Parma. Josephine's allowance as the ex-wife of the ex-emperor was reduced to 1 million francs. Napoleon himself was to be paid 2 million francs a year by France and was allowed a guard of four hundred soldiers on Elba.[3]

Afterwards, the palace of Fontainebleau was deserted. Almost all Napoleon's loyal generals, courtiers and servants left him. In empty echoing rooms he looked listlessly at maps of Elba and selected almost seven hundred books from the library that he wanted to take with him; books on botany and mineralogy to help him understand Elba's flora, fauna and natural history; travel narratives like William Coxe's *Voyage en Suisse* (1790); a full bound set of the *Moniteur* newspaper to help him write his memoirs; translations of Latin and Greek classics; books by Voltaire, Rousseau and other companions in exile. To one of his valets, Louis Constant, who had no intention of following him into exile, he quipped, 'Prepare your cart, we will go and plant our cabbages.'[4] He spent a lot of time in the Garden of Diana, sitting on a stone bench near the restored fountain and its bronze statue of the huntress goddess. The bench faced a vista at the end of which was Mercury on a pedestal. On one occasion he sat for three hours, kicking a hole a foot deep with his heel in the gravel.[5] Every so often he heard carriage wheels in the courtyard and asked, 'Is not Berthier returned?' But Marshal Berthier, Napoleon's Chief of Staff since the Italian campaign of 1796, was busy making peace with Louis XVIII and getting ready to accompany the restored Bourbon king on his ceremonial entrance into Paris. Within a week of Napoleon's abdication, a ceremony of cleansing took place on the Place de la Concorde, where Louis XVI and Marie Antoinette had been guillotined during the Revolution.

In the early hours of the morning of 13 April, Napoleon had tried to kill himself.[6] Since the Russian campaign, he had carried a tiny black silk bag around his neck containing something the size of a clove of garlic. Some people thought it was an amulet, but it turned out to be a vial of poison, a mixture of belladonna, white hellebore and opium. Around 4 a.m. he called for a light from another of his valets, a man named Hubert who was on duty that night, and sat down to write to Marie Louise in his dressing gown and slippers. Hubert withdrew to the antechamber, but left the door ajar and saw Napoleon begin his letter three times, each time throwing what he had written into the fire. Then came the sound of water being poured into a glass and stirred with a spoon as though to dissolve something. He then asked his valet to send for the Duke of Vicenza, the Duke of Bassano, Grand Marshal Bertrand and Baron Fain, his *secrétaire archiviste*. When they arrived he told them that, unable to survive the dishonour of France, he had poisoned himself. They sent for a doctor, the surgeon Alexandre-Urbain Yvan, to administer an antidote. Napoleon vomited violently for the next hour and by 6 a.m. was feeling better. As soon as he could, he went down the external spiral staircase that led to the Garden of Diana, and walked there for a long time with the close confidants he had summoned when he thought his life was about to end. Somewhere in the palace his Polish mistress, Marie Walewska, was waiting for him to visit her. 'Poor woman, she will think she was forgotten!' he said when he remembered her the next morning. He wrote to reassure her:

Marie . . . the feelings that move you touch me greatly. They are worthy of your fine soul and the kindness of your heart. When you have settled your affairs, should you wish to go and take the waters at Lucca or Pisa, I shall see you with great pleasure, as well as your son, towards whom my feelings never change. Take care of yourself, think of me with pleasure, and never doubt me![7]

The English officer Colonel Campbell, entrusted by British Foreign Minister Lord Castlereagh with accompanying the *ci-devant* Emperor from Fontainebleau to the island of Elba, observed him unawares, 'rapidly pacing the length of his apartment, like some wild animal in a cell'.[8] He was dressed in an old green uniform with gold epaulettes, blue pantaloons and red-topped boots. He was unshaven, his hair was uncombed, and particles of snuff were scattered profusely over his upper lip and chest. At morning Mass in the palace chapel, Napoleon anxiously rubbed his forehead and chewed his fingers in a state of great agitation.[9] He was most deeply distressed by the absence of his wife and son, and Campbell saw him weep openly at the separation from them. After the abdication, Marie Louise took the King of Rome to Rambouillet, a chateau and game park fifty kilometres outside Paris, where the imperial family had spent private time together. But she was soon persuaded by her father to leave Rambouillet for Vienna in a hurry.

A few days after her departure, the artist Benjamin Robert Haydon, travelling in France in his late twenties and already obsessed with Napoleon, found the King of Rome's rocking horse and other toys abandoned in the chateau garden.[10] The child, no longer heir to his father's lost empire, had been snatched up in the middle of a game. Haydon's own childhood had been spent in Plymouth playing with toy bone guillotines made and sold by French prisoners of war.[11] On the journey to Rambouillet, he made his coachman stop to give a lift to a nineteen-year-old grenadier. The young man told Haydon that he had been wounded at the Battle of Chaumont and was the only survivor of his cohort of sixty recruits from his home town of Chartres. 'If Bonaparte had reigned longer, he would have murdered all the world, then made war on the animals,' the grenadier declared.[12] But despite the cruelty and bloodshed, Haydon could not help being fascinated by the fallen emperor. He was shown Napoleon's *salle de repos secret* at Rambouillet, a small private room furnished with a satin couch beneath a vaulted alcove decorated with representations of the battles of Austerlitz, Marengo, Friedland and other triumphs. In this room, Haydon began to tremble and felt himself in touch with Napoleon's soul. 'Here he used to retire when exhausted . . . here was his private, secret, sacred closet, painted and arranged by his own orders and for his own particular gratification . . . here he lay in dim twilight, revelled in associations of dominion, and visions of conquest.'[13]

As he left Fontainebleau on the morning of 20 April, Napoleon called for his standard-bearers to advance so he could embrace the eagle, the emblem beneath which his soldiers had gone into battle and, in so many cases, died. They inclined the standard within his reach and he embraced it three times with deepest emotion. All who witnessed the scene cried. Old men, guards, soldiers, even foreign officers, had tears running down their cheeks. To shouts of '*Vive l'Empereur!*', he entered his carriage, wound down the window, almost suffocated by his feelings, and began the journey to Elba. Afterwards, officers in the crowd broke their swords and resigned their commissions.

The day before he set sail from Fréjus on HMS *Undaunted*, a British warship bedecked to receive a monarch, he wrote from the Chapeau Rouge, the small town's only hotel, to General Dalesme, the Commandant of Elba:

Circumstances having led me to renounce the French throne, sacrificing my rights to the welfare and interests of my country, I have reserved for myself the sovereignty and proprietorship of the island of Elba . . . I am therefore sending General Drouot, so that you may make over the island to him without delay, with its stores of food and ammunition, and all the properties belonging to my Imperial Domain. Announce this new order of things to the inhabitants, and tell them that I have chosen the island for my residence because I know the kindness of their character and the excellence of their climate. They will always be an object of liveliest interest to me.[14]

Fréjus was where Napoleon had disembarked when he returned to France from Egypt in 1799. Then he had been in the early stages of his dramatic rise to power; now, despite his authoritative tone to General Dalesme, he had lost his empire. In bright moonlight a regiment of cavalry waited under trees by the harbour and a crowd assembled to wish the ex-emperor farewell. As he boarded the ship, Napoleon conversed courteously with those among the crew who could speak French. The ship's captain was Thomas Ussher, an Anglo-Irish officer of the Royal Navy, instructed by Castlereagh to convey Napoleon to Elba and wait there with him until the English ships that would follow with the ex-emperor's troops, horses, carriages and baggage had arrived. As it left Fréjus, the cannon of HMS *Undaunted* fired a royal salvo, despite the prohibition on doing so after sunset. Napoleon turned his back on France. 'Only the dead never come back,' he said. Did he remember the provenance of this infamous phrase? It originated in the revolutionary Terror, in the signing of Louis XVI's death warrant and in a report to the revolutionary government on the regular guillotining taking place on the Place de la Concorde in 1794.[15] In appropriating it, Napoleon might have been accepting his fate – he sometimes referred to himself as a 'dead man' on Elba.[16] Or he might have been clinging to the possibility of a return to France and his former glory. No one had done more than he had, he felt, to heal the wounds of the Revolution. Now he was an exile from the country he had saved.

Just weeks before Napoleon arrived on Elba, an effigy of him was burned in the village square of Marciana, tricolour flags were torn up and the French local commander was shot and hacked to pieces in Porto Longone. Those on the island, cut off from trade and news by the blockades, knew nothing of the peace negotiated in Paris. General Dalesme put down the revolt against the French with brutal efficiency: the rebels were shot and their weapons exported to the continent. But in the western part of the island there were insurgents who would not surrender. In addition, the island was quarantined because of fears that the plague, virulent in Malta, had reached its shores. Ahead of Napoleon, the British arrived on 27 April with news of the fall of Paris and the emperor's abdication. For about a week, no one on Elba knew if the island was going to be ruled by the British or the French. It turned out to be neither when, on 4 May, Napoleon disembarked at Portoferraio.[17]

It took him five days to sail to Elba. HMS *Undaunted* tacked towards the Ligurian coast and Napoleon gazed at the Alps, almost in a trance, looking up at their immense height from sea level, amazed by his memories of crossing those mountains with an army in 1800. A storm arose and the ship tacked again, towards Corsica. During the voyage the ship's tailors sewed new flags for Elba. Napoleon chose an old Tuscan design, white with a red band running diagonally. He added three golden bees to the red band. By the time the ship reached Portoferraio, two flags were ready to be hoisted above the town's fortifications. There were gun salutes as Napoleon ceremoniously disembarked, wearing the uniform of the chasseurs of his guard, with the addition of a cockade of Elban colours on his bicorne hat. A crowd collected from all parts of the island to welcome him. Even the British seamen cheered 'Farewell' from the decks of their ship. As soon as Napoleon stepped onto firm land, the mayor, Signor Pietro Traditi, handed him the keys to Elba on a silver platter. Under a grand canopy, he processed to the cathedral where the choir sang a *Te Deum*. It was not Notre-Dame, but it was not nothing. At the height of his power he had sent early-career administrators to Elba and reserved the revenue of its mines for the fatherless children of his soldiers killed in battle. Now the small island was his whole kingdom.

Napoleon spent his first night on Elba sleeping on his campaign camp bed in an apartment on the second floor of the town hall which had been designated his temporary residence. The same rooms had been occupied a decade earlier by General Joseph-Léopold Hugo and his three young sons, the youngest of whom was Victor, the future

novelist.[18] Restless through the night, Napoleon's mind turned immediately to finding more suitable permanent accommodation. The hills
of Elba were covered with luxurious vegetation, pomegranate, orange
and lemon trees in flower, honeysuckle, vines and olive groves. A great
profusion of produce grew on the island, including chestnuts, almonds,
figs, walnuts and prickly pears. The region's wines were good. There
was abundance of fish and fowl. Aromatic plants such as rosemary, gum
cistus and aloes scented the air. Later in the nineteenth century, a
German professor from Berlin visited Elba to study its natural resources.
If Elba were in Prussia, he thought, it would be turned into a great
peripatetic school offering inexhaustible lessons for students of nature.[19]
But there were no grand houses, nothing to compare to Malmaison,
still less any of the palaces Napoleon had occupied in France.

The Treaty of Fontainebleau allowed Napoleon a force of four
hundred soldiers to protect Elba. In fact 566 soldiers of the elite
Imperial Guard followed him into exile. They joined a battalion of
grenadiers, who were mostly Corsican, and some local gendarmes. In
total Napoleon ended up commanding about a thousand armed men
on Elba.[20] In preparation for the arrival of the Imperial Guard, he
ordered the conversion of tuna-fishing storehouses into stables. The
old Franciscan convent and Fort Stella were turned into barracks. He
waited anxiously for his troops, regularly scanning the horizon for
sight of approaching ships. To distract himself he began a tour around
his new kingdom. On 6 May, just two days after arriving on Elba, he
went to visit the principal mine at Rio Marina. Iron ore had been
mined here since the time of the ancient Etruscans. While he was
visiting there was a planned explosion, during which he took a pinch
of snuff, then moved calmly on to the local church, where another *Te
Deum* was sung in his honour. There was no fuel on Elba to smelt the
iron ore, so it was exported. Four hundred men and a hundred horses
and oxen were employed in the mine. The manager was paid 15,000
francs a year; the miners received 1 franc 20 centimes a day.

Before Napoleon arrived, the inhabitants of Elba paid tax to the Grand Duchy of Tuscany at Piombino. The island's municipal councils determined the manner in which the levy was raised, but no tax had been paid for the past year because of the war.[21] Napoleon immediately imposed a direct tax on the whole island and a deadline for paying arrears. He knew the tax would be unpopular, but his finances demanded it. Archpriest Bartolini of the small town of Capoliveri dared to ask at a council meeting: 'Who is this Napoleon who presumes to give us laws? Whence does he come?' Napoleon soon went to visit Capoliveri and made Bartolini one of his councillors. A crowd of local people including young children watched the island's new ruler process into the town under a ceremonial canopy. Afterwards the tax was paid.[22] Tax revenue became extremely important to Napoleon when France refused to pay his allowance of 2 million francs a year. Aside from tax, the only resource he had left was his personal wealth, which he still had access to in exile.[23]

Napoleon chose the Villa dei Mulini for his primary residence on Elba and stipulated that it should be renamed the Palais Impérial des Mulini.[24] It was situated under the walls of Fort Stella, on top of a cliff with a sea view, overlooking the harbour. It was named after two nearby windmills, already partially demolished by the time he arrived. His rooms were on the ground floor of the two-storey building, facing the garden, which he wanted redesigned and improved. Paolo Bargigli, a professor at the Fine Art Academy in Carrara who had worked for Napoleon's sister Eliza, the Grand Duchess of Tuscany, was appointed architect, and the painter and decorator Vincenzo Antonio Revelli came from Turin to collaborate on the project. Napoleon moved in at the end of May, amid the renovations, which were not finished until September. After his troops landed on Elba, early in the morning of 27 May, he got the grenadiers and chasseurs who were not on duty to help. They demolished the furnaces near the house, which were once used to heat cannon shot, and other shacks cluttering the upper plateau of the Portoferraio hillside. It was hard labour and the soldiers bargained with him for bonuses.

The Villa dei Mulini was a small unobtrusive building, but still one of the best on Elba. Before Napoleon's alterations it consisted of two houses of two storeys used as barracks linked by a single-storey building. He added a large reception room to this connecting building, raising it slightly above the height of the other two houses. This became the best and only grand part of the house, and from here it was possible to see the sea on both sides. He hoped his wife and son would come and occupy it. He also converted the barn-like building adjoining the house into a small theatre. Napoleon had the early volumes of the *Description de l'Égypte* with him in exile and extracted some of the plates to frame them for his walls.[25] There was so little good glass on Elba that it proved impossible to find pieces large enough to cover the engravings. Two pieces were used inside each frame.[26] Napoleon's bathroom was decorated with small coloured Italian engravings of the pagan gods as described by Ovid.[27] Outside there was soon a fine terrace from which he could hear the waves breaking on the shore sixty metres below.[28] He had the garden designed in the formal style he had always favoured. There were two pilasters, marking the entrance, on which there were two large alabaster vases into which lights could be placed at night.[29] The topiary included a large 'N' laid out in heliotrope. Heliotrope was a plant that had rich associations for him, because while they were still married the Empress Josephine took the flower as her emblem along with the motto '*Vers le Soleil*' (Towards the Sun).[30] He liked to remind himself on Elba that he had once warranted comparison with the Sun King. Despite the shortage of glass, he somehow added a greenhouse to propagate the plants for his new garden. At the back of the house there was a flagged walk, bordered by a small parapet, where Napoleon exercised, walking rapidly up and down, looking through his telescope to see if there were any arrivals to the port below. Some boards, roughly nailed together, provided a rest for the telescope, sometimes for a book. His other diversion was a favourite monkey called Jénar, often to be seen playing in the garden.[31]

As his gardener, Napoleon chose Claude Hollard, who had visited Fontainebleau in 1807. Hollard first went to Fontainebleau hoping to recover money owed him from his time as port administrator, protecting French interests in Breskens, in West Flanders.[32] While he was there, he made contacts with highly influential people and ended up being offered a job as gardener to Napoleon's sister in Piombino. Eliza Bonaparte was impressed by Hollard's success at cultivating vegetables and plants, and in 1810 promoted him to Director of the Royal Park of Piombino; in 1813, after she had become Grand Duchess of Tuscany, she awarded him a landed estate. From these favourable circumstances, which suited his health well, Hollard was summoned to Elba to assist Napoleon in his favourite pastime. Together they planted Mediterranean flowers and shrubs, apricot, cherry, apple, pear, citron and peach trees. Napoleon adored citrus fruits: 150 orange and 50 lemon trees were shipped from Naples for planting at the Villa dei Mulini. He was also determined to import mulberry trees from various parts of Italy. Given the role played by these trees in his early life, the ill-fated nursery on Corsica that bankrupted his family after his father's death, this was a strange choice. But he was insistent. Perhaps in a small way he wanted to overwrite bad memories with good; or maybe he just liked mulberry trees and thought they would thrive on Elba.

Hollard spent a lot of time with Napoleon whose rooms opened onto the garden. One morning the gardener got up early to surprise his employer by laying out the names of all the members of the imperial family across the lawn in arrangements of small flowerpots. Napoleon also woke early and came out into the garden before Hollard had finished. He was delighted, but with his customary attention to detail, pointed out that Hortense, Josephine's daughter, was missing. Hollard immediately produced a basket of flowers spelling out her name which he had not yet placed in the garden. Napoleon pulled his ear and said affectionately: 'I have not found you to fail yet!'[33] But later in the year, when he went through his accounts for September, he did find fault with Hollard. He wrote to Grand Marshal Bertrand complaining in precise detail about supplementary expenditure, and gardens were top of his list. 'Reprimand the gardener for employing three men all the month on a garden the size of my hand, and eleven grenadiers for loading up a few cartfuls of earth.'[34] Napoleon disapproved of the money that had been spent on turf and would have preferred the cheaper option of grass seed. He thought the gardener should have bargained with the grenadiers to accept payment per cubic metre of earth moved. The grenadiers should have been supplied with just enough carts to keep them permanently employed; he did not want to pay them to stand around doing nothing. He estimated that moving the remaining earth should not cost more than 80 francs. Further excavations in the garden needed to be negotiated between the grenadiers and engineers whom he had employed as designers. In his estimate, another 400 francs would be needed, so he would allow a budget of 480 francs for the gardens during October. A further 600 francs was assigned to building stables. 'It's impossible to do things on the same scale in this country as in Paris,' Napoleon reminded Bertrand, as though the Grand Marshal might have not noticed or understood the dramatic shrinkage of his master's empire.

Every morning on Elba, as Napoleon left his house, he was accompanied by a drum roll. At the beginning of June the drums fell silent. They were not heard for three consecutive days, during which no one in Portoferraio saw their emperor. Usually he exercised every day, but suddenly he stopped: he had learned of the death of Josephine from newspapers sent to the island. She had died, probably from pneumonia, at Malmaison on 29 May. Her final words were reported to have been 'Napoleon' and 'Elba'. In her last letter to her former husband she had offered to share his exile, as long as she could be sure that Marie Louise would not be joining him. Josephine had been the wife of his youth and the wife who accompanied him on his rise to power. Grieving for her he was grieving, at least in part, for himself.

Napoleon often walked in his garden at night, enjoying the cool scented air and the sound of the waves breaking below the terrace. Sometimes he was overheard singing, intoning the same words over and over again, rarely in tune. 'Had the King given me Paris, his large city,' he would sing, or 'Give me back Paris'. The Revolution was still on his mind, 'Marat, the people's avenger' was one of his refrains, along with 'Yes it's done, I'm getting married' and 'Here's daylight, Colette is not coming'. A sympathetic interpretation is that Napoleon paid no attention to what he was singing while his mind was busy with other thoughts. But there is also the possibility that he was starting to lose his mind, singing nonsense to himself in the middle of the night, not caring who heard him. 'He seemed to be urging the night to end and waiting impatiently for daylight,' his attendant Marchand remarked.[35]

Napoleon could not afford the wide-ranging improvements he planned for Elba. In addition to renovating his residence at Villa dei Mulini, he wanted to finance new roads, stables, a hospital, a quarantine ground and a system for pumping seawater up the cliff to his new garden. Napoleon's favourite sister, Princess Pauline, arrived at Portoferraio on a Neapolitan frigate called the *Princess Letitia* for a brief visit. She had recovered from the illness which prevented her sailing to Elba with Napoleon earlier that year and stayed in the rooms her brother had prepared in the Villa dei Mulini. But before work on that house was finished, Napoleon decided he needed a second residence, further into the countryside. Borrowing money from his sister, who sold some of her diamonds to help him, he purchased land covered with vines near San Martino, on the road to Marciana, about ten kilometres from Portoferraio. Working again with the architect Paolo Bargigli and the painter Vincenzo Antonio Revelli, he drew up plans for another building project, with a provisional budget of a million francs. It would be nicknamed Saint-Cloud in memory of the country retreat outside Paris where he first seized power in the orangery in 1799. The spot he chose was halfway up a steep mountain, backed by oak groves, with a fine panoramic view. Despite the heat, he went on horseback or by carriage to visit the site every day, escorted by a guard of Polish lancers who had travelled from Parma with their horses to join his guard on Elba. To one of his attendants he quipped: 'It will be the house of a rich bourgeois man with an annuity of fifteen thousand livres.'[36]

The San Martino villa was even more modest than the Villa dei Mulini. It had four whitewashed outer walls, three windows either side of a narrow door on the ground floor and seven on the second floor that was level with the garden at the rear, due to the steep slope of the terrain. Napoleon filled the garden, from which there was a spectacular view, with various trees: oaks, mulberries and acacias. He personally planted a Mediterranean elm. Inside the house, Revelli decorated the central hall with *trompe l'œil* Egyptian columns, hiero-glyphics and frescoes inspired by the illustrations in the *Description de l'Égypte*. The bathroom was also decorated with a panorama of Egyptian views – pyramids, the Sphinx, obelisks and temples.[37] In other rooms, the faux-coffered ceilings were stamped with golden bees and the Legion of Honour stars, pearls and laurel wreaths. The recep-tion room had *trompe l'œil* drapery around the walls and on the ceiling a canopy with a pair of painted doves at the centre clasping a blue knotted ribbon in their beaks. This represented the love knot between Napoleon and Marie Louise, still closely connected, even though far apart. But as the weeks and months went by it became clearer that his wife and son were not going to come and share his exile.

Napoleon's gatekeeper at San Martino was a young woman in her early twenties called Mademoiselle Durgy. He called her his madwoman. She was a Napoleon fanatic, wholly devoted to him. She had no income until he employed her in the grounds of his country house. She had an extraordinary imagination and wrote poetry in praise of the Emperor of Elba. Every time he visited, she could be heard reciting her verse in the garden.[38] The company of women, which he had sometimes dismissed in the past, became particularly

Caricatures of the architects Pierre Fontaine and Charles Percier, who pioneered the Empire style of interior decoration favoured by Napoleon

The botanist and gardener André Thouin, whose revolutionary principles made him unwilling to accept the Legion of Honour from Napoleon

The triumphal arch on the Place du Carrousel in Paris, designed by
Percier and Fontaine and built in 1806–8 to commemorate
Napoleon's diplomatic and military victories

Napoleon and his son, Napoléon François Joseph Charles Bonaparte,
known as the King of Rome, in the Tuileries gardens

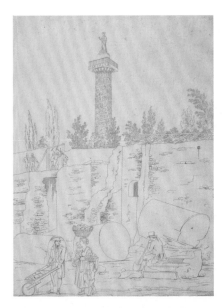

Workers excavating below Trajan's Column in Rome. Napoleon ordered extensive digs in Rome and the creation of two vast gardens: the Jardin du Capitole and the Jardin du Grand César

The architect and garden designer Louis-Martin Berthault's plan for the Jardin du Grand César, viewed from the Piazza del Popolo, 1813

Madame de Staël, the political theorist and novelist, who was highly critical of Napoleon and exiled by him

Laure Junot, Duchess of Abrantès, was married to Napoleon's friend and supporter General Jean-Andoche Junot

Antonio Canova's colossal sculpture of Napoleon as Mars the Peacemaker, made in 1803–6 in Rome. When Napoleon finally saw it in Paris he refused to have it on public display, fearing ridicule

The plan for the enormous palace for the King of Rome
on Chaillot Hill in Paris was reduced to a mere garden pavilion

An English satirical print showing
Napoleon's pedigree, starting with
a dunghill, from which he arises
as a republican officer before
growing into an emperor

The garden wall of the chateau Hougoumont, a farm with an
orchard and formal garden on the site of the Battle of Waterloo,
which both sides wanted to capture

Burying bodies outside the chateau Hougoumont after
the Battle of Waterloo in 1815

Napoleon, corpulent and exiled,
in his garden on St Helena

Napoleon's birdcage, which was built by Chinese workers on St Helena

Longwood House, St Helena, looking out over Napoleon's final garden

Napoleon leaning on his spade

important for him here. His sister Pauline's presence galvanised him into improving his surroundings, devoting time and energy to the many building projects he initiated on the island. When his mother arrived at Portoferraio on 2 August, escorted by Colonel Campbell on board HMS *Grasshopper*, he kissed her several times, drying her tears of joy at their reunion.[39] Under the terms of the Treaty of Fontainebleau, she had been guaranteed 300,000 francs a year and had moved to Rome, but chose to join her son in exile. He arranged a separate residence for her in the Casa Vantini, close to the Villa dei Mulini, and spent time with her in the evenings playing cards. She was the only person who dared reprimand him for cheating.

During his first few days on Elba, Napoleon told Captain Ussher of his plan to occupy the neighbouring island of Pianosa. It amused him to imagine the European powers receiving news that his habit of territorial expansion had not ended with his abdication. Pianosa is a small, flat triangular island fourteen kilometres south-west of Elba. It is the fifth largest island in the Tuscan archipelago. From his reading of Tacitus, Napoleon knew that the Roman Emperor Augustus had banished his grandson, Marcus Agrippa Postumus, to Pianosa in AD 7.[40] Marcus Agrippa Postumus lived on the island for about seven years until he was assassinated, but the remains of his villa, thermal baths and small theatre had not been uncovered when Napoleon claimed Pianosa as an extension of his Elban empire. In 1810, British forces had invaded the island and destroyed the fort at Teglia. Napoleon set up a garrison and ordered repairs to the fort. He made these plans as though he were launching a great military campaign. 'You will go,' he said to his officer, 'to Pianosa with a detachment of so many men and eight pieces of cannon; you will erect batteries, and you will fire on any who may present themselves.' Then laughingly he turned to Captain Ussher and said: 'Europe will say I have already made a conquest!'[41] He thought the flat, low surface of Pianosa would be easier to irrigate than mountainous Elba and hoped it would be possible to grow corn on the island to feed his troops. He intended to plant acorns that would become tall oak trees, and citrus orchards, and vineyards. The reality never measured up to his grand vision for the place. Pianosa was almost a desert, inhabited only by wild horses.

On 27 June, Napoleon went in state to watch the drawing-in of the tuna nets. Tuna fishing was one of Elba's most important sources of revenue and a national sport. The fishery at Portoferraio dated back to ancient times and had been revived by the Grand Duke Francis I in 1585. When the sea was sufficiently calm, nets were placed in the bay to catch the tuna swimming towards Elba from far out in the Atlantic. To encourage the fish to keep moving through the nets, the fishermen threw great quantities of earth into the water: seeking the sun, the enormous fish moved further into the trap. Once they were inside the men harpooned them with spears, turning the seawater red. The fishermen hummed as they hauled the fish on board the barges, pulling rhythmically on the nets. When Napoleon wanted to take his turn, they selected a vast tuna for him to pull out of the sea. The gardener Hollard was watching and saw that the Emperor of Elba did not have the strength to land the fish. There was so much general jubilation, young boys jumping into the water trying to catch the smaller fish caught up with the tuna, boats everywhere across the bay, sparkling in the sunshine, that Napoleon easily laughed off this small humiliation. But it was a very public reminder that his physical strength was declining, not as sharply as his political power had done, but enough for him and others close to him to notice. He was now forty-four years old, his complexion sallow, his eyes deep-set, he was gaining weight and his hair was thinning.[42]

Napoleon was restless, regularly moving between residences and launching new building projects to distract himself from the reality of exile, from how little he had left to occupy him. His power was gone, his wife and child were absent, and his finances were stretched even by the constrained life he was now living. But each project brought him closer to nature, to more remote, more naturally majestic settings. On the other side of the bay, opposite Portoferraio, is a high-peaked mountain called Volterraio, topped by a ruined fortress dating back to the ancient Etruscans. The fortress was enlarged in the thirteenth and fourteenth centuries, and was a refuge for Elbans when their island was attacked by Turkish pirates or other invaders. Napoleon climbed the mountain to visit the ancient walls. He was accompanied by Captain Ussher, an Elban named M. Lapi, who later became governor of the island, and a local guide who knew the mountain well. Just before he reached the entrance to the fortress, he stopped at the tiny church which could hold no more than twenty people. At that height, he remarked, a priest might say anything he wanted. Religion for him was always a practical matter, a means of securing secular political power, but he could see immediately that a preacher in such a remote place, almost four hundred metres above sea level, would be above the control of the state. He carved the date of his visit on a stone and left it behind in the church, where it remained until revolutionaries removed it in 1848. From the crumbling fortress walls at the summit of the mountain, Portoferraio was scarcely visible. All around were fertile valleys and distant hills, with only birdsong to interrupt the quiet.

Napoleon visited many of the churches on Elba. He went to the Madonna delle Grazie in Capoliveri and admired a beautiful painting of the Virgin Mary which some Elbans venerated. The painting was by a student of Michelangelo's, Marcello Venusti, but many thought it was by the master himself. He also visited the Sanctuary of the Madonna del Monte in Marciana, which was surrounded by majestic chestnut trees, the largest on the island. The chestnuts were a source of sustenance and revenue. Their luxuriant dark green foliage offered welcome shade as Napoleon ascended the mountain, glimpsing the blue sky and sea above and below. The sanctuary's facade is decorated with frescoes dating from the thirteenth century, one of them depicting the Madonna of the Assumption looking up to the sky. When Napoleon visited it he noticed a small house next to the chapel occupied by two hermits. It had just four rooms and fragile walls, but was beautifully situated. It was shaded by trees, including a fig whose branches had grown downwards into the ground and taken root, so a circle of smaller fig trees surrounded it.[43] Napoleon imagined that the place must look wonderful in a thunderstorm. Impulsively, he decided to acquire another summer house and the hermits moved out to accommodate him. Near the chapel, facing the main door, was a semicircular fountain of classical design, out of which flowed an abundant spring of pure clear water from the mountainside that disappeared into the chestnut grove below. Napoleon loved the secluded spot and enjoyed dining outside under the trees. Lilies of the valley, heliotropes and violets scented the shade and dampness of the deep forest. The thick grass was more agreeable to his feet than the best carpets in Paris. People speculated that his own thoughts in this modest abode could not have been very different from those of the hermits who had occupied it before him: the fickleness of fortune, the fleeting nature of worldly success and power, the inconstancy of lovers and friends. He went hunting in the woods but could find neither birds nor animals to shoot at: his loaded gun remained undischarged. 'What a difference there is between this hunt and those which I had at Versailles, at Saint-Germain, at Fontainebleau, where I killed so many head of game!' he remarked.[44]

Not far from the fountain, higher up the peak of Mount Campana, there was a bare rock, from which there was a view of the Tuscan archipelago, the Corsican sea, Pianosa and Montecristo. The rock was called the Affacciatoio, or sometimes the Rock of the Eagle because from a distance it looked like a bird of prey with spread wings waiting to fly. Napoleon often sat on it, his eyes fixed toward the island where he was born, his power in France and on the battlefields of Europe, his Egyptian and Russian campaigns, all just memories. Captain Mellini, an Elban engineering officer who had previously guarded the incomplete pyramid erected to commemorate the Battle of Marengo, sketched Napoleon on the rock.[45] 'It must be confessed, my isle is very small,' the Emperor of Elba remarked. Close to the rock there was a ruined semaphore, a reminder of the signalling system that he had inherited from the French revolutionaries and that spread throughout France and beyond so that messages from Paris could reach the border in under four hours. It would have been easy to restore the semaphore on Elba, to send messages to Corsica and on to France, but there would have been no point now he was powerless. In England the semaphore towers that had been set up to rival the French were being dismantled following his abdication.

He often thought of Corsica, which was under the command of General Jean-Baptiste Bruny. In March 1814, Bruny had been the first general to sanction the fall of Napoleon and give his support to the new provisional government. Louis XVIII lost no time making him Chevalier de Saint-Louis and sending him to Ajaccio to keep the peace in the ex-emperor's birthplace. While Napoleon gazed wistfully across the water towards Corsica, there were riots in Ajaccio. Part of Bruny's brutal repression involved having the walls of the botanical garden knocked down. Since its establishment in 1800 the garden had seen good and bad times. Even after it was affiliated to the Jardin des Plantes in Paris, funding was not forthcoming. By 1811 it was derelict, but the following year a new greenhouse had been built and two gardeners came from Paris to revive the garden. They tried to plant cotton, but the summer was too dry and the autumn not hot enough for the plants to thrive. The gardeners fell ill with fever. One returned to Toulon, the other died. Then two more gardeners, deportees from Saint-Domingue, now Haiti, were appointed. They grew vegetables in between the exotic plants. When General Bruny razed the walls the two gardeners almost died trying to defend it from plunderers and vandals.

Looking out to sea one day in late August, Napoleon saw a Genoese felucca, luxuriously fitted out, arrive in the bay of Portoferraio. A lady and a child disembarked and the rumour spread that the Empress

Marie Louise and the King of Rome had at last arrived on Elba. In fact, Marie Louise was in Aix in Savoy at the time and her son was in Vienna with her parents. The woman who had arrived was Napoleon's Polish mistress Marie Walewska and her son, Alexandre, who was his child, conceived in 1809 just after the Battle of Wagram. To avoid gossip and to enjoy the privacy that had always mattered to him, he took his visitors straight to the little house in the woods at Marciana Alta. The next day, as the child played under the chestnut trees, he was overheard calling Napoleon 'Papa'. Napoleon asked one of his attendants what the Elbans were saying about his visitors and was told they assumed their island had been honoured by the presence of the empress and his son. Napoleon replied, 'He may well be my son and yet not be the King of Rome.' Local people struggled to understand why Napoleon wanted to live in the humble hermit house, but the time he spent with his mistress and child in a remote woodland idyll on Elba, surrounded by nature – whether it was a week or only a day – might have been the most privately happy of his life.[46]

In the autumn of 1814 the ambassadors of Europe, representing more than two hundred states and princely houses, met for the Congress of Vienna, hoping to agree a peace plan. Europe had suffered twenty-two years of war, interrupted only by the brief Peace of Amiens. The delegates started arriving in late September, and at the congress chaired by the Austrian statesman Klemens von Metternich, Talleyrand negotiated a settlement for France that involved undoing almost all Napoleon's conquests. From Elba, Napoleon sent forth his spies. Captain Loubets of the Imperial Guard and his butler, Cipriani, sailed in a brig to Genoa on the pretext of buying supplies for the battalion and furniture and crystal for the Emperor of Elba's new residences.[47] The spies carried letters between the emperor and Marie Louise and through a network of contacts they tried to find out what was going on in diplomatic circles in Vienna. Napoleon hoped for a weekly bulletin on the gathering of European power brokers, which previously he would have expected to dominate. To his great dismay, he learned that there was talk of moving him from Elba to the South Atlantic island of St Helena to get him further away from the coasts of Italy and France. Soon even the newspapers were openly talking about this plan. Napoleon was incredulous. 'I do not believe that Europe wishes to take up arms against me; I would however not suggest that they attack me here, they would pay dearly for their endeavour. I have six months' provisions, good artillery, and brave soldiers to defend me. I was guaranteed the sovereignty of Elba; I am at home here, and do not advise anyone to come and disturb me.'[48]

At the Congress of Vienna, an alliance was formed between France, Austria and England against Russia and Prussia. The restored Bourbons wanted Naples and Parma returned to their control. The Treaty of Fontainebleau had given Marie Louise and the King of Rome the duchies of Parma and Placentia, but now, like many of the other terms of the treaty, that promise seemed insecure. On the night that the brig bringing his spies back to Elba was due to return, a terrible storm blew up. Amid the howling wind and rain cannon shots of distress could be heard. Napoleon woke and went out on his terrace to see what was happening at sea. He was nearly knocked over by the wind. Clinging to the terrace wall, he could see nothing but the waves furiously breaking on the rocks far below. He insisted on riding down to the shore, where he found the brig beached but safe. He ordered a bonfire and impromptu feast in celebration.[49]

Napoleon became a tourist attraction. Many visitors came to Elba from Corsica, Italy and France, some of them looking for work. English visitors came too, eager for a glimpse of the man so long demonised in the British press. Lord and Lady Holland, his loyal English supporters, were in Italy, hoping to get to Elba. The French consul at Leghorn, Chevalier Mariotti, warned Talleyrand in August that 'The English have an intense admiration for Napoleon. They have bought up all his alabaster busts in Florence. All the English captains have his portrait in their cabins.'[50] At the beginning of December, Viscount

Ebrington arrived to see Napoleon. He reported that he 'found no devil in him'.[51] He met him twice at the Villa dei Mulini and wrote a detailed account of their conversations. In their talks, Napoleon insisted that France could not be content under the restored Bourbons. He claimed to know this not from spies or newspapers or visitors, but from his understanding of French vanity. He told Ebrington that he had always tried to encourage the old nobility to serve in his army and at court, but this was a highly sensitive matter in the aftermath of the Revolution; he had had to proceed with great caution, otherwise French 'spirits would quiver, like those of a horse whose reins are too tight'.[52] France, he thought, wanted an aristocracy, but would only accept one with time. He had been able to create princes and dukes and give them great wealth, but he had not been able to make them real nobles. Only intermarriage with the old nobility would have achieved that. He greatly admired the English constitution, especially the House of Lords. As to French finances, he explained to Ebrington that his civil list had been 30 million francs, of which he claimed to have seldom spent more than 18 million, and from which he had finished two of his three planned palaces. All this was stretching the truth. The unfinished palace in Napoleon's mind must have been the one intended for the King of Rome on the banks of the Seine. He did not draw Ebrington's attention to his dramatically reduced finances on Elba, or his series of new, also unfinished, modest residences.

The first conversation between Napoleon and Ebrington lasted from 8 p.m. until around 11.30 p.m. They talked freely about forms of government, heads of state, generals, the Egyptian campaign and the execution of the Duc d'Enghien. As he paced up and down at the Villa dei Mulini, answering Ebrington's questions, Napoleon was rehearsing his memoirs. Either before or after Ebrington's visit, he started writing them. Ebrington was struck by the fact that at no point did Napoleon 'betray, either by his countenance or his manner, a single emotion of resentment or regret'.[53] Two days later he went back to the Villa dei Mulini for dinner and they talked again about England's politics and constitution. Ebrington shifted the comparison between England and France to the question of agriculture, remarking on how cultivated France was. Napoleon attributed this to the division of property and his own encouragement; agriculture, he told Ebrington, had always been his first priority, ahead of manufacture and commerce. Then he returned to the problem of re-establishing the nobility in France, confiding to his visitor that he had always intended his 'Temple de la Gloire' in Paris to become a church dedicated to expiating the massacres of the Revolution, but he thought it would have taken about twenty years for this to become acceptable. The bloodshed of the Revolution, especially the murder of the Swiss Guard in the Tuileries gardens, still haunted him, even though he had seen so much life lost on battlefields in the intervening decades.

In early January, Napoleon invaded Palmaiolo, another tiny island in the Tuscan archipelago, and planned to add the rocky island of Montecristo to his territory. But on 8 January more snow fell in Portoferraio than anyone could remember. It was like the unusual rainfall in Cairo that had been attributed to General Bonaparte's presence back in 1798. Now on Elba there were those who thought the snowfall something to do with Napoleon, as though he could command the weather.[54] The bad weather meant that almost all the construction projects that had kept him busy and sane had to be suspended. Only work on the new roads continued. Napoleon's mind turned increasingly to France. He believed that, aside from a few thousand schemers, the whole nation was still attached to him and to the principles of national sovereignty and French honour. Out of 30 million inhabitants, he anticipated that 29.5 million would be in favour of overthrowing the restored Bourbon monarchy.[55] He started to imagine setting sail from Elba with his small number of troops and striking the soil of France with his foot, as Caesar had done to produce armed legions as he marched through the country.

Fleury du Chaboulon, a redundant French official who had lost his position as sub-prefect of Reims after Napoleon abdicated, was sent

to Elba in disguise by the Duke of Bassano, Napoleon's former Foreign
Minister and a diehard Bonapartist, charged with giving the Emperor
of Elba a detailed description of the discontent in France.[56] This would
be a much fuller account than the newspapers provided. Fleury was
told not to advise Napoleon to return, but simply to explain the situation and leave the great man to make his own mind up. First Fleury
won Bertrand's trust. Then he was advised to stroll up to the perimeter
of Napoleon's garden at the Villa dei Mulini, as though he was one of
the many tourists trying to catch a glimpse of the most famous man
in the world. He walked up casually on 12 February and encountered
Napoleon at the garden gate. In his memoirs, Fleury records his first
impressions of the emperor in exile. He seemed, at least superficially,
to have lost his ambition and to be enjoying a peaceful retiring life
devoted to the study of botany, the care of his houses and the cultivation of his gardens and newly planted trees and vines. 'Like [the retired
Roman Emperor] Diocletian, he could say to the men who suspected
him of regretting the throne: "Come and see me in my retreat; I will
show you the gardens that I have planted, and you will no longer tell
me about the empire."'[57] Fleury claimed that without the reports of
the support waiting for him in France, Napoleon would have continued
tending the soil on Elba.

Napoleon's new municipal theatre for Elba had opened on 24
January for performances by actors selected from among the soldiers
and supported by the military band.[58] It had been financed by selling
sixty-five private boxes to wealthy Elbans. The architect Paolo Bargigli
converted the interior of the deconsecrated church of the Madonna
del Carmine into a horseshoe-shaped theatre. The boxes were arranged
in four tiers and at the top there was a public gallery. Vincenzo Antonio
Revelli designed and painted a curtain in egg tempera that portrayed
Napoleon as Apollo tending herds of cows during his year of exile
and servitude. According to the ancient myth, Apollo was sent to the
home of Admetus, King of Thessaly, to serve as his cowherd after he
killed Delphyne, the serpent at Delphi. Revelli's message to the rich

and poor Elbans in the audience was that Napoleon, also an exile, was still comparable to a god. He depicted Apollo in a mountainous landscape, surrounded by panoramic views of the kind enjoyed from all the emperor's residences on Elba. Bursting through the clouds at the top of the curtain, there was a horse-drawn chariot, a messenger from the gods announcing the end of Apollo's exile and, prophetically, the end of Napoleon's too.

In France, among those hostile to the restoration of the Bourbons, Napoleon was known at this time as Corporal Violette. Violets were his favourite flower, and his loyal supporters exchanged rings and other tokens decorated with violets in the hope that, like the perennial plant, he would return in the spring. A story circulated that when he was walking in the garden at Fontainebleau, after attempting suicide and before leaving for Elba, he promised to return in the violet season.[59] A popular print featured a bunch of violets, among which were cleverly disguised profiles of Napoleon, Marie Louise and their son. This was a 'puzzle' portrait of the imperial family, dating back to 1810, but after the abdication in April 1814 the profiles hidden among the violets took on new significance for those still hoping that Napoleon would return to power. The print was satirised in the British press. George Cruikshank's *The Peddigree of Corporal Violet* showed a tall plant emerging from a dungheap. At its base is the head of Napoleon as a young republican officer, wearing a hat shaped like a mushroom, decorated with a revolutionary cockade. Further up, a second head appears, inside a sunflower, wearing a crown composed of stamens. Even higher up, the stamens have grown together to form the scraggy neck of a third Napoleon, emaciated and desperate, wearing a much bigger fungus on his head, from which the bunch of violets from the 'puzzle' portrait are growing. Beneath the print's title is the following explanation of Napoleon's rise and fall: 'First as a Consular Toadstool, rising from a Corsican Dunghill, then changing to an Imperial Sun Flower, from that to an Elban Fungus and lastly to a bunch of Violets, which are so disposed as to represent a Whole length Profile of Buonaparte, with a Bust of Maria Louisa, and her son the Prince of Rome.'

Napoleon's last activity on Elba was tree planting. Once the snow had melted and the weather improved, he ordered his guard to make a new garden around their barracks.[60] In just three days, the ground was dug up and levelled, walks laid out and trees planted.[61] The soldiers were given new allotments and told to plant them up ready for spring and an avenue of mulberry trees was planted on the road between Portoferraio and Napoleon's villa at San Martino. But by now all this gardening activity was a facade, intended only as a distraction from the serious plans that were being made to return to France. The sailors repainted HMS *Inconstant* in the colours of a British merchant ship and stocked it with supplies to last 120 men three months at sea.[62] While the soldiers were still working on their garden, a British corvette sailed into the roadstead of Portoferraio. Napoleon was extremely concerned, afraid he had aroused the suspicions of the English spies, but the ship sailed away again on 24 February and the final preparations for leaving Elba went ahead undisturbed.[63] Napoleon dined with General Drouot and discussed the ammunition that was available to load onto the seven ships that would form his convoy to France. He explained to the general that his mother's carriage would be loaded onto one of the vessels, to fool people into thinking it was taking her to Naples. When he had gone through all the practical arrangements, he began to reminisce about his Egyptian campaign. He contrasted the Muslim religion with Christianity. The first he considered sensual, 'promising blue-eyed houris, verdant copses, streams full of milk'. The second was spiritual, focused on love and charity. Of the two, he said he preferred the earthy sensuality of the Muslim religion, adding, 'I was perfectly suited to settle in that country, given the little religion of my army.'[64]

A month after the opening of the theatre, Napoleon's sister Pauline chose it as the venue for a grand carnival ball and Napoleon made a brief appearance. At the same time, he was getting ready to leave Elba.

The horses of the Polish Lancers were brought back to Elba from Pianosa where they had been allowed to run wild; the saddlers were busy and the troops were expectant of some great event. Napoleon believed there were plots against him. He avidly read the English newspapers that Lady Holland sent him. It was clear that his future was a subject of great debate in England, and by no means clear that he would be allowed to stay on Elba. During his last evening on the island, Napoleon strolled on the terrace of the Villa dei Mulini with his mother who afterwards claimed to have told him: 'If Heaven intends that you shall die, my son, and has spared you in this time of ignominious exile, I hope you will not perish by poison but with your sword in your hand!'[65] Perhaps they had discussed his suicide attempt at Fontainebleau. On the morning of Sunday 26 February, Napoleon addressed a crowd that had gathered outside his house, his imminent departure now an open secret. 'I leave you peace. I leave you prosperity. I leave you a clean, fair city. I leave you my roads and trees, for which your children at least will thank me.'[66] In the afternoon, the soldiers worked in their gardens as usual, but when they returned to their barracks they were told to dress for battle.[67] That evening, after dark, as Napoleon boarded HMS *Inconstant*, the Elbans sobbed to see him go.

Hollard followed Napoleon to Paris and became a gardener at Malmaison during the Hundred Days, the period between Napoleon's return to Paris on 20 March 1815 and the second restoration of Louis XVIII on 8 July 1815. Like many of the humbler people devoted to the *ci-devant* Emperor, his loyalty was limitless. As a reviewer for the British journal the *Athenaeum* remarked of Napoleon, 'The men he raised the highest were the first to turn from him when the clouds of misfortune darkened his path: the men for whom the sunshine of his glory had ripened only a moderate harvest prayed for the satisfaction of serving him in exile.'[68] After Napoleon's second fall from power, Hollard tried to follow him into exile on St Helena, but he ended up back on Elba in a house near Portoferraio, where Henry Drummond Wolff, another young man obsessed by Napoleon, at the start of a brilliant diplomatic career, tracked him down in 1854. In his eighties, Hollard told Drummond Wolff all he could remember of Napoleon's time on Elba. In Hollard's last garden, where they sat drinking lemonade and eating strawberries, an ancient geranium had grown into a small tree with a trunk as large as a sapling. Drummond Wolff estimated that it was as old as Hollard and certainly old enough to have been on the island during the stay of Napoleon.[69]

9

The Walled Garden at Waterloo

'Had he been able to take it, this patch of ground might perhaps have given him the world.'
Victor Hugo[1]

On 20 March 1815, the architect Fontaine saw Louis XVIII leave the Tuileries Palace at one in the morning and Napoleon return at nine in the evening.[2] Louis XVIII, infirm, in his sixties, surrounded by old nobles and ancient prejudices, seemed to let the reins of power fall from his hands, sliding rather than falling from the throne. His kindness and affability during the ten months of the First Restoration had won the hearts of many in the palace who cried as he left. As he fled, he gave them his blessing and promised to return soon. Napoleon, who Fontaine believed had been abandoned, betrayed and forced into exile after fifteen brilliant years in power, had returned with extraordinary daring. His supporters hoped that the disastrous Russian campaign and the subsequent invasion of France by the allies which led to his exile would be forgiven. After marching hundreds of kilometres from Cannes, gathering supporters all along the way, he was carried into the Tuileries Palace on the shoulders of an immense crowd, and regained the throne using no force beyond his name. Louis XVIII's supporters were courtiers, keen to recover the titles and privileges stripped from them during the Revolution. Napoleon's supporters were war heroes, many of them honourably wounded, loyal to the chief who had so often led them into victory. Fontaine, who saw himself as a custodian of the Tuileries Palace, watched in amazement the regime change that occurred in a single day. During the twenty-hour interregnum, after Louis XVIII left and before Napoleon arrived, he worried that the crowd alongside the Tuileries gardens crying 'Long Live the King' might come to blows with the crowd in the Place du Carrousel crying 'Long Live the Emperor'. He feared that the palace would be pillaged but his fears were not realised.

Napoleon resumed his intimacy with Fontaine. He told him that after escaping from Elba he could have established himself on Corsica, where 30,000 men would have been willing to support him, but he knew that France needed him. He had no concerns for his personal safety, believing that being fearless and having no fixed habits were the best guarantors of security for any head of state, and that everything else would depend on destiny.[3] To Fontaine, he seemed calm and in perfect health, although others thought him obese and old before his time.[4] Napoleon thought that France was too proud of its recent military glory to submit to a monarch like Louis XVIII who did not lead from the front. He presented himself as a liberator. 'I want to make France happy, restore her rank and make her respected by all world powers.' He set about mobilising the cities and countryside in a national effort that reminded Fontaine of the revolutionary enthusiasm of 1793. New regiments were formed to complement the old. Everywhere, preparations were under way for an immense war. 'Death before shame!' the people cried. The problem was time. During the Revolution there had been three years after 1789 to raise a national guard, impose conscription and send an enormous people's army into battle. Napoleon had just over two months. By June, without resorting to conscription, he had raised an army of some 300,000 soldiers, most of them veterans already deeply loyal to him.

Fontaine was entrusted with designing a festival, the Champ de Mai, on the Champ de Mars where 15,000 deputies from the departments of France, together with contingents of the army, would assemble to accept the new constitution, hastily drafted since Napoleon's return. Despite the financial demands of the impending War of the Seventh Coalition, Napoleon set aside more than 300,000 francs for illuminations during the festival from public funds. He also allowed 66,000 francs for repairs to the Tuileries Palace and a further 28,000 for work on the garden.[5] On 1 June, the weather was beautiful. Napoleon and his brothers processed across the Champ de Mars and were seated outside a pavilion tent, Napoleon on a throne. The new constitution was announced to the assembled crowd of political and military personnel, arranged on stands in the shape of an amphitheatre. On a specially constructed Altar of the Fatherland, Napoleon, his hand on the Bible, swore an oath of loyalty to the new constitution. There was a solemn Mass and *Te Deum*, then the eagle standards were distributed and the emperor reviewed the troops who paraded past. Fontaine thought the festival he had designed the best that had ever taken place on the Champ de Mars, where there had been celebrations of national unity ever since the first Fête de la Fédération was held on the first anniversary of the Fall of the Bastille on 14 July 1790.[6] Napoleon's valet Marchand, who had returned with him from Elba, thought that the spirit of the festival was the same as it had been in 1790 and hoped the successes of the French revolutionary army would be replicated by Napoleon's new forces. On 4 June, there were further celebrations in honour of the newly accepted constitution, with a concert on the terrace of the illuminated Tuileries Palace, dancing and free food and wine in the gardens, and fireworks on the Place de la Concorde. On 12 June, Napoleon left the Élysée Palace at 4 a.m. to place himself at the head of the army ready to invade Belgium.

Three days later the French army crossed the Sambre River at the town of Charleroi and the emperor ordered his generals to take up position on the road to Fleurus before entering the plain that had, almost exactly twenty-one years earlier, been the site of the French revolutionary army's greatest victory against a coalition of British,

Dutch, Austrian and Prussian forces. In the midst of the Terror, on 26 June 1794, under the command of General Jourdan and supervised by Saint-Just, Robespierre's closest friend and a member of the Committee of Public Safety, the French had defeated their opponents at Fleurus and destroyed the Dutch Republic, a victory helped by the first recorded use of a hot-air balloon for military reconnaissance.[7] As Napoleon positioned his troops on the same terrain, he knew that he needed an equally decisive victory for France as the revolutionaries had won in 1794. He had long presented himself as the only man who could bring an end to the revolution and provide stable government, but now he himself was fighting the forces of counter-revolution. The future of France was once again in the balance. If he lost, there would be a second restoration of the Bourbon kings and Louis XVIII would resume the throne which he had so recently and swiftly relinquished. Losing was unimaginable to Napoleon.

After he escaped from Elba and before he reached Paris, Napoleon was declared an outlaw at the Congress of Vienna, and Britain, Russia, Austria and Prussia formed an alliance, each promising to commit 150,000 troops to a coalition army. He knew that his only chance of survival depended on defeating the existing armies of each country separately before they could be reinforced or united. The speed and decisiveness of Napoleon's advance surprised the Duke of Wellington, who was in Brussels in command of the Anglo-Allied army. On the evening of 15 June, Wellington was at the Duchess of Richmond's ball when he learned that Napoleon had crossed the border and had occupied a position between the Anglo-Allied army and the Prussian forces commanded by Gebhard von Blücher, thus dividing the two forces.[8] The next day, Napoleon faced Blücher's army at the Battle of Ligny, thirty-two kilometres south of Waterloo. The Prussian army, ranged on a hillside behind the villages of Saint-Amand and Ligny, could not withstand the French full-frontal assault and started to fall back. Napoleon then sent the right wing of his army, 33,000 men under the command of General Grouchy, to pursue the retreating troops and ensure they did not join a separate body of Prussian forces stationed at Wavre, under the command of General Friedrich von Bülow. Meanwhile he prepared to engage in battle again the next day with Wellington's forces, now in position on the ridge of Mont Saint-Jean, south of the village of Waterloo.

Napoleon and Wellington had never faced each other on a battlefield before. When they did so at Waterloo, both commanders decided that the chateau of Hougoumont, in a hollow just south of the Mont Saint-Jean ridge, was a crucial stronghold to be kept or taken at whatever cost. Hougoumont was a set of buildings, including a chapel, manor house and farm, arranged around two courtyards and mostly enclosed by high garden walls. In 1661 it had been purchased by the Arazola de Onate family, who later added 'Gomont' to their title.[9] Large pine trees grew nearby and the 'Gomont' might have been a reference to the pine resin or *gomme*. As they developed the site, the family added an arboretum and a large garden laid out in the formal French style perfected by André le Nôtre, with strictly geometric box hedges and gravel paths. A hornbeam avenue ran down the south side parallel to the wall which was two metres high. During the Battle of Fleurus in 1794, when French émigré forces opposing the revolutionary army had occupied Hougoumont, they found it to be a fully functioning farm, with all kinds of agricultural equipment and livestock.[10] At that time they knocked loopholes in the garden walls so that they could fire at the enemy without being seen. Some of the loopholes were still there when Wellington sent his forces to occupy Hougoumont twenty-one years later.

Colonel Macdonnell, commanding the Light Companies of the Coldstream Guards, ordered his soldiers to knock new loopholes in the garden walls as soon as they took possession of the chateau. Wellington arrived for an early-morning visit on 18 June to see how preparations for the defence of the site were progressing. He reinforced the two hundred Coldstream Guards with eight hundred soldiers from the Nassau Regiment, ordered to garrison the chateau and surrounding woods. Other troops were added until the Hougoumont area was guarded by approximately 1,200 troops, most of them German-speaking, from the King's Hanoverian regiments. The Earl of Uxbridge, nominated as Wellington's second in command, asked him to explain the battle plan in case something happened to the Duke and he had to take over. 'Keep Hougoumont' was Wellington's response.[11] His strategy was defensive. He hoped to withstand the battery from Napoleon's forces until the Prussian reinforcements from Wavre arrived. Wellington was playing for time. Soon after the Anglo-Allied troops occupied Hougoumont some French soldiers arrived, either cavalry, with a definite mission to take the stronghold, or opportunistic scavengers looking for food. But they were too late: Hougoumont had been firmly claimed for the other side.

The night before the battle saw heavy rainfall and thunderstorms. In the morning, Napoleon judged it necessary to wait until the ground had started to dry out before beginning an artillery attack, to avoid moving heavy guns through thick wet mud. He planned a head-on full-frontal attack on the British infantry. He inspected his troops outside La Belle Alliance, an inn just south of the battle lines that had become the French army headquarters, and as he rode through the ranks they greeted him with loud cries of '*Vive l'Empereur!*'. Then he retired south to the farm of Rossomme with his Imperial Guard, on a hill from where he could spread out his maps and watch the battle before him. Next he instructed his brother Jérôme to attack Hougoumont as a diversionary tactic before the start of the main battle; he thought Wellington would weaken the centre of his army by sending more troops to defend Hougoumont.[12] Unlike Wellington, Napoleon had not seen the chateau up close and had certainly had not been inside its high walls. Although his valet Marchand implied that it was easy to watch the attack on Hougoumont from the Rossomme farm, it is much more likely that the chateau was hidden behind trees.[13] Marchand was keen to protect Napoleon from criticism and did not want to admit that rather than being able to watch and direct the attack on Hougoumont from a distance, all Napoleon could see was a heavily wooded valley rising towards the ridge of Mont Saint-Jean.

Wellington came back again to Hougoumont around 11 a.m. and told Colonel Macdonnell to 'defend the post to the last extremity'.[14] Some of the soldiers doubted that this was possible with only 1,200 men to defend it, but Wellington insisted he could rely on the colonel. The first shot of the battle came from English artillery firing on a column of French infantry from Jérôme Bonaparte's 6th Division at around 11.30 a.m. General Baudin's 1st Brigade then engaged in hand-to-hand fighting in the woods around Hougoumont. For approximately forty-five minutes, every single tree was fought for. Painfully advancing through the undergrowth and across uneven ground, the French troops eventually reached the northern edge of the wood and faced a ditch and a dense, quickset hawthorn hedge, which hid the garden wall behind it. Between the garden wall and the hedge there was a strip of land known as the small orchard. When the French pushed through the hedge and saw the wall for the first time, about thirty metres away, one witness remembered, 'A deadly fire bursting forth from the loopholes and platforms along the garden wall, which was parallel to and about thirty yards distance from the hedge, laid prostrate the leading files. Those who came up in rapid succession were staggered by the sudden and unexpected appearance of this little fortress!'[15] The soldiers fell, shot down in the small orchard by bullets fired through the loopholes. General Baudin was among the dead. Some French forces made it into the large orchard next to the formal garden, which had once been the arboretum, but they were pushed back by the defending Anglo-Allied forces. It proved impossible to scale the wall without breaching it. The French soldiers who made it from the hedge across the open ground and started climbing the wall were easily shot as soon as their heads and upper bodies appeared at the top, targets for the many muskets waiting for them in the formal garden. A French grenadier climbed on the back of one of his comrades and aimed his musket over the wall, but before he could discharge it, he was shot in the face by a Coldstream Guard.[16] Bodies began piling up alongside the wall in the small orchard, which became known as the Killing Ground.

A second French attack was launched at 12.30 on the west side of the chateau. Soye's 2nd Brigade 6th Division entered the wood behind Baudin's Brigade. These reinforcements meant that Colonel Cubières could lead the new offensive on Hougoumont. The Coldstream Guards under Colonel Macdonnell were driven back northwards until they began retreating through Hougoumont's north gate, which comprised two wide solid wooden doors that could be secured from the inside by a metal crossbar. Macdonnell himself led the drive to close the gates. Despite fierce fighting from around thirty attacking French soldiers, some of whom managed to get inside the gates first, they were eventually closed and all the French intruders were hunted down and killed, except for a young drummer boy, whose life was spared. Wellington later attributed the successful defence of Hougoumont to the closing of the north gates, a scene celebrated in many artistic representations of the Battle of Waterloo.[17]

Around 1 p.m. the main battle began on the ridge Mont Saint-Jean. Napoleon aimed eighty guns at the Anglo-Allied left flank, thrusting towards Brussels, and d'Erlon's corps advanced across the fields to the east of the main road, but were pushed back, sustaining around 7,000 casualties and losing two eagle standards.[18] By 2 p.m. a third French attack on Hougoumont was under way, even though Napoleon had only ever intended to cause a diversion from the main focus of the attack when he sent Jérôme to assault the chateau. The fight over Hougoumont turned into a battle within the battle, with the French committing more and more troops to trying to break through the walled enclosure. Soon controlling Hougoumont stood for wider victory on the battlefield and in Europe. The future of France depended on conquering a single walled garden. This time the south gate was attacked. The French chopped down trees and crashed the gate, which was smaller than the north gate, managing to enter Hougoumont for the first time. They were shot at from the windows of the farm buildings so fast, so accurately, that their bodies piled up in the courtyard: French soldiers streaming in behind tripped over their dead or wounded comrades. Those who weren't killed were driven back out through the gate by bayonet.

The 9th Division of Marshal Foy's troops now began a new attack on the great orchard. As it was still proving impossible to push through the hedge or scale the wall, Napoleon ordered a howitzer battery near the south-east corner of the garden and fired incendiary 'carcass' projectiles at the farm buildings.[19] The 1st Foot Guards tried to over-turn the howitzer but could not do so before Hougoumont was on fire. Wounded Anglo-Allied soldiers were sheltering inside buildings that now burst into flames and there were horrific scenes as they dragged themselves, despite their injuries, back into the courtyard, rolling on the ground in agony to try and put out the flames consuming their uniforms and injured flesh. Corporal James Graham of the Coldstream Guards, who had helped close the north gate, asked for and received permission to leave his post in the firing line in the garden, because he knew that his wounded brother, Joseph, was inside one of the burning buildings and he wanted to carry him to safety.[20] Taking advantage of the conflagration, the French once again broke into Hougoumont, this time through a small side door into the upper courtyard. An English battalion drove them back out. Both sides took prisoners, but Hougoumont still did not fall to the French. When Wellington saw from afar that the chateau was on fire, he sent a message repeating his instructions to hold it at all cost:

I see that the fire has communicated from the Hay Stack to the Roof of the chateau. You must however still keep your men in those parts to which the fire does not reach. Take care that no men are lost by the falling-in of the Roof or Floors. After they

have both fallen in, occupy the ruined walls inside of the Garden;
particularly if it should be possible for the enemy to pass through
the Embers in the inside of the House.[21]

Carrying out these orders, officers stood at the doors to the burning
buildings, preventing the soldiers defending them from leaving until
the last moments before they collapsed. The chapel caught fire. Inside
there were wounded soldiers and a large fifteenth-century wooden
crucifix. The flames reached the feet of the figure of Christ and badly
charred them, but then receded. For the wounded, propped up against
the sanctuary's whitewashed walls, this seemed like a miracle.[22] Ensign
George Standen of the 3rd Guards wrote to his relatives afterwards:
'The anecdote of the fire only burning to the feet of the Cross is
perfectly true, which in so superstitious a country made a great sensa-
tion.'[23] By around 3.30 p.m., the last serious French attack on the
chateau was over, although skirmishes continued throughout the rest
of the afternoon.

It was hard, if not impossible, for Napoleon to see what was
happening at Hougoumont through his telescope from the farm of
Rossomme. As he impatiently scanned the horizon, he suddenly
noticed something happening in the east. A body of troops had
appeared near the village of Chapelle-Saint-Lambert, seven kilometres
away. From a distance, Napoleon could not tell whose troops they
were. They were only about four and a half kilometres from the
Prussian troops at Wavre. It was vital to find out the allegiance of these
troops that had suddenly appeared so close to the battlefield. Napoleon
sent General Bernard, his aide-de-camp, with an escort to discover
more details. His only hope was that they were a detachment of the
troops he had sent to pursue the Prussians, returning now to help
their French comrades. Bernard soon returned to tell him that the
troops on the horizon were Prussian infantry. The only remaining
uncertainty was their strength. Was the approaching force merely the
remains of the army Napoleon had already defeated at Ligny, or a new

and much larger Prussian army? It turned out to be the latter, 30,000 soldiers under the command of General Bülow. The reinforcements Wellington was waiting for had arrived.

Because Napoleon had failed to take Hougoumont, when he sent his cavalry into the main battle, his horses and soldiers came under fire from the chateau's defenders, still aiming through the loopholes of the garden wall. This concentrated Napoleon's cavalry at the centre of the battlefield, making it an easier target for enemy artillery.[24] Eventually, in desperation, knowing that he was now substantially outnumbered, Napoleon committed his Imperial Guard to the battle, hoping to break the line of the Anglo-Allied forces. But as the Imperial Guard approached the slopes of Mont Saint-Jean, Maitland's 1st Guards Brigade, which had been hidden in dead ground behind the ridge, stood up and overwhelmed them.[25] Around three hundred of the Imperial Guard were slaughtered. The rest fell back, retreating past the walls of Hougoumont. The French had lost approximately 5,000 men trying to take the stronghold. In failing to take that single patch of ground, they had lost the wider Battle of Waterloo.

As dusk fell on the battlefield, the chaotic exodus of soldiers began, many of them walking wounded. Johannes (Jean) Hornn, the Dutch driver who had accompanied Napoleon on his campaigns since 1804, managed to drive the emperor's carriage as far as Genappe, thirteen kilometres from Waterloo, where he lost two fingers (some claim a whole arm) trying to defend it in the scrum of fleeing soldiers.[26] The emperor had already abandoned the carriage. The Prussian commander Blücher claimed to have seen him jump out, throw himself onto a horse without his sword and gallop away as his bicorne hat fell off. 'His hat on the battlefield is worth 40,000 men,' Wellington said of Napoleon before Waterloo, but it was no longer true.[27] When Blücher arrived and learned that Hornn was the driver, he abused him, instead of ordering his wounds to be dressed. Hatred for Napoleon and all associated with him overran the scene of his defeat. The carriage had been Napoleon's portable office, bedroom, dressing room, kitchen and dining room. It was exquisitely fitted out with telescopes, an atlas and an inkwell. It held a mattress and bedding and shaving and grooming equipment, as well as dining plates, cutlery, candlesticks, gold tea and coffee pots and a sugar basin. And the carriage was also a travelling treasure chest, containing diamonds and cash that Napoleon had no time to pack before fleeing on horseback. The Prussians sent the carriage to London as a war trophy. It was exhibited in the Egyptian Hall of Mr Bullock's museum of natural curiosities in Piccadilly, and hundreds of thousands of visitors enjoyed climbing into it and sitting where Napoleon had sat. Bullock claimed to have tracked down Hornn, whom he employed to stand beside Napoleon's mobile home giving a guided tour to the spectators. Bullock also published *The Narrative of Jean Hornn, Military Coachman to Napoleon Bonaparte*, assuring readers in the preface that Hornn was not an impostor, but a genuine eyewitness to extraordinary events. On the orders of the Prince Regent, the carriage then toured the country, allowing even more people a chance to gloat over the fall of Napoleon.

In the immediate aftermath of the battle, wounded soldiers from both sides lay in pain among the dead in the garden and orchards of Hougoumont. The next day, Private Matthew Clay and his corporal went back inside the walled enclosure and found the bodies of some of their comrades, still recognisable despite having been burnt to death. They began moving the wounded to Brussels. New fires were lit to burn, or in some cases to finish burning, the bodies. They were collected from the formal garden, covered in mud and already stripped naked by pillagers. The walls of the ruined buildings were pockmarked with bullet holes. The trees and hedges were broken and destroyed. The terrace had been smashed. Captain Mercer, visiting Hougoumont the day after the battle, described what survived of the garden in positive and romantic terms:

... the garden was an ordinary one, but pretty-long straight walks of turf overshadowed by fruit-trees, and between these beds of vegetables, the whole enclosed by a tolerably high brick-wall. The leaves were green, roses and other flowers bloomed forth in all their sweetness, and the very turf when crushed under my feet smelt sweet and fresh.[28]

In July, however, an Englishman, a very early battlefield tourist, gave a grim account of how Hougoumont looked just weeks after Waterloo:

Every tree in the wood at Hougoumont is pierced with balls; in one alone I counted the holes where upwards of thirty had lodged ... huge piles of human ashes, dreadfully offensive in smell, are all that now remain of the heroes who fought and fell upon this fatal spot ... the poor countryman who, with his wife and family, occupied the gardener's house still inhabits a miserable shed among the deserted ruins, and pointed out with superstitious reverence the little chapel belonging to the chateau which stood alone uninjured in the midst of the blackened walls and fallen beams ... A more mournful scene than this ruined chateau and wood cannot possibly be imagined.[29]

The figure of the countryman, or gardener, became one of the many legends of Waterloo. Before the battle, Hougoumont was owned by the Chevalier de Louville, an octogenarian living in Nivelle, who rented the chateau to a tenant farmer, Antoine Dumonceau. The formal garden and vegetable gardens were cared for by Jean-Joseph Carlier, who lived in the house by the south gate.[30] The gardener's house was one of the few buildings at Hougoumont to survive the fighting and fire. Some accounts of the battle claim Carlier was present throughout and afterwards wandered around the scene of devastation, horrified and disorientated. Others claim that his small daughter remained with

the gardener for part of the battle until they were led out of the chateau
to safety, together or separately, by Coldstream Guards. In none of
the accounts was the gardener's wife present.

After the battle, the Chevalier de Louville decided to sell
Hougoumont. It was bought by Count François-Xavier de Robiano
for 40,000 francs, but was still occupied by a tenant farmer. For years,
tourists came to the battleground, picking up mementoes and
collecting anecdotes from local people claiming to remember Waterloo.
In 1861, Victor Hugo spent two months exploring the battlefield and
the remains of Hougoumont, which was once again a functioning
farm. He stayed at the Hôtel des Colonnes at Mont Saint-Jean,
immersing himself in the 'mournful field' and imaginatively reconstructing the bloodshed.[31] During this time Hugo met a middle-aged
grey-haired local woman, living in the gardener's house inside the
walls of the chateau, who claimed to be the daughter of the gardener
at the time of Waterloo. She told him that she remembered being with
her father at Hougoumont as a very young child in the midst of the
fighting. Hugo recorded the name of her dead father as William Van
Kylsom and wrote him into his account of the Battle of Waterloo in
Les Misérables. Records show that there was a gardener called Van
Custem, not Van Kylsom, who lived at Hougoumont with his wife
and four children, but as he moved to the chateau only in 1823 none
of them could have been at Hougoumont during the battle. The woman
Hugo spoke to either had a false memory of her childhood, or was
an impostor.[32] Hugo's novel was published in 1862. Fourteen years
later, in 1876, an elderly widow calling herself Madame Van Custem
came to England to stay with a Captain Kerrish in Gedelston, Norfolk.
She repeated a version of the story that had been told to Hugo to the
local newspaper, the Norwich Argus, and it was reprinted in newspapers
all over England:

Madame Van Custem, now the farmer of Hougoumont, was at
that time the gardener's daughter at the Chateau of Hougoumont,

and aged five years. Her father, the gardener, stuck to his post,
retaining his little daughter as company. The chateau itself was
occupied by the British Guards, and was throughout the whole
of the memorable 18th June, 1815, the grand and principal
object of attack. Madame has a very vivid recollection of the
kindness of our soldiers, who treated her as a pet, and kept
throwing her bits of biscuit out of their haversacks wherewith
to amuse her. At last the chateau was shelled in the afternoon
and set fire to by Jérôme Bonaparte. Madame was then conducted
by a sergeant of the Guards to a back gate, and her retreat secured
into the forest of Soignies.[33]

The woman who visited Captain Kerrish could have been the same
or different from the one who told her story to Hugo. For the novelist,
the idea of the gardener who witnessed the fall of Napoleon mattered
more than checking the source or truth of the story that had sparked
his imagination. At Hougoumont Hugo was deeply impressed, like
many others before and since, by the resurgence of the natural world
in a small space that had contained a man-made hell. He described
Hougoumont as 'a fateful place, the initial obstruction, the first resistance encountered at Waterloo by that great tree-feller of Europe whose
name was Napoleon: the first knot under the fall of his axe'.[34] In Hugo's
mind the chateau became part of a tree that Napoleon could not fell.
He described a blossoming pear tree espaliered along the chapel wall
inside the yard that Napoleon only dreamed of conquering. In the
chapel, Hugo saw the charred feet of the wooden figure of Christ on
the cross. He imagined the gardener sending away his family to keep
them safe but staying behind himself to take care of Hougoumont,
hiding in a cellar as the fighting began. He imagined the gardener was
discovered and forced to fetch water from the well in the yard for the
thirsty soldiers. He imagined that the gardener was the last man to
draw water from that well before it became a tomb for the three
hundred bodies thrown into it, some of them not yet dead. In *Les*

Misérables he writes, 'And it seems that, on the night after the burial, feeble voices were heard calling from the well.'[35]

Hugo wandered around the garden. He could see that it had once been a 'seigneurial' garden in the old formal French style, but he found it full of gooseberry bushes and overgrown by brambles. He counted forty-three of the stone balustrades on the terrace still intact, but others were lying on the ground, marked by bullet holes, and one stood on its stem 'like a broken leg'. Hugo walked in the orchard and counted thirty-eight loopholes in the garden wall enclosing it. He thought the wall looked ready for renewed fighting. And yet the orchard was 'as susceptible to the month of May as any other'.[36] There were buttercups and daisies and high grass, carthorses grazing and washing hanging out to dry on ropes suspended between the trees. One frail apple tree had been bandaged, like a wounded soldier, with a poultice of straw and clay. It was not the only ailing or dying tree. 'Nearly all the apple trees are decrepit with age. There is not one which does not have its bullet or biscayen ball. The skeletons of dead trees abound in this orchard. Crows fly in their branches, and at the far end is a wood full of violets.'[37]

There was deep irony and melancholy in the carpet of violets, the symbol of hope for Napoleon's return from Elba, that Hugo saw or imagined in the wood beyond Hougoumont. As he understood it, Napoleon's defeat at Waterloo was also the definitive defeat of the French Revolution. 'the mounted Robespierre was unseated,' he claimed at the end of the chapter in *Les Misérables* entitled 'Is Waterloo to be Considered Good?'[38] Robespierre never fought in a battle, might not even have known how to ride a horse, and almost certainly never owned one. There could not have been a greater contrast between Robespierre, the academic lawyer whose name became synonymous with the revolutionary Terror, and the soldier Napoleon who had devoted himself to France's glory. 'If glory lies in the sword made sceptre, the Empire was glory itself,' Hugo wrote.[39] Yet Napoleon owed his opportunities and all his power to the disruption caused by the

Revolution of 1789: when he finally lost everything at Waterloo, what remained of the Revolution fell with him.

In Paris news from the battlefield arrived slowly. On the morning of Sunday 18 June 1815, cannon fire announced the French victory at the Battle of Ligny two days earlier. The news from the front line was jubilant: on the very same ground where the French revolutionary army won the Battle of Fleurus in 1794, Napoleon had triumphed over Prussian forces, driving them back to Namur and Brussels. 'The wind of victory, which for a long time had not blown for us, seemed to have returned in our favour,' the architect Fontaine wrote in his diary.[40] While Parisians waited for more detailed reports, they started imagining a bright future and a glorious new horizon for France. For twenty-four hours or more, Fontaine dared to hope that the palace for the King of Rome might still arise on the banks of the Seine, that Napoleon's power would rebound stronger than ever. These illusions were soon shattered as reports of the defeat at Waterloo arrived. Fontaine was woken in the middle of the night on 21 June, and told that the emperor was on his way back to the Élysée Palace. He hastily ordered the return of the locks and items of furniture that had been sent away for repair, and went straight to the palace, where he saw Napoleon and Grand Marshal Marchand return at around 6 a.m., in a shabby postal carriage with almost no entourage.

To Fontaine the disaster seemed supernatural, beyond human comprehension. How was it possible that such an enterprising man as Napoleon, who had won so many formidable victories, who had even returned from exile and resumed his title and throne and raised a new army, was so utterly and comprehensively defeated? Fontaine understood that Napoleon had lost everything and was now a fugitive in Paris. He noticed insensitivity, almost indifference, in his former master's expression and speech that might have been taken for insanity. His prestige was gone, he no longer seemed an extraordinary man, and the only sentiment he inspired in Fontaine was regret at seeing

such a famous man shamefully survive his fall.[41] As more and more
of the wounded followed Napoleon back to Paris and described what
had happened at Waterloo, the city convulsed with panic.

Napoleon accepted that his political life was over. He wanted to
abdicate, as he had hoped to do the previous year, in favour of the
King of Rome. But this scheme, which had been rejected after his first
abdication, did not prevail after his second either. A provisional
government of five – Fouché, Carnot, Caulaincourt, Grenier and
Quinette – took over as head of state awaiting the return of Louis
XVIII. Fouché had been Minister of Police when Napoleon expelled
the Directory, which also had five members, at the beginning of his
rise to power in the coup of 18 Brumaire in 1799. Carnot had been
a member of the Directory. Both men had worked closely with
Napoleon since. They had seen his immense power come from
nowhere and disappear again after only fifteen years.

The ex-emperor decided to leave the Élysée Palace at 1 p.m. on
Sunday 25 June, exactly a week after Waterloo. Public turmoil around
the residence was increasing. He wanted to avoid attracting attention,
so he left without an escort in a borrowed carriage that waited for him
at the garden gate on the Champs-Élysées. His Swiss valet Jean-Abram
Noverraz and Comte Henri Gatien Bertrand, who had accompanied
him to Egypt, were with him. He climbed into his own carriage only
after passing through the city gates.[42] He went to Malmaison, where
he once had so many dreams of glory.[43] Josephine had been dead for
over a year, but the house was still fully furnished, inhabited by her
staff and made ready for him by his stepdaughter Hortense. He arrived
around 1.30 p.m. with an Imperial Guard of three hundred men and
entered his old rooms. Napoleon's old friend, the distinguished mathematician Gaspard Monge, came to visit him the day he arrived at
Malmaison. The ex-emperor confided that, without an army and an
empire, only the sciences could make a strong impression on him
now. He had been reading a volume of Alexander von Humboldt's
Voyage to the Equinoctial Regions of the New Continent, and was

planning a new scholarly career. But simply learning what others had already done would not be enough for him:

> I want to make a new career and leave behind work and discoveries worthy of me. I need a companion who can bring me rapidly up to date with the current state of the sciences. Then we will travel the New Continent together, from Canada to Cape Horn, and during that immense voyage, we will study all the great phenomena of the physical world.[44]

Monge, aged sixty-nine, gallantly volunteered to accompany Napoleon, as he had done to Egypt, but his offer was kindly declined. He was too old for such a long voyage. Three years later Monge died, stripped of his honours and excluded from the institute because his association with Napoleon overshadowed all his achievements.

Later in the day, General Becker arrived at Malmaison to assume command of the Imperial Guard, charged by the provisional government with guaranteeing Napoleon's safety. Hortense panicked when she saw Becker arriving because she thought he had come to arrest her stepfather. He reassured her that this was not the case and was shown into the library to meet him. The library was exactly as Napoleon had left it when he divorced Josephine in 1810. Afterwards, Josephine insisted that none of the books, which she treated like relics, should be moved; she dusted them herself and allowed very few people even to enter the library, where some of the volumes still had bookmarks keeping her ex-husband's place. Becker treated Napoleon with the greatest respect. He explained that he had accepted the role imposed on him on the condition that he was appointed only to protect, not to guard or spy on, Napoleon. The ex-emperor was moved by Becker's loyalty and devotion. They walked together in the garden, discussing the mood of Paris, news of the army, the expectations of the provisional government.[45] Night fell as they walked. Napoleon explained his plan to emigrate to America.

He was waiting for the government to provide him with passports and two frigates at Rochefort.

The 26th of June was a very hot day. Napoleon spent it at Malmaison reminiscing about the past. He walked up and down with his hands behind his back in what had once been his personal garden, just outside his library. The garden was a large rectangle that had been demarcated by four alleys of lime trees with a vast star-shaped flower bed at the centre. In 1815 only one of the alleys survived, leading from Napoleon's library to the octagonal garden pavilion that he called his work cabin. It was a short walk he had often done in the past, alone or in company, but this time there were no tame gazelles, like the ones brought from Egypt, no pink flamingos like those that once stood in the reeds of the shallow ponds. He asked Hortense to walk around Malmaison's grounds with him. They lingered among the exotic trees that Josephine had always insisted on planting herself: honey locusts, cedars of Lebanon, Louisiana cypresses, Japanese varnish trees, Japanese pagodas, Double Belle Fleur apple trees and tulip trees. They visited Josephine's grand greenhouse and remembered her, surrounded by colour and fragrance, checking on her tropical flowers every day. Outside in the flower beds there were tulips, hyacinths, dahlias and 250 different roses. Over and over again Napoleon exclaimed, 'How beautiful Malmaison is!' Then he added, 'Poor Josephine. I cannot get used to living here without her. I seem always to see her emerging from an avenue of trees, gathering one of the roses she loved so much. She was the most graceful woman I ever saw.'[46] To the servant who had been Josephine's first gentleman-in-waiting he remarked, 'She wanted everything.'[47]

Two of Napoleon's mistresses visited him at Malmaison to say goodbye: Marie Walewska, who brought her son to see his natural father for the last time, and Françoise-Marie Pellapra.[48] Napoleon's brothers came too. Fontaine also tried. He had noticed that before the ex-emperor left Paris he was completely apathetic and indifferent to the momentous events he had caused. His defeat seemed to have deranged him. But perhaps madness, Fontaine speculated, was all that was stopping him from killing himself. Aware of what he owed Napoleon, Fontaine went to Malmaison, not out of curiosity, but because his conscience would not allow him to abandon, as so many others had, his former patron and friend in his fallen circumstances. He arrived around 11 a.m. and was told Napoleon was still asleep. Waiting for him to wake, Fontaine wandered around the house and gardens, talking to the servants, whose accounts of Napoleon's state of mind only added to his sadness and anxiety. Haunted by the past, Fontaine found memories reborn with every step he took at Malmaison, once the cradle of Napoleon's grandeur, but now the tomb. He walked there for two hours, but by 1 p.m. the ex-emperor had still not appeared. Worried that he would be prevented from returning to Paris if he left much later, Fontaine went away with a heavy heart, but almost relieved not to have seen Napoleon. When he reached the Neuilly Bridge he found it barricaded: the invading coalition forces had reached Saint-Denis. With great difficulty, Fontaine passed back into the centre of Paris and never saw Napoleon again.

In his *Mémoires d'Outre-Tombe*, published posthumously in 1849 and 1850, Chateaubriand imagined Napoleon at Malmaison after Waterloo. He pictured him alone 'in those gardens where the feet of the mob once scarred those sandy paths', walking among brambles and overgrown grass. The exotic trees would have been languishing uncared for, the black swans would no longer have been gliding on the ponds, the aviary would have been empty of exotic birds. The birds, Chateaubriand fantasised, had flown back to their native lands, some to the island of St Helena, where they awaited the ex-emperor:

At the sight of those abandoned gardens, those uninhabited rooms, those galleries faded from entertainments, those rooms in which music and song had ceased, Napoleon could review his career: he could ask himself whether a little more moderation might have maintained his happiness.[49]

Chateaubriand emphasised that it was not foreigners or enemies who banished Napoleon, but Frenchmen, his friends, asking him 'to quit the soil over which he had poured glory as much as suffering'. He was completely deserted, 'misfortune merely returned him to the wilderness that was his life'. Thinking about Napoleon preparing in the gardens of Malmaison for his second exile, Chateaubriand drew a contrast between him and George Washington. When he relinquished power, Washington had been able to retire to the fields of Virginia without any of Napoleon's regrets. Washington simply went back to his modest habits because he had never 'elevated himself above the happiness of the ploughmen he had liberated'. But Napoleon had promoted himself to, then fallen from, such a great height that everything in his life was overthrown.

The provisional government wanted Napoleon to leave Malmaison for Rochefort and to set sail from there as soon as possible. Initially, he refused to do so until his passports for America arrived. He feared being taken prisoner in Rochefort. He finally agreed to leave on the morning of 29 June. He dressed in his uniform and visited once more the bedroom in which Josephine had died. A carriage was brought round to the side of the chateau. Napoleon said goodbye to his friends and family. Hortense was too deeply distressed to go outside with him, but she watched from the threshold as he took a last rapid look about him before stepping into the carriage.[50] Later an alley of laurels was planted to the right of the main courtyard. It was called the Alley of Exile and at the end a stone marked Napoleon's final footstep at Malmaison. The carriage went via a back road. Napoleon insisted on stopping at Rambouillet, where he was recognised and greeted with cries of 'Vive l'Empereur!'. He had the park and chateau opened at sunset.[51] He was indisposed and disheartened.

During the five days that Napoleon was at Rochefort, the telegraph between the port city and Paris was in constant use. The provisional government was still pressing him to set sail, but it was unclear which ship he should go on and what his destination would be. On 8 July he went to sleep on the *Saale*.[52] But he was very uncomfortable on board the French frigate, so decided on the 12th to go and stay on the small island close to Rochefort, the Île d'Aix. There were now British ships guarding the bay, and as he disembarked he was greeted by a crowd lining the shore, begging him not to abandon France. He moved into the commanding officer's headquarters, the best house on the island, the construction of which he had ordered during his visit to view the island's fortifications in 1808. In the walled garden there is a magnificent tree, an ash grafted onto an elm. A recent commemorative plaque reads:

NAPOLÉON
Jardinier intermittent capable de greffer un frêne sur un orme.
(Intermittent gardener, capable of grafting an ash tree on an elm.)[53]

If Napoleon grafted the tree himself, he did so either on his first visit to the Île d'Aix, when he was close to the height of his power, or on his second when he was in limbo, waiting to go into exile. He would have known about grafting from classical sources such as Virgil and Pliny, from his youthful experience in his father's mulberry nursery on Corsica, from Josephine's horticultural circle and his own scientific colleagues at the institute. The choice of graft, though, is not a common one: the purpose can only have been to prove that it could be done. He might have planted the tree in celebration of man's power over nature in 1808, or as a distraction from the vicissitudes of fortune in 1815.

Napoleon's brother Joseph came to visit him on the Île d'Aix the day after he arrived, offering to give himself up to the British pretending to be the ex-emperor. Napoleon embraced him, rejected his generous proposal, and told him to leave and look after himself. Joseph made it to America where he lived the life in exile that Napoleon could have had if he had been prepared to change places. While he was still deliberating about what to do, a fledgling sparrow flew in through the open window and beat its body against the walls. General Baron Gourgaud, who had fought at Waterloo and remained loyal to Napoleon after his abdication, caught it. 'There is enough unhappiness in the world!' Napoleon said. 'Set it free!' Gourgaud did so and they watched as the bird found the window again and flew off in the direction of the British ships.[54] Later the same day Napoleon wrote a letter to the Prince Regent, sitting in a first-floor room that overlooked the garden and the grafted elm and ash tree.

Royal Highness,

Prey to the factions which are dividing my country, and the enmity of the greatest powers of Europe, I have ended my political career, and I come, like Themistocles to 'sit at the hearth' of the British people. I place myself under the protection of their laws, which I ask of Your Royal Highness as the most powerful, most constant and most generous of my enemies.

Rochefort, the 13th of July, 1815.[55]

Napoleon knew the story of the ancient Greek general Themistocles from his reading of Plutarch's *Lives*. The life of a hero from a family 'too obscure to further his reputation' attracted him. He had a certain amount in common with Themistocles, whose 'ambition surpassed all men', who was very fond of honour and on good terms with the common people of Athens because he memorised all their names. Now he hoped he would be as fortunate in exile as Themistocles who made a new life for himself in Asia Minor, became a governor and died of natural causes. Napoleon never suggested that he could have a new political life in England, but he did think he could live peacefully and happily in a country whose laws, army and culture he had always respected. For these reasons, early on the morning of 15 July, he went on board the brig *Épervier* and surrendered to the English. He was transferred to HMS *Bellerophon*, a British ship that had fought in the Battle of the Nile, and was taken to the English south coast, but not allowed to disembark at Plymouth, where huge crowds gathered to see him, flocking round the ship in small boats. Soon afterwards, the idea of sending him to the remote South Atlantic island of St Helena, the destination that had horrified him on Elba, was revived.

'Men anticipate the throne of the world, and perceive Saint Helena,' Victor Hugo wrote of the gap between what Napoleon expected from Waterloo and what happened.[56] While the ex-emperor went into an unwelcome and uncomfortable exile in the South Atlantic, 'the sixty thousand men who fell at Waterloo rotted calmly, and something of their peace spread over the world. The Congress of Vienna converted it into the treaties of 1815, and Europe called that the restoration.' Even when in exile, Hugo claimed, Napoleon continued to terrify the European kings because of 'how much of the revolutionary there was in him'.[57]

At Waterloo today there is a campaign to replant the significant trees and hedges that existed at the time of the battle, which were either destroyed in the fighting or subsequently cleared to create arable land. Replanting would make it easier for visitors to understand what happened in the walled garden and orchard of Hougoumont, the small patch of land that Napoleon needed to conquer to change the course of European history. Funds have been raised and the planting proposals have been approved by the Intercommunale Bataille de Waterloo 1815, which now owns Hougoumont, and by Kléber Rossillon, the French company which operates the site, but planning permission from the Walloon Region is not forthcoming. Nevertheless, in the hope that their replanting project will ultimately prevail, those involved with the charity Project Hougoumont have collaborated with classicist and garden writer Robin Lane Fox and plant scientist Professor Barrie Juniper of Oxford University, to identify and source old varieties of apple tree to replant at Hougoumont. The trees are rare ones that were common in Brabant and northern France in the eighteenth century.

They are being grafted by a specialist in Kent ready for transplanting in 2023. Another English firm, Majestic Trees of Harpenden, will supply the forest trees and hedgerow plants; and Penelope Milburn, a former director of Project Hougoumont, has grown sweet chestnuts (*Castanea sativa*) from seeds from one of the three old trees by the south gate of the chateau, thought to date back to the original wood.[58] All three of the old trees have been struck by lightning; two of them are dead though still standing, their massive skeletons stark against the sky. One is still alive despite storm damage. There is a fourth, smaller, much younger tree, planted by the 8th Duke of Wellington in the 1970s. In 2016, these trees outside the south gate of Hougoumont were declared European Trees of Peace and Memory, by the Fondation Wallonne pour la Conservation des Habitats.

Wellington had an elm at Waterloo. It was situated south-west of the road between Genappe and Brussels, and the Duke made it his command post for much of the battle. The elm did not long survive the souvenir hunters who crowded to Waterloo after 1815.[59] Stripped of its bark and foliage the tree died and was felled in 1818. But before this happened, it was drawn by the teenager Anna Children, on a trip to the battlefield with her father John George Children, an entomologist and librarian in the Department of Antiquities at the British Museum. When he heard that Wellington's elm was to be cut down, Children purchased the timber and had it made into furniture and other mementoes, including a Chippendale chair for George IV and a quaich for Walter Scott. Children's daughter grew up to become the botanist and pioneering photographer Anna Atkins. Her youthful drawing of Wellington's elm, the first two metres or so of its trunk bare like a bone, the sparse branches above struggling to rejuvenate, was purchased by Queen Victoria, who ordered a monument to the British dead to be built in the Brussels Cemetery in Evere in 1890. The monument to the French dead at Hougoumont was inaugurated in 1913 on the initiative of the Belgian novelist and historian Hector

Fleischmann, president of Les Amis de Waterloo. It is inscribed with words spoken by Napoleon remembering the battle in exile on St Helena:

La terre paraissait orgueilleuse de porter tant de braves.[60]
(The earth seemed proud to carry so many brave men.)

10

Last Garden

'The glory of Napoleon grew in a night, like Jonah's vine,
and within a night it withered.'
Charlotte Brontë, 'The Death of Napoleon'[1]

During Napoleon's voyage to St Helena, sailors on HMS *Northumberland* caught an enormous shark and hauled it onto the deck. Curious about the ugly, dangerous fish, Napoleon went too close and only narrowly escaped serious injury.[2] Afterwards it amused him to nickname Admiral Cockburn, in charge of conveying him to the remote volcanic island, 1,930 kilometres off the west coast of Africa, 'the Shark'. They were on acerbic terms, even though the admiral treated the ex-emperor with respect and granted his request to divert the ship so he could see the Teide Peak at Tenerife from the sea; though when they sailed between Gomera and Palma thick fog covered the sea and Napoleon saw nothing.[3] On board HMS *Northumberland*, he was a prisoner of the British state. 'Let them call me what they wish,' he said. 'They cannot stop me being me.'[4] As they approached their final destination, Cockburn agreed that Napoleon should disembark after dark to avoid being gawped at. 'I should have done better to have stayed in Egypt,' he quipped as the island's purple and brown rocks, precipices and craters came into view.[5]

On the evening of 17 October 1815, Napoleon was rowed ashore to Jamestown, the island's only town. The route from the quay to the inn, the Maison Porteous, where he and his small entourage of followers spent the first night on St Helena, was lined with wide-eyed inhabitants, holding up lanterns to catch a glimpse of the most dangerous man in the world. They saw a prematurely aged figure, pale and losing his hair. There were shadows under his eyes, but his gaze had lost nothing of the penetrating character for which it was known.[6] The inn was opposite the East India Company's botanical gardens, established in 1787 as a resting station for plants on their journeys across the globe, and Henry Porteous, the *super-intendant* of the gardens, also ran the inn, the only one on the island. Napoleon slept badly, deepening the shadows under his grey eyes. Since Waterloo, four months earlier, he had lost the ability to sleep at will. From his bedroom on the first floor, he could hear voices talking about him in the street below.

Early the next morning, Cockburn took him to see Longwood, the house that was still being made ready for him, nine kilometres outside Jamestown. His valets, Saint-Denis and Marchand, went too. Both had shared his exile on Elba and neither had hesitated to accompany him to St Helena. The small party set off down the main street in Jamestown, lined by houses with verandas displaying exotic plants, Napoleon riding a beautiful black Arab horse that Cockburn had provided.[7] Outside Jamestown they took a path that climbed the cliff. The terrain was immediately mountainous. At first there were giant tree aloes (*Aloidendron barberae*), some of them eighteen metres tall, and cacti, palm trees and bananas. But soon the tropical vegetation gave way to pines, olive trees and African willows. At the centre of the island was a deep, barren, chalky hollow known as the Devil's Punch Bowl, 572 metres above sea level. At its rim, they turned left towards Longwood. The horses sometimes slipped on the steep, dry stony path. They reached the high, flat area known as Deadwood Plateau and finally arrived at the two stone pillars that marked the entrance to Napoleon's last home.

The house was approached by a broad drive flanked by gum trees (*Commidendrum robustum*) endemic to the island, five to six metres high, filled with fragrant sap and large flies. Longwood had previously been used as a summer house for the East India Company's lieutenant governor, and the buildings were small and wooden with pitch roofs: more like a farmstead than a formal residence. Napoleon viewed the rooms in silence, walked around the garden of yellowing grass, and was ready to leave. On the way back, about two kilometres outside Jamestown, he noticed a charming house surrounded by a luxurious garden with fig, mango, banana, lemon and pomegranate trees. He stopped and discovered it belonged to William Balcombe, the East India Company's administrator, rumoured to be the illegitimate son of the Prince Regent. At the end of the garden was a natural waterfall and an elegant pavilion, the size of a large room, where the Duke of Wellington had stayed when he visited St Helena on his way back from India in 1805.[8]

Napoleon immediately befriended the Balcombe family, sent his valets to fetch his belongings from Jamestown, and within a couple of hours was dining al fresco in an exotic setting that reminded him of his favourite novel, Bernardin de Saint Pierre's *Paul et Virginie*. He refused to return to the Maison Porteous and the Balcombes invited him to stay with them at the Briars until Longwood was ready. He became very fond of the family and their garden, where he spent many happy hours dictating his memoirs to his friend and confidant, the Councillor of State and atlas-maker the Comte de Las Cases. When he was tired from working, he reread Rousseau's *La Nouvelle Héloïse* and was as charmed by it as he had been at school.[9] The garden at the Briars was not a wilderness like the old orchard in the novel, but still he felt close to nature and revived. He walked on the rocky terraces examining the plants: white roses, geraniums, magnolias, camellias and African snowdrops. The Balcombes had several slaves, among them Toby, an old Malay, who cultivated the garden. Napoleon questioned Toby, using Las Cases, who spoke fluent English, as an interpreter. He learned that Toby had been kidnapped as a child and sold by English sailors on St Helena. Slave trading had been banned throughout the British Empire since 1807, but the ban did not free existing slaves or their children. Napoleon liked Toby and planned to buy him his freedom. Toby called Napoleon 'the good gentleman'.[10]

Longwood was ready for him to move into on 10 December 1815, midsummer on St Helena. The altitude of the house meant that even in high summer, thick fog could descend without warning, making it impossible to see a metre ahead, and it rained frequently throughout the year. Everything at Longwood was damp. Soon the hundreds of books Napoleon brought with him were too. During the day he was allowed to walk or ride within the estate's twenty-kilometre perimeter, but could not go beyond without being accompanied by a British officer. The guards were stationed at Deadwood Barracks, within sight of Longwood. At 9 p.m., sentries entered the Longwood garden and surrounded the house for the night. Colonel Bingham, the commander of the garrison, sent home a favourable description of the terrain:

> I have an excellent suite of barrack rooms, from the windows of which is seen a very grand, and noble view comprising sea, wood, a fine extensive plain, immense heights, rugged rocks, fortifications, barracks, tents and people of all colours, even the whole making a pretty panorama.[11]

The gum trees at Longwood reminded Bingham of broken umbrellas. They were filled with sweetly singing canary birds, java sparrows with red beaks and avadavats. Golden pheasants and peacocks, which had been registered as present on St Helena in Buffon's *Natural History*, strutted back and forth on the ground.[12] There was a marquee near the house, erected by Bingham's deputy, Lieutenant Colonel Fehrzen, where Napoleon often ate or worked on his memoirs. If he closed his eyes he could imagine himself back on campaign, or in one of the many ceremonial tents that his architects Percier and Fontaine had designed in happier times. At first, Napoleon enjoyed exploring his surroundings, on foot, by horse or in a small carriage. Wearing a green hunting coat with silver buttons and medals, a white waistcoat and breeches, he climbed Diana's Peak, the highest point on the island, and visited the Mulberry Gut ravine where local farmers tended vegetable gardens and orchards. But everywhere he went there were sentries to annoy him. 'Only a bird could get out of here,' he complained. 'What good are these sentries on the crest of the hills?'[13]

On 14 April 1816, as the summer was ending, the island's new governor, Sir Hudson Lowe, arrived and took up residence at Plantation House, the best building on the island. The weather was starting to deteriorate. 'In this *isola maladetta*, there is neither sun nor moon to be seen, just constant rain and fog,' Napoleon grumbled.[14] He hated Lowe almost from the start. Lowe had taken part in the British occupation of Corsica in 1794 and afterwards became an aide-de-camp to the British governor of Ajaccio. He was even rumoured to have lodged in the Casa Buonaparte, which Napoleon and his family had abandoned when they fled to France.[15] At their first meeting, Napoleon scathingly insisted they speak Italian. 'Didn't you command a Corsican regiment?' he asked with contempt. Lowe was small, thin, red-headed and almost exactly the same age as Napoleon. The ex-emperor could not reconcile himself to the fact that someone so mediocre had complete power over his daily life. Before Lowe left England, the aristocrats Lord and Lady Holland had repeatedly invited him to Holland House to try and soften his attitude to Napoleon and make arrangements for sending gifts to Longwood. They met with no success and soon afterwards Lowe signed a letter advocating outlawing Napoleon for life. A bill ratifying this lifelong exile was debated in Parliament in the month that Lowe arrived on St Helena and Lord Holland protested against it in the House of Lords, calling Napoleon's exile 'repugnant', but the bill passed. Under the new Act, the ex-emperor was classified as a prisoner of war: any English subject attempting to help him escape would face the death penalty. Despite this, Lady Holland found ways to circumvent the restrictions on the mail and communications Napoleon could receive and managed to send clothing, fine eau de cologne, wine and sugared plums, which he called '*les pruneaux de Lady Holland*'.[16] She also sent around 475 books, which Saint-Denis, acting as Longwood's librarian, catalogued and ordered on the mildewed shelves.

Lowe introduced new restrictions on Napoleon's movements. The sentries were placed around the garden at sunset and drew nearer to the house during the night, where they remained until morning. No letters or gifts addressed to Napoleon as Emperor were delivered. John Cam Hobhouse tried to send a copy of his account of the Hundred Days, *The Substance of some letters written by an Englishman resident at Paris, during the last reign of the Emperor Napoleon*, but he inscribed it 'Imperatori Napoleon', so Lowe confiscated it and kept it at Plantation House.[17] When Napoleon tried to free the slave Toby, who worked in the garden at the Briars, Lowe stopped him. Lowe's attitude had more to do with his intense suspicion of Napoleon than with his views on slavery.[18] He thought the ex-emperor's philanthropic gesture must be a front for some nefarious scheme or other. The new regime soured Napoleon's mood. One Saturday, two months after Lowe's arrival, he took a three-hour bath and read *La Nouvelle Héloïse* again, revisiting the character Julie's Élysée orchard and its natural-seeming wilderness. Afterwards he called for Las Cases and tore into the text he had previously admired with devastating criticisms.[19] In the following months he turned to other books, such as Homer's *Odyssey*, for solace.

Philippe Welle, a young Austrian botanist who worked at the Schönbrunn Gardens, came to St Helena in 1817, in the party of the Austrian commissioner, Baron Stürmer, officially appointed to study the island's plants. Welle was following in a grand tradition of botanists who had collected plants on the island, including Joseph Banks and

Daniel Solander who travelled with Captain Cook's *Endeavour* voyage, and Johann Forster and his son Georg who joined Cook's *Resolution* expedition. Welle had often seen Napoleon's wife, the Empress Marie Louise, and son, the King of Rome, in Vienna in the Schönbrunn Gardens, and since Napoleon had had no news of his family for two years, he was desperate to meet him. But Lowe prevented it.

In a letter to Lord Liverpool, Napoleon mocked, among other absurdities, Lowe's fear that a botanist might have been entrusted with a battle or escape plan.[20] But despite Lowe's precautions, a lock of the King of Rome's hair, which had been passed to Welle in the Schönbrunn Gardens by Marchand's mother, who was the King of Rome's governess, did reach Napoleon at Longwood. He received it with great emotion.[21] Soon after, he had a dream about losing his wife and son. In his dream he saw the empress looking as fresh as when he saw her in Compiègne. He took her in his arms: 'but no matter how hard I tried to keep her, I felt her escape me; and when I wanted to hold her again, everything had disappeared'. He told Marchand that it was better to bear his misery on St Helena alone without having his family as witnesses.[22] Thinking about his brother Joseph, who had been able to get to America, Napoleon commented, 'Joseph will build a great establishment in America. It will be the refuge of all my relatives. If I was in his place I would found a great empire of all Spanish America, but you will see that he will be a bourgeois American and spend his fortune in making gardens.'[23]

When Napoleon first moved into Longwood, the garden had been damaged by the building work. Around the house there was nothing but dry trampled grass. The buildings he occupied were T-shaped, one long, single-storey structure intersecting at right angles with the centre of another. He had two small rectangular gardens marked out in the formal French style that he always preferred, squaring off the T-shape; both were approximately 9 × 18 metres. He could see one garden from his bedroom, the other from his library. He named the two gardens after his two faithful valets who accompanied him in exile: Marchand and Saint-Denis, nicknamed Mameluke Ali. The memoirs of the valets are important sources of information about Napoleon's life at Longwood, even if, like all memoirs, they are personal and liable to exaggeration or distortion. Sometimes they overlap, sometimes they disagree, as though the petty quarrels of Napoleon's last household have continued after death. The first garden, known as the Jardin Marchand, had a diamond of grass at the centre. In the middle of the diamond, Napoleon planted a coffee tree which was given to him as a present. He claimed that the island's coffee, originally transplanted from Yemen in 1733, was the only good thing to come out of St Helena. Around the four sides of the diamond were four triangular flower beds, planted with rose bushes and strawberry plants. Napoleon called this little garden his parterre and installed a glass door in place of one of the windows in his bedroom, so he could walk out into it at any time of the day or night. This door was hidden behind a trellis covered in greenery.

The second garden, onto which the library looked, had an oval of grass at the centre. It was named the Jardin Ali. This garden was planted with citrus, peach and acacia trees and Napoleon called it his grove. In the middle of the oval he placed a wooden basin, a metre in diameter, full of water; but this attracted too many mosquitoes, so had to be moved elsewhere. Mosquitoes were not the only pests to plague the inhabitants of Longwood. Rats came out of the pantry floor at night and climbed the walls and jumped onto the meat suspended from the ceiling on iron hooks. The servants baited large traps and carried them each morning into the garden where eight or ten rats, fighting to get out, would be released for their backs to be broken by the teeth of the stable dogs. Occasionally one of the dogs was bitten by a rat.[24]

Across the garden, what had previously been only scorched lawn was turned into ground suitable for trees and plants. The most remarkable were two pairs of lemon trees that were transplanted into the

Jardin Marchand to form an arbour beneath which six people could dine. Another arbour in the Jardin Ali was covered with the evergreen *Passiflora*, or passion flower, which was also trained around the fencing and trellis surrounding both gardens. The showy purple and white flowers looked like decorative plaques and had a distinctive corona ripening into an orange-yellow fruit. The passion flowers grew extraordinarily fast here because of the heat during the day and abundant dew at night. The vines threw out shoots ten centimetres long in just twenty-four hours, and covered the fences with thick hedges in a mere three months. Inside the arbours in these small gardens, Napoleon enjoyed disappearing from the sight of the duty captain. He took an interest in the development of the trees, rose bushes and flowers.[25] Sometimes he played ninepins with his generals on the grass.[26]

Lunch was served in the Jardin Marchand. The meal consisted of soup, a vegetable dish, a meat dish, then coffee poured over sugar in one of the Sèvres cups decorated with scenes from Napoleon's Egypt campaign. In the shade of his lemon trees he reminisced about his time in Cairo and his retreat from Syria. Among the pieces of Sèvres porcelain that he brought with him were dinner plates depicting views of battlefields or major cities he had conquered. He had commissioned the service in 1807 for his personal use and stipulated that none of the plates should bear 'images of battles or names of men' but only indirect, allusive subjects evoking pleasant memories. He paused over a plate representing his visit to Ajaccio in 1799, on his way back to France after fleeing Egypt on board the frigate *Muiron*.[27] Looking at the plate, Napoleon remembered his wet nurse, Camilla Illari, who was one of the first to welcome him, as well as the gang leaders who controlled Ajaccio and the chaos of its administration. He claimed the whole population of Corsica had lined the shore to catch a glimpse of him and that a garrison of soldiers was positioned along the route to his home. His desire to go ashore was granted and the usual quarantine period waived after he insisted, with sheer force of personality rather than medical evidence, that there was no disease on board the

Muiron. He found the soldiers on Ajaccio poorly dressed and discovered they had been without pay for seven or eight months. Beneath the transplanted lemon trees in his newly made garden at Longwood, he remembered paying the arrears in the Corsican soldiers' wages himself by borrowing 40,000 francs from his mother.[28] These events, already commemorated on porcelain, were unpacked on St Helena, the memories as brittle as the plates.

Despite the pleasure Napoleon found in his small gardens, his thoughts turned to suicide, a subject that had interested him throughout his life. He dictated a fragment on suicide as 'a literary relaxation on this miserable rock'. Despite the fact that he had tried to kill himself after abdicating his throne at Fontainebleau in 1814, and may have tried again after Waterloo, Napoleon argued against suicide:

> The man who would have killed himself on Monday will want to live on Saturday, and yet you can only kill yourself once. Man's life is made up of the past, the present and the future, or at least the present and the future.[29]

Napoleon spent most of his time on St Helena dictating his memoirs. He was preoccupied with his legacy. He knew that he was seriously ill from the persistent pain in his stomach and that he might die on the island, yet he was still intensely alive and focused on making the most of the present. He understood that the present and the future are all anyone, even the grandest of historical figures whose names echo through the centuries of recorded time, really has. He was prepared to wait patiently for nature to run its course. He insisted he had no fear of death. 'As to my body, it will become carrots or turnips. I have no dread of death. In the army I have seen many men perish who were talking to me.'[30] He was not suicidal, but he was increasingly depressed.

Lowe arrested Las Cases on 25 November 1816 for writing a letter complaining about Napoleon's treatment on the island and attempting

to evade censorship. Las Cases was sent away from St Helena early in
the new year and the manuscript of the memoirs he had transcribed
for Napoleon was confiscated. Afterwards Napoleon's mood darkened.
He stopped going out for walks and rides. He went less often into his
gardens. He began playing games to avoid surveillance, hiding from
the officers charged with sighting him at least once a day. His health
deteriorated. His Irish doctor, Barry O'Meara, removed a rotten tooth
from his swollen gum and urged him to resume exercising. Napoleon
said death would be a release, he had no motivation to take care of
his health. Lowe became concerned about Napoleon's lack of exercise.[31] The ex-emperor was gaining weight. Towards the end of 1817,
on her journey back to England from the Cape of Good Hope, a ten-
year-old girl named Helen Sheridan was taken by her recently widowed
mother to get a look at Napoleon when their ship stopped at St Helena.
She saw him walking in his garden: 'he was enormously fat with a
large straw hat'.[32]

Lowe ordered O'Meara to make regular reports on Napoleon and
his household. The doctor was an unwilling messenger between
Longwood and Plantation House. He believed Napoleon was suffering
from hepatitis, but Lowe feared this would be blamed on the conditions at Longwood and disputed the diagnosis, which he did not want
reported in the press. O'Meara found the interference irksome and
stopped cooperating. Soon relations between them deteriorated
dramatically, and the doctor resigned before he was sacked. He sailed
back to England in July 1818, where his attempts to persuade the
British government that Napoleon was seriously ill and should return
to England for treatment ended in him being dismissed from the navy
and struck off the medical register. He rented rooms on the Edgware
Road and set up as a dentist, displaying Napoleon's tooth in the
window. He made a fortune from the diary of his time on St Helena,
which Napoleon had wisely advised him to keep.

After O'Meara left, Napoleon was without a doctor in his household
until his mother sent François Carlo Antommarchi, a Corsican

physician who had trained at the University of Florence, and two Italian priests, to look after him. Soon after Antommarchi arrived at Longwood in September 1819, he urged Napoleon to resume exercise. 'Where?' asked the patient. 'In the gardens, in the fields, in the open air,' the doctor advised. Although he was feeling better, Napoleon remained resistant to exercising under the surveillance of the British 'redcoats', so Antommarchi suggested gardening. 'You must dig the ground, turn up the earth, and thus escape from inactivity and insult at the same time.' The suggestion was well received. 'Dig the ground! Yes, doctor you are right, I will dig the ground.'[33] By the next morning, he had appointed his Swiss servant Jean-Abram Noverraz, who had previous agricultural experience, as his chief gardener.[34] They were already discussing elaborate plans for expanding the existing garden. Napoleon seized on Antommarchi's idea for at least two reasons. Gardening would boost his levels of physical activity and would also increase his privacy. He hoped to devise a means of screening from view the barracks and the telegraph pole that sent daily updates on his whereabouts to Plantation House. Suddenly, nothing but gardens was talked of at Longwood.[35] Napoleon wanted to grow fruit and vegetables, to construct shady walkways and to hide the sentinels from his windows, so that he looked out on greenery, rather than being reminded of the surveillance to which he was subject.

He was annoyed by the wind that blew across Deadwood Plateau and through his grove, so had a semicircular turf wall, approximately 2.7 metres tall, built around a new garden, beyond the grove and about five times bigger. He hoped the berm, or tall grass bank, would provide some shelter at Longwood.[36] He also wanted to distract himself and his household from boredom and provide a barrier between his house and the English sentries. He sent his butler, Pierron, to Jamestown to buy wheelbarrows, pickaxes, shovels and all the gardening tools necessary for clearing a large area of land. He had his own rake and spade, which he sometimes used as a walking stick, or to lean on as he watched the work progress. He tried to use a pickaxe, but found the tool unsuited to his hands.[37] He summoned Antommarchi to admire his gardening prowess, teasing the doctor by claiming that spadework and fresh air had done more for his health than medicine.[38] 'I have always accustomed my body to bend to my will, and I shall bring it to do so now, and inure it to this exercise.'[39]

The gardening became more and more ambitious. Inspired by his memories of fortifications, Napoleon designed a maze of straight and curving sunken paths to be dug between symmetrically arranged flower beds within about 10,000 square metres of land surrounding Longwood. He hoped he would be able to walk along the sunken paths without being observed by his guards.[40] The gardening began at daybreak and involved the whole household. Four Chinese labourers were hired to work on the construction of the gardens and afterwards two were kept on to maintain them. Napoleon used to watch the Chinese work and on one occasion gave them a bottle of wine as a present.[41] They were paid 30 shillings a month in addition to their government wages and food. Early in the eighteenth century, the then governor of St Helena had suggested that the East India Company bring Chinese workers to St Helena from Pinang and Macau as 'they are excellent artisans and farmers, who provide quality labour at a good price'.[42] By 1818 there were approximately six hundred of these labourers living on the island. Because their names were hard for the English to pronounce, they were known by numbers.

One of the Chinese was a skilled carpenter who helped build a Chinese pavilion at the extremity of the turf wall so Napoleon could sit there looking out to sea. The pavilion was decorated with white muslin and furnished with a Chinese armchair and bamboo chaise longue. From here Napoleon could see the panorama around Longwood and use his telescope to watch ships arriving in the distant bay. The canopy and walls of the square pavilion were canvas and it had glass diamond-shaped windows. It was painted light green with grey window frames and was approached via a grass-covered staircase supported by pickets which followed the curve of the turf wall. On the top of the pavilion there was a Chinese dragon weathervane.

One day one of the Chinese labourers was digging too close to a tall yew tree and Marchand reprimanded him, worried about damage to the tree's roots. Napoleon intervened to defend him. 'If a fine table is served behind you, and you are hungry and allowed to sit down, you will certainly find a way to turn around to satisfy your appetite. It will be the same for this tree: it will take from its remaining roots on the other side the substance that has been withdrawn from it.'[43] Far from being intimidated by Napoleon, or awed to be working for an ex-emperor, the Chinese labourers were simply amused by his gardening outfit, a nankeen jacket like a farmer's, a pair of trousers of the same fabric, red slippers and a wide-brimmed straw hat. The hat still exists. It has a black taffeta ribbon round the deep crown, which is lined inside with white silk and reinforced with a clipping from an English newspaper dated September 1813. It forms a poignant contrast to the bicorne hat that has become integral to the instantly recognisable silhouette and legend of Napoleon.

In 1829, the printer Jean-Georges Frey produced a lithograph entitled *Le jardinier de Sainte-Hélène*. The subtitle of the anonymous illustration is: 'no longer be astonished that Mars is a gardener'. Napoleon, previously associated with the god of war, is shown pensively leaning on a spade, holding his straw hat in his hand amid a rural idyll of his own creation. He has exposed his balding head to the sun temporarily while he rests among his plants and tools, observed from afar by a man, woman and child. The man is in military dress and wearing a bicorne hat sideways, so the two corners frame his face, in the manner immortalised in Napoleon's silhouette. Perhaps he is the younger Napoleon, or even the Emperor Napoleon, showing viewers of the lithograph where his career ended, in a garden on St Helena.

The bicorne hat that Napoleon was wearing at the Battle of Waterloo in 1815 – which reputedly fell off as he fled and was collected from the battlefield by a Dutch captain, Baron Arnout Jacques van

Zuijlen van Nijevelt – sold at auction in 2018 for just under €350,000. That bicorne is one of nineteen that survive of the estimated 150 that Napoleon wore during the ascent and descent of his career, from the time he was made First Consul in 1799 to his defeat at Waterloo. He bought them all from Poupard et Delaunay, whose shop in the Palais Royal arcade opened in 1811. He was buried in one of his bicorne hats. He brought four with him to St Helena, but only one straw hat, strengthened by newspaper when it started to wear out.

The straw hat appears in a nineteenth-century coloured lithograph by the Austrian artist Franz Gerasch, after Horace Vernet, entitled *Napoléon Ier en planteur à Sainte-Hélène*. Overweight and glum, Napoleon leans heavily on his elbow over the newspaper he has stopped reading, seated on a plain garden bench. The straw hat he is wearing closely resembles the one listed in the inventory of Napoleon's belongings prepared after his death. Comte Henri Gatien Bertrand, who had accompanied Napoleon on his expedition to Egypt and shared his exile on St Helena, inherited this hat and bequeathed it to his daughter, who in turn bequeathed it to Victor-Napoleon, the grandson of Napoleon's youngest brother and the Bonapartist pretender to the French throne, until his death in 1926. The hat is now in the Musée national des châteaux de Malmaison et Bois-Préau. In the same museum, there is a garden bench made of juniper wood, acquired by Napoleon III from a seller on St Helena, which is reputedly 'the bench on which the Emperor often sat during his exile'. The back of the bench is divided into three sections, one of which still has a lattice of simply nailed wooden slats.

Lowe was initially suspicious about Napoleon's gardening. He asked Antommarchi, 'Is it by your advice that General Bonaparte takes this violent exercise?' When the doctor confirmed that it was, Lowe was dismissive. 'You harass yourselves in transplanting trees in a soil without humidity, and exposed to a burning sun; it is labour lost, they will die – not one will grow up.'[44] But he had no serious objections, not even to the turf wall, which ended up being 2.7 metres tall and wide, and 24 metres long. To begin with Lowe believed it was merely a windbreak, and was pleased that the gardening made Napoleon easier to spot by the guards. When he realised that the enlargement of the garden had moved the guards further from the house, he was more concerned, but still did not intervene in Napoleon's new passion. He even came to Longwood and offered help with the gardening from the English soldiers. Marchand remembered that this help was refused, but Saint-Denis claimed it was accepted.[45] Napoleon's hatred of Lowe did not extend to his relatives. When Lowe's attractive stepdaughter came to see the gardens at Longwood, hoping to catch a glimpse of the ex-emperor, he served the young girl sweets and presented her with a rose.

To grow roses at Longwood they had to overcome the obstacle of dry soil. Water was scarce on the Deadwood Plateau. The water for Napoleon's regular long baths, which he considered essential to his mental and physical health, had to be brought from a natural spring over a kilometre away in barrels pulled on a cart by the Chinese labourers. This spring, which provided Longwood with drinking water, also supplied the English camp. Lowe arranged for a reservoir to be built at Diana's Peak, and for conduits to bring water to both Longwood and the soldiers' barracks opposite. A pump and hose were purchased in Jamestown and mounted on wheels so that water could be moved around the garden to areas of new planting or drought.

Perhaps remembering the oak transplanted in his honour in Lausanne in 1800, Napoleon attempted to move mature oak trees into his garden on St Helena. Oak trees did not grow tall on the island, but spread their branches out like apple trees in France, the main trunks seldom reaching over two or three metres.[46] Oaks had been introduced onto St Helena in 1749, at the same time as they were extensively planted on the Cape in an attempt to alleviate timber shortages. Transplanting the trees required the strength of twenty men, and great care was taken to move them with a large clump of earth beneath their roots. They were watered every day but even so most of them died after a fortnight. One survived and became known as 'the Emperor's oak', under which he arranged a table and several chairs.

Napoleon decided he wanted the sound of water. Because the gardens were on a slight incline, he set up a series of basins, channelling the overflow from one to another. The first, on the highest elevation, was a semicircle, the same shape as his bicorne hat, 4 metres in diameter and 0.8 metres deep, made of masonry. The second was an enormous vat, 3.6 metres in diameter and 1.2 metres deep, and the third was 1.8 metres in diameter by 1.2 metres deep. The first semicircular basin, or pond, cost 1,000 francs, the second and third together cost 1,800 francs. Water could run through these basins down into the vegetable garden, located on lower ground. Earth from the construction of the basins was added to the turf wall, which was terraced to form what Marchand called an amphitheatre, and planted with grass, flowers and rose bushes to hold the earth back.

Napoleon laughed at himself for being entertained by the small hydraulics of his garden. Every day around sunset he said to Saint-Denis, 'Come, let us make the fountains play!' Then one of the valets would turn the principal and secondary stopcocks, and water would run into the basins and little canals that had been built in the garden. But often there was only enough water in the reservoir for the needs of the household, and in the dry season especially it had to be sparingly used. The water at Longwood would often dry up when the stopcock at the barracks was open and there was a high demand on the shared resource from the soldiers.[47]

The largest semicircular basin was lined with stone and cement, then covered with layers of oil paint to make it watertight. Napoleon purchased some carp and personally placed them in it. But the next day, the basin was half empty and some of the fish were floating dead on the surface of the remaining water. Saint-Denis thought they might have been poisoned by the oil paint. Recognising that the basin was not properly watertight, Napoleon decided to have it lined with lead. The remaining fish were removed and stored in a barrel while the plumber carried out this work. In the process of building the pond, the roots of a pine tree had been damaged and gradually that tree dried up and died. In its place, Napoleon commissioned the Chinese carpenter to construct a large three-storeyed bamboo aviary.

The semicircular aviary was beautifully constructed from painted wood and metal. The three Chinese artisans who worked on it were known as numbers 146, 174 and 178.[48] They raised it above the ground on clawed feet and decorated it with Chinese motifs, including a flower basket, egret and ribbon that formed a rebus representing longevity. The word 'peony' formed a second rebus meaning wealth and rank, and birds among crab-apple blossoms along the bottom spelt out the message 'May your noble house be blessed with wealth and honour'. The domed green roof was topped with a wooden carving of an eagle, until Napoleon ordered it removed. It was too absurd that the emblem his soldiers had followed into battle and sacrificed their lives for should end up as a garden ornament.[49] Canaries were kept in cages until the aviary was finished, but nearly all became diseased and died. The few that survived were killed by cats. When the aviary was ready its first inhabitants were a lame pheasant and some chickens. The pheasant died inside, but the chickens were let out. Then pigeons were found to fill it, but they soon escaped. 'The cage remained without birds as the basin did without fish,' Saint-Denis noted. His grandfather, an officer of the royal kitchens, had made a birdcage from nougat that was presented to the court at Versailles before the Revolution; when the nougat was broken, the bird flew out of the cage and perched on Marie Antoinette's head. Saint-Denis's father had lost his position in the royal stables at Versailles after the Revolution, but moved to Paris, started a riding school, and placed his son in the emperor's household in 1806. Now that son was watching the ex-emperor, a prisoner on St Helena, struggling to find occupants for his birdcage in a garden too dry and inhospitable for roses.

Napoleon also had an artificial cave dug in the turf wall. Since the vault was only soil, it had to be reinforced with wooden beams. The cave was made big enough to contain turf benches, a round table and some chairs. A channel of water ran through it to a wooden basin on the other side of the wall, which could be emptied by means of a tap into another channel leading to the pavilion. To make the inside of the cave more seemly, Napoleon lined it with wooden panels decorated by one of the Chinese artisans with serpents, dragons, birds and a melee of fantastical Chinese figures. But drought soon made the turf wall crumble and the cave started to fill up and subside. In less than fifteen days all the roses planted on ledges along the turf wall shrivelled. Every day they were well watered and still the earth was too dry. Napoleon managed to eat at the table inside the crumbling cave only two or three times.

A fence was erected inside the turf wall to keep animals out of the garden. When the sunken paths and irrigation channels and basins were finished and the flower beds and vegetables beds planted, Napoleon noticed straying chickens in his gardens. Maddened by the damage they were doing, he fetched a shotgun and put an end to it: three chickens fell with one shot and a fourth was shot where it perched on a wall. These were the first shots he had fired in a long time and they made him reminisce about his hunting days.[50] A few days later he shot at a goat and her kids that were grazing on the lawn and doing no harm. For a few weeks afterwards he had kids brought into the garden so he could prove his skill at shooting them. Remembering Corsica and the damage the goats did to young trees on the island, he told Marchand, 'I was always in favour of destroying them, and I had tremendous arguments with my old uncle the archdeacon, who owned many of them. One day when he had reached the peak of his furore, he accused me of being an upstart.'[51] Napoleon also shot a suckling pig on St Helena, boasting to his companions, 'I am going to offer you a roast worthy of Odysseus.' His final shot, according to Marchand, was into the head of a plough ox belonging to the East India Company, which had got into the gardens and was trampling them.

Napoleon's household found all the gardening extremely tiring and moaned that if they were made to extend the gardens still further, it would kill them.[52] Many of them had never handled a pickaxe, shovel or spade, or even pushed a wheelbarrow before. When Napoleon was present, overseeing operations, they all worked as hard as they could from five or six in the morning. 'Never had Longwood been so animated as it was while we were working in these gardens; the activity seemed to have revived us,' Saint-Denis wrote. It seemed as though Napoleon's health had never been better while on St Helena: he was always in good humour, impatient every morning to get into the garden and advance it before the midday sun became too hot for work to continue. In the last months of 1819, it seemed as though nature had come to Napoleon's aid, that his health was improving and he had found distraction in his work and small gardens. But this, Marchand claims, was an illusion.[53] He remembered commenting on Napoleon's improved health and receiving the response: 'Don't believe it . . . I haven't long to live. It is right here,' Napoleon said, pointing to his liver, 'this is only a moment of rest granted me by nature; the illness will again gain the upper hand and do me in.'[54]

Arranging a bed of French beans, Napoleon noticed some tiny roots which led him to discuss the phenomenon of vegetation with Antommarchi. He told his doctor that he believed in the existence of a Superior Being who presides over the wonders of Nature, and asked him if he had ever met with a soul under his scalpel. 'Where does the soul reside? In what organ?' Napoleon was convinced that most doctors were atheists, unlike, in his experience, mathematicians. His own views were agnostic. Sometimes he seemed to side with the materialists. 'When I have had stags cut open in hunting, I saw that their interior was like that of man. Man is only a more perfect being than dogs and trees. Plants are the first link in the chain of which man is the last. I know this is contrary to religion, but it is my opinion. We are all matter.' On other occasions, he seemed sure there was a divine intelligence responsible for ordering the world. But he told General Baron Gourgaud, 'If I had to choose a religion I think I should become a worshipper of the sun. The sun gives to all things life and fertility. It is the true God of the earth.'[55]

The dry soil at Longwood did not repay the effort spent on cultivating it, and the caterpillars could devastate in a single night anything that had been successfully grown.[56] Produce from the garden did, however, end up on Napoleon's table, the occasional bowl of salad and some radishes. He always asked if what they were about to eat had been home-grown. The peas and string beans were hard and the cauliflower did not form properly.[57] Only the cabbage did well. The strawberry plants were covered in flowers but bore little fruit. The transplanted peach trees did better. Every other day they ate a salad of haricot beans made with olive oil, tarragon vinegar, chervil, parsley, chives and the astringent herb burnet.[58] As he sat down to eat Napoleon remarked, 'After all, our trouble has not been wholly lost. Our gardens are feeding us.' Then he pretended to chide those in his household who could not hide their smiles, smiling himself at the fiction.

In May 1820, Lowe wrote to Lord Bathurst, Secretary for War and the Colonies, about the vegetable growing at Longwood. He reported that he had heard that the French commissioner, the Marquis de Montchenu, had been offered both green and white beans – *haricots verts* and *haricots blancs* – from Napoleon's kitchen garden.[59] Since green was the Bonapartist colour and white the Bourbon colour, Lowe wondered, in a completely paranoid frame of mind, if a political message was being communicated to the marquis via the vegetable patch. He made himself look ridiculous by suggesting that the French commissioner had compromised himself by accepting the green beans when he should have 'limited himself to a demand for the white alone'. Of more political seriousness was Montchenu's report that Napoleon had told one of his valets: 'It is a great misfortune for France that my son lives because he has great rights.'[60]

Napoleon's thoughts often turned to the Revolution, out of which his power had come. He reminisced about the fall of the monarchy and the massacre in the Tuileries gardens. 'The French Revolution,' he said, 'was a general movement of the mass of the people against the privileged classes. The chief object of the Revolution was to destroy those privileges and abuses. It established equality of rights. Any citizen might succeed to any office according to his talent.' Napoleon thought that the Revolution had started the process of centralising and rationalising France which he had continued. France became one nation with the same civil and criminal laws and taxes throughout the land. He believed that when the people voted to establish an imperial throne and place him on it, 'no person ever ascended a throne with more legitimate rights'. His power came from the people, and the people had voted to make his power hereditary. He still hoped, against all the odds, that his son would one day be emperor of the French.[61]

The determination to make a last garden was Napoleon's final blaze of energy. The life of the man who had conquered and transformed Europe was almost spent. But before surrendering completely to the natural decline of his own body, Napoleon found the strength to impose himself one more time on the earth. Like a fire that had burned brighter, hotter and higher than any other, the flame of his will revived one last time before it flickered out. This was the first time since school that he had time to dig the ground, sow seeds and plan a garden. It was also the first time since school that he was so unfree. At school he was not free to roam as he had done as a small child in Corsican orchards; the institution had rules and routines that he, along with all the other boys, had to observe. On St Helena he was under constant surveillance, lest he attempt to leave the remote island. Here the rules and routines had been invented solely for him, an ex-emperor, still considered the most dangerous man in Europe.

Lady Holland, who had only seen Napoleon once, from a distance, during the Peace of Amiens, continued her support for him in exile. She acquired one of Canova's bronze busts of Napoleon from Rome, and set it in her garden at Holland House on a column of Scotch granite, inscribed with a verse from *The Odyssey* translated by Lord Holland:

> He is not dead, he breathes the air
> In lands beyond the deep,
> Some distant sea-girt island where
> Harsh men the hero keep.

Lady Holland herself was an accomplished gardener, responsible for introducing the dahlia to England in 1804. She supported Napoleon's horticultural ambitions on St Helena by sending him seeds of *Xerochrysum bracteatum*, or everlasting daisy. This plant had been catalogued in 1803 in the book documenting the rare plants grown in the Empress Josephine's garden at Malmaison. Originally from Australia, it had been grown in England since 1791. Descendants of the seeds Lady Holland sent to St Helena flourish on the island to this day and are sold to tourists at Longwood. Another Australian plant catalogued in the book of rare plants at Malmaison was *Acacia subulata*, or golden wattle.[62] This too Napoleon propagated on St Helena. In a candid moment, he told General Baron Gourgaud that if he had not been a captive, the life he lived on St. Helena would have suited him very well. 'I should like to live in the country; I should like to see the soil improved by others, for I do not know enough about gardening to improve it myself. That kind of thing is the noblest existence.' At the end of his life he believed, 'Man's true vocation is to cultivate the ground.'[63]

Despite all the good that gardening had done him, Napoleon's health declined. He talked at length to Antommarchi about the stomach cancer that had killed his father. He was obsessed by the idea that the disease was hereditary and worried that the King of Rome might develop it too. The pond had now been filled with fish again and he sat watching them for hours even as he became 'so weak he could hardly support himself'. He amused himself throwing bread to the fish, observing their interactions and trying to find parallels between the behaviour of fish and mankind. But in spite of all the care and the precautions which were taken to preserve them, four or five months later not one was left alive.[64] When the fish started to die, Napoleon complained that 'There is a fatality attached to me. Everything I love, everything that belongs to me, is immediately struck: heaven and mankind unite to persecute me.'[65] But he did not give up searching for the precise cause of the poisoning of his fish, which turned out to be a coppery cement that had been plastered on the bottom of the basin.

By the end of 1820, Napoleon was so ill that he could hardly walk and needed help even to reach his garden chair. Around this time, news of his sister Eliza's death in Trieste from malaria affected him deeply.[66] He had made her Grand Duchess of Tuscany in happier times. When he was too ill to go out into his garden, he sat with the doors into it open and often asked one of his valets to fetch him a flower.[67] He wanted to breathe fresh air and have roses close enough to enjoy their fragrance.[68] He refused medicine and repeated his favourite saying: 'Everything that must happen is written down: our hour is marked, and it is not in our power to take from time a portion which nature refuses us.'[69] Antommarchi recorded his directions for his body:

> After my death, which cannot be far off, I wish you to open my body: I wish also, nay, I require, that you will not suffer any English physician to touch me. If, however, you find it indispensable to have someone to assist you, Dr. Arnott is the only one I am willing you should employ. I am desirous, further, that you should take out my heart, that you put it in spirits of wine, and

that you carry it to Parma to my dear Maria Louisa: you will tell
her how tenderly I have loved her, that I have never ceased to
love her; and you will report to her all that you have witnessed,
all that relates to my situation and my death. I recommend you
above all carefully to examine my stomach, to make an exact,
detailed report of it, which you will convey to my son. The
vomitings which succeed each other without intermission lead
me to suppose that the stomach is the one of my organs which
is the most deranged; and I am inclined to believe that it is
affected with the disease which conducted my father to the grave;
I mean a cancer in the lower stomach. What think you?[70]

Before he died, Napoleon added codicils to his will, including one
bequeathing to Lady Holland a snuffbox decorated with a fine cameo,
which had been given to him by Pope Pius VI after the Treaty of
Tolentino. For all his religious doubts, his will clearly asserted: 'I die
in the Apostolical Roman religion, in the bosom of which I was born
more than fifty years since.' To his son, he left his houses and gardens
in Ajaccio. He also left him other articles, such as his Sèvres china,
his field bed, saddles, spurs, chapel plate, books and the linen he had
worn on St Helena, hoping that these items would be treasured 'as
coming from a father of whom the whole world will remind him'.
When a comet appeared in the sky above St Helena in 1821, Napoleon
believed it would mark his death. He had spent time in exile working
on his commentary on Caesar's campaigns and knew that a comet
had appeared after Caesar's assassination.[71] He believed that Caesar's
right to rule, like his own, had come from the people.

While Antommarchi was watching and following the progress of
Napoleon's pain and distress in the last few days of his life, he
suddenly saw him collect his strength, jump up and insist that he
would walk in the garden. 'I ran to receive him in my arms, but his
legs buckled under the weight of his body: he fell backwards, and I
had the mortification of being unable to prevent his falling,' the

doctor remembered.[72] Napoleon's attendants got him back into his bed, which was one of the low narrow camp beds he had used on military campaigns, but he no longer recognised anyone. In the midst of his confusion he kept insisting that he wanted to go into the garden. He showed no understanding of what was going on around him and did not stop hiccoughing from this point until he died at 5.49 p.m. on 5 May 1821, just after the sun went down. The doctor recorded that the day before Napoleon's attempt to go into his garden one last time, there was a terrible storm that threatened to destroy everything at Longwood. The new plantings were torn up by the roots and a willow tree that Napoleon liked to sit under fell in the tempestuous wind. 'It seemed,' Antommarchi claimed, 'as if none of the things the Emperor valued were to survive him.'[73]

Before he lost the power of speech, Napoleon told his companions that after death he would be reunited with his brave soldiers on the Elysian Fields. In the *Odyssey* those fields are the final resting place of heroic souls: 'where life glides on in immortal ease for mortal man; no snow, no winter onslaught, never a downpour there but night and day the Ocean River sends up breezes, singing winds of the West refreshing all mankind'.[74] As he lay on his camp bed waiting for his soul to reach the Elysian Fields, the green space beyond his last garden, he thought of the soldiers who had gone before him. His final delirious words were '*à la tête d'armée*' (at the head of the army), almost inaudible in the death rattle of his breath. Perhaps he recalled the other fields, the battlefields, where his soldiers had been assembled, ready to follow him to glory. At Longwood there was no sumptuous alcove with paintings representing the battles of Austerlitz, Marengo and Friedland, as there had been above the couch in his private resting room at Rambouillet. But during his last long day his eyes were mostly closed and no one knows what images of triumphant warfare his mind projected. Or perhaps what he saw were the gardens: the gardens of his childhood at school and on Corsica; the Tuileries, the Jardin des Plantes, and other Parisian gardens; Egyptian gardens;

Malmaison; Saint-Cloud; Compiègne; the gardens and the forest at
Fontainebleau; imagined gardens in Rome and at Chaillot for the
King of Rome; unfinished gardens on Elba; the garden at Waterloo
that became an inferno; and finally, his last garden, just beyond the
open windows, darkened by the long evening shadows of the trees
he had planted: the garden he could no longer get to, except in his
dreams.

In his will, Napoleon asked to be buried in Paris, 'on the banks of
the Seine, in the midst of the French people [whom I] loved so much'.
But on his deathbed he changed his mind and said he would like to
be buried with his ancestors in the Cathedral of Ajaccio. If his body
could not leave St Helena, then he requested burial near the spring
from which the Chinese labourers drew his drinking water. This was
a verdant spot, adorned with wild flowers, roses and geraniums, and
overhung by willow trees. It was more green and shady than anywhere
else in the neighbourhood.[75]

In 1836, a letter in the *Morning Chronicle* appealed for information
about the willows near Napoleon's grave for inclusion in the *Arboretum
Britannicum*. Many people who had visited the site sent in responses,
including engravings, drawings, dried samples and one living plant.
The editors of the *Arboretum Britannicum* published their conclusions
in the *Gardener's Magazine*.[76] No species of willow is indigenous to St
Helena. In 1810, when General Beatson was governor, he had introduced a large number of trees and shrubs. The *St Helena Gazette* of
1811–12 records the difficulty the governor had protecting his plantations from goats, but several of the tree varieties survived, including
Salix babylonica, which eventually became known as Napoleon's
willow. According to this report, the willow tree destroyed in the
storm before Napoleon's death grew close to the spring and the site
of his future grave. After he was buried, Bertrand's wife planted several
cuttings from the uprooted tree around his tombstones, which were
slabs taken from the kitchen hearth at Longwood, together with some
forget-me-nots. By 1828, the trees grown from these cuttings were

dying and twenty-eight new ones were planted to replace them. At this point the grave was covered in 'a profusion of scarlet-blossomed pelargoniums' and surrounded by iron railings. In 1835, visitors to the tomb reported that the new willow trees were also dying, largely due to being stripped for relics. By then there was already a tree in the garden of the Roebuck Tavern on Richmond Hill with a plaque inscribed:

This willow, which was taken from the tomb of Buonaparte in St. Helena, in the year 1823, was presented by General Walker, Governor of the island and successor to Sir Hudson Lowe, to John Townsend Farquhar Esq., Governor of Mauritius, who brought it to England.[77]

There were also examples of Napoleon's willow growing in the Horticultural Society's Garden at Chiswick, at Kew, in the Twickenham Botanical Garden, in Kensington Gravel Pits, at Chatsworth, and in various private gardens in London and elsewhere in the country. The authors of the *Gardener's Magazine* article conceded that there were at least two types of willow in question, and it was unclear which had originally grown beside Napoleon's grave. They quoted anecdotes collected by 'a zealous young naturalist', J.H. Fennell, preparing a work on historical and literary botany. Among the eyewitness accounts of the grave that Fennell had collected was this from Captain Mundy's *Pen and Pencil Sketches of India*, 1832: 'The willows are decaying fast; and one of them rests upon the sharp spears of the railing, which are buried in its trunk, as though it were committing suicide for very grief.'[78]

The artist Benjamin Robert Haydon owned several hundred prints of Napoleon and repeatedly depicted him on St Helena, looking out to sea or contemplating his grave in a pose of romantic isolation and melancholy. After seeing one of Haydon's paintings, William Wordsworth composed a sonnet contrasting Napoleon with the setting sun. The sun, an 'unguilty' power, will rise again, unlike Napoleon's fallen fortunes:

> Sky without cloud – ocean without a wave;
> And the one Man that laboured to enslave
> The World, sole-standing high on the bare hill –
> Back turned, arms folded, the unapparent face
> Tinged, we may fancy, in this dreary place
> With light reflected from the invisible sun
> Set, like his fortunes; but not set for aye
> Like them. The unguilty power pursues his way.
> And before *him* doth dawn perpetual run.[79]

In a journal entry for 14 October 1832, Haydon noted that he had seen Sir Hudson Lowe in the street in London when out walking with friends. They all stopped and stared. Lowe looked fiercely at them then crossed the road. 'A meaner face no assassin ever had. He answered Napoleon's description to a T.'[80] Haydon purchased a copy of Napoleon's death mask and tried on one of his bicorne hats and found it fitted him perfectly – 'My skull is like Napoleon's,' he noted delightedly in his diary.[81] Haydon believed that 'all that ever happened of Romance, of degradation, of Poetry, was realized in Napoleon'. In September 1840, he looked forward in awed anticipation to the return of Napoleon's remains to France. 'What a condition the world will be in against the ashes [*sic*] of Napoleon come back to France – the very moving of them seems to have already roused the very devils in Hell and made the Earth tremble!' Haydon continued to paint Napoleon until he slit his own throat in his studio on 22 June 1846, wondering if 'the glitter of his genius rather dazzled me'.[82]

Saint-Denis and Marchand returned to St Helena in 1840 with the delegation that exhumed Napoleon's body in October 1840 and brought it back to France, where it was received at Les Invalides in Paris on 15 December. In his travel journal, Saint-Denis noted that the gardens at Longwood were already in ruins. The two small rectangular plots, closest to the house, Napoleon's parterre and grove, were completely destroyed. There were only a few old peach trees left. The two larger gardens, which had been surrounded by turf walls, were empty. Only a small section of the turf wall around the garden beside the grove remained and almost all the masonry of Napoleon's pond. The pavilion was still standing. The aviary had been taken away for safekeeping and the new governor of St Helena, George Middlemore, sent it back to France as a memento. The canal and the sunken paths, where Napoleon had walked without being observed by English guards, had all crumbled. Faced with these ruins, Saint-Denis found it took some time to remember and map how different the gardens had been twenty years earlier: here and there were patches of ground that had once been cultivated, which were now separated from each other by ditches filled with brambles and weeds; trees grew where they once had not, and areas that had been planted were now naked. 'All that we had before our eyes was abandoned to the greatest disorder.'[83] Marchand found no trace of the gardens: 'everything had disappeared'.[84] Only the oak tree was still standing, the remains of Napoleon's pond and a small section of the berm.

Acknowledgements

This is the third book I have worked on with Jenny Uglow and I wish to express my heartfelt thanks for her brilliant editing, her deep historical and textual understanding, and her friendship.

Thank you to all at Chatto & Windus: Clara Farmer and Greg Clowes especially, my copy-editor Katherine Fry and my proof-reader Anthony Hippisley.

Thank you to all at W.W. Norton & Company Ltd: Bob Weil, Gabriel Kachuck, Steve Attardo and my cover designer Eric C. Wilder.

Thank you as always to Peter Straus, my agent and friend of many years, and to Melanie Jackson, my agent in the US.

Thank you to Peter Stothard for all his encouragement of my writing.

Thank you to the Master, fellows and students of Gonville and Caius College, Cambridge.

Thank you to Joanna Evans, my picture researcher, and to Alex Bell who made my index.

Thank you to the staff at Cambridge University Library and to Kirstie Preest at Murray Edwards College Library, for making it possible for me to check references during the pandemic.

For professional and personal help of many different kinds, thank you: Nadine Abell, Stig Abell, David Abulafia, Mary Beard, John Casey, Raphael Cormack, Robin Cormack, Charles Dunn,

Richard J. Evans, Biancamaria Fontana, Antonia Fraser, Heather Glen, Kate Gregory, Alexandra Harris, Justin Higgins, Niall Hobhouse, Olivia Horsfall-Turner, Sarah Houghton-Walker, John Kerrigan, Yuri Kim, Adam Lebovitz, Maren Meinhardt, Alan Mikhail, Christopher Prendergast, Munro Price, Michael Sonenscher, Gillian Scurr, Ingrid Scurr, James Scurr, John Scurr, Alina Trabattoni, Paul Wingfield, Brian Young.

Finally, thank you to my daughters, Polly and Rosalind Dunn, wonderful young women and avid readers, to whom this book is dedicated.

Notes

Introduction

1   Lonoff, p. 272.
2   Coleridge (1957), p. 1166.
3   Coleridge (1911) vol. 2, p. 69; Sewell, p. 346.
4   Stendhal (2002), p. 15.
5   Carlyle, p. 29.
6   Sorensen, pp. 296, 284.
7   Ibid., p. 284.
8   Lonoff, p. 272.
9   Ibid., p. 278.
10 Ibid., p. 305. Heger's friend and colleague was Joachim-Joseph Lebel.
11 Holland, vol. 2, p. 101; O'Meara, vol. 2, p. 67.
12 Holland, vol. 2, p. 101; Bourrienne, vol. 3, p. 155.
13 Staël (2008), p. 271.
14 Woolf, p. 35.
15 Coats (1977) p. 45.
16 Saint-Hilaire, p. 2.
17 Stäel (2008), p. 272.

1: First Gardens

1   Jeanson, Le Bon, Zellal, p. 15.
2   Las Cases (2017), p. 97.
3   Ibid., p. 314.
4   Chuquet, p. 118.
5   Dumas, vol. 4, p. 318.
6   Ibid.
7   Bourrienne (1836), vol. 1, p. 3.

8   Chuquet, p. 122.

9   Ibid.

10   Bourrienne (1836), vol. 1, p. 3.

11   Delille (1834), p. 50.

12   Bonaparte (1929), p. 48.

13   Rousseau (1968), p. 305; Hendel, pp. 49–50; Chagneau, p. 37; Williams, p. 90.

14   Chagneau, p. 9.

15   Gueniffey, p. 55.

16   Las Cases (2017), p. 254.

17   Scott (1827), vol. 3, p. 10.

18   Gueniffey, p. 70.

19   *CG*, vol. 1, no. 29. p. 76.

20   Bonaparte (2009b), pp. 95–6.

21   *CG*, vol. 1, no. 2, p. 45.

22   Boswell, p. 191.

23   Conrad, p. 5.

24   Ibid., pp. 5–6.

25   Branda, p. 22.

26   *CG*, vol. 1, nos 4, 5, pp. 47–8.

27   Conrad, pp. 6–7.

28   Gueniffey, p. 23; Bertrand, vol. 3, p. 64.

29   *CG*, vol. 1, no. 24, p. 71; Falk, p. 66.

30   *CG*, vol. 1, no. 23, p. 70.

31   Healey, p. 41.

32   Bonaparte (1907), p. 282.

33   Roger, p. 421.

34   Ibid.

35   *CG*, vol. 1, no. 29, p. 76.

36   Ibid., no. 31, pp. 78–9.

37   Bonaparte (2009b), p. 149.

38   Gueniffey, p. 95.

39   Las Cases (2017), p. 478.

40   Abrantès, vol. 1, p. 56.

41   Monge, p. 91.

42   Bourrienne (1836), vol. 1, p. 12.

43   Las Cases (2017), p. 105.

44   Hillairet, p. 132.

45   Scurr, p. 142.

46   Bourrienne (1836), vol. 1, p. 13.

47   Jordan, p. 21.

48   Bourrienne (1836), vol. 1, p. 13.

49   Las Cases (2017), p. 105.
50   Roudinesco, p. 114.
51   Las Cases (2017), p. 105; Price, pp. 50–1.
52   Price, pp. 50–1.

2: Revolutionary Regeneration

1   *Gazette Nationale ou le Moniteur*, vol. XVII, p. 367.
2   Williams, pp. 46, 126.
3   Spary (2000), p. 183, Williams, p. 142.
4   Scurr, p. 263.
5   Letouzey, p. 361.
6   Ibid., pp. 368–9; Spary (2000), p. 141.
7   Chandler, pp. 27–8.
8   Gueniffey, p. 143.
9   Las Cases (2017), p. 116.
10   Abrantès, vol. 1, p. 62.
11   Bernard, Couailhac, Lemaout, pp. 232–3.
12   Saint-Pierre, p. 56.
13   Bernard, Couailhac, Lemaout, p. x.
14   Robespierre, p. 274.
15   Gueniffey, pp. 151–2.
16   Englund, p. 68.
17   Las Cases (2017), p. 195; Gueniffey, p. 159.
18   Chagneau, p. 64.
19   Bertrand, vol. 1, pp. 175–9.
20   Gueniffey, pp. 153–4.
21   Bertrand, vol. 1, pp. 175–9.
22   *CG*, vol. 1, no. 235, p. 197.
23   Ibid., p. 198.
24   Abrantès, vol. 1, p. 61.
25   Ibid.
26   Robbins, p. 225.
27   Abrantès, vol. 1, p. 60.
28   Ibid., p. 19.
29   Ibid., p. 67.
30   Bourrienne (1836), vol. 1, p. 30.
31   Dard, p. 219.
32   Bonaparte (2009a), p. 15.
33   Ibid., p. 16.
34   Ibid., p. 17.
35   Abrantès, vol. 1, pp. 102–3.

36   Ibid., p. 104.
37   CG, vol. 1, no. 1068, p. 672.
38   Gueniffey, p. 201.
39   O'Meara, vol. 1, pp. 270–1; Gueniffey, p. 179.
40   CG, vol. 1, no. 380, pp. 282–3.
41   Gueniffey, p. 183.
42   Coats (1977), p. 45.
43   Stendhal (2000), p. 3.
44   Thompson (1988), p. 70.
45   Letouzey, p. 464.
46   Ibid.
47   Bonaparte (2009), pp. 30, 37.
48   Ibid., p. 39.
49   CG, vol. 1, no. 993, p. 628.
50   Mainardi, p. 156.
51   Jacques, p. 19.
52   Letouzey, p. 478.
53   Ibid., p. 484.
54   Scott (1827), vol. 3, p. 310.
55   Ibid., p. 292.
56   Ibid., p. 295.
57   Letouzey, p. 489.
58   Ibid.
59   Lytton, p. 166.
60   Las Cases (2017), pp. 292–3.
61   Ibid.
62   Ibid., p. 437.
63   W. von Humboldt, p. 28; https://www.napoleon.org/en/history-of-the-two-empires/articles/a-physical-description-of-napoleon-and-josephine-in-1798-eyewitness-accounts-by-alexander-wilhelm-von-humboldt/
64   Letouzey, p. 545.
65   https://www.napoleon.org/en/history-of-the-two-empires/articles/a-physical-description-of-napoleon-and-josephine-in-1798-eyewitness-accounts-by-alexander-wilhelm-von-humboldt/
66   Letouzey, p. 505.

3: Egyptian Gardens

1   Wright, pp. 235–6; Las Cases (2017), p. 141; Strathern, pp. 45–6.
2   Gueniffey, p. 400.
3   CG, vol. 2, no. 2315, pp. 36–9, Napoleon's report to the Directory on 23 February 1798.

4   Tooke, p. x.
5   Burleigh, p. 16.
6   Cole, pp.13–14.
7   Ibid.
8   Wright, p. 148.
9   Krettly, p. 42; Cole, p. 17.
10 Strathern, p. 38;
11 Letouzey, p. 495.
12 Herold, p. 53.
13 Kete, p. 152.
14 Ibid., p. 163.
15 Wright, p. 108.
16 Burleigh, p. 38.
17 Ibid., p. 55.
18 Ibid., p. 46.
19 Wright, p. 55.
20 Ibid., p. 119.
21 Cole, p. 40.
22 Cole, p. 57.
23 Wright, p. vii.
24 CG, vol. 2, no. 2625, pp. 193–5.
25 Gueniffey, p. 384.
26 Wright, pp. 23–4.
27 Burleigh, p. 68.
28 Wright, p. 59.
29 Behrens-Abouseif (1985), p. 71.
30 Ibid.
31 Al-Jabarti, p. 110.
32 Behrens-Abouseif (1985), p. 71.
33 Las Cases (1836), p. 249.
34 Ibid., p. 294; Gourgaud (1823), vol. 2, p. 294.
35 Fairchild Ruggles, p. 169; Behrens-Abouseif (1985), p. 74.
36 Behrens-Abouseif (1985), p. 74; Al-Jabarti, p. 115.
37 Al-Jabarti, p. 107.
38 Behrens-Abouseif (1985), p. 74.
39 Raymond, p. 299.
40 Fay, p.157.
41 Wright, p. 181.
42 Ibid., p. 208.
43 Cole, p. 110.
44 CG, vol. 2, no. 2654, p. 208.

45   CG, vol. 2, no. 2857, p. 290.

46   Wright, p. 182.

47   Wright, p. 183.

48   *CG*, vol. 2, no. 2635, pp. 199–200; Strathern, p. 258.

49   *CG*, vol. 2, no. 2635, pp. 199–200.

50   Holland, vol. 1, p. 200.

51   Ibid.

52   Strathern, p. 259.

53   Khaldi, p. 21.

54   Ibid., p. 22; Strathern, p. 259; Cole, p. 188.

55   Said, p. 190.

56   Gueniffey, p. 468.

57   Las Cases (2017), p. 139.

58   Guitry, p. 228.

59   Gourgaud (1823), vol. 2, p. 208.

60   Burleigh, p. 51.

61   *Description de l'Égypte*, vol. 19, p. 35.

62   Rabbat, p. 47.

63   Strathern, p. 179.

64   Monge, Berthollet and Magallon were the three members of a commission for putting seals on all the possessions of the Mamelukes. See *CG*, vol. 2, nos 2602, 2808.

65   Gourgaud (1823), p. 288.

66   Behrens-Abouseif (1985), p. 107.

67   Hamilton (1999), p. 3.

68   Al-Jabarti, p. 117.

69   Mikhail, p. 6.

70   Ibid, p. 1.

71   Burleigh, p. 74.

72   Behrens-Abouseif (1985), p. 303.

73   Ibid.

74   Al-Jabarti, p. 115.

75   Burleigh, p. 71.

76   *La Décade*, vol. 1, p. 10.

77   Gourgaud (1823), p. 289.

78   Ibid., p. 288.

79   *La Décade*, vol. 1, pp. 37–46.

80   Bourrienne (1836), vol. 1, p. 161.

81   Bellaigue (2017), p. 4.

82   Burleigh, p. 79; Las Cases (2017), p. 409.

83   Englund, p. 134.

84 Cole, p. 186.

85 Ibid., p. 188.

86 *Journal des Défenseurs de la Patrie*, no. 1493 (29 Nivôse, an 8).

87 Martel, p. xiii.

88 Burleigh, p. 242.

89 Villiers du Terrage, p. 83.

90 Cole, p. 211.

91 Ibid., p. 213.

92 *CG*, vol. 4, no. 2907, pp. 286–7; Cole, p. 105.

93 Burleigh, p. 48.

94 Al-Jabarti, p. 113

95 Strathern, p. 256.

96 Gourgaud (1823), p. 294.

97 Al-Jabarti, p. 114; Behrens-Abouseif (1985), p. 77.

98 Strathern, p. 257.

99 Masson, p. 66.

100 Burleigh, p. 175; p. 177.

101 Ibid., p. 167.

102 Ibid., p. 177.

103 Ibid., p. 185.

104 Ibid., p. 187.

105 *Description de l'Égypte*, vol. 4, p. 457; Bourne, p. 78; *Literary Gazette*, vol. 7, p. 579; *Transactions of the Horticultural Society of London*, 7 July (1818), p. 178.

106 Burleigh, p. 108.

107 Gourgaud (1823), p. 227.

108 Ibid., p. 226.

109 Karabell, p. 20.

110 Ibid., p. 21.

111 Strathern, p. 267.

112 Cole, p. 233; Las Cases (2017), p. 143.

113 Hamilton (2000), p. 25.

114 Ibid., p. 28.

115 Cole, p. 229.

116 Roberts, p. 183.

117 Kete, p. 154.

118 Hamilton (1999), p. 103.

119 Martel, p. 1.

120 Elmarsafy, p. 149; Bonaparte (1907), p. 337.

121 Hamilton (2000), p. 37.

122 Burleigh, pp. 144–5.

123 Cole, p. 244.

124 Behrens-Abouseif (1985), p. 81.

125 Herold, pp. 365–6.

126 Potenza, p. 42.

127 Kennedy, vol. 4, p. 394.

128 Bourrienne (1836), vol. 2, p. 19.

129 Behrens-Abouseif (1985), p. 84; Gillot, p. 418.

130 Behrens-Abouseif (1985), pp. 88–9.

4: Growing a Crown

1   Hicks, p. 45.

2   Lack, p. 10; Williams, p. 147.

3   DeLorme, p. 75.

4   Vigée-Lebrun, vol.1, p. 117

5   Lack, p. 8; DeLorme, p. 79.

6   Lack, p. 22.

7   Ibid., p. 24.

8   Garric (2012), p. 69.

9   Moon, p. 132.

10 Fontaine, vol. 1, p. 7.

11 Ibid., p. 31.

12 In a letter to an unidentified recipient of 10 Prairial, Year 8 (30 May 1800).

13 Fontaine, vol. 1, p. 15.

14 Coats (1977), p. 40.

15 Fontaine, vol. 1, p. 12.

16 Ibid., p. 11.

17 Truffer, Verdan.

18 Moon, p. 125.

19 Fontaine, vol. 1, p. 31.

20 Lemercier, pp. 208–22; https://www.napoleon.org/en/history-of-the-two-empires/articles/the-poet-and-the-consul-a-late-night-conversation-at-malmaison/

21 Rousseau (1816), p. 9; Williams, p. 101.

22 Calder, p. 129.

23 Gueniffey, p. 431.

24 Rœderer, vol. 3, p. 336.

25 Hamilton (1999), p. 48; Ducrest, vol. 2, p. 292.

26 Granger, p. 2728.

27 Ducrest, vol. 2, pp. 284–5.

28 Lenôtre, pp. 51–8.

29 North, pp. 172–9.

30 Las Cases (2017), p. 211.

31 Ibid., pp. 211–12.

32   Webster, p. 154.

33   Rœderer, vol. 3, p. 363.

34   Ibid. p. 357.

35   Ibid.

36   Staël (1821), p. 34.

37   Lenôtre, pp. 51–8; North, p. 133.

38   Staël (1821), p. 34; Lentz, p. 586.

39   Fisher, p. 9.

40   Ducrest, vol. 1, p. 221.

41   Ibid, p. 222.

42   Freud, pp. 130–1.

43   Fontaine, vol. 1, p. 19.

44   Ibid., p. 25.

45   Bourrienne (1836), vol. 2, p. 32.

46   Englund, p. 214.

47   Bourrienne (1836), vol. 2, p. 34; Alison, vol. 4, p. 655.

48   Englund, p. 215.

49   Vovk, p. 344.

50   Fontaine, vol. 1, p. 27.

51   Ibid., p. 26.

52   Staël (1821), p. 50.

53   Ibid., pp. 50–1.

54   Alison, vol. 4, p. 654; Staël (1821), p. 50.

55   DeLorme, p. 81; Disponzio, p. 158.

56   Fontaine, vol. 1, pp. 31–2.

57   Rœderer, vol. 3, p. 342.

58   Alison, vol. 4, p. 672.

59   Ibid.

60   Rœderer, vol. 3, p. 589.

61   Dwyer (2013), p. 82.

62   Ibid., p. 83.

63   DeLorme, p. 194.

64   Staël (1821), p. 59.

65   Ibid., p. 60.

66   Ibid., p. 93.

67   Reinhard, pp. 271–2.

68   Grainger, p. 95.

69   Staël (1821), p. 72.

70   Holland, vol. 2, p. 150.

71   Holmes (2009), p. 200–1; Lubbock, p. 311.

72   Biver, p. 424.

73   Granger, p. 2729.

74   Holland, vol. 2, pp. 151–2.

5: Terre Napoléon

1   Coleridge (1957), vol. 1, p. 1166; Vallins, Oishi, Perry, p. 43.

2   Harrison, p. 35; Tombs, Tombs, p. 148; Sivasundaram, p. 44.

3   Harrison, p. 34.

4   Ibid., p. 35.

5   Scott (1910), p. 146.

6   Humboldt (1814–29), vol. 1, p. 7; Scott (1910), p. 154.

7   Bourgoin, Taillemite, p. 6.

8   Scott (1910), p. 166.

9   Letouzey, p. 529.

10   Conrad, p. 7.

11   Ibid., p. 8.

12   Letouzey, p. 557.

13   Ibid., p. 644.

14   Alison, vol. 4, p. 659.

15   Ibid., p. 663.

16   Ibid., p. 664.

17   Ibid., pp. 664–5.

18   Letouzey, p. 529.

19   Arneville et al., p. 24.

20   Letouzey, p. 536.

21   Ibid., p. 541.

22   Arneville et al., p. 83. Letter dated 26 October 1803. Nelson, Rouke, p. 668.

23   Coats (1969), p. 260.

24   Arneville et al., p. 133.

25   Ibid., p. 111.

26   Jones, p. 58; Arneville et al., p. 25.

27   Archives Parlementaires, 6 August 1803.

28   Letouzey, p. 558.

29   Ibid., p. 560.

30   Scott (1910), p. 248.; *Gazette Nationale ou le Moniteur*, 14 Messidor, Year 11 (3 July 1803).

31   Arneville et al., p. 135.

32   Ibid., pp. 127–8, 122.

33   Ibid., pp. 142–5.

34   Milgrom, p. 5.

35   Ibid.; Farber, p. 561.

36   Arneville et al., p. 69.

37   DeLorme, p. 85.

38   Arneville et al., p. 23.

39   Coats (1977), p. 46.

40   Williams, p. 148.

41   Thompson (1934), pp. 111–12. Letter dated 1 March 1805.

42   Letouzey, p. 533.

43   Ibid., p. 584.

44   Arneville et al., pp. 50–1.

45   Staël (1821), p. 52.

46   Hazareesingh, p. 190.

47   Ibid., p. 298.

48   Ibid., p. 158.

49   Girard, p. 70.

50   Hazareesingh, p. 306.

51   Wordsworth, p. 126.

52   Hazareesingh, p. 301.

53   Beckett, p. 6; Leadlay, pp. 4–5; Michal, Jackson, pp. 50–3.

54   Las Cases (2017), p. 516; Hazareesingh, p. 301.

55   Hazareesingh (2020), pp. 301–2.

56   Arneville et al., p. 26.

57   Ibid., p. 132.

58   Ibid., pp. 113, 128.

59   Ibid., p.136.

60   Rémusat, vol.2, p. 122.

61   Las Cases (2017), p. 216.

62   *Gazette Nationale ou le Moniteur*, 30 Pluviôse, Year 12 (20 February 1804).

63   Staël (1821), p. 122.

64   Letouzey, pp. 560, 568.

65   Ibid., p. 603.

66   Ibid., p. 654.

67   Ibid., p. 562.

68   Ibid., p. 565.

69   Ibid., p. 550.

70   Ibid., p. 584.

71   Robertson, p. 295.

72   Arneville et al., p. 21.

73   Ibid., p. 51.

74   Ibid.

75   Ibid., p. 93; Letouzey, p. 651.

76   Arneville et al., p. 32.

77   Ibid., p. 113.

78   Croix (1805), p. 358.

79   Ibid, p. 360.

80   June 1805, letter from Banks to Flinders; Scott (1910), p. 78.

81   Arneville et al., p. 114.

82   Chandler, pp. 412–13.

83   Ibid., p. 413.

84   Ibid., p. 439.

85   C. Fraser, p. 109.

86   Ibid., pp. 112–13.

87   Ibid., p. 119.

88   Ibid., pp. 116–17.

89   Arneville et al., p. 137.

90   Ibid., p. 145.

91   Letouzey, p. 561.

92   Ibid.

93   Arneville et al., p. 44, p.183.

94   Ibid., p. 26.

95   Scott (1910), p. 261.

96   Ibid., p. 88.

97   Ibid., p. 70.

98   Ibid., p. 83.

99   Ibid., p. 82.

6: The Forest of Fontainebleau

1   Fontaine, vol. 1, p. 352.

2   Tendron, p. 7.

3   A. Fraser, p. 35.

4   Terrasse, p. 20.

5   Tylus, p. 121.

6   Olson, p. 79.

7   Fontaine, vol. 1, p. 91.

8   Ricard, p. 251.

9   Fontaine, vol. 1, p. 88.

10   Ibid., p. 91.

11   Englund, p. 245.

12   Dwyer (2013), p. 180.

13   Fontaine, vol. 1, pp. 92–3.

14   Vittet, p. 9.

15   Rémusat, vol. 2, p. 455.

16   Tendron, p. 22.

17   Ibid.

18   Ibid., p. 23; Rémusat, vol. 2, p. 641.

19   Rémusat, vol. 2, p. 644.

20   Tendron, p. 23.

21   Rémusat, vol. 2, p. 644

22   *Secret History of St Cloud*, pp. 33–4.

23   Matteson, p. 116.

24   Ibid., p. 106.

25   Ibid., p. 152.

26   Ibid., p. 155.

27   Ibid., p. 157.

28   Ibid., p. 171.

29   Rémusat, vol. 2, pp. 447–8.

30   Matteson, p. 173.

31   Ibid.

32   Lormant, p. 31.

33   Ibid., p. 32.

34   Matteson, p. 34.

35   Lormant, p. 33.

36   Rémusat, vol. 2, p. 452.

37   Lormant, p. 35.

38   Ibid.

39   Compare letter to Josephine mentioning royal boxes in four great Parisian theatres, 17 March 1807.

40   Thompson (1934), p. 143.

41   Lormant, p. 35.

42   Matteson, p. 165.

43   Ibid., p. 177; Williams, p. 166.

44   Ibid., p. 180.

45   Ibid., p. 182.

46   Ibid., p. 252.

47   Ibid., p. 183; Williams, p. 172.

48   Matteson, p. 175.

49   Vittet, p. 19.

50   *CG*, vol. 8, no. 19042, pp. 1126–7.

51   Thompson (1934), p. 227.

52   Talleyrand, pp. 330–1.

53   Thompson (1988), p. 296.

54   Ibid., p. 300.

55   Geiringer, Geiringer, p. 192.

56   Wheelock Thayer, Hermann, Reimann, vol. 2, p. 150.

57   Las Cases (2017), p. 383.

58   Rapp, p. 147.

59   Staël (1821), p. 261.

60   Rapp, p. 149.

61   Thompson (1934), p. 258.

62   Williams, p. 61.

63   Arago (1859), pp. 82–3.

64   Ibid., pp. 78, 83.

65   Stafleu, p. 436.

66   Packard, p. 82.

67   Riskin, p. 5.

68   Ibid.

69   Barthélemy-Maudle, p. 37.

70   Vittet, p. 21.

71   Verlet (2014), p. 16.

72   Courajod, p. 12.

73   Castellan, p. 400.

74   Ibid., p. 9.

7: Imperial Gardens

1   Boyer, pp. 103–4.

2   Bourrienne (1836), vol. 4, pp. 370–8.

3   Tacitus, Book II, p. 313.

4   Bourrienne (1836), vol. 4, p. 371.

5   Tardieu, p. 14; Tollfree, p. 209; Huet, p. 63.

6   Ridley, p. 248.

7   Fontaine, vol. 1, p. 268.

8   Johns (1998), p. 117.

9   Ridley, p. 86.

10   Boyer, pp. 103–4.

11   Ibid., p. 104.

12   Ridley, p. 300.

13   Ibid., pp. 49–50.

14   Ibid., p. 81.

15   Ibid., p. 58.

16   Ibid., p. 57.

17   Ibid., p. 141.

18   Ibid., p. 54.

19   Ibid., p. 57.

20   Ibid., p. 67.

21   Ibid., p. 143.

22   Ibid., p. 139.

23 Ibid., p. 143.

24 Ibid., pp. 80–1.

25 Ibid., p. 144.

26 Ibid., p. 143.

27 Ibid., p. 144.

28 Ibid.

29 Fontaine, vol. 1, p. 133.

30 Tollfree, p. 173.

31 Ibid., p. 199.

32 Ibid., p. 184, Fontaine, vol. 1, p. 145.

33 Garric (2012), p. 133.

34 Tollfree, p. 187.

35 Fontaine, vol. 1, pp. 284–5.

36 Ibid., p. 269.

37 Ibid., p. 290.

38 Ibid., pp. 312, 299, 302.

39 CG, vol. 7, no. 14483, p. 265; Chagneau, p. 23.

40 Prod'homme, Martens, p. 598.

41 Johns (1998), p. 125.

42 Ibid., p. 126.

43 Huet, p. 59.

44 Plant, p. 57.

45 Ibid., p. 59.

46 Ibid., p. 57.

47 Ibid., p. 53.

48 Ibid., pp. 61, 59.

49 Ibid., p. 59.

50 Ibid., p. 60.

51 Bourrienne (1836), vol. 4, p. 376.

52 Plant, p. 71.

53 Fontaine, vol. 1, p. 261.

54 Ibid., p. xxvii.

55 Ibid., p. 262.

56 Ibid., p. 264.

57 Gaillard, p. 26

58 Gaillard, p. 28

59 Thompson (1934), p. 251.

60 Gaillard, p. 28.

61 Ibid., p. 30.

62 Fontaine, vol. 1, p. 376.

63 Ibid., vol. 1, pp. 146, 281.

64 Garric (2012), p. 143.

65 Fontaine, vol. 1, p. 274.

66 Ibid., p. 271.

67 Ibid., p. 276.

68 Ibid., p. 278.

69 Ibid., p. 288.

70 Ibid., pp. 289, 290; Garric (2016), p. 255.

71 Garric (2012), p. 139.

72 Ibid.

73 Fontaine, vol. 1, p. 310.

74 Ridley, p. 144.

75 Ibid., p. 68.

76 Ridley, p. 144.

77 Fontaine, vol. 1, p. 283.

78 Ibid., pp. 297–8.

79 Tollfree (1999), p. 181.

80 Ridley, p. 66.

81 Ibid.

82 Kirk, p. 116.

83 Ridley, p. 72.

84 Kirk, p. 119.

85 Ridley, p. 151.

86 Ibid., p. 152.

87 Fontaine, vol. 1, pp. 294, 316.

88 Ibid., p. 317.

89 Ibid., p. 323.

90 Ibid., p. 234.

91 Ibid., p. 334; Garric (2012), p. 146.

92 Mikaberidze, pp. 79, 86; Saint-Denis, p. 23.

93 Shvidkovsky, Reteyum, p. 30.

94 Garric (2012), pp. 147–8.

95 Garric (2016), p. 256.

96 Roustam (1911), p. 166.

8: Gardens on Elba

1 Thompson (1934), p. 355.

2 Hobhouse, vol. 1, p. 193.

3 Hicks, p. 53.

4 Roberts, p. 717.

5 Hobhouse, vol. 1, p. 193.

6 Saint-Denis (1922), pp. 67–70.

7   Marchand, p. 116.
8   Campbell, p. 18.
9   Thompson (1949), p. 7.
10 Ibid., p. 6.
11 Olney, p. 5.
12 O'Keeffe, p. 134.
13 Ibid., p. 135.
14 Thompson (1934), p. 353.
15 By Bertrand Barère de Vieuzac.
16 Hicks, p. 67.
17 Dallas, p. 262.
18 Halsall, p. 5.
19 Wolff, p. 131.
20 Hicks, p. 58.
21 Braude, p. 99.
22 Wolff, p. 124.
23 Branda, p. 60.
24 Hicks, p. 60.
25 Saint-Denis, p. 75.
26 Ibid.
27 Ibid.
28 Ibid., p. 89.
29 Ibid., p. 76.
30 Coats (1977), p. 45.
31 Braude, p. 102.
32 Arrigoni, pp. 11–13.
33 Wolff, p. 55.
34 Thompson (1934), p. 355.
35 Marchand, p. 88.
36 Wolff, p. 230.
37 Saint-Denis, p. 83.
38 Ibid.
39 Marchand, p. 104.
40 Higginbotham, p. 72.
41 Braude, p. 72.
42 Marchand, p. 90.
43 Braude, p. 104.
44 Saint-Denis, p. 94.
45 Marchand, p. 103.
46 Saint-Denis, p. 97, claims stay was ten days; Marchand, p. 113, claims stay was twenty-four hours.

47   Marchand, p. 127. Cipriani had been a trusted deputy of the Corsican Saliceti.
48   Marchand, p. 130.
49   Marchand, pp. 133–4.
50   Dallas, p. 264.
51   Fortescue, p. 23.
52   Ibid., p. 8.
53   Fortescue, p. 19.
54   Marchand, p. 138.
55   Ibid.
56   Braude, p. 201.
57   Chaboulon, vol. 1, p. 81.
58   Hicks, p. 65.
59   Meehan, p. 58.
60   Marchand, p. 141.
61   Saint-Denis, p. 100.
62   Braude, p. 204.
63   Saint-Denis, pp. 100–1.
64   Marchand, pp. 142–3.
65   Braude, p. 219.
66   Ibid., p. 225.
67   Ibid., p. 226.
68   Wolff, p. 166.
69   Wolff, p. 42.

9: The Walled Garden at Waterloo

1   Hugo, p. 279.
2   Fontaine, vol. 1, p. 447.
3   Ibid., p. 449.
4   Ibid.; Charras, p. 85.
5   Fontaine, vol. 1, p. 457.
6   Ibid.; Marchand, pp. 238–9.
7   Scurr, pp. 307–8.
8   Dallas, p. 367.
9   Paget, Saunders, p. 7; Damiens (2012), p. 6.
10   White, p. 30.
11   Paget, Saunders, p. 24.
12   Ibid., p. 34.
13   Marchand, pp. 243–4.
14   Paget, Saunders, p. 35.
15   Ibid., p. 39.

16 Crumplin https://ageofrevolution.org/themes/science-technology/keep-hougoumont-at-what-price/
17 Paget, Saunders, p. 45.
18 Ibid., p. 49.
19 Paget, Saunders, p. 53.
20 Ibid.
21 Ibid., p. 54.
22 Ibid., p. 56.
23 Ibid., p. 54.
24 Ibid., p. 60.
25 Ibid., pp. 62–3.
26 Marchand, p. 247; Saint-Denis, p. 133; Pascoe, p. 101.
27 Price, p. 10.
28 Mercer, pp. 90–1.
29 Paget, Saunders, pp. 71–2.
30 White, p. 5.
31 Hugo, p. 296.
32 Damiens, p. 42.
33 *Ipswich Journal*, 16 December 1876, p. 7.
34 Hugo, p. 278.
35 Ibid., p. 281.
36 Ibid., p. 283.
37 Ibid.
38 Ibid., p. 319.
39 Ibid.
40 Fontaine, vol. 1, p. 459.
41 Ibid., vol. 1, p. 460.
42 Marchand, p. 257.
43 Pincemaille, Tamisier-Vétois, p. 54.
44 Arago (1848), p. 131.
45 Bourguignon, pp. 15–21.
46 Lack, p. 55.
47 DeLorme, p. 100; Jouanin, p. 58.
48 Lentz, p. 371.
49 Chateaubriand, Book XXIV, Chapter 1, Section 1.
50 Marchand, p. 142.
51 Ibid., p. 144.
52 Ibid., p. 152.
53 https://ilesjardinsilesparadis.com/le-regard-de-gilles-clement-dans-le-paysage-de-lile-daix-et-au-fort-liedot/
54 Gourgaud (1823), vol. 1, p. 36.

55　CG, vol. 15, no. 40066, p. 1103.
56　Hugo, p. 321.
57　Ibid.
58　https://projecthougoumont.com/restoration-of-hougoumont-the-next-phase/
59　Bellaigue (1978), pp. 14–18.
60　Las Cases (1836), vol. 1, p. 319; http://napoleon-monuments.eu/Napoleon1er/1815Goumont.htm

10: Last Garden

1　Lonoff, p. 278.
2　Bourrienne (1836), vol. 4, pp. 261, 235.
3　Cockburn, p. 74; Las Cases (2017), p. 95.
4　Las Cases (1836), vol. 1, p. 102.
5　Roberts, p. 781.
6　Marchand, p. 560.
7　Aubry, p. 123.
8　Ibid., p. 128.
9　Las Cases (2017), p. 490.
10　Aubry, pp. 133–4.
11　Shorter, p. 335.
12　Buffon, vol. 12, p. 259.
13　Malcolm, p. 41.
14　O'Meara, vol. 1, p. 33; Las Cases (2017), p. 393.
15　Gregory, p. 22.
16　Kelly, p. 93.
17　Daniels, p. 105.
18　O'Meara, vol. 1, p. 19; http://www.sthelenaisland.info/slavery/
19　Las Cases (2017), pp. 490, 670–1.
20　CG, vol. 15, no. 40090, pp. 1116–31.
21　Ibid., p. 1120.
22　Marchand, p. 621.
23　Tyson Stroud, p. 77.
24　Marchand, p. 568.
25　Ibid., pp. 507–8.
26　O'Meara, vol. 1, p. 59.
27　Chuquet, p. 78.
28　Marchand, p. 620.
29　Ibid.
30　Roberts, p. 793.
31　O'Meara, vol. 1, p. 169.
32　Atkinson, p. 36.

33 Antommarchi, vol.1, p. 261.

34 In the appendix of persons in Napoleon's household on St Helena at the end of Walter Scott's biography, there is also one unnamed English gardener.

35 Saint-Denis, p. 201.

36 Marchand, p. 591.

37 Ibid., p. 592.

38 Antommarchi, vol. 1, p. 261.

39 Ibid., p. 262.

40 Saint-Denis, p. 211.

41 Marchand, p. 613.

42 Naturel, Vigo, p. 304.

43 Marchand, p. 597.

44 Antommarchi, vol. 1, p. 263.

45 Ibid., p. 203; Marchand, p. 592.

46 Cronk, p. 22.

47 Saint-Denis, p. 205.

48 Saint-Denis, pp. 206–7; Naturel, Vigo, p. 304.

49 Musée-hôtel Bertrand, Châteauroux.

50 Marchand, p. 611.

51 Ibid., p. 612.

52 Saint-Denis, p. 207.

53 Marchand, p. 555.

54 Ibid., p. 564.

55 Gourgaud (1903), p. 273

56 Marchand, p. 612.

57 Ibid., p. 613.

58 Grigson, p. 153.

59 Roberts, p. 788; Unwin, p. 185; Forsyth, p. 225.

60 Forsyth, p. 225.

61 O'Meara, vol. 2, p. 351.

62 Lack, p. 42.

63 Gourgaud (1823), p. 252.

64 Saint-Denis, p. 204.

65 Antommarchi, vol. 2, p. 363.

66 She died on 7 August 1820, but the news did not reach Napoleon until later in the year.

67 Marchand, p. 639.

68 Ibid., p. 654.

69 Bourrienne (1836), vol. 4, p. 294.

70 Ibid., pp. 296–7.

71 Marchand, p. 644.

72   Bourrienne (1836), vol. 4, p. 296.
73   Ibid., p. 299.
74   Homer, p. 142.
75   Bourrienne (1836), vol. 4, p. 297.
76   Loudon, pp. 700–2.
77   Ibid., pp. 700–1.
78   Ibid., p. 702.
79   Wordsworth, p. 108.
80   Haydon, p. 503.
81   Ibid., p. 477.
82   Ibid., p. 651.
83   Ali (2003), pp. 160–1.
84   Marchand, p. 608.

Bibliography

Napoleon's Letters

CG *Correspondance générale, Napoléon Bonaparte*, présentation du baron Gourgaud, introduction générale de Jacques-Olivier Boudon, 15 vols, Paris: Fayard, 2004–18.

Journals

Archives Parlementaires de 1787 à 1860, Débats Législatifs et Politiques des chambres Françaises, sous la direction de M.J. Mavidal et de M.E. Laurent, Paris: Librairie administrative de Paul Dupont.

La Décade égyptienne: Journal littéraire et d'économie politique, 3 vols, Cairo: Imprimerie Nationale, 1798–9.

Description de l'Égypte publiée par les ordres de Sa Majesté l'Empereur Napoléon le Grand, complete digital version, Le Mans: Harpocrate, 2006.

Gazette nationale ou le Moniteur universel, Société canadienne du microfilm, Montréal.

Ipswich Journal, and Suffolk, Norfolk, Essex and Cambridgeshire Advertiser, est. 1725.

Journal des Défenseurs de la Patrie, nos 1–2278, 17 avril 1796–20 mars 1802, Paris.

Journal de Paris, 21 févr. 1795–30 sept. 1811, Paris: Imprimerie du Journal de Paris.

Literary Gazette: A Weekly Journal of Literature, Science, and the Fine Arts, 1823, ed. W. Jerdan, W. Ring Workman, F. Arnold, J. Morley, C. Wycliffe Goodwin, London: Henry Colburn.

Transactions of the Horticultural Society of London, London, 1812–48.

Books and Articles

Abrantès, L.J. duchesse d' (1836), *Memoirs of Napoleon, his Court and Family*, 2 vols, London: Richard Bentley.

Ali, M. (Louis-Étienne Saint-Denis) (2000), *Souvenirs sur L'Empereur Napoléon*, ed. C. Bourachot, Paris: Arléa.

Ali, M. (Louis-Étienne Saint-Denis) (2003), *Journal inédit du Retour des Cendres 1840*, ed. J. Jourquin, Paris: Tallandier Éditions.

Alison, A. (1835), *History of Europe during the French Revolution*, vols 3 and 4, Edinburgh: William Blackwood and Sons.

Al-Jabarti, A. al-R. (1975), *Al-Jabarti's Chronicle of the First Seven Months of the French Occupation of Egypt*, trans. S. Moreh, Leiden: E.J. Brill.

Anon. (1807), *The Secret History of the Court and Cabinet of Saint Cloud*, New York: Brisban & Brannan.

Antommarchi, F. (1826), *Memoirs of the last two years of Napoleon's exile*, 2 vols, London: Henry Colburn.

Arago, F. (1848), 'Éloges de Gaspard Monge', *Mémoires de l'Académie des sciences*, XXIV, 131–3.

Arago, F. (1859), *The History of My Youth: An Autobiography of Francis Arago*, Boston: Ticknor and Fields.

Arneville, M.-B. d', Benoît, J., Chevallier, B., Chiappero, P.-J., Jouanin, C., Ledoux-Lebard, G., (1997), *L'Impératrice Joséphine et Les Sciences Naturelles*, Paris: Réunion des musées nationaux.

Arrigoni, T. (2014), *Il Giardiniere di Napoleone: Vita e Avventure di Claude Hollard*, Piombino: La Bancarella Editrice.

Atkinson, D. (2012), *The Criminal Conversation of Mrs Norton*, Canada: Preface Publishing.

Aubry, O. (1937), *St. Helena*, trans. A. Livingston, London: Victor Gollancz Ltd.

Bailleux, N. (2016), ed., *La Conquête de la Mémoire: Napoléon à Sainte Hélène*, Paris: Gallimard/Musée de l'Armée.

Barthélemy-Maudle, M. (1982), *Lamarck, the Mythical Precursor: a Study of the Relations between Science and Ideology*, Massachusetts: MIT Press.

Beckett, G. (2004), 'Master of the Wood: Moral Authority and Political Imaginaries in Haiti', *Political and Legal Anthropology Review*, vol. 27, no. 2, pp. 1–19.

Behrens-Abouseif, D. (1985), *Azbakiyya and its environs: From Azbak to Ismāʿīl, 1476–1879*, Cairo: Institut français d'archéologie orientale.

Behrens-Abouseif, D. (1992), 'Gardens in Islamic Egypt', *Der Islam*, 69 (2), pp. 302–12.

Bellaigue, C. de (2017), *The Islamic Enlightenment: The Modern Struggle between Faith and Reason*, London: The Bodley Head.

Bellaigue, G. de (1978), 'The Waterloo Elm', *Furniture History*, vol. 14, pp. 14–18.

Bernard, P., Couailhac, L., Lemaout, G. and E. (1842), *Le Jardin des Plantes*, 2 vols, Paris: L. Curmer.

Bertrand, H.-G. (1949–59), *Cahiers de Sainte-Hélène*, ed. P.F. de Langle, 3 vols, Paris: Sulliver-Albin Michel.

Beyeler, C. (2015), ed., *Pie VII face à Napoléon: La tiare dans les serres de l'Aigle, Rome, Paris, Fontainebleau, 1796–1814*, Paris: Réunion des musées nationaux.

Biver, M.L. (1963) 'Le "Napoléon" de Canova', *Revue des Deux Mondes*, pp. 424–9.

Bonaparte, N. (1907), *Manuscrits inédits, 1786–1791 / Napoléon, publ. d'après les originaux autographes*, ed. F. Masson et G. Biagi, Paris: Librairie Paul Ollendorff.

Bonaparte, N. (1929), *Le discours de Lyon par le lieutenant Napoléon Bonaparte*, intro. E. Driault, Paris: Éditions Albert Morancé.

Bonaparte, N. (2001), *Œuvres littéraires et écrits militaires*, ed. J. Tulard, 3 vols, Paris: Bibliothèque des Introuvables.

Bonaparte, N. (2009a), *Clisson et Eugénie*, trans. P. Hicks, London: Gallic Books.

Bonaparte, N. (2009b), *La Corse du jeune Bonaparte: Manuscrits de jeunesse*, ed. A. Casanova, Ajaccio: Albiana.

Bonaparte, N. (2018), *Napoleon's Commentaries on the Wars of Julius Caesar*, trans. R.A. Maguire, South Yorkshire: Pen & Sword Military.

Boswell, J. (1768), *An Account of Corsica: The Journal of a Tour to that Island, and Memoirs of Pascal Paoli*, London: Edward and Charles Dilly.

Bourgoin, J., Taillemite, E. (2002), 'The Baudin Expedition to Australia 1800-1804', *International Hydrographic Review*, vol. 3, no.1, pp. 6–19.

Bourguigonon, J. (1947), *Les Adieux de Malmaison (29 Juin, 1815)*, Paris: Paul Lechevalier.

Bourne, H. (1833), *Flores Poetici: The Florist's Manual: Designed as an Introduction to Vegetable Physiology and Systematic Botany for Cultivators of Flowers. With More*

Than Eighty Beautifully-coloured Engravings of Poetic Flowers, Boston: Munro and Francis.

Bourrienne, L.A.F. de (1831), *Mémoires sur Napoléon, le Directoire, le Consulat, l'Empire et la Restauration*, 10 vols, Paris: Ladvocat.

Bourrienne, L.A.F. de (1836), *Memoirs of Napoleon Bonaparte by M. de Bourrienne, his Private Secretary*, 4 vols, London: Richard Bentley.

Boyer, F. (1943), 'La conservation des monuments antiques à Rome sous Napoléon', in *Comptes rendus des séances de l'Académie des Inscriptions et Belles-Lettres*, 87e année, N. 1, pp. 101–8.

Branda, P. (2007), *Napoléon et l'argent*, Paris: Fayard.

Braude, M. (2018), *The Invisible Emperor: Napoleon on Elba*, London: Profile Books.

Broers, M. (2002), *The Politics of Religion in Napoleonic Italy: The War against God, 1801–1814*, London and New York: Routledge.

Broers, M. (2018), *Napoleon: The Spirit of the Age*, London: Faber & Faber.

Buffon, G.-L.L. Comte de, Daubenton, L.-J.-M, Montbeillard, P.G. de, Bexon, G.-L.-C.A. (1749–89), *Histoire naturelle, générale et particulière, avec la description du Cabinet du Roi*, 36 vols, Paris: Imprimerie Royale.

Burleigh, N. (2007), *Mirage: Napoleon's Scientists and the Unveiling of Egypt*, New York: HarperCollins.

Calder, M. (2006), ed., *Experiencing the Garden in the Eighteenth Century*, Bern: Verlag Peter Lang.

Campbell, N. (2004), *Napoleon on Elba: Diary of an Eyewitness to Exile*, Welwyn Garden City: Ravenhall Books.

Carlyle, T. (2010), *On Heroes, Hero-Worship and the Heroic in History, The Works of Thomas Carlyle*, vol. 5, Cambridge: Cambridge University Press.

Castellan, A.L. (1840), *Fontainebleau: Études Pittoresques et Historiques sur ce Château*, Paris: Gaillot.

Chaboulon, le Baron Fleury de (1820), *Memoirs of the Private Life, Return and Reign of Napoleon in 1815*, 2 vols, London: John Murray.

Chagneau, C. (1978), ed., *Jardins en France 1760–1820*, trans. W. Wheeler, Paris: Caisse nationale des monuments historiques et des sites.

Chambers, N. (1999), 'The correspondence of Sir Joseph Banks', *Notes and Records of the Royal Society of London*, vol. 53, no. 1, pp. 27–57.

Chandler, D.G. (2009), *The Campaigns of Napoleon*, New York: Scribner.

Charras, J.B.A. (1857), *Histoire de la campagne de 1815*, Leipzig: A. Dürr

Chateaubriand, F. (2005), *Mémoires d'Outre-Tombe*, trans. A.S. Kline, Poetry in Translation. https://www.poetryintranslation.com/PITBR/Chateaubriand/Chathome.php

Chuquet, A. (1898), *La jeunesse de Napoléon: Brienne*, Paris: Librairie Armand Colin.

Clayton, T., O'Connell, S. (2015), *Bonaparte and the British: Prints and Propaganda in the Age of Napoleon*, London: British Museum.

Coats, A.M. (1969), *The Quest for Plants*, London: Studio Vista.

Coats, A.M. (1977), 'The Empress Josephine', *Garden History*, vol. 5, no. 3, pp. 40–6.

Cockburn, G. (1888), *Extract from a Diary of Rear-Admiral Sir George Cockburn, with particular reference to Gen. Napoleon Buonaparte, on passage from England to St. Helena, in 1815. On board H. M. S. 'Northumberland'*, London: Simpkin, Marshall.

Cole, J. (2007), *Napoleon's Egypt: Invading the Middle East*, London: Palgrave Macmillan.

Coleridge, S.T. (1911), *Biographia Epistolaris: being the biographical supplement of Coleridge's Biographia Literaria*, ed. A. Turnbull, London: G. Bell and Sons Ltd.

Coleridge, S.T. (1957), *The Notebooks of Samuel Taylor Coleridge, Volume 1, 1794–1804*, ed. K. Coburn, New York: Pantheon, Bollingen series L.

Collectif (1978), *Jardins en France 1760–1820*, Paris: Caisse nationale des monuments historiques et des sites.

Conrad, M. (1961), 'Jardins disparus', *Revue d'études historiques, littéraires et scientifiques Corses*, no. 1, Ajaccio: Archives départementales de la Corse, pp. 5–12.

Cordier, S. (2018), ed., *Napoleon: The Imperial Household*, New Haven and London: Yale University Press.

Courajod L. (1886), 'La Diane de Bronze du Chateau de Fontainebleau', *Revue Archéologique*, 3rd series, vol. 7, January–June 1886, pp. 10–19.

Croix, N. de la (1752), *Géographie moderne*, Paris: Delalain l'aîné.

Croix, N. de la (1805), *Géographie moderne*, ed. M. Fontenai, Paris: Delalain Fils.

Cronin, V. (1972), *Napoleon Bonaparte: An Intimate Biography*, London: William Collins.

Cronk, Q.C.B. (2000), *The Endemic Flora of St Helena*, England: Anthony Nelson.

Crumplin, M.K.H. (Waterloo 2000, 2014–2020), https://ageofrevolution.org/themes/science-technology/keep-hougoumont-at-what-price/

Cruysen, Y.V. (2015), *Waterloo: Busting the Myths*, Waterloo: Éditions Jourdan.

Dallas, G. (1996), *1815: The Roads to Waterloo*, London: Richard Cohen Books.

Damiens, M. (2012), *Hougoumont: une clé de la bataille de Waterloo*, San Francisco: Scribd.

Daniels, M. (1991), 'A Memento of Napoleon', *The British Library Journal*, vol. 17, no.1, pp. 104–8.

Dard, E. (1939) 'Napoléon Romancier', *Revue des Deux Mondes (1829–1971)*, vol. 54, no. 2, pp. 214–28.

Delille, J. (1832), *Œuvres de Delille: Les Géorgiques*, Paris: Furne, Libraire-Éditeur.

Delille, J. (1834), *Œuvres de Delille: Les Jardins,* Paris and Avignon: Lebailly & Chaillot.

DeLorme, E.P. (2005), *Josephine and the Arts of the Empire*, Los Angeles: Paul Getty Museum.

Disponzio, J. (2001), 'Jean-Marie Morel', *Studies in the History of Gardens and Designed Landscapes*, nos. 3–4, pp. 158–61.

Droguet, V. (2011), *Fontainebleau le temps des jardins*, no. 5, Amis du Château de Fontainebleau.

Ducrest, G. (1829), *Memoirs of the Empress Josephine, with anecdotes of the courts of Navarre and Malmaison*, 2 vols, London: Henry Colburn.

Dufresnes (1803), *Nouveau dictionnaire d'histoire naturelle appliquée aux arts: principalement à l'économie rurale et domestique,* Paris: Deterville.

Dumas, A. (1842), *Œuvres d'Alex. Dumas: Napoléon*, vol. 4, Brussels: Méline, Cans et Compagnie.

Dwyer, P. (2007), *The Path to Power (1769–1799)*, London: Bloomsbury.

Dwyer, P. (2013), *Citizen Emperor: Napoleon in Power (1799–1815)*, London: Bloomsbury.

Dwyer, P. (2018), *Napoleon: Passion, Death and Resurrection 1815–1840*, London: Bloomsbury.

Edwards, C. (1999), ed., *Receptions of Rome in European Culture 1789–1945*, Cambridge: Cambridge University Press.

Elmarsafy, Z. (2009), *The Enlightenment Qur'an: The Politics of Translation and the Construction of Islam*, Oxford: One World.

Englund, S. (2004), *Napoleon: A Political Life*, Cambridge, MA: Harvard University Press.

Fairchild Ruggles, D. (2008), *Islamic Gardens and Landscapes*, Pennsylvania: Penn Studies in Landscape Architecture.

Falk, A. (2007), *Napoleon Against Himself: A Psychobiography*, Charlottesville, Virginia: Pitchstone Publishing.

Farber, P.L. (1977), 'The Development of Taxidermy and the History of Ornithology', *Isis*, vol. 68, no. 4, pp. 550–66.

Fay, M.A. (2012), *Unveiling the Harem: Elite Women and the Paradox of Seclusion in Eighteenth-Century Cairo*, Syracuse, New York: Syracuse University Press.

Fisher, H. A. L. (1914), *Bonapartism: Six Lectures*, Oxford, Clarendon Press.

Fontaine, P.-F.-L. (1987), *Journal: 1799–1853*, 2 vols, Paris: École nationale supérieure des beaux-arts.

Fornasiero, J., Lawton, L., West-Sooby, J. (2016), eds, *The Art of Science: Nicolas Baudin's Voyagers 1800–1804*, Adelaide: Wakefield Press.

Forsyth, W. (1853), *History of the Captivity of Napoleon at St. Helena: from the letters of the late Lieut.-Gen Sir Hudson Lowe, and official documents not before made public*, London: J. Murray.

Fortescue, H.F. (1823), *Memorandum of Two Conversations Between the Emperor Napoleon and Viscount Ebrington at Porto Ferrajo, on the 6th and 8th of December, 1814*, London: J. Ridgway.

Fraser, A. (2006), *Love and Louis XIV: The Women in the Life of the Sun King*, London: Weidenfeld & Nicolson.

Fraser, E. (1912), *War Drama of the Eagles*, London: John Murray.

Freud, S. (1997), *The Interpretation of Dreams*, trans. A.A. Brill, Hertfordshire: Wordsworth Editions.

Gaillard, M. (1998), *L'Arc de Triomphe*, trans. N. Randall, Amiens: Martelle Éditions.

Garric, J.-P. (2012), *Percier et Fontaine: Les architectes de Napoléon*, Paris: Belin.

Garric, J.-P. (2016), ed., *Charles Percier: Architecture and Design in an Age of Revolutions*, New York: Bard Graduate Center Gallery.

Geiringer, K., Geiringer, I. (1982), *Haydn: A Creative Life in Music*, California: University of California Press.

Gershenowitz, H. (1980), 'Napoleon and Lamarck', *Indian Journal of History of Science*, 15(2), pp. 204–9.

Gillispie, C.C. (2004), *Science and Polity in France: The Revolutionary and Napoleonic Years*, Princeton: Princeton University Press.

Gillot, G. (2006), 'Du paradis à Dream Park, les jardins dans le monde arabe: Damas, Le Caire, Rabat', *Annales de géographie*, no. 650, pp. 409–33.

Girard, P.R. (2011), *The Slaves Who Defeated Napoleon: Toussaint Louverture and the Haitian War of Independence 1801–1804*, Tuscaloosa: University of Alabama Press.

Glover, G., (2015), *Waterloo in 100 Objects*, Cheltenham: The History Press.

Gourgaud, B.G. (1823), *Memoirs of the History of France during the Reign of Napoleon, dictated by the Emperor at Saint Helena to the Generals who shared his captivity*, 3 vols, London: Henry Colburn.

Gourgaud, B.G. (1903), *Talks of Napoleon at St Helena with General Baron Gourgaud: together with the journal kept by Gourgaud on their journey from Waterloo to St Helena*, Chicago: A.C. McClurg & Co.

Grainger, J.D. (2004), *The Amiens Truce: Britain and Bonaparte 1801–1803*, London: Boydell Press.

Granger, W. (1808), *The New Original and Complete Wonderful Museum and Magazine Extraordinary*, vol. 6, London: Alex Hogg & Co.

Gregory, D. (1996), *Napoleon's Jailer: Lt. Gen. Sir Hudson Lowe, a Life*, Madison: Fairleigh Dickinson University Press.

Grigson, J. (2007), *Good Things*, London: Grub Street.

Gueniffey, P. (2015), *Bonaparte 1769–1802*, trans. S. Rendall, Cambridge, MA, and London: Belknap Press of Harvard University Press.

Guitry, P.G.M. (1897), *L'Armée de Bonaparte en Egypte 1798–99*, Paris: Ernest Flammarion.

Halsall, A.W. (1998), *Victor Hugo and the Romantic Drama*, Toronto: University of Toronto Press.

Hamilton, J. Duchess of (1999), *Napoleon, the Empress and the Artist: The Story of Napoleon, Josephine's Garden at Malmaison, Redouté & the Australian Plants*, Sydney: Kangaroo Press.

Hamilton, J. Duchess of (2000) *Marengo: The Myth of Napoleon's Horse*, London: Fourth Estate.

Hamy, E.T. (1901), ed., *Lettres écrites d'Égypte à Cuvier, Jussieu, Lacépède, Monge, Desgenettes, Redouté jeune, Norry, Etc., aux professeurs du Muséum et à sa famille,* Paris: Librairie Hachette et Cie.

Harrison, C.E. (2009), 'Projections of the Revolutionary Nation: French Expeditions in the Pacific, 1791–1803', *Osiris,* vol. 24, no. 1, pp. 33–52, Chicago: University of Chicago Press on behalf of The History of Science Society.

Haydon, B.R. (1950), *The Autobiography and Journals of Benjamin Robert Haydon (1786–1846),* ed. M. Elwin, London: Macdonald.

Hazareesingh, S. (2020), *Black Spartacus: The Epic Life of Toussaint Louverture,* London: Allen Lane.

Healey, F.G. (1959), *The Literary Culture of Napoleon,* Geneva: Droz, and Paris: Librairie Minard.

Hendel, W.T. (2003), 'The Theatrical Representation of Landscape in Rousseau's *La Nouvelle Héloïse, Paroles gelées,* UCLA French Studies 21(1), pp. 47–52.

Herold, J.C. (1962), *Bonaparte in Egypt,* London: Hamish Hamilton.

Hicks, P. (2014), 'Napoleon On Elba – An Exile Of Consent', *Napoleonica. La Revue,* 1, no. 19, pp. 53–67.

Higginbotham, J.A. (1997), *Piscinae: Artificial Fish Ponds in Roman Italy,* Chapel Hill, North Carolina: University of North Carolina Press.

Hillairet, J. (1965), *Le Palais des Tuileries: Le Palais Royal et Impérial et son Jardin,* Paris: Les Éditions de Minuit.

Hobhouse, J.C. (1816), *The Substance of some letters written by an Englishman resident at Paris during the last reign of the Emperor Napoleon,* 2 vols, London: Ridgways.

Holland, E. (1908), *The Journal of Elizabeth Lady Holland (1791–1811),* ed. Earl of Ilchester, 2 vols, London: Longmans, Green and Co.

Holmes, R. (2008), *The Hottentot Venus: The Life and Death of Saartjie Baartman, Born 1789 – Buried 2002,* London: Bloomsbury.

Holmes, R. (2009), *The Age of Wonder: How the Romantic Generation Discovered the Beauty and Terror of Science,* London: HarperCollins.

Homer, (1996), *The Odyssey,* trans. R. Fagles, London: Penguin Books.

Horn, J. (1816), *The Narrative of Jean Horn, Military Coachman to Napoleon Bonaparte,* London: London Museum.

Huet, V. (1999), 'Napoleon I: a new Augustus?', in *Receptions of Rome in European Culture 1789–1945*, ed. C. Edwards, Cambridge: Cambridge University Press.

Hugo, V. (2016), *Les Misérables*, trans. C. Donougher, London: Penguin Classics, Penguin Random House.

Humboldt, A. von (1814–29), *Personal narrative of travels to the equinoctial regions of the New Continent, during the years 1799–1804, By Alexander de Humboldt, and Aimé Bonpland; with maps, plans, &c. written in French by Alexander de Humboldt, and trans. into English by Helen Maria Williams*, 7 vols, London: Longman, Hurst, Rees, Orme and Brown.

Humboldt, W. von (2001), *Wilhelm von Humboldt Journal Parisien (1797–1799)*, trans. E. Beyer, Arles: Solin/Actes Sud.

Hunt, S., Carter, C. (1999), eds, *Terre Napoléon: Australia through French Eyes 1800–1804*, New South Wales: Historic Houses Trust.

Jacques, S. (2018), *The Caesar of Paris: Napoleon Bonaparte, Rome, and the Artistic Obsession that Shaped an Empire*, New York: Pegasus Books Ltd.

Jeanson, M., Le Bon, L., Zellal, C. (2017), *Jardins*, catalogue to the exhibition *Jardins*, Paris: Éditions de la Réunion des Musées Nationaux – Grand Palais.

Johns, C.M.S. (1994), 'Portrait Mythology: Antonio Canova's Portraits of the Bonapartes', *Eighteenth-Century Studies*, vol. 28, no. 1, pp. 115–29.

Johns, C.M.S. (1998), *Antonio Canova and the Politics of Patriotism*, Berkeley, California: University of California Press.

Jones, D.S. (2017), 'A Lasting Legacy: the Baudin Expedition in Australian Waters (1801–1803)', *The Great Circle*, vol. 39, no. 2, Special Issue: French Exploration, pp. 56–85.

Jordan, D.P. (2012), *Napoleon and the Revolution*, London: Palgrave Macmillan.

Jouanin, C. (1977), 'Josephine and the Natural Sciences', *Apollo*, pp. 50–9.

Karabell, Z. (2003), *Parting the Desert: the Creation of the Suez Canal*, London: John Murray.

Kelly, L. (2013), *Holland House: A History of London's Most Celebrated Salon*, London: I.B. Tauris.

Kennedy, W.P. (1845–6), 'Eloge historique de Joseph Fourier, par M. Arago, Secrétaire Perpétual de l'Académie Royale des Sciences de l'Institut de France', pp. 380–413, in *The North British Review*, vol.4, 1845–6.

Kete, K. (2012), *Making Way for Genius: The Irish Aristocracy in the Seventeenth Century*, New Haven: Yale University Press.

Khaldi, B. (2012), *Egypt Awakening in the Early Twentieth Century: Mayy Ziyadah's Intellectual Circles* New York: Palgrave Macmillan.

Kirk, T. (2005), *The Architecture of Modern Italy, Volume 1: The Challenge of Tradition 1750–1900*, Princeton: Princeton Architectural Press.

Krettly, E. (2003), *Souvenirs Historiques du capitaine Krettly*, Paris: Nouveau Monde Éditions.

Lack, H.W. (2004), *Jardin de la Malmaison: Empress Josephine's garden; with an essay by Marina Heilmeyer*, trans. M. Walters, Munich, Berlin and London: Prestel.

Lamarck, J.B.P.A. de Monet (2011), *Zoological Philosophy: An Exposition with Regard to the Natural History of Animals*, Cambridge: Cambridge University Press.

Las Cases, E. (1836), *Memoirs of the Life, Exile and Conversations of the Emperor Napoleon*, 4 vols, London: Henry Colburn.

Las Cases, E. (2017), *Le Mémorial de Sainte-Hélène: Le manuscrit retrouvé*, ed. T. Lentz, P. Hicks, F. Houdecek, C. Prévot, Paris: Perrin.

Launay, L. de (1932), 'Gaspard Monge: II: Un ami de Bonaparte', *Revue des Deux Mondes* (1829–1971), vol. 10, no. 4, pp. 813–39.

Leadlay, E. (1993), 'Botanic Gardens News', *Botanic Gardens Conservation News*, vol. 2, no. 2, pp. 4–10.

Lemercier, N.L. (1823), *Moyse, Poème en quatre chants*, Paris: Bossange père.

Lenôtre, G. (1932), *Napoléon: Croquis de l'épopée*, Paris: Bernard Grasset.

Lentz, T. (2020), *Napoléon: Dictionnaire historique*, Paris: Perrin.

Leroy, E. (2019), *Waterloo: une porte ouverte sur l'histoire*, Norderstedt: Books on Demand.

Letouzey, Y. (1989), *Le Jardin des Plantes à la Croisée des Chemins avec André Thouin 1747–1824*, Paris: Éditions du Muséum national d'Histoire naturelle.

Leys, S. (2006), *The Death of Napoleon*, trans. P. Clancy and S. Leys, New York: New York Review Books.

Lonoff, S. (1996), *The Belgian Essays: Charlotte Brontë and Emily Brontë*, New Haven and London: Yale University Press.

Lormant, F. (2008), 'La politique de la forêt sous le Consulat et l'Empire. L'exemple du département de la Meurthe', *Napoleonica. La Revue* 1 (no. 1), pp. 69–100. https://www.cairn.info/revue-napoleonica-la-revue-2008-1-page-69. htm (online pagination used in notes).

Loudon, J.C. (1836), *The Gardener's Magazine*, vol. 12, London: Longman, Rees, Orme, Brown, Green and Longman.

Lubbock, C.A. (1933), ed., *The Herschel Chronicle: The Life-Story of William Herschel and his Sister Caroline Herschel*, Cambridge: Cambridge University Press.

Lytton, E.B. (1860), *The Poetical Works of Sir Edward Bulwer Lytton*, London: Routledge.

McClellan, A.L. (1988), 'The Musée du Louvre as Revolutionary Metaphor During the Terror', *The Art Bulletin*, vol. 70, no. 2, pp. 300–13.

Macé, J. (2004), *Dictionnaire historique de Sainte-Hélène*, Paris: Tallandier Éditions.

Mainardi, P. (1989), 'Assuring the Empire of the Future: The 1798 Fête de la Liberté', *Art Journal*, 48, pp. 155–63.

Malcolm, C.E. (1899), *A Diary of St Helena (1816, 1817), the Journal of Lady Malcolm*, ed. A. Wilson, London: A.D. Innes & Co.

Marchand, L.-J. (1998), *In Napoleon's shadow: being the first English language edition of the complete memoirs of Louis-Joseph Marchand, valet and friend of the Emperor 1811–1821, including the original notes of Jean Bourguignon and Henry Lachouque*, San Franscisco: Proctor Jones Publishing Company.

Martel, T. (1926), *Mémoires et Œuvres de Napoléon*, Paris: Albin Michel.

Masson, F. (1894), *Napoleon, Lover and Husband*, trans. J.M. Howell, New York: Merriam Company.

Matteson, K. (2015), *Forests in Revolutionary France: Conservation, Community and Conflict (1669–1848)*, Cambridge: Cambridge University Press.

Meehan, T. (1887), ed. *The Gardener's Monthly and Horticulturalist*, vol. 29, Philadelphia: Charles H. Marot.

Mercer, C. (2012), *Journal of the Waterloo Campaign*, ed. A. Uffindell, Barnsley: Pen & Sword.

Michal, S., Jackson, P.W. (1997), 'Developing an in-country capacity for biodiversity conservation in Haiti: the Haitian Botanical Foundation', *Botanic Gardens Conservation News*, vol. 2, no. 9, pp. 50–3.

Mikaberidze, A. (2014), *The Burning of Moscow: Napoleon's Trial by Fire, 1812,* Barnsley: Pen & Sword.

Mikhail, A. (2014), *The Animal in Ottoman Egypt,* Oxford: Oxford University Press.

Milgrom, M. (2011), *Still Life: Adventures in Taxidermy,* Boston, Massachusetts: Houghton Mifflin Harcourt.

Monge, G. (1851), *An Elementary Treatise on Descriptive Geometry: with a Theory of Shadows and of Perspective,* trans. J.F. Heather, London: John Weale.

Moon, I. (2017), *The Architecture of Percier and Fontaine and the Struggle for Sovereignty in Revolutionary France,* New York: Routledge.

Murat, L. (2014), *The Man Who Thought He Was Napoleon: Towards a Political History of Madness,* trans. D. Dusinberre, Chicago and London: University of Chicago Press.

Naturel, M., Vigo, L. (2018), 'The Birdcage at Saint Helena', in *Napoleon: The Imperial Household,* ed. S. Cordier, New Haven and London: Yale University Press.

Nelson, E.C., Rourke, J.P. (1993), 'James Niven (1776–1827), a Scottish Botanical Collector at the Cape of Good Hope. His Hortus siccus at the National Botanic Gardens, Glasnevin, Dublin (DBN), and the Royal Botanic Gardens, Kew (K)', *Kew Bulletin,* vol. 48, no. 4, pp. 663–82.

North, J. (2019), *Killing Napoleon: The Plot to Blow up Bonaparte,* Gloucestershire: Amberley.

O'Connor, H. (2017), *Napoleon's Doctor: The St Helena Diary of Barry O'Meara,* Dublin: The O'Brien Press Ltd.

O'Keeffe, P. (2009), *A Genius for Failure: The Life of Benjamin Robert Haydon,* London: Bodley Head.

Olney, C. (1952), *Benjamin Robert Haydon: Historical Painter,* Athens, GA: University of Georgia Press.

Olson, R.J.M. (1986), 'Representations of Pope Pius VII: The First Risorgimento Hero', *The Art Bulletin,* vol. 68, no. 1, pp. 77–93.

O'Meara, B.E. (1822), *Napoleon in Exile,* 2 vols, London: Simpkin & Marshall.

Packard, A.S. (1901), *Lamarck, the Founder of Evolution: His Life and Work,* London: Longmans.

Paget, J., Saunders, D. (1992), *Hougoumont: The Key to Victory at Waterloo,* London: Leo Cooper.

Pascoe, J. (2006), *The Hummingbird Cabinet: A Rare and Curious History of Romantic Collectors*, Ithaca and London: Cornell University Press.

Pesme, G. (1936), *Les dernières heures de Napoléon avant l'exil*, Bordeaux: Éditions Delmas.

Peters, E. A. (2009), 'The Napoleonic Egyptian Scientific Expedition and the Nineteenth-Century Survey Museum', Theses, 37. https://scholarship.shu.edu/theses/37

Pincemaille, C., Tamisier-Vétois, I. (2015), *Cap sur l'Amérique: la dernière utopie de Napoléon*, Paris: Art Lys, and Malmaison: Musée national des châteaux de Malmaison et Bois-Préau.

Plant, M. (2002), *Venice, Fragile City 1797–1997*, New Haven: Yale University Press.

Potenza, D. (2018), *L'effet kaléidoscope. La réécriture dans la production dramaturgique d'Alfred Farag comme stratégie multifunctionnelle pour une création à plusieurs niveaux*, Paris: Sorbonne.

Price, M. (2014), *Napoleon: The End of Glory*, Oxford: Oxford University Press.

Prod'homme, J.-G., Martens, F.H. (1921), 'Napoleon, Music and Musicians', *The Musical Quarterly*, vol. 7, no. 4, pp. 579–605.

Rabbat, N. (2004) 'A Brief History of Green Spaces in Cairo' in *Cairo: Revitalising a Historic Metropolis*, S. Bianca and P. Jodidio, eds., Turin: Umberto Allemandi & C. for Aga Khan Trust for Culture, pp. 43–53.

Rapp, J. (1823) *Memoirs of General Count Rapp, First aide-de-camp to Napoleon*, 2 vols, London: Henry Colburn.

Raymond, A. (2000), *Cairo*, trans. W. Wood, Cambridge, MA: Harvard University Press.

Reinhard, M.R. (1994), *Le Grand Carnot: Lazare Carnot 1753–1823*, Paris: Hachette.

Rémusat, M. de (1910), *Memoirs of the Empress Josephine*, 2 vols, New York: P.F. Collier & Son.

Ricard, A. (1893), *Le Cardinal Fesch, Archevêque de Lyon: 1763–1839*, Paris: E. Dentu.

Ridley, R.T. (1992), *The Eagle and the Spade: Archaeology in Rome during the Napoleonic era*, Cambridge: Cambridge University Press.

Riskin, J. (2018a), 'The Naturalist and the Emperor, a Tragedy in Three Acts; or, How History Fell Out of Favor as a Way of Knowing Nature', *KNOW: A Journal on the Formation of Knowledge*, University of Chicago Press Journals, vol. 2, no. 1, pp. 85–110.

Riskin, J. (2018b), 'Evolution, the Science Napoleon Hated', *Republics of Letters*, vol. 6, issue 1, pp. 1–10.

Robbins, L.E. (2002), *Elephant Slaves and Pampered Parrots: Exotic Animals in Eighteenth-Century Paris*, Baltimore: Johns Hopkins University Press.

Roberts, A. (2014), *Napoleon the Great*, London: Allen Lane.

Robertson, J.W. (1814), *The Life and Campaigns of Bonaparte*, Newcastle upon Tyne: Mackenzie and Dent.

Robespierre, M. (2000), *Œuvres de Maximilien Robespierre, Volume 3: Correspondance*, Paris: Phénix Éditions.

Rœderer, P.-L. (1853–9), *Œuvres du comte P.-L. Rœderer*, ed. A.M. Rœderer, 8 vols, Paris: Typ. de Firmin Didot frères.

Roger, J. (1997), *Buffon: A Life in Natural History*, trans. S.F. Bonnefoi, Ithaca and London: Cornell University Press.

Rose, J.H. (1929), *The Personality of Napoleon*, London: G. Bell and Sons.

Roudinesco, E. (1992), *Madness and Revolution: The Lives and Legends of Thérogine de Méricourt*, trans. M. Thom, London and New York: Verso.

Rousseau, J.-J. (1816), *Émile: ou de l'éducation*, Paris: Pierre Didot et Firmin Didot.

Rousseau, J.-J. (1968), *La Nouvelle Héloïse*, trans. J.H. McDowell, Pennsylvania: Pennsylvania State University Press.

Roustam (1911), *Souvenirs de Roustam, mamelouck de Napoléon 1er*, ed. P. Cottin, Paris: Librairie Paul Ollendorff.

Said, E.W. (2014), *Orientalism: Western Conceptions of the Orient*, New York: Knopf Doubleday.

Saint-Denis, L.-E. (1922), *Napoleon from the Tuileries to St. Helena: personal recollections of the emperor's second mameluke and valet, Louis Etienne St. Denis (known as Ali)*, trans. F.H. Potter, introduction by G. Michaut, New York and London: Harper & Brothers.

Saint-Hilaire, G. (1835), *Sur une vue scientifique de l'adolescence de Napoléon Bonaparte, formulée dans son âge mûr sous le nom de 'Monde des détails'*, Paris: Brun.

Saint-Pierre, J.H.B. de (1799), *Paul et Virginie*, London: Baylis.

Scott, E. (1910), *Terre Napoléon: A History of French Explorations and Projects in Australia*, London: Methuen & Co.

Scott, W. (1827), *The Life of Napoleon Buonaparte, Emperor of the French*, 9 vols, Edinburgh: Longman, Rees, Orme, Brown & Green.

Scurr, R. (2006), *Fatal Purity: Robespierre and the French Revolution*, London: Chatto & Windus.

Sewell, E. (1972), 'Coleridge on Revolution', *Studies in Romanticism*, vol. 11, no. 4, pp. 342–59.

Shorter, C. (1908), ed., *Napoleon and his Fellow Travellers: being a reprint of certain narratives of the dethroned emperor on the Bellerophon and the Northumberland to exile in Saint Helena, the romantic stories told by George Home, Captain Ross, Lord Lyttelton and William Warden*, London: Cassell and Company.

Shvidkovsky, D., Reteyum, A. (1999), 'Botany in a Cold Climate', *Historic Gardens Review*, no. 4, pp. 29–34.

Sivasundaram, S. (2020), *Waves Across the South: A New History of Revolution and Empire*, London: William Collins.

Smith, J.E.H. (2018), 'The Ibis and the Crocodile: Napoleon's Egyptian Campaign and Evolutionary Theory in France 1801–1835', *Republics of Letters*, vol. 6, issue 1, pp. 1–20.

Sorensen, D.R. (2006), 'Je suis la Révolution Française', *Carlyle Studies Annual*, no. 22, pp. 283–302.

Spary, E.C. (1998), 'L'invention de l' "expédition scientifique". L'histoire naturelle, Bonaparte et l'Égypte', in *L'invention scientifique de la Méditerranée: Égypte, Morée, Algérie*, ed. M-N. Bourguet, B. Lepetit, D. Nordman, Paris: École des hautes études en sciences sociales.

Spary, E.C. (2000), *Utopia's Garden: French Natural History from Old Regime to Revolution*, Chicago: University of Chicago Press.

Staël, A.L.G. Madame de (1821), *Ten Years' Exile: Or, Memoirs of that Interesting Period of the Life of the Baroness de Stael-Holstein*, trans. A.L. Baron de Staël-Holstein, London: Treuttel and Würtz.

Staël, G. Madame de (2008), *Considerations on the Principal Events of the French Revolution*, ed. A. Craiutu, Indianapolis: Liberty Fund Edition.

Stafleu, F.A. (1971), 'Lamarck: The Birth of Biology', *Taxon*, vol. 20, no. 4, pp. 397–442.

Stendhal (2000), *The Charterhouse of Parma*, trans. R. Howard, New York: The Modern Library.

Stendhal (2002), *The Life of Henry Brulard*, trans. J. Sturrock, New York: New York Review Books.

Strathern, P. (2008), *Napoleon in Egypt*, London: Vintage.

Tacitus (1925), *The Histories*, Books 1–3, trans. C.H. Moore, Cambridge, Massachusetts, London: Loeb, Harvard University Press.

Talleyrand-Périgord, C.M. de (2007), *Mémoires du Prince de Talleyrand*, ed. E. de Waresquiel, Paris: R. Laffont.

Tardieu, A. (1822), *La Colonne de La Grande Armée d'Austerlitz ou de la Victoire*, Paris: Librairie Le Feu Follet.

Taylor-Leduc, S. (2019), 'Joséphine at Malmaison: Acclimatizing Self and Other in the Garden', *Journal 18*, issue 8.

Tendron, G. (2015), *Napoléon 1er à Fontainebleau*, no. 11, Amis du Château de Fontainebleau.

Terrasse, C. (1952), *Napoléon à Fontainebleau*, Paris: Grasset.

Thompson, J.M. (1934), *Letters of Napoleon*, Oxford: Basil Blackwell.

Thompson, J.M. (1949), 'Napoleon's Journey to Elba in 1814. Part I. By Land', *American Historical Review*, vol. 55, no. 1, pp. 1–21.

Thompson, J.M. (1950), 'Napoleon's Journey to Elba in 1814. Part II. By Sea', *American Historical Review*, vol. 55, no. 2, pp. 301–20.

Thompson, J.M. (1988), *Napoleon Bonaparte*, Oxford: Basil Blackwell.

Tollfree, E. (1999), 'Napoleon and the "new Rome": rebuilding imperial Rome in the late eighteenth- and early nineteenth-century Paris', PhD thesis, University of Bristol.

Tombs, I., Tombs, R. (2006), *That Sweet Enemy: The British and the French from the Sun King to the Present*, London: William Heinemann.

Tooke, W. (1798), *Observations on the Expedition of General Buonaparte to the East, and the Probability of its Success Considered*, London: George Cawthorn, British Library.

Truffer, M., Verdan, N. (1995), https://www2.unil.ch/dorigny40/files/2010/07/US243_1995_Histoiredusite5.pdf

Tylus, J. (1999), 'Tasso's Trees: Epic and Local Culture', in *Epic Traditions in the Contemporary World*, ed. M. Beissinger, J. Tylus, S. Wofford, Berkeley and Oxford: University of California Press.

Tyson Stroud, P. (2005), *The Man Who Had Been King: The American Exile of Napoleon's Brother*, Pennsylvania: University of Pennsylvania Press.

Unwin, B. (2010), *Terrible Exile: The Last Days of Napoleon on St Helena*, London: I.B. Tauris.

Vallins, D., Oishi, K., Perry, S. (2013), eds, *Coleridge, Romanticism and the Orient: Cultural Negotiations*, London; New York: Bloomsbury Academic.

Verlet, H. (2012), *Les Belles eaux de Fontainebleau*, no. 6, Amis du Château de Fontainebleau.

Verlet, H. (2014), *Le Jardin de Diane à Fontainebleau*, no. 10, Amis du Château de Fontainebleau.

Vial, C.-É. (2018), *Napoléon à Sainte-Hélène: L'encre de l'exil*, Paris: Perrin/BNF.

Vigée-Lebrun, L.-É. (1870), *Souvenirs (1755–1789)*, 2 vols. Paris: Bibliothèque Charpentier.

Villiers du Terrage, É. (1899), *Journal et souvenirs sur l'expédition d'Égypte (1798–1801)*, Paris: Librairie Plon.

Vittet, J. (2018), *L'appartement de Napoléon 1er à Fontainebleau: Histoire et Métamorphoses*, no. 15, Amis du Château de Fontainebleau.

Vovk, J.C. (2010), *In Destiny's Hands: Five Tragic Rulers, Children of Maria Theresa*, New York, Bloomington: iUniverse.

Watkin, D. (2011), *The Roman Forum*, London: Profile Books.

Webster, J. (2005), 'The sublime and the pastoral' in *The Creation* and *The Seasons*, pp. 150–63, in C. Clark (ed.) *The Cambridge Companion to Music*, Cambridge: Cambridge University Press.

Wheelock Thayer, A., Hermann, D., Reimann, H. (2013), *The Life of Ludwig Van Beethoven*, Cambridge: Cambridge University Press.

White, A. (2016), *Of Hedges, Myths and Memories: A Historical Reappraisal of the Château/Ferme d'Hougoumont, Battlefield of Waterloo, Belgium*, Belgium: White & MacLean Publishing.

Williams, R.L. (2001), *Botanophilia in Eighteenth-Century France: The Spirit of the Enlightenment*, Dordrecht: Kluwer Academic Publishers.

Wolff, H.D. (1855), *The Island Empire, or, The Scenes of the First Exile of Emperor Napoleon I*, Philadelphia: Parry & McMillan.

Woolf, V. (2016), *A Room of One's Own*, London: Vintage Classics.

Wordsworth, W. (1838), *The Sonnets of William Wordsworth: collected in one volume*, London: Edward Moxon.

Wright, J. (1798), *Copies of Original Letters from the Army of General Bonaparte in Egypt, Intercepted by the Fleet under the Control of Admiral Lord Nelson*, London: J. Wright.

Zamoyski, A. (2018), *Napoleon: A Life*, New York: Basic Books.

List of Illustrations

Plate Section I

1. Storming of the Tuileries in Paris, 10 August 1792 (© Hôtel Carnavalet, Paris / akg-images / De Agostini Picture library)
2. Jardin du Roy by Jean-Baptiste Hilaire, 1794 (© Bibliothèque nationale de France)
3. The gardens of the institute in Egypt by André Dutertre, 1798–1809 (© Bibliothèque nationale de France)
4. The interior of the institute in Egypt by Jean Constantin Protain, 1798–1809 (© Bibliothèque nationale de France)
5. Porcelain plates, clockwise from top left: dromedaries from the Sèvres Egyptian Service, 1810–1812 (© Victoria and Albert Museum, London)
6. French scientists measuring the Sphynx from the Sèvres Egyptian Service, 1810–1812 (© Victoria and Albert Museum, London)
7. *Mesembryanthemum carinatum* from the Sèvres Exotic Plants Service, 1802–1805 (© RMN-Grand Palais (musée des châteaux de Malmaison et de Bois-Préau) / Franck Raux)
8. *Iris Susiana* from the Sèvres Liliacées Service, 1802–1805 (© RMN-Grand Palais (musée des châteaux de Malmaison et de Bois-Préau) / Gérard Blot)
9. Bonaparte depicted as a crocodile in the orangery of the chateau of Saint-Cloud, 10 November 1799 (© The Trustees of the British Museum)

10. Napoleon and George III depicted as rival gardeners by Charles Williams, 10 February 1803 (Courtesy of the Library of Congress Prints and Photographs Division Washington, DC)

11. Napoleon and Josephine in the gardens at Malmaison by George Cruikshank, 1824 (© The Trustees of the British Museum)

12. An Allegory of Empress Josephine as Patroness of the Gardens at Malmaison by François Gérard, *c.* 1805–6 (© The Met, New York, USA / Purchase, Guy Wildenstein Gift, 2003 / (CC0 1.0))

13. The frontispiece to the *Voyage de Découverte aux Terres Australes* by François Péron, 1807 (© RMN-Grand Palais (musée des châteaux de Malmaison et de Bois-Préau) / Gérard Blot)

14. Napoleon crosses the Alps over the Great St Bernard Pass by Jacques-Louis David, 20 May 1800 (© Rueil-Malmaison, Musée du Château / akg-images / Laurent Lecat)

15. Meeting between Napoleon and Pope Pius VII in the Forest of Fontainebleau in 1804 by Alexandre-Hyacinthe Dunouy, 1808 (© Chateau de Fontainebleau, Seine-et-Marne, France / Bridgeman Images)

16. The entry of the Emperor (Napoleon) and Empress (Marie Louise, daughter of Francis II of Austria) to the Tuileries gardens on the day of their wedding, 1810 (© Bibliotheque Nationale, Paris, France / Bridgeman Images)

Plate Section II

1. Caricature of the architects Pierre Fontaine and Charles Percier by Julien-Léopold Boilly (© RMN-Grand Palais (Institut de France) / Gérard Blot)

2. Caricature of botanist and gardener André Thouin by Julien-Léopold Boilly (© RMN-Grand Palais (Institut de France) / Gérard Blot)

3. View of the Arc de Triomphe du Carrousel, Paris, designed by Charles Percier and Pierre Fontaine (© National Maritime Museum, Greenwich, London, Herschel Collection)

4. Napoleon and his son, Napoléon François Joseph Charles Bonaparte, in the Tuileries gardens (© Musée Carnavalet / Roger-Viollet / Topfoto)

5. Workers excavating below Trajan's Column in Rome (© Roma / Sovrintendenza Capitolina ai Beni Culturali / Museo di Roma)

6. Louis-Martin Berthault's plan for the Jardin du Grand César, 1813 (© Roma / Sovrintendenza Capitolina ai Beni Culturali / Museo di Roma)

7. Madame de Staël, *c.* 1815–7 (Royal Collection Trust / © Her Majesty Queen Elizabeth II 2020)

8. Laure Junot, Duchess of Abrantès (© Fondation Napoléon / Vincent Mercier / Missionning)

9. Sculpture of Napoleon as Mars the Peacemaker by Antonio Canova, 1803–6 (© akg-images / Rabatti & Domingie)

10. Project for the palace of the King of Rome on Chaillot Hill, Paris (© Beaux-Arts de Paris, Dist. RMN-Grand Palais / image Beaux-arts de Paris)

11. The pedigree of Corporal Violet by George Cruikshank, 1815 (© The Trustees of the British Museum)

12. The garden wall of the chateau Hougoumont on the site of the Battle of Waterloo, 1816 (Royal Collection Trust / © Her Majesty Queen Elizabeth II 2020)

13. The chateau Hougoumont by Denis Dighton, 1815 (Royal Collection Trust / © Her Majesty Queen Elizabeth II 2020)

14. Napoleon in his garden on St Helena (© RMN-Grand Palais (musée des châteaux de Malmaison et de Bois-Préau) / André Martin)

15. Napoleon's birdcage from St Helena (© Collections Bertrand Museum of the City of Châteauroux, France)

16. View of Longwood House by Louis Joseph Marchand, 1 January 1820 (© RMN-Grand Palais (musée des châteaux de Malmaison et de Bois-Préau) / Gérard Blot)

17. The gardener of St Helena, 1829 (© Bibliothèque nationale de France)

Index

Aboukir Bay, Egypt, 68
Abyssinia, 72
Académie royale d'architecture, 200
Academy of Lyons, 14
Accademia di San Luca, 195, 198
Account of Corsica (Boswell), 20
Acre, Ottoman Empire, 88, 90
Adige River, 51
Affacciatoio, 236
Ah Sam, 132
Ajaccio, Corsica, 1, 12, 16, 17, 20, 22, 26,
    89, 282–3
  British occupation (1794–6), 278
  British occupation (1814), 237
  burial request (1821), 300
  Casa Buonaparte, 16, 17, 278
  Cathedral, 300
  Jardin d'Expériences, 132
  Napoleon's Grotto, 17–18
  in Napoleon's will (1821), 298
Alaska, 129
L'Alceste, 63
Aleppo, Syria, 91
Alessandria, Piedmont, 100, 155
Alexander I, Emperor of Russia, 149, 156,
    157, 180, 181, 215, 217–18
Alexander the Great, 3, 7, 50, 62, 64, 89
Alexandria, Egypt, 62, 63–4
al-Alfi Bey, 66
Alfi Palace, Cairo, 66, 78, 91, 92–3
Algiers, Ottoman Empire, 72

Alps, 51, 53, 100–102, 159, 164
Altar of Victory, Champs de Mars, 59–60
Alvinczi, Jozsef, 52
Amis de Waterloo, Les, 273
Ancien Régime, 7, 23, 95, 123, 176
  Bastille and, 25
  Brienne-le-Château and, 16
  divorce and, 167
  executions and, 92
  forests and, 174, 191
  hunting and, 171
  Malmaison and, 121
  Mamelukes, comparison with, 77
  natural history and, 33
  Royal Touch, 87
  Spanish sheep and, 140
d'Anjou, David, 155
Antibes, France, 41
Antommarchi, François Carlo, 284–5, 286,
    288, 293, 296–9
Apollo, 242
Apothecaries' Garden, Moscow, 217
Appian Way, Rome, 194
Appiani, Andrea, 54
Arago, François, 186
Arazola de Onate family, 251
Arboretum Britannicum, 300
Arc du Carrousel, Paris, 200–202, 208
Arc d'Orange, France, 200
Arc de Triomphe, Paris, 209–10, 218
Arch of Severus, Rome, 197

Arch of Titus, Rome, 198
el-Arish, Egypt, 87
Armenians, 90
Army of the Interior, 49
artillery, 23, 47, 129
    Battle of Austerlitz (1805), 156
    Battle of the Pyramids (1798), 86
    Battle of Rivoli (1797), 52
    Battle of Smolensk (1812), 216
    Battle of Waterloo (1815), 252, 253,
        254, 257
    Siege of Toulon (1793), 36, 39
    theory of shadows and, 27
    Vendémiaire revolt (1795), 47–8
L'Astrolabe, 129
atheism, 39–40, 186, 293
Athenaeum, 245
Atkins, Anna, 272
Augusta, Princess of Bavaria, 159
Augustus, Roman Emperor, 97
Australasia, 129, 130, 132, 137–43, 146–7,
    154, 160–61, 296
Austria, 180, 181
    Congress of Vienna (1814–15), 238–9,
        250, 271
    St Helena exile (1815–21), 279
    Treaty of Fontainebleau (1814), 219
    War of the First Coalition (1792–7),
        26, 48, 49, 51–2, 53–4, 250
    War of the Second Coalition
        (1798–1801), 100–104
    War of the Third Coalition (1803–6),
        156, 181, 185
    War of the Fifth Coalition (1809), 181,
        201, 238
    War of the Sixth Coalition (1813–14),
        219
Auvergne, France, 189
Auxonne, Bourgogne, 23, 24, 25, 61
Avignon, 52
Azbakiyya Square, Cairo, 66, 67, 73, 78,
    80, 93
al-Azhar University, 91

Baden, 147, 159
Bagatelle Pavilion, Bois de Boulogne, 203,
    212

al-Bakri, Khalil, 71–2, 90
al-Bakri, Zeinab, 71–2
Balcombe family, 276
Balcombe, William, 276
balloon flight, 29, 77, 79–80, 152–3, 169
Banks, Joseph, 131, 132, 140, 155, 279
Barbary Coast, 84, 86
Bargigli, Paolo, 227, 231, 242
Barras, Paul, 46, 47, 48, 177
Bartolini, Archpriest, 227
Bassano, Hugues-Bernard Maret, Duc,
    221, 242
Bastia, Corsica, 26
Bastille, Paris, 25, 215, 249
Bathurst, Henry, 3rd Earl, 294
Battle of Acre (1799), 88, 90
Battle of Arcole (1796), 51–2, 104, 116, 123
Battle of Aspern (1801), 181
Battle of Austerlitz (1805), 155–8, 181,
    194, 200, 223, 299
Battle of Borodino (1812), 216
Battle of Brienne (1814), 16, 217
Battle of Chaumont (1814), 222
Battle of Chobrakit (1798), 65
Battle of Fleurus (1794), 249–50, 251, 263
Battle of Friedland (1807), 215, 223, 299
Battle of Jena (1806), 180
Battle of Leipzig (1813), 217
Battle of Ligny (1815), 250, 256, 263
Battle of Lodi (1796), 50
Battle of Marengo (1800), 101, 103, 104,
    120, 155, 223, 236, 299
Battle of Montebello (1800), 101
Battle of the Nile (1798), 68–70, 77, 86,
    271
Battle of Paris (1814), 219
Battle of the Pyramids (1798), 65, 77, 86
Battle of Rivoli (1797), 51–2, 104, 123
Battle of Rothière (1814), 217
Battle of Smolensk (1812), 216
Battle of Wagram (1809), 238
Battle of Waterloo (1815), 1, 3, 4, 78, 86,
    251–63, 287–8
Battle of Zama (202 BC), 103
Baudin, Charles, 253–4
Baudin, Nicolas, 130–32, 138, 146, 154,
    160–61, 154, 160, 161

Bavaria, 159

Beatson, Alexander, 300

de Beauharnais, Alexandre, 46, 95

de Beauharnais, Eugène, 46, 57, 71, 81, 159, 206

de Beauharnais, Hortense, 46, 95, 108, 159, 172, 229, 264, 265

de Beauharnais, Josephine, 6, 45–7
  assassination attempt (1800), 108–9, 110, 111, 115–16
  Australasia medallion, 160
  Canova commissions, 195
  coronation (1804), 168–9
  death (1814), 230, 264
  dinner services, 159–60
  divorce from Napoleon (1809), 180, 184–5, 188, 265
  d'Enghien execution (1804), 148
  Fontainebleau, life at, 164, 166
  Géographe cargo (1804), 146–7, 154
  heliotrope emblem, 228
  Humboldt, meeting with (1798), 58–9
  hunting trips, 172
  infidelity, reports of, 70
  Louverture, relationship with, 144
  Malmaison, life at, *see* Château de Malmaison
  marriage to Napoleon (1796), 46–7, 49–50, 70
  menagerie, 140, 146–7, 154, 155, 158
  Mignonette d'Égypte gift, 83–4
  Milan, arrival in (1797), 54
  monkey, gift of, 90
  Naturaliste cargo (1803), 138–43, 154
  Pius VII's visit (1804), 166, 167–8
  Rousseau bust, 106
  Talleyrand, relationship with, 181
  taxidermy collection, 141
  Thermidor coup (1794), 41
  Thouin, relationship with, 149
  'Vers le Soleil' motto, 6, 228
  weight gain, 195

de Beauharnais, Stéphanie, 159

Beausset, France, 35–6

des Beaux-Monts, Percée, 191

Becker, Nicolas Léonard, 265

bees, 151, 163, 232

van Beethoven, Ludwig, 181, 182

Beirut, Ottoman Empire, 196

Belgium, 152

La Belle Alliance, Waterloo, 252

Bellerophon, HMS, 270

Bellisle, Marguerite-Pauline, 80, 81–2, 83, 91

Belvedere Gardens, Vienna, 136

Béraud, Henri, 104

de la Bergerie, Rougier, 175, 176

Bernard, Simon, 256

Berthault, Louis-Martin, 99–100, 195, 214–15, 217

Berthier, Louis-Alexandre, 52, 101, 109, 171, 173, 178, 182, 220

Berthollet, Claude, 62, 65, 73–4, 76, 79, 84, 88

Bertrand, Henri Gatien, Comte, 47, 221, 230, 242, 264, 288, 300

bicorne hats, 2, 98, 102, 127, 225, 257, 287–8, 302

Bingham, George Ridout, 277

Bitter Lakes, Egypt, 85

black swans, 140, 158

Blanchard, Jean-Pierre, 152

Blanchard, Sophie, 152–3

Blanquet du Chayla, Armand, 68

von Blücher, Gebhard Leberecht, 217, 250, 257

Bois de Boulogne, Paris, 203, 212

Bois-Préau, France, 97

Bologna, Italy, 50, 52, 171

Bonaparte, Carlo, 16, 20–21

Bonaparte, Caroline, 16

Bonaparte, Charles-Louis Napoléon, 50, 154, 288

Bonaparte, Eliza, 16, 227, 229, 297

Bonaparte, Jérôme, 16, 100, 180, 253, 254

Bonaparte, Joseph, 16, 21, 26, 30, 43, 70, 100, 155, 157, 180, 269, 280

Bonaparte, Josephine, *see* Beauharnais, Josephine

Bonaparte, Letizia, 16, 21, 49, 100, 233, 245, 284

Bonaparte, Louis, 16, 100, 155

Bonaparte, Lucien, 16, 97, 100, 118–19, 135

Bonaparte, Pauline, 16, 42, 144, 145, 172, 173, 231, 233, 244

Bonaparte, Napoleon
accent, 1, 11, 78
arrest (1794), 41
assassination attempt (1800), 107–17, 139, 175, 200
assassination attempt (1809), 182–3
bicorne hats, 2, 98, 102, 127, 225, 257, 287–8, 302
biographies of, 3–7
birth of Napoleon François (1811), 202–5
Brienne-le-Château, studies at (1779–84), 1, 2, 11–16, 80, 85
Brumaire coup (1799), 95, 96, 97, 110, 120, 128, 177
Cadoudal Affair (1804), 147, 165
Canova commissions, 127, 192–5, 204, 205–6, 207, 296
carriage, 257–8
Civil Code (1804), 167, 176, 179, 185
Clary, relationship with, 45
Clisson et Eugénie (1795), 45, 51
Compiègne, life at, 190–91, 208
Concordat (1801), 122–4, 139
Congress of Erfurt (1808), 180
Constitution (1799), 97, 107
Constitution (1804), 149
Constitution (1815), 249
coronation as Emperor (1804), 151, 164, 165, 167–70
coronation as King of Italy (1805), 16, 170–71
Corsica, life in, *see under* Corsica
death (1821), 299
death mask, 302
death of Josephine (1814), 230
divorce from Josephine (1809), 180, 184–5, 188, 265
Duchâtel, relationship with, 167
Egypt and Syria campaign (1798–9), *see* Egypt; Syria
Elba, exile on (1814–15), 1, 8, 219–46
d'Enghien execution (1804), 147–9, 177, 240
Ermenonville visit (1800), 104–5

Etruria, creation of (1801), 119
Fontainebleau, life at, 162–6, 171–3, 184, 189–90, 219–23
forest administration, 175–80
Fourès, relationship with, 81–2, 83
Gregorian calendar, reinstatement of (1806), 158
Haiti invasion (1802), 144–6
horse riding style, 86, 172
Hundred Days (1815), 245, 247–71
hunting trips, 162–6, 171–3, 184, 203, 236
internment of remains (1840), 4, 302–3
Malmaison, life at, 94–100, 119–20, 121, 147–8, 153, 245, 264, 266
marriage to Josephine (1796), 46–7, 49–50, 70
marriage to Marie Louise (1810), 190–91
Military Academy, studies at (1784–5), 16, 22
Napoleonic Wars (1803–15), *see* Napoleonic Wars
Paris redevelopment, 199–202, 215
Pellapra, relationship with, 266
Permond, relationship with, 43
Pius VII, relations with, *see* Pius VII
religion, views on, 123, 168, 235, 244, 293–4, 298
Revolution (1789–99), 24–31, 47–9, 241, 295
Revolutionary Wars (1792–1802), *see* French Revolutionary Wars
Rome redevelopment, 192–9, 213–15, 216
Saint-Pierre, relationship with, 56
shooting style, 172–3
St Helena, exile on (1815–21), *see* St Helena
'straw-nose' nickname, 11, 13
succession, 155, 163, 218
suicide attempt (1814), 221, 243, 245, 283
titles, 103, 209
Treaty of Fontainebleau (1814), 219–20, 226

Venice redevelopment, 206–7
Walewska, relationship with, 221, 238, 266
will (1821), 297–8
women, views on, 5–6
Bonaparte, Napoleon François, 8, 202–5, 207–8, 216, 218
  birth (1811), 202–5
  Chaillot Palace, 208, 210–12, 215, 216, 217, 218, 240
  Château de Meudon, life at, 216
  exile of father (1814–21), 222, 232, 238, 243
  Hundred Days (1815), 263, 264
  lock of hair gift (1817), 280
  Rambouillet, life at, 222
  Schönbrunn Gardens visits, 280
  Treaty of Fontainebleau (1814), 239
Bonaparte, Victor, 288
Bonaparte visitant les pestiférés de Jaffa (Gros), 87
bonnets rouge, 29, 34, 96, 166
Bonpland, Aimé, 159
Bordeaux, France, 40
Borghese family, 173, 193
Borghese gardens, Rome, 53, 214
Bormida River, 101
Borsato, Giuseppe, 207
Boswell, James, 20
Bougainville, Louis-Antoine, Comte, 14, 37
Boulevard des Italiens, Paris, 42
Boulogne, France, 151, 152, 178
Bourbon, House of, 119, 147–8, 219, 239, 240, 241, 243, 250, 294
Bourgogne, France, 23
de Bourrienne, Fauvelet, 27
de Bourrienne, Louis Antoine, 12–13, 27–8, 30, 44–5, 121
Boussole, Le, 129
Brabant, 271
Brazil, 37, 91
Brescia, Italy, 50, 171
Breskens, West Flanders, 229
Brest, France, 144
Brienne-le-Château, Champagne, 1, 2, 11–16, 80, 85
British Museum, 272

Brontë, Charlotte, 1, 4–5, 9
de Brueys, François-Paul Brueys d'Aigalliers, comte, 65, 68 , 69
Brûlon, Angélique, 135
Brumaire coup (1799), 95, 96, 97, 110, 120, 128, 177
Brunswick, Charles William Ferdinand, Duke, 147
Bruny, Jean-Baptiste, 237
Brussels, Flanders, 250, 258, 263
Brutus, Lucius Junius, 52, 59–60, 103
Brutus, Marcus Junius, 52, 183
bubonic plague, 87, 225
Buffon, Georges-Louis Leclerc, Comte, 23–4, 32, 37, 56, 151, 185, 277
Bullock, William, 258
von Bülow, Friedrich, 251, 257
Burgundy, France, 70, 189
Burrini, Giovanni Antonio, 166

Cabarrus, Thérésa, 40–41, 46, 70
cacti, 17
cadastre, 179
Cadoudal Affair (1804), 147, 165
Caelian hill, Rome, 196
Caesar, Julius, 50, 62, 103, 118, 183, 207, 209, 213, 241, 298
Café d'Apollon, Paris, 107
Caffarelli du Falga, Louis-Marie-Joseph, 78, 79, 85, 87, 88
Cairo, Egypt, 8, 63, 65–7, 73–5, 143
  Alfi Palace, 66, 78, 91, 92–3
  Azbakiyya, 66, 67, 73, 78, 80, 93
  Kléber assassination (1800), 91–2, 101
  Mokattam quarries, 89
  Republic Day (1798), 77–8
  Revolt (1798), 78–9
  Tivoli gardens, 80–81, 93
California, 129
Calonne, Charles-Alexandre de, 22
de Cambacérès, Jean-Jacques-Régis, 97
camels, 85–7
Campbell, Neil, 222, 233
Camporese, Giuseppe, 196–7, 198, 213
Canal d'Ourcq, 208
Canal of the Pharaohs, 72, 84–5
cancer, 296–7

Cannes, France, 247

Canova, Antonio, 127, 192–5, 204, 205–6, 207, 296

Cap des Adieux, New Holland, 160

Cape Banks, Australia, 161

Cape of Good Hope, 72, 136, 137, 146, 160, 284

Capitol, Rome, 52, 60, 194, 196, 198

Capitoline Venus, 59

Capoliveri, Elba, 227, 235

Caprara, Giovanni Battista, 170, 171

Carbon, François-Jean, 113, 115

Carlier, Jean-Joseph, 259

Carlyle, Thomas, 4

Carnot, Lazare, 48, 49, 126, 264

Carrara, Italy, 227

Carteaux, Jean François, 36

Carthage, 90

Casa Buonaparte, Ajaccio, 16, 17, 278

Casa Vantini, Elba, 233

Casabianca, Giocante, 69

de Casabianca, Luc-Julien-Joseph, 69

'Casabianca' (Hemans), 69

de las Cases, Emmanuel, comte, 56, 276, 279, 283–4

Castellan, Antoine-Laurent, 190

Castlereagh, Robert Stewart, Viscount, 222, 224

Casuarina, Le, 161

Catherine of Württemberg, 180

Catholicism, 40, 122–4, 167, 173, 187–8, 204, 298

de Caulaincourt, Armand-Augustin-Louis, Marquis, 264

Cento, Italy, 50

Cerf, Le, 65

du Chaboulon, Fleury, 241–2

Chaillot, Paris, 208

   Arc de Triomphe, 209–10

   Palace, 208, 210–12, 215, 216, 217, 218, 240

Chalgrin, Jean, 209–10

Champ de Mai Festival (1815), 248–9

Champagne, France, 1, 2, 11–16

Champs de Mars, Paris, 40, 59–60, 170, 248–9

Champs-Élysées, Paris, 264

Chapelle-Saint-Lambert, Wallonia, 256

Chaptal, Jean-Antoine, 135–6, 138, 140

Charlemagne (Lemercier), 104

Charlemagne, Emperor of the Romans, 102–3, 165, 167, 169

Charleroi, Wallonia, 249

Charles IV, King of Spain, 102, 119

Charles IX, King of France, 29

Charles, Duke of Teschen, 53–4, 181

Charles, Grand Duke of Baden, 159

Charles, Hippolyte, 70, 95

Charterhouse of Parma, The (Stendhal), 50

Château de Compiègne, France, 190–91, 208, 280

Château de Fontainebleau, France, 8, 162–6, 170–71, 189–90, 219–23

   Battle of Jena anniversary (1807), 180

   Cascades, 171

   Garden of Diana, 163, 170–71, 189, 220, 221

   Grand Parterre, 180

   Great Court of the White Horse, 162

   Mail, 171

   obelisk, 166, 189

   orangery, 162, 189, 190

   Oval Court, 166

   pleasure garden, 190

   Porte Dorée, 166

   Queen's Gallery, 163, 170

Château d'Hougoumont, Wallonia, 3, 251–62, 271–2

Château d'If, France, 92

Château de Malmaison, France, 8, 94–102, 122, 123, 127, 136, 211

   Alley of Exile, 268

   Australian plants at, 296

   assassination attempts at, 111, 147

   books on, 159

   Britain, plants from, 136–7, 153

   dairy, 140

   Diana statue, 189

   divorce settlement (1809), 185

   Etrurian royal visit (1801), 119–20, 168

   Géographe cargo (1804), 146–7, 154

   Grand Serre Chaud, 153

   Hundred Days (1815), 245, 264–8

Lebanese cedars, 101, 266
Lemercier's visit (1800), 103
library, 117, 265–6
menagerie, 140, 146–7, 154, 155, 158, 266
Naturaliste cargo (1803), 138–43, 154
orangery, 99, 136, 153
purchase (1799), 94
renovation, 97–102, 120–21
Rousseau bust, 106
rustic hamlet, 121
Schönbrunn, plants from, 158
Château de Navarre, France, 185
Château de Saint-Cloud, France, 96, 120–21, 127–8, 165, 198, 231
Château de Vincennes, Paris, 147–8
Château du Raincy, France, 38
de Chateaubriand, François-René, 124, 267–8
de Châteaureine, Madame, 173
Chatsworth House, Derbyshire, 301
Chêne Napoléon, Le, 100–101
Chevalier de Saint-Louis, 237
Childeric I, King of the Salian Franks, 151
Children, Anna, 272
Children, John George, 272
Chile, 129
China, 132, 160, 203, 286–7, 289, 291, 300
Chippendale furniture, 272
Chiswick, Middlesex, 301
Christ en croix, Le (Rubens), 166
Christianity, 122–4, 173, 204, 235, 244
Concordat (1801), 122–4, 139
divorce and, 167
evolution and, 187–8
Mass, 123, 124, 169, 181, 185, 205, 222, 249
Robespierre and, 40
Waterloo miracle (1815), 256, 261
Church Saint-Roch, Paris, 108
Cicogna, Emmanuele, 207
City of Victories, 155
Civil Code (1804), 167, 176, 179, 185
Civitavecchia, Italy, 62
Clary, Eugénie Désirée, 45
Clay, Matthew, 258

clematis, 17
Clisson et Eugénie (Bonaparte), 45, 51
Cloaca Maxima, Rome, 198
Cockburn, George, 274, 275
coffee, 281
Colbert, Jean-Baptiste, 174
Coldstream Guards, 251–2, 254, 255, 260
Coleridge, Samuel Taylor, 3, 129
Collège de France, 14
Colosseum, Rome, 197, 204, 213
Column of Phocas, Rome, 199
comet (1821), 298
Commission des Monuments et Bâtiments Civils, 197
Commission of Arts and Sciences, 50–51, 52–3, 62, 73, 79, 83
Committee of Public Safety, 35, 48, 122, 210, 250
Compiègne, France, 177, 190–91, 208, 280
Concord, 195
Concordat (1801), 122–4, 139
Congress of Erfurt (1808), 180
Congress of Vienna (1814–15), 238–9, 271
Coni, Piedmont, 39
Consalvi, Ercole, 127
Constant, Louis, 220
Constantine, Roman Emperor, 200, 204
Constitution
  1791 28
  1795 47
  1799 97, 107
  1804 149
  1815 249
Conté, Nicolas-Jacques, 79
Convention of Alessandria (1800), 101
Convention, 41, 43–4, 46, 47, 98
Conversations Across the Water, 153
Cook, James, 62, 129, 280
Corfu, 219
Corsica, 1, 3, 8, 11–13, 16–23, 25, 26, 27, 43, 47, 180, 237, 282–3
  British occupation (1794–6), 278
  British occupation (1814), 237
  Casa Buonaparte, 278
  Egyptian campaign (1798), 62, 69

Corsica (*Continued*)
French invasion (1769), 17, 19
French Revolution (1789–99), 26
horse riding in, 86
Hundred Days (1815), 248
Jardin d'Expériences, 132
Les Milelli, 16, 17–19, 22
mulberry trees, 8, 15, 20–22, 25, 229
Napoleon's Grotto, 17–19
Republic of (1755–69), 19–20, 23
Les Salines, 20–22
Treaty of Fontainebleau (1814), 219
Cossacks, 16
cotton, 193, 237
Council of Five Hundred, 96
Council of State, 111, 114, 133–5, 151
Council of the Ancients, 96
Courrier de L'Égypte, 73
Le Couteulx du Molay, Jacques-Jean, 94–5, 96, 100
Coxe, William, 220
Creation, The (Haydn), 107, 109–10, 123, 181
Creticus, Caecilius, 199
Croix de St Hérem, Fontainebleau, 166
de la Croix, Nicolle, 129
Cromwell, Oliver, 118
Cruikshank, George, 243
de Cubières Amédée Louis, 254
Cult of Reason, 40, 124
Cult of the Supreme Being, 39–40, 59–60, 123, 124
Cuvier, Georges, 63, 151, 187–8

dahlias, 150–51, 296
Dalesme, Jean Baptiste, 224
Dancer, The (Canova), 195
Danube River, 181, 183
Daru, Martial, 214
Daubenton, Louis Jean-Marie, 33, 37, 185
David, Jacques-Louis, 25, 39, 52, 57, 97–8, 102, 127, 205, 208
Deadwood Barracks, St Helena, 277
Deadwood Plain, St Helena, 8, 275, 285, 289
'Death of Napoleon, The' (Brontë), 1, 4–5, 9
Decadi, 100

Declaration of Rights, 97
deforestation, 174–5, 178–9
Delile, Alire Raffeneau, 75, 143
Delille, Jacques, 14
Dendera, Egypt, 82
Denon, Dominique Vivant, 64, 82–3, 88, 90, 192, 196, 199, 200, 215
Des Dames St Marie, Paris, 210
Desaix, Louis, 82, 101
Description de l'Égypte, 73, 75, 83, 228, 232
Desgenettes, René-Nicolas Dufriche, 87, 88
Devil's Punch Bowl, St Helena, 275
Diana, 163
Diana's Peak, St Helena, 278, 289
Diocletian, Roman Emperor, 242
Directory, 48–9, 50, 52, 59, 62, 63, 64, 95, 128, 177, 207
divorce, 167–8, 180, 184, 188
de Dolomieu, Déodat, 64
Doringy estate, Saint-Sulpice, 100
Dresden, Saxony, 216
Drouot, Antoine, 223, 244
Drummond Wolff, Henry, 245–6
Dubois, Louis-Nicolas, 112, 209
Duchâtel, Marie-Antoinette Adele, 167
Ducrest, Georgette, 106
Dufresne, Louis, 141, 147
Dumas, Alexandre, 12
Dumonceau, Antoine, 259
Dunham, Katherine, 145–6
Duomo, Milan, 61
Durgy, Mademoiselle, 232
Dutch Cape Colony (1652–1806), 136, 137, 146
Dutch Republic (1588–1795), 58, 250
Dying Gaul, The, 59

eagles, 17, 150, 151, 155, 156, 157, 223
East India Company, 137, 275, 276, 286, 293
Eaux et Forêts, 174
Ebrington, Hugh Fortescue, Viscount, 239–41
Edgware Road, London, 284
Égalité, 131, 133, 139
d'Églantine, Philippe Fabre, 33
L'Éguillette, Toulon, 36–7

Egypt, 8, 60, 61–93, 95, 105, 143, 224, 228, 232, 240
  Alfi Palace, 66, 78, 91, 92–3
  Azbakiyya, 66, 67, 73, 78, 80, 93
  balloon flight demonstration (1798), 79–80, 169
  Battle of Chobrakit (1798), 65
  Battle of the Nile (1798), 68–70, 77, 86, 271
  Battle of the Pyramids (1798), 65, 77, 86
  Cairo Revolt (1798), 78–9
  camels in, 85–7
  Canal of the Pharaohs, 72, 84–5, 87
  Festival of the Nile (1798), 73
  horses in, 86–7, 90, 102
  Institut d'Égypt, 73–7, 78
  Islam in, 73, 76–7, 122
  Kléber assassination (1800), 91–2, 101
  Nile River, 72–3, 76, 84–5
  Pyramids, 78
  Republic Day (1798), 77–8
  Sèvres service depiction, 83, 282
  slavery in, 71, 72, 90
  Tivoli gardens, 80–81, 93
Egyptian Hall, London, 258
Elba, 1, 8, 219–46
  Casa Vantini, 233
  drum roll at, 230
  Fort Stella, 226, 227
  Imperial Guard, 226
  iron ore mining, 226
  Sanctuary of the Madonna del Monte, 235–6
  snowfall in, 241
  taxation on, 227
  theatre, 242, 244
  tourism, 239–41
  tree planting on, 244
  tuna fishing, 234
  Villa dei Mulini, 227–31, 240, 242, 245
  Villa San Martino, 231–2, 244
elephants, 58
Eliza, Grand Duchess of Tuscany, 16, 227, 229, 297
Élysée Palace, Paris, 185, 249, 263, 264
Elysian Fields, 299
Encounter Bay, Australia, 138, 160

Endeavour, 280
d'Enghien, Louis Antoine de Bourbon, duc, 147–9, 177, 240
Enlightenment (c. 1715–89), 74, 75, 77, 105
Ennery, France, 144
d'Entrecasteaux Channel, Australia, 137
Épervier, 270
epilepsy, 108, 119
Epochs of Nature (Leclerc), 24
Erfurt, Prussia, 180
d'Erlon, Jean-Baptiste Drouet, comte, 254
Eroica Symphony (Beethoven), 182
Estates General, 22–3, 24–5
Etruria, Kingdom of (1801–7), 119–20
Etruscan civilization (900–27 BC), 226, 235
Ettenheim, Baden, 147
Études de la Nature (de Saint-Pierre), 56
Eugène, Prince of Savoy, 104
European Trees of Peace and Memory, 272
everlasting daisy, 296

Fabre, Jean-Antoine, 178
Fain, Agathon Jean François, 221
famine, 42–3
Farnborough Abbey, Hampshire, 50
Farnese Palace, Rome, 211
Faubourg Saint-Antoine, Paris, 44
Fehrzen, Olof Godlieb, 277
Fennell, J.H., 301
Féraud, Jean Bertrand, 43–4
Ferdinand, Duke of Parma, 119
Fère regiment, La, 19
Ferrara, Italy, 50, 52
Fesch, Joseph, 17, 100, 168, 188, 204
Festa della Federazione (1798), 197
Festival of Liberty (1798), 59–60
Festival of the Nile (1798), 73
Festival of St Louis, 13, 29
Festival of the Supreme Being (1794), 39–40, 59–60, 123
Fête de la Fédération (1790), 249
feudalism, 171
Fez, Morocco, 72
First Consul (David), 102

Fleischmann, Hector, 272–3
fleur-de-lis, 163
Fleurus, Wallonia, 249
Flinders, Matthew, 138, 160
Florence, Italy, 239, 285
Fondation Wallonne pour la Conservation
    des Habitats, 272
Fontaine, Pierre-François-Léonard, 278
    and assassination attempt (1800),
        117–18
    and Bagatelle Pavilion, 203, 212
    and Borsato, 207
    and Canova's visit (1802), 127
    and Chaillot, 208, 210–11, 212, 216
    and Champ de Mai Festival (1815),
        248–9
    and Compiègne, 190
    and coronation (1804), 151, 168, 170
    and Fontainebleau, 163, 165, 170
    and Hundred Days (1815), 247, 248,
        263, 267
    and Lyons, 208
    and Malmaison, 98–100, 102, 117–18,
        119–20, 168, 211, 267
    and Parc Monceau, 203–4
    and Paris redevelopment, 200, 215
    and Peyre, 208
    and Saint-Cloud, 120–21
    and Tuileries, 202, 203, 212, 247
    and Valadier, 214
Fontainebleau, France, 8, 162–8, 283
    Château, 8, 162–6, 170–71, 189–90
    Croix de St Hérem, 166
    forest, 164–5, 173, 177
    hunting at, 162, 163, 164, 165, 166,
        171–3, 184
    obelisk, 166, 189
    Pius VII's visit (1804), 165–8, 170
Fontanone stream, 101
Fontenay, Jean Jacques, 40
Fores, Samuel William, 125
forests, 173–80
Forster, Georg, 280
Forster, Johann, 280
Fort Carré, Antibes, 41
Fort Stella, Elba, 226, 227
Forum of Trajan, Rome, 194, 198

Forum, Rome, 192, 194, 196, 197, 198,
    206, 213
Foucault, Michel, 11
Fouché, Joseph, 110–16, 118–19, 148,
    176, 177, 183, 264
Fountain of Regeneration, Paris, 215
Fountains of Moses, Sinai, 85
Fourès, Marguerite-Pauline, 80, 81–2, 83, 91
Fourier, Joseph, 92
Fourth Line Regiment, 157
Fox, Charles James, 71, 126–7
Foy, Maximilien Sébastien, 255
Francis II, Emperor of Austria, 156, 190, 202
Francis I, Grand Duke of Tuscany, 234
Francis II, King of France, 29
Frederick I, King of Württemberg, 158, 184
Frederick II 'the Great', King of Prussia, 142
Fréjus, France, 223–4
French Revolution (1789–99), 2, 3, 7,
    24–31, 32–49, 231, 240, 241, 295
    1789 Tennis Court Oath, 24–5, 28;
        Storming of the Bastille, 25, 249
    1790 Fête de la Fédération, 249
    1791 Champs de Mars massacre, 40;
        new constitution adopted, 28
    1792 June 20 demonstration, 28–30;
        Tuileries assault, 3, 30–31, 47, 110,
        241, 295
    1793 execution of Louis XVI, 48–9,
        107, 120, 122, 124, 130, 220, 224;
        Revolutionary calendar adopted,
        33–4; siege of Toulon, 35–7, 39, 47;
        execution of Marie Antoinette,
        120, 220
    1794 Festival of the Supreme Being,
        39–40; Thermidor coup, 41, 43, 115
    1795 famine in cities, 42–3; Prairial
        insurrection, 43–4; new constitution
        adopted, 47; Vendémiaire revolt,
        47–8
    1798 Festival of Liberty, 59–60
    1799 Brumaire coup, 95, 96, 97, 110,
        120
French Revolutionary Wars (1792–1802),
    48–55, 61–90, 100–104
    1792 France declares war on Austria,
        26; Brunswick invades France, 147

1793 siege of Toulon, 35–7, 39, 47
1794 Battle of Fleurus, 249–50, 251, 263
1795 French occupation of Netherlands, 58
1796 Battle of Lodi, 50; French occupation of Milan, 50; Battle of Arcole, 51–2, 104, 116, 123
1797 Battle of Rivoli, 51–2, 104, 123; Treaty of Tolentino, 52, 298; Austria sues for peace, 54
1798 Battle of Chobrakit, 65; Battle of the Pyramids, 65, 77, 86; Battle of the Nile, 68–70, 77, 86, 271
1799 Battle of Acre, 88, 90
1800 Battle of Montebello, 101; Battle of Marengo, 101, 103, 104, 120, 155, 223, 236, 299
1802 Treaty of Amiens, 124, 126, 137, 138, 140, 145, 149, 152, 296
Freud, Sigmund, 116–17
Frey, Jean-Georges, 287
Freycinet, Louis, 161

Gardener's Dictionary (Miller), 84
Gardener's Magazine, 300, 301
Garnerin, André Jacques, 152
Garnier, Adolphe, 116
Gaudin, Martin-Michel-Charles, 176, 204
Gaza, 87
Gedelston, Norfolk, 260
Genappe, Wallonia, 257
Genesis, 109
Génie du christianisme, Le (Chateaubriand), 124
Genoa, Italy, 19, 23, 41, 62, 171, 211, 237
Géographe, Le, 130–32, 137–8, 146–7, 154
Géographie moderne (de la Croix), 129, 154
George III, King of the United Kingdom, 125, 137
George IV, King of the United Kingdom, 258, 270, 272, 276
Georgics (Virgil), 14
de Gérando, Joseph-Marie, 197
Gerasch, Franz, 288
Ghayt al-Nubi, Cairo, 80
Giani, Felice, 213
Gillray, James, 127

de Girardin, René, 104, 105–6
goats, 178–9, 292
golden wattle, 296
Göttingen University, 217
Gourgaud, Gaspard, 270, 294, 296
grafting, 269
Graham, James, 255
Grand Mosque, Cairo, 78–9
Grand Serre Chaud, 153
Grand Trianon, Versailles, 201
Grande Armée, *see* Napoleonic Wars
Grandisca, Italy, 54
Grasshopper, HMS, 233
greenhouses, 153, 228, 237
Gregorian calendar, 33, 34, 158
Grenier, Paul, 264
Gros, Antoine-Jean, 54, 87
de Grouchy, Emmanuel, 250
Guadeloupe, 145
Guastalla, Italy, 220
guillotine, 38, 40, 41, 92, 114, 177, 222, 224
Guyana, 145

L'Habitation Leclerc, Saint-Domingue, 145
Habsburg, House of, 184
Haiti, 143–6, 173, 237
al-Halabi, Sulayman, 91–2
Hamelin, Jacques, 138–40
Hannibal, 100, 102, 103–4
Hassan Bey Kachef, 73, 75
Haura, Egypt, 84
Le Havre, France, 130, 131, 138–9
Hawaii, 129
Haydn, Joseph, 107, 109–10, 123, 181
Haydon, Benjamin Robert, 222–3, 301–2
Hazlitt, William, 4
Héger, Constantin, 5
heliotrope, 228
Hemans, Felicia, 69
Henri II, King of France, 29, 163
Henri III, King of France, 29
Henri IV, King of France, 171
hepatitis, 284
Herschel, Mary, 127
Herschel, William, 127
Histoire des Arabes (Marigny), 89

Histoire Naturelle (Leclerc), 23, 32, 56, 277

Hobhouse, John Cam, 279

Hoffmann, Georg, 217

Holland House, London, 71, 278, 296

Holland, Elizabeth Vassall-Fox, Lady, 71, 126, 127, 239, 245, 278–9, 296, 298

Holland, Henry Vassall-Fox, 3rd Baron, 71, 126, 239, 278–9, 296

Hollard, Claude, 229–30, 234, 245–6

Homer, 103, 279, 292, 296, 299

Homère, Alexandre, Poèmes (Lemercier), 103

Hop, Step and Jump, 153

Hornn, Johannes, 257, 258

horses, 86, 90, 102, 275

Horticultural Society, 301

Hôtel de la Tranquillité, Paris, 43

Hôtel des Anglais, Cairo, 93

Hôtel des Colonnes, Mont Saint-Jean, 260

Hougoumont, Wallonia, 3, 251–62, 271–2

House of Lords, 240, 278

Howatson, Alexander, 99

Hudrée Valley, France, 97

Hugo, Joseph-Léopold, 225

Hugo, Victor, 225, 247, 260, 261, 271

von Humboldt, Alexander, 131, 159, 264

von Humboldt, Wilhelm, 57–9, 131

Hundred Days (1815), 245, 247–71

hunting, 162–6, 171–3, 184, 203, 236

Hurtault, Maximilien-Joseph, 189

Husraw, Muhammad, 92

Ibn Khaldun, 65

Ibrahim Efendi, 67

Île d'Aix, France, 86, 269–70

Île de Bourbon, 132

Île de France, 38, 132

Île de Ré, France, 130

Île des Peupliers, Ermenonville, 105

Illari, Camilla, 282

Imperial Guard, 226, 238, 252, 257, 264–5

Inconstant, HMS, 244, 245

India, 61, 72, 276, 301

Institut d'Égypte, 73–7

Institut de France, 56–8, 62, 73, 133, 134, 139, 149, 155, 185, 209, 269

Intercommunale Bataille de Waterloo, 271

Interpretation of Dreams, The (Freud), 116–17

Introduction of Citizen Volpone (Gillray), 127

Les Invalides, Paris, 4, 98, 117, 302

iron ore, 226

Islam, 73, 76–7, 122, 244

Isola Bella, Italy, 54–5

Israel, 87

Italian War (1551–9), 163

Italy
 Napoleon's coronation (1805), 16, 170–71
 Papal States annexation (1809), 192–3
 Rome excavations, 192–9
 War of the First Coalition (1792–7), 49–55, 98
 War of the Second Coalition (1798–1801), 100–104, 120, 155, 125

al-Jabarti, Abd al-Rahman, 66, 67, 74, 75, 80, 81, 91

Jacob, Georges, 210

Jacob Frères, 165, 210

Jacobin Club, 29, 41, 47, 95, 109, 111–16, 139

Jaffa, Ottoman Empire, 87, 88

Jamestown, St Helena, 275, 276, 285

Janssens, Jan Willem, 146

Japan, 129, 160

jardin à l'anglaise, 15, 94, 97, 99, 104, 121, 189, 190, 197

jardin à la française, 29

Jardin Ali, Longwood, 281–2

Jardin du Capitole, Rome, 196–7, 199, 213, 214, 217

Jardin du Général en Chef, Alfi Palace, 66, 78, 91, 92

Jardin d'Expériences, Ajaccio, 132

Jardin du Grand César, Rome, 214–15, 217

Jardin du Luxembourg, Paris, 203, 209

Jardin Marchand, Longwood, 281–2

Jardin National, Paris, 28

Jardin des Plantes, Paris, 8, 32–3, 37–9, 74, 132–3, 237
 Buffon and, 37
 Chaptal and, 135–6, 138
 Commission of Arts and Sciences and, 50, 83

Géographe cargo (1804), 147
greenhouses, 37
Humboldt in, 58–9
Lamarck and, 185, 187
menagerie, 33, 38, 42, 58, 86, 135–6
museum, *see* Muséum national
    d'histoire naturelle
Napoleon in, 35, 42, 45, 58–9
Naturaliste cargo (1803), 138–9, 140, 143
Rotunda, 135
Saint-Pierre and, 38
Thouin and, 32–3, 35, 62, 132–40, 143,
    149–51
vegetables, 37
Jardin des Plantes de la Malmaison
    (Ventenat), 159
Jardin du Roi, Paris, 32
Jardin Rosetti, Cairo, 93
Jardinier de Sainte-Hélène, Le (Frey), 287
Jardins, Les (Delille), 14
Jefferson, Thomas, 151
Jénar, 229
Jerusalem Delivered (Tasso), 164
Jerusalem, 164
Jesuit, 203
Jomard, Edme-François, 75
Josephine, Empress consort of the French,
    see Beauharnais, Josephine
Joubert, Barthélemy, 52
Jourdan, Jean-Baptiste, 250
Journal de Paris, 152
Juniper, Barrie, 271
Junot, Jean-Andoche, 35–6, 41–2, 45, 63,
    100

Kangaroo Island, Australia, 138, 154
Kazan Cathedral, St Petersburg, 157
Kennedy, John, 137
Kensington, London, 301
de Kersaint, Armand, 28
Kew Gardens, London, 136, 137, 140
Khalidj Canal, 73
Killing Ground, Waterloo, 254
King Island, Australia, 154
King, Philip Gidley, 132
King's Hanoverian regiments, 252
Kléber Rossillon, 271

Kléber, Jean-Baptiste, 87, 88, 90, 91–2, 101
Koran, 76
Korea, 129

de Lacépède, Bernard Germain, 57,
    149–50
Lafitte, Louis, 209
Lake Bracciano, 169
Lake Como, 54
Lake Maggiore, 54
Lamarck, Jean-Baptiste, 185–8
Lane Fox, Robin, 271
Languedoc marble, 201
Lannes, Jean, 100, 109, 123, 157
Laocoön and His Sons, 98
Lapi, M., 235
Laplace, Pierre-Simon, marquis, 127, 187–8
Lauriston, Jacques Alexandre, 109
Lausanne, Switzerland, 100, 289
Lebanon, 87, 101
Lebon, Philippe, 205
Lebrun, Charles-François, 97
Leclerc, Charles-Victoire Emmanuel,
    143–6, 173
Leclerc, Georges-Louis, 23–4, 32, 37, 56,
    151, 185, 277
Lecomte, Étienne, 102, 117, 121
Lee and Kennedy Vineyard Nursery,
    London, 137
Legion of Honour, 133–5, 142, 149–50
    151–2, 163, 169, 232
Legislative Assembly, 28, 30, 114
Legnano, Italy, 171
Lemercier, Louis-Jean-Népomucène,
    103–4
Leroy, Étienne, 170
Leroy, Louis-Hippolyte, 172, 189
Lesueur, Charles-Alexandre, 160, 161
Letourneur, Étienne-François, 48
Liberté, 131, 133, 139
Liberty trees, 34–5, 40
Life of Napoleon Buonaparte, The (Scott), 3
Liliacées, Les (Redouté), 159
de Limoëlan, Chevalier Pierre Picot, 113
Lisonzo River, 54
Liverpool, Robert Jenkinson, 2nd Earl, 280
Livorno, Italy, 53

Lombardy, 16, 49–55, 120
de Loménie de Brienne, Étienne Charles, 22
London, England, 23, 25, 71, 86, 125,
    136, 137, 258, 301, 302
Longwood House, St Helena, 8, 275–99
    aviary, 291, 303
    cave, 292
    Chinese pavilion, 286, 303
    Jardin Ali, 281–2
    Jardin Marchand, 281–2
    library, 279
    mosquitoes, 281
    oak trees, 289–90
    pond, 290–91, 297, 303
    produce, 294
    rats, 281
    sunken paths, 2, 286, 292
    turf walls, 285, 287, 288, 290, 292, 303
    water features, 290–91
    wind, 285
Loreto, Italy, 50
Louis I, King of Etruria, 119–20
Louis XIII, King of France, 32
Louis XIV, King of France, 29, 147, 163,
    174, 175–6, 179, 201, 228
Louis XV, King of France, 166, 190
Louis XVI, King of France, 13, 16, 20, 113
    1789 Estates General summoning, 22;
        moves to Tuileries Palace, 28
    1790 Paoli visits Paris, 26
    1791 escape attempt, 28; new
        constitution adopted, 28
    1792 June 20 demonstration, 28–30;
        Tuileries assault, 3, 30–31, 47, 110
    1793 execution, 48–9, 107, 120, 122,
        124, 130, 220, 224
Louis XVIII, King of France, 220, 237,
    243, 247, 248, 250
Louis Philippe II, Duc d'Orléans, 38, 203
Louverture, Toussaint, 144–5
de Louville, Philippe Gouret, Chevalier,
    259, 260
Louvre, Paris, 82, 87, 99, 163, 166,
    199–201, 205, 218
Lowe, Hudson, 278–80, 283–4, 288–9,
    294, 301, 302
de Loys, Étienne, 100

Lucca, Italy, 119
Luxembourg Palace, Paris, 48, 203, 209
Lyons, France, 14, 115, 121, 168, 208
Lytton, Edward Bulwer, 55

al-Ma'diyya, Cairo, 67
Macau, 286
Macdonnell, James, 251, 253, 254
Machiavelli, Niccolò, 207
Macpherson, James, 103
Madame de Châteaureine
Madrid, Spain, 119
Maghribi Bridge, Cairo, 66
Maison Porteous, Jamestown, 275, 276
Maitland, Peregrine, 257
Majestic Trees of Harpenden, 272
Malaya, 277, 286
Malmaison, France
Malta, 225
Mamelukes, 65, 77, 80, 82, 86, 102, 166, 218
Mantua, Italy, 52, 171
Maori, 143
Marat, Jean-Paul, 231
marble, 201
Marchand, Louis Joseph
    Battle of Waterloo (1815), 252, 263
    Champ de Mai Festival (1815), 249
    Elba, life in, 231
    internment of Napoleon's remains
        (1840), 302–3
    St Helena, life in, 275, 280, 281, 287,
        289, 290, 292
Marciana, Elba, 224, 231, 235, 238
Marengo, 86, 90, 102
Maria Luisa, Queen consort of Etruria,
    119, 120
Maria Theresa, Holy Roman Empress, 158
Marie Antoinette, Queen consort of
        France, 98, 140, 190
    dairy, 140
    Compiègne, life at, 190
    execution (1793), 120, 220
    Fontainebleau, life at, 164, 166
    menagerie, 38, 140
    nougat birdcage, 291
    rustic hamlet, 121
    Saint-Cloud, life at, 128

Marie Louise, Empress consort of France
   birth of Napoleon François (1811),
      202–3
   Canova, modelling for (1810), 192, 195
   Dresden visit (1812), 216
   exile of Napoleon (1814–21), 221, 222,
      230, 232, 238, 243
   marriage to Napoleon (1810), 190–91
   Rambouillet, life at, 222
   Schönbrunn Gardens visits, 280
   Treaty of Fontainebleau (1814), 220,
      239
Marigny, Abbé, 89
Mariotti, Chevalier, 239
Mars, 201, 205–6, 287
'Marseillaise, La' 49
Marseilles, France, 53, 92
Martinique, 46, 106, 145, 154
Martyrdom of St Erasmus, The (Poussin), 59
Martyre d'une sainte, Le (Burrini), 166
'Masque Prophète, Le' (Bonaparte), 89
Mass (Paisiello), 169
Mass, 123, 124, 169, 181, 185, 205, 222,
   249
Masséna, André, 53, 123, 173
Mauritius, 38, 132, 160, 301
Maximilian I Joseph, King of Bavaria, 159
Mecca, Ottoman Empire, 72, 84
de'Medici, Catherine, 29
von Melas, Michael, 101
de Mélito, Miot, 50
Melk Abbey, Austria, 183
Mellini, Captain, 236
Mémoires d'Outre-Tombe (Chateaubriand),
   267
menageries, 74
   Jardin des Plantes, 33, 38, 42, 58, 86,
      135–6
   Malmaison, 140, 146–7, 154, 155, 158,
      266
   Parc Monceau, 203–4
   Tivoli gardens, 93
   Versailles, 38, 140
Mercer, Alexander Cavalié, 258
de Méricourt, Théroigne, 31
merino wool, 140
Merovingian dynasty (458–751), 151

von Metternich, Klemens, 238
Metz, Nicolas Francin, Bishop of, 37
Mexico, 150, 160
Michelangelo, 235
Middlemore, George, 303
Mignonette d'Égypte, 84
Milan, Italy, 16, 50, 54, 61, 101, 170
Milburn, Penelope, 272
Les Milelli, Corsica, 16, 17–19, 22
Military Academy, Paris, 16, 22
Milius, Pierre Bernard, 146
Miller, Philip, 84
Milton, John, 103, 109, 124
Milvian Bridge, Rome, 197
Ministry of the Interior, 135, 138
mirages, 76
de Mirbel, Charles-François Brisseau, 142,
   143
Misbah, Cairo, 67
Misérables, Les (Hugo), 260, 261–2
Modena, Italy, 50, 119, 171
Mokattam quarries, Cairo, 88
Molinos, Jacques, 135
Mon ami Robespierre (Béraud), 104
Monck, George, 1st Duke of Albemarle,
   118
Monge, Gaspard, 16, 26–7, 50, 264–5
   balloon flight demonstration (1798), 80
   Cairo Revolt (1798), 79
   Egypt invasion (1798), 62–5
   exile offer (1815), 264–5
   Institut d'Égypt, 73–6
   Republic Day (1798), 78
   Revolutionary calendar, 33
   Suez investigation (1798), 84
   Syria invasion (1799), 88
Monge, Louis, 16, 26
Moniteur Universel, 52–3
Moniteur, Le, 139, 149, 155, 220
monkeys, 90, 173, 229
Mont Cenis, Alps, 51
Mont Saint-Jean ridge, Waterloo, 251, 253,
   254, 257, 260
Montbard, France, 32
de Montchenu, Victor François, 294
Montebello Castle, Italy, 54
Montecristo, 236, 241

Montesquieu, 88
de Montesquiou, Louise Charlotte, 215
de Montmorency, Charlotte, Duchess, 176
Moreau, Jean Victor Marie, 165
Morel, Jean-Marie, 94, 121, 153
Morning Chronicle, 71, 300
Morocco, 72
Moscow, Russia, 216–17
Mosque of al-Zahir Baybars, Cairo, 67
mosquitoes, 145, 281
Mount Campana, Elba, 236
Mount Carmel, 87
Moustache, 157
Mozart, Wolfgang Amadeus, 181
Muhammad Ali, Wali of Egypt, 93
Muiron, 282–3
Muiron, Jean-Baptiste, 51
Mulberry Gut ravine, St Helena, 278
mulberry trees, 8, 15, 20–22, 25, 229, 269
mules, 102
Mundy, Godfrey, 301
Munich, Bavaria, 201
Murad Bey, 65, 82, 134
Murat, Caroline, 108
Murion, Le, 90
Murray River, 161
Musée Africain de l'île d'Aix, 86
Musée de l'Homme, Paris, 92
Musée Napoléon, Paris, 166
Muséum national d'histoire naturelle,
    Paris, 33, 37, 38, 99
  black swans at, 140, 158
  camel at, 86
  emus at, 154
  Etrurian royal visit (1801), 119–20
  Festival of Liberty (1798), 59
  Géographe cargo (1804), 147
  Naturaliste cargo (1803), 136, 138–9,
    140–41
  Redouté brothers at, 83
  taxidermy at, 141, 147
  Thouin at, 132, 133, 135
Muski Bridge, Cairo, 67
Mussolini, Benito, 6

Namur, Wallonia, 263
Naples, Italy, 239, 244

Napoleon as Mars the Peacemaker
    (Canova), 205–6
Napoleon I, Emperor of the French, *see*
    Bonaparte, Napoleon
Napoleon II, King of Rome, *see* Bonaparte,
    Napoleon François
Napoleon III, Emperor of the French, 50,
    154, 288
Napoleon's Grotto, 17–18
Napoleonic Wars (1803–15), 7
  1803 Britain declares war on France, 152
  1805 Ulm campaign, 156, 201; Battle of
      Austerlitz, 155–8, 181, 194, 200, 201,
      223, 299; Treaty of Presbourg, 201
  1806 Battle of Jena, 180
  1807 Battle of Friedland, 215, 223,
      299; Treaty of Tilsit, 180, 201
  1809 siege of Vienna, 181, 201; France
      annexes Papal States, 192–3; Battle of
      Aspern, 181; Battle of Wagram, 238
  1812 French invasion of Russia,
      215–17, 221, 247
  1813 Battle of Leipzig, 217
  1814 Battle of Brienne, 16, 217; Battle
      of Rothière, 217; Battle of
      Chaumont, 222; Battle of Paris, 219;
      Treaty of Fontainebleau, 219–20,
      226, 233
  1815 Battle of Ligny, 250, 256, 263;
      Battle of Waterloo, 1, 3, 4, 78, 86,
      251–63
Nasiri Canal, Cairo, 66
al-Nasiriyya, Cairo, 73
Nassau, 252
National Army Museum, London, 86–7
National Assembly, 26, 110
National Guard, 39, 47, 49
National Institute, 56–8, 62, 73
Naturaliste, Le, 130–32, 137–43, 154, 161
Nectanebo II, Pharaoh of Egypt, 64
Nemours, France, 166
de Nerval, Gérard, 93
Nettement, M., 210
New Holland, 129, 130, 138, 160–61
New South Wales, 129, 130, 132, 139, 161
New Zealand, 143
Newton, Isaac, 7, 89

Nice, France, 41
Nile River, 72–3, 76, 84–5
Niven, James David, 137
Normandy, France, 185
Northumberland, HMS, 274
Norwich Argus, 260–61
Notre-Dame, Paris, 123, 126, 168–9, 203, 204
le Nôtre, André le, 29, 128, 251
Nouvelle Dictionnaire d'Histoire Naturelle, 141
Nouvelle Héloïse, La (Rousseau), 15, 104, 105, 276, 279
Noverraz, Jean-Abram, 264, 285

O'Hara, Charles, 36–7
O'Meara, Barry, 284
oak trees, 5, 35, 100, 125, 151, 191, 232, 234, 289–90
obelisks, 55, 152, 158, 166, 189
Océan, 144
Odyssey (Homer), 279, 292, 296, 299
Office of Foreign Affairs, 27
On Heroes (Carlyle), 4
Only the dead never come back', 224
opera, 98
opium, 88
Oppian hill, Rome, 196
Oriani, Barnaba, 54
L'Orient, 63, 68, 69
Orléanais, France, 189
d'Orléans, Louis Philippe Joseph, 38, 203
Ossian, 103
Ostend, Belgium, 152
Otto, Louis, 136–7
Ottoman Empire, 61, 65, 73, 77, 87
Ovid, 228
Oxford University, 271

Paisiello, Giovanni, 45, 124, 126, 169, 205
Palais Royal, Paris, 28
Palatine Hill, Rome, 196, 211
Palazzo Borromeo, Isola Bella, 54–5
Palmaiolo, 241
Paoli, Pasquale, 19, 20, 23, 25, 26
Papal States (754–1870), 52, 122–4, 127, 139, 163, 165, 192–3
Paradise Lost (Milton), 109, 124

Parallel among Caesar, Cromwell, Monck and Bonaparte, A', 118–19
Parc Monceau, Paris, 203–4
Paris, France, 8, 26–31, 98, 199–202, 215
    Arc du Carrousel, 200–202, 208
    Arc de Triomphe, 209–10, 218
    Bastille, 25, 215, 249
    Canal d'Ourcq, 208
    Chaillot, 208–12, 215, 216
    Champs de Mars, 40, 59–60, 169, 248–9
    Champs-Élysées, 264
    Château de Vincennes, 147–8
    Coalition invasion (1814), 219
    coronation of Napoleon (1804), 168–70
    elephant statue plan, 215–16
    Élysée Palace, 185, 249, 264
    Festival of Liberty (1798), 59–60
    Festival of the Supreme Being (1794), 39–40, 59–60
    Fountain of Regeneration, 215
    Les Invalides, 4, 98, 117, 302
    Jardin des Plantes, *see* Jardin des Plantes
    Jardin du Luxembourg, 203
    Louvre, 82, 87, 99, 163, 166, 199–201, 205, 218
    Luxembourg Palace, 48, 203, 209
    Military Academy, 16, 22
    Musée de l'Homme, 92
    Muséum national d'histoire naturelle, 33, 37, 38, 59, 83, 86
    Napoleon assassination attempt (1800), 107–17
    Notre-Dame, 123, 126, 168–9, 203, 204
    Place de la Concorde, 199, 220, 224, 249
    Place de Vendôme, 194, 200
    Place du Carrousel, 27, 127, 200
    Rue Rivoli, 199
    Tivoli gardens, 80, 81
    Tuileries Palace, *see* Tuileries Palace
Paris (Canova), 195
Parma, Italy, 50, 119, 220, 232, 239, 298
passion flower, 282
Paul et Virginie (de Saint-Pierre), 38, 45, 56, 276
Paul IV, Pope, 163

Pavia, Italy, 50
Peace of Amiens (1802), 124, 126, 137,
138, 140, 145, 149, 152, 296
Peace of Presbourg (1805), 201
Peace of Tilsit (1807), 180, 201
Peddigree of Corporal Violet, The
(Cruikshank), 243
Pellapra, Françoise-Marie, 266
Pen and Pencil Sketches of India (Mundy),
301
Penang, Malaya, 286
Percier, Charles, 278
and assassination attempt (1800), 117
and Borsato, 207
and Canova's visit (1802), 127
and Chaillot, 208, 210–11
and Compiègne, 190
and coronation (1804), 151, 168, 170
and Fontainebleau, 165
and Malmaison, 98–100, 102, 119–20,
168, 211
and Paris redevelopment, 199–200
and Peyre, 208
and Saint-Cloud, 120–21
and Valadier, 214
Le Père, Gratien, 85
Le Père, Jacques-Marie, 85
de Permond, Laure Martin, 37, 43–5,
46–7
de Permond, Panoria, 46
Péron, François, 160, 161
La Pérouse, Jean François de Galaup,
Comte, 129–30, 132
Perugia, Italy, 50
Peter I 'the Great', Emperor of Russia, 217
Petit Trianon, Versailles, 53
Peusol, Marianne, 107–8, 112–15
Peyre, Marie-Joseph, 208
Phaethon, 65
Philae, Egypt, 82
Philosophie Zoologique (Lamarck), 186–8
phrenology, 181
Piacenza, Italy, 50, 171
Pianosa, 233–4, 236, 245
Piazza del Popolo, Rome, 213, 214
Piedmont, 39, 49, 101
Pincian Hill, Rome, 213–14

Piombino, Italy, 227, 229
Pius VI, Pope, 52, 298
Pius VII, Pope
annexation Papal States (1809), 192–3
arrest (1809), 195, 204
Canova commission persuasion (1802),
127
Colosseum buttressing (1807–20), 197
Concordat (1801), 122–4, 139
coronations of Napoleon (1804), 163,
165–8, 170, 171
Fontainebleau, imprisonment at (1812–
14), 216
return to Rome (1814), 217
Place d'Austerlitz, Ajaccio, 17
Place de la Concorde, Paris, 199, 220,
224, 249
Place de Vendôme, Paris, 194, 200
Place du Carrousel, Paris, 27, 127, 200
Placentia, Italy, 220, 239
Plantation House, St Helena, 278, 279,
284, 285
Pliny the Elder, 269
Plutarch, 8, 26, 270
Plymouth, England, 222, 271
Poland, 221, 232, 238, 245
de Pompadour, Jeanne Antoinette
Poisson, Marquise, 190
Port Jackson, New South Wales, 132, 139,
161
Port Western, New Holland, 160
Port-au-Prince, Saint-Domingue, 144
Porteous, Henry, 275
Porto Longone, Elba, 224
Portoferraio, Elba, 225, 228, 230, 231,
233, 234, 235, 237, 241, 244, 245
Portsmouth, New Hampshire, 141
Portugal, 219
Postumus, Marcus Agrippa, 233
Potaveri, 14–15
Poussin, Nicolas, 59
Pratzen Heights, Austria, 156
Princess Letitia, 231
Prix Décennal d'Architecture, 200
Protain, Jean Constantin, 75, 91
Prud'hon, Pierre-Paul, 202
Prussia

Congress of Vienna (1814–15), 238–9, 250, 271
Treaty of Fontainebleau (1814), 219
Treaty of Tilsit (1807), 180
War of the First Coalition (1792–7), 250, 263
War of the Fourth Coalition (1806–7), 180
War of the Sixth Coalition (1813–14), 16, 217, 219
War of the Seventh Coalition (1815), 250–51, 252, 256–8
Ptolemy, Claudius, 72
Pyramid of Cestius, Rome, 198
pyramids, 18, 78, 101, 152, 155, 236
Pyramids, Giza, 78
Pyrenees, 159, 219

Qasim Bey, 73, 74
Quarterly Review, 160
Quinette, Nicolas, 264
Quirinal Palace, Rome, 213

Rambouillet, France, 177, 222, 299
Raphael, 59
Rapp, Jean, 182, 184
Réal, Pierre-François, 177
Red Sea, 61, 62, 85
Redouté, Henri-Joseph, 83
Redouté, Pierre-Joseph, 83, 159
Reims, France, 241
religion, 123, 168, 235, 244, 293–4, 298
see also Christianity; Islam
de Rémusat, Claire Élisabeth, 148
Republic of Corsica (1755–69), 19–20, 23
Republic of Genoa (958–1797), 19, 23, 41
Resolution, 280
Reuil, France, 123
Réunion, 132
Revelli, Vincenzo Antonio, 227, 231, 242
de la Révellière-Lépeaux, Louis Marie, 48
Revolutionary calendar, 33–4, 44, 100, 107, 158
Rewbell, Jean-François, 48
Rhine River, 219
Rhône River, 19
Richmond, Charlotte Lennox, Duchess, 250

Richmond, Surrey, 301
Rigo, Michel, 77
Rio Marina, Elba, 226
Rival Gardeners, The (Fores), 125
Robespierre, Augustin, 35–7, 39, 41
Robespierre, Maximilien, 26, 29, 35, 39–41, 43, 46, 68, 104, 262
Cult of the Supreme Being, 39–40, 59–60, 123, 124
execution (1794), 46
Thermidor coup (1794), 41, 43, 115, 177
de Robiano, François-Xavier, 260
Rochefort, France, 266, 268
Rock of the Eagle, 236
Roebuck Tavern, Richmond, 301
Rœderer, Pierre-Louis, 110–11, 119, 122–3, 119, 122–3
de Rohan, Charlotte, 147
Romagna, Italy, 52
Rome, ancient (753 BC–476 AD), 52, 60, 200
antiquities from, 52–3, 60, 192–9
architecture, 192–9
Battle of Zama (202 BC), 103
Caesar assassination (44 BC), 52, 183, 298
Dacian Wars (101–106), 200
eagle symbol in, 151
Egypt as granary, 72
Empire founded (27 BC), 97
honours system in, 134
legions, 135
pottery, 159
Postumus, exile of (7 AD), 233
Republic founded (509 BC), 52, 60
Rome, city of, 59, 192–9, 213–15
Appian Way, 194
Arch of Constantine, 204
Arch of Severus, 197, 204
Arch of Titus, 198
balloon crash (1804), 169
Borghese gardens, 53, 214
Caelian hill, 196
Capitol, 52, 60, 194, 196, 198
Charlemagne coronation (800), 165
Cloaca Maxima, 198

Rome, city of (*Continued*)
  Colosseum, 197, 204, 213
  Column of Phocas, 199
  Commission of Arts and Sciences in,
    52–3, 60
  excavations, 192–9
  Farnese Palace, 211
  Fontaine in, 98, 121
  Forum, 192, 194, 196, 197, 198, 213
  Forum of Trajan, 194, 198
  Jardin du Capitole, 196–7, 199, 213,
    214, 217
  Jardin du Grand César, 214–15, 217
  Milvian Bridge, 197
  Oppian hill, 196
  Palatine Hill, 196, 211
  Percier in, 98, 121
  Piazza del Popolo, 213, 214
  Pincian Hill, 213–14
  Pyramid of Cestius, 198
  Quirinal Palace, 213
  Sacred Way, 194
  St Peter's, 166, 197, 205, 208
  Tabularium, 213
  Temple of Antoninus, 199, 204
  Temple of Concord, 204
  Temple of the Dioscuri, 199
  Temple of Faustina, 199, 204
  Temple of Jupiter Stator, 204
  Temple of Peace, 204
  Temple of Saturn, 213
  Temple of Vespasian, 199
  Trajan's Column, 194, 200
Romme, Charles-Gilbert, 31, 33, 44, 133,
  158
Room of One's Own, A (Woolf), 6
Rosetta Stone, 83
Rosetta, Egypt, 68, 73
Rossomme, Waterloo, 252, 256
Roudah Island, Cairo, 73
Rousseau, Jean-Jacques, 15, 53, 104–6,
  185, 220, 276, 279
Roustam Raza, 90, 166, 218
Royal Society, 131
Royal Touch, 87
Rubens, Peter Paul, 166
Rue Chantereine, France, 46

Rue d'Antin, Paris, 49
Rue des Filles Saint-Thomas, Paris, 43
Rue du Bac, Paris, 107
Rue Montholon, Paris, 27
Rue Notre-Dame-des-Champs, Paris, 113
Rue Rivoli, Paris, 199
Rue Saint-Honoré, Paris, 28, 29, 108
Rue Saint-Nicaise, Paris, 107, 108,
  112–13, 116, 139, 175, 200
Rueil, France, 121
Russia, 129, 149
  Congress of Erfurt (1808), 180
  Congress of Vienna (1814–15), 238–9,
    250, 271
  French invasion (1812), 215–17, 221, 247
  Treaty of Fontainebleau (1814), 219
  Treaty of Tilsit (1807), 180
  War of the Third Coalition (1803–6),
    156–7
  War of the Fourth Coalition (1806–7),
    180
  War of the Sixth Coalition (1813–14),
    16, 217, 219

Saale, 269
Sacred Way, Rome, 194
al-Sadd Bridge, Cairo, 73
Saint-Amand, Fleurus, 250
Saint-Cucufa Pond, Malmaison, 97
Saint-Denis, France, 267
Saint-Denis, Louis Étienne, 216, 275, 279,
  281, 289–91, 293, 302–3
Saint-Domingue, 143–6, 173, 237
Saint-Germain forest, France, 177
Saint Helena, 1, 2, 8, 9, 129, 137, 239,
  271, 274–303
  Briars, 276, 279
  Brienne, reminiscence of, 16
  burial on, 4, 5, 300
  Chateaubriand on, 267
  Chinese labourers on, 286–7, 289, 291,
    300
  coffee in, 281
  comet (1821), 298
  Deadwood Barracks, 277
  Deadwood Plain, 8, 275, 285, 289
  Diana's Peak, 278, 289

d'Enghien, reminiscence of, 148
fog in, 277, 278
gardening outfit in, 287–8
Institut de France, reminiscence of, 56
Josephine, reminiscence of, 47
Longwood House, *see* Longwood
    House
Maison Porteous, 275, 276
memoirs, writing of, 72, 220, 283
mosquitoes in, 281
New Zealand flax on, 143
oak trees on, 289–90
Paoli, reminiscence of, 26
Plantation House, 278, 279, 284, 285
rats, 281
Saint-Domingue, reminiscence of, 146
straw hat in, 2, 284, 287–8
Waterloo, reminiscence of, 273
weight gain in, 284–5, 288
Saint-Hilaire, Étienne Geoffroy, 8, 63, 74,
    83, 88, 89, 146
de Saint-Just, Louis Antoine, 250
Saint Lucia, 145
Saint Mark's Basilica, Venice, 59, 98, 201,
    206
Saint-Maur, France, 44
de Saint-Pierre, Jacques-Henri Bernardin,
    38, 45, 56, 276
Saint Peter's, Rome, 166, 197, 205, 208
Saint Petersburg, Russia, 157
de Saint-Régent, Pierre Robinault, 113,
    114
Saint-Sulpice, Switzerland, 100
Saliceti, Antoine, 35–6, 44
Les Salines, Corsica, 20–22
Salzburg, Austria, 159
Sambre River, 249
San Martino, Elba, 231–2, 244
Sardinia, Italy, 119
Savary, Claude-Étienne, 61, 185
Savoy, 104, 119
Schönbrunn Palace, Vienna, 136, 157,
    181–2, 191, 279, 280
School of Practical Agriculture, 143
Schwarzenberg, Karl Philipp, Prince, 217
Scipio Africanus, 103
Scott, Walter, 3, 53, 272

Scottish Gaelic, 103
scrofula, 87
Ségur, Philippe-Paul, comte, 157
Seine River, 202
    Chaillot Palace and, 208, 211, 218
    Jardin des Plantes and, 32, 42
    Malmaison and, 94
    Rue Rivoli and, 199
    Saint-Cloud and, 128
    Tuileries Palace and, 28, 59, 203
Selva, Giannantonio, 206
semaphore, 237
Septimius Severus, Roman Emperor, 200,
    204
Serjent, Louis, 133
Sèvres porcelain, 83, 159, 282, 298
Seychelles, 114
shadows, 27
Shepheard, Samuel, 93
Sheridan, Helen, 284
Sieyès, Emmanuel-Joseph, 95–6
Simonetta, Carlo, 55
Sinai, 85
Sistine Chapel, Vatican, 205
slavery, 71, 72, 90, 144, 145, 146, 276–7,
    279
Société d'Agriculture et d'Économie
    Rurale, 132
Société des amis de la loi, 31
Solander, Daniel, 280
Soult, Jean-de-Dieu, 156, 157
Spain, 102
    Italian War (1551–9), 163
    War of the First Coalition (1792–5),
        36–7
    War of the Sixth Coalition (1813–14),
        219
Spanish sheep, 140
Sphinx, Giza, 78
Spoleto, Italy, 211
Sri Lanka, 58
St Helena Gazette, 300
de Staël, Germaine, 5, 10, 112, 114, 120,
    125–6, 149, 183
Standen, George, 256
Staps, Friedrich, 182–3
Stendhal, 3–4, 50

Stern, Raffaele, 213
Strasbourg, France, 92, 147
straw hat, 2, 284, 287–8
Stresa, Italy, 55
von Stürmer, Bartholomäus, 279
Stuttgart, Württemberg, 158, 184
Sudan, 82
Suerre, France, 24
Suez, Egypt, 72, 84–5, 87
sugar cane, 154
suicide, 19, 221, 243, 245, 267, 283
Sulémy, Clément, 181
Sulla, 199
Sweden, 136, 219
Swiss cows, 140
Swiss Guard, 3, 28, 30–31, 98, 241
Switzerland, 100, 125, 159
Sydney, New South Wales, 132, 139, 161
Syria, 61, 84, 87, 282

Tabularium, Rome, 213
Tacitus, 193, 233
Tagaste, Ottoman Empire, 72
Tagliamento River, 53, 109, 116
Tahiti, 14
de Talleyrand-Périgord, Charles-Maurice,
    110, 170, 173, 176, 180–81, 238, 239
Tallien, Jean-Lambert, 40–41, 46, 68,
    69–70
Tamerlan, 86
Tasso, Torquato, 103, 164, 190
Taunay, Nicolas-Antoine, 120
taxidermy, 141, 147
Te Deum (Paisiello), 124, 126, 169, 205,
    206, 225, 226, 249
Teglia, Pianosa, 233
du Teil, Jean-Pierre, 25
Temple of Antoninus, Rome, 199, 204
Temple of Concord, Rome, 204
Temple of the Dioscuri, Rome, 199
Temple of Faustina, Rome, 199, 204
Temple of Glory, Compiègne, 191
Temple of Glory, Paris, 241
Temple of Hathor, Dendera, 82
Temple of Jupiter Stator, Rome, 204
Temple of Peace, Rome, 204
Temple of Saturn, Rome, 213

Temple of Vespasian, Rome, 199
Tenerife, 274
Tennis Court Oath (1789), 24–5, 28
du Terrage, Villiers, 79
Terre Napoléon, 138, 160–61
Terror (1793–4), 39–42, 44, 68, 104, 117,
    120, 121, 130, 147, 262
    Académie royale d'architecture and, 200
    Beauharnais execution (1794), 46, 95
    Château de Fontainebleau and, 163
    Committee of Public Safety, 35, 48,
        122, 210, 250
    Fontaine and, 98, 121
    Le Couteulx arrest (1794), 95
    Moreau and, 165
    'Only the dead never come back', 224
    Percier and, 98, 121
    Réal and, 177
Théâtre des Arts, Paris, 107, 109, 116
Thebes, Egypt, 82, 90
Themistocles, 270
Théorie des Jardins (Morel), 94
theory of shadows, 27
thermolampe, 205
Thibaudeau, Antoine Claire, 122–3
Thibault, Jean-Thomas, 153
Thouin, André, 32–5, 54, 143
    Chaptal, relationship with, 135–6, 140
    Commission of Arts and Sciences,
        50–51, 52, 54, 59
    constitution (1804), 149–50
    dahlia cultivation, 150–51
    Egypt, invitation to (1798), 62
    Festival of Liberty (1798), 59–60
    Legion of Honour refusal (1804),
        149–50
    Liberty tree planting, 34–5
    Naturaliste cargo (1803), 138–9, 140,
        143
    Revolutionary calendar and, 33–4,
        158–9
    Serjent decommissioning (1799),
        132–3
Thouin, Jacques, 51
Thouin, Jean, 50–51
Three Graces, The (Canova), 195
Thunberg, Carl Peter, 136

Tiber River, 60, 197, 202
Ticino River, 101
Tivoli gardens, Cairo, 80–81, 93
Tivoli, Italy, 211
Tobago, 145
Toby, 277, 279
'Toi et Moi', 49
Toulon, France, 35–7, 39, 47, 62, 237
de Tournon, Camille, 196, 205, 213, 214
Townsend Farquhar, John, 301
Traditi, Pietro, 225
Traité des facultés de l'âme (Garnier), 116
Trajan's Column, Rome, 194, 200
Trambasore Heights, Italy, 52
Transactions of the Horticultural Society, 84
Transfiguration (Raphael), 59
Treaty of Amiens (1802), 124, 126, 137,
    138, 140, 145, 149, 152, 296
Treaty of Fontainebleau (1814), 219–20,
    226, 233
Treaty of Presbourg (1805), 201
Treaty of Tilsit (1807), 180, 201
Treaty of Tolentino (1797), 52, 298
Trepsat, Guillaume, 117–18
Trieste, Italy, 297
Tripoli, Ottoman Empire, 72
Les Trois-Ilets, Martinique, 46
trompe l'œil, 209, 232
Tuileries Palace, Paris, 27, 39, 59, 95, 98,
    99, 102, 107, 109, 117, 127
    Arc du Carrousel, 200–202
    divorce (1809), 184
    extension plan, 212
    Hundred Days (1815), 247–8, 249
    Institut de France summons (1809), 185
    Insurrection (1792), 3, 30–31, 47, 241,
        295
    June 20 demonstration (1792), 28–30
    Napoleon II and, 218
    orangery, 202
    pavilion, 203, 211
    Rue Rivoli and, 199
    underground passage, 202, 203
    Venetian horses, 127, 201
tuna fishing, 234
Tunisia, 72
Tuscany, Italy, 99, 119, 219, 227

Twickenham, Middlesex, 301
Tyrol, 159

Ulm campaign (1805), 156, 201
Undaunted, HMS, 223, 224, 225
United Kingdom, 103, 124–7
    Battle of the Nile (1798), 68–70, 77,
        86, 271
    botany in, 136–7, 149, 153
    Congress of Vienna (1814–15), 238–9,
        250, 271
    East India Company, 137, 275, 276,
        286, 293
    Elba exile (1814–15), 222, 223, 224,
        225, 239, 243, 244
    House of Lords, 240, 278
    Indian colonies, 61
    interception of letters, 71
    Kew Gardens, 136, 137
    Lee and Kennedy Vineyard Nursery, 137
    naval blockade, 84
    New South Wales colony, 129, 130,
        132, 139
    Pianosa invasion (1810), 233
    semaphore in, 237
    Slave Trade Act (1807), 277
    St Helena exile (1815–21), 2, 269,
        270–71, 274–80, 283–4, 288, 294
    Toulon, siege of (1793), 36–7
    Treaty of Amiens (1802), 124, 126,
        137, 138, 140, 145, 149, 152
    War of the First Coalition (1792–7),
        36–7, 48, 249–50
    War of the Third Coalition (1803–6), 152
    War of the Sixth Coalition (1813–14),
        219
    War of the Seventh Coalition (1815),
        250–63
United States, 124, 141, 143, 160, 165,
    268, 269, 280
Uppsala, Sweden, 136
Ussher, Thomas, 224, 233, 235
Uxbridge, Henry Paget, Earl, 252

Valadier, Giuseppe, 196–7, 198, 213, 214
Valence, France, 19
Van Custem family, 260–61

Van Diemen's Land, 137
Van Kylsom, William, 260
Vassall-Fox, Elizabeth, 71, 126, 127, 239, 245, 278–9, 296, 298
Vassall-Fox, Henry, 71, 126, 239, 278–9, 296
Vauvray, René de Girardin, Marquis, 104, 105–6
Venice, Italy, 59, 98, 127, 201, 206–7, 211
Ventenat, Étienne, 159
Venusti, Marcello, 235
Vernet, Horace, 288
Verona, Italy, 50, 51, 171
Veronese, Paolo, 59
Versailles, France, 24, 25, 28, 38, 53, 121, 128, 185, 201, 208, 291
Versailles et du Roule nursery, 141–2
Versailles forest, France, 177
Vicenza, Armand-Augustin-Louis, Duc, 221
Victor, Prince Napoléon, 288
Victoria, Queen of the United Kingdom, 272
Vienna, Austria, 53, 54, 156, 157, 181–4, 191
  assassination attempt (1809), 182–3
  Belvedere Gardens, 136
  Congress (1814–15), 238–9, 271
  Schönbrunn Palace, 136, 157, 181–2, 191, 279, 280
  Siege (1809), 181–2, 201
  Volksgarten, 183
Vignon, Barthélemy, 153
Villa dei Mulini, Elba, 227–31, 240, 242, 245
violets, 50, 243, 262
Virgil, 14, 103, 269
Vitellius, Roman Emperor, 193
Volksgarten, Vienna, 183
Volney, Constantin de Chassebœuf, Comte, 61
Voltaire, 220
Volterraio, Elba, 235
voodoo, 146
Voyage de Découvertes aux Terres Australes, 160–61
Voyage en Égypte et en Syrie (Chassebœuf), 61
Voyage en Suisse (Coxe), 220
Voyages (Cook), 62

Walewska, Alexandre, 238
Walewska, Marie, 221, 238, 266
Walker, Alexander 301
War of the First Coalition (1792–7), 26, 36–7, 39, 47–55, 104, 116, 123, 147, 249–50, 263
War of the Second Coalition (1798–1801), 61–90, 100–104, 120, 155, 223, 236
War of the Third Coalition (1803–6), 152, 156–8, 181, 194, 200, 201, 223
War of the Fourth Coalition (1806–7), 180, 201, 215, 223
War of the Fifth Coalition (1809), 181, 192–3, 201, 238
War of the Sixth Coalition (1813–14), 16, 217, 219–20, 222
War of the Seventh Coalition (1815), 249–63
War Office, 27
Washington, George, 268
Waterloo, Wallonia, 1, 3, 4, 8, 78, 86, 251–63, 287–8
Wavre, Wallonia, 251, 252, 256
Wedding at Cana (Veronese), 59
Weimar, Thuringia, 180
Welle, Philippe, 279–80
Wellington, Arthur Wellesley, 1st Duke, 5, 250, 251, 253, 254, 255, 257, 272, 276
Wellington, Valerian Wellesley, 8th Duke, 272
West Bank, 87
Western Australia, 161
William V, Prince of Orange, 58
Williams, Charles, 125
willow trees, 300–301
Wilmington, North Carolina, 143
women, 5–6
Woolf, Virginia, 6
Wordsworth, William, 144–5, 301–2
Württemberg, 158, 180, 184

Yemen, 281
Yvan, Alexandre-Urbain, 221

Zingarelli, Niccolò, 205
zoos, *see* menageries
van Zuijlen van Nijevelt, Arnout Jacques, 287–8